FEMINIST PERSPECTIVES ON CANADIAN FOREIGN POLICY

FEMINIST PERSPECTIVES ON CANADIAN FOREIGN POLICY

Edited by

CLAIRE TURENNE SJOLANDER

HEATHER A. SMITH

AND DEBORAH STIENSTRA

OXFORD
UNIVERSITY PRESS

70 Wynford Drive, Don Mills, Ontario M3C 1J9
www.oupcan.com

Oxford University Press is a department of the University of Oxford.
It furthers the University's objective of excellence in research, scholarship,
and education by publishing worldwide in

Oxford New York

Auckland Bangkok Buenos Aires Cape Town
Chennai Dar es Salaam Delhi Hong Kong Istanbul Karachi
Kolkata Kuala Lumpur Madrid Melbourne Mexico City Mumbai Nairobi
São Paulo Shanghai Taipei Tokyo Toronto

Oxford is a trade mark of Oxford University Press
in the UK and in certain other countries

Published in Canada by Oxford University Press

First published 2003

National Library of Canada Cataloguing in Publication

Feminist perspectives on Canadian foreign policy / edited by Claire Turenne Sjolander,
Heather Smith and Deborah Stienstra.

Includes bibliographical references and index.
ISBN 0-19-541836-0

1. Canada--Foreign relations--1945- 2. Women in development--Canada. 3. Sex discrimination against women. 4. Feminism--Political aspects--Canada. I. Sjolander, Claire Dorothy Turenne, 1959- II. Stienstra, Deborah, 1960- III. Smith, Heather A. (Heather Ann), 1964-

FC602.F45 2003 327.71 C2003-901118-6
F1029.F45 2003

Cover Design: Brett J. Miller

1 2 3 4 - 06 05 04 03

This book is printed on permanent (acid-free) paper ♾.
Printed in Canada

Contents

Contributors

Erin K. Baines, Social Sciences and Humanities Research Council Post-doctoral fellow at the Centre for International Relations, University of British Columbia, and the Department of Geography, Simon Fraser University. External Associate, Centre for Refugee Studies, York University and the Centre for Foreign Policy, Dalhousie University.

Ann Denholm Crosby, Associate Professor and Graduate Program Director, Department of Political Science, York University.

Shelagh Day is a member of the Steering Committee of the Feminist Alliance for International Action, human rights advisor to the National Association of Women and the Law, and a Director of the Poverty and Human Rights Project (Vancouver, British Columbia).

Teresa Healy, Senior Research Officer, National Research Branch, Canadian Union of Public Employees (Ottawa, Ontario).

Edna Keeble, Associate Professor, Department of Political Science, St Mary's University.

Laura Macdonald, Associate Professor, Department of Political Science and Institute of Political Economy, and Director, Centre on North American Politics and Society, Carleton University.

Meredith Ralston, Associate Professor and Chair, Department of Women's Studies, Mount St Vincent University.

Elizabeth Riddell-Dixon, Professor, Department of Political Science, University of Western Ontario.

Claire Turenne Sjolander, Associate Professor, Department of Political Science and Associate Dean (Academic), Faculty of Social Sciences, University of Ottawa.

Heather Smith, Associate Professor and Chair, International Studies Program, University of Northern British Columbia.

Deborah Stienstra, Royal Bank Research Chair in Disability Studies, Canadian Centre on Disability Studies, Winnipeg, Manitoba, and Associate Professor, Department of Politics, University of Winnipeg.

Rebecca Tiessen, Assistant Professor, Department of International Development Studies, Dalhousie University.

Sandra Whitworth, Associate Professor, Departments of Political Science and Women's Studies, York University, and Faculty Associate, Centre for International and Security Studies, York University.

Acronyms

APEC	Asia Pacific Economic Cooperation
AUCC	Association of University and Colleges
CATW	Coalition Against the Trafficking of Women
CBFC	Canadian Beijing Facilitating Committee
CCD	Convention to Combat Desertification
CCFFD	Canadian Centre for Foreign Policy Development
CCR	Canadian Council for Refugees
CEDAW	Convention on the Elimination of All Forms of Discrimination Against Women
CERD	Convention on the Elimination of Racial Discrimination
CESD	Commissioner of the Environment and Sustainable Development
CFB	Canadian Forces base
CFP	Canadian foreign policy
CIC	Citizenship and Immigration Canada
CIDA	Canadian International Development Agency
CO_2	carbon dioxide
CPC	Canadian Preparatory Committee
CRIAW	Canadian Research Institute for the Advancement of Women
CSD	Commission on Sustainable Development
CWMC	Canadian Women's March Committee
DFAIT	Department of Foreign Affairs and International Trade
DND	Department of National Defence
EPZ	Export Processing Zone
FAFIA	Feminist Alliance for International Action
FTA	Free Trade Agreement
FTAA	Free Trade Area of the Americas
FWCW	Fourth World Conference on Women
GAATW	Global Alliance Against the Traffic in Women
GATS	General Agreement on Trade in Services
GATT	General Agreement on Tariffs and Trade
GBA	gender-based analysis
GNP	gross national product
GO	government organization
HAS	Hemispheric Social Alliance
HRDC	Human Resources Development Canada
ICCPR	International Covenant on Civil and Political Rights
ICESCR	International Covenant on Economic, Social and Cultural Rights
ICFTU	International Congress of Free Trade Unions
ICRC	International Committee of the Red Cross

IDP	internally displaced person
IFA	integrated feminist analysis
IFI	international financial institution
ILO	International Labour Organization
IMADR	International Movement Against Racism and All Forms of Discrimination
IMF	International Monetary Fund
IOM	International Organization for Migration
IPE	international political economy
LIFT	Low Income Families Together
MAI	Multilateral Agreement on Investment
NAC	National Action Committee on the Status of Women
NAFTA	North American Free Trade Agreement
NATO	North Atlantic Treaty Organization
NAWL	National Association of Women and the Law
NORAD	North American Aerospace Defence Command
OAS	Organization of American States
ODA	Overseas Development Assistance
OECD	Organization of for Economic Co-operation and Development
SAP	structural adjustment program
SDS	sustainable development strategy
SEAFILD	Southeast Asia Fund for Legal and Institutional Development
SME	small and medium-sized enterprise
SWC	Status of Women Canada
TRC	Trade-Research Coalition
UN	United Nations
UNCED	United Nations Conference on Environment and Development
UNCTAD	United Nations Conference on Trade and Development
UNDP	United Nations Development Program
UNHCR	United Nations High Commissioner for Refugees
UNIFEM	United Nations Development Fund for Women
UPCD	university partnerships in co-operation and development
VOW	Voice of Women
WEDPRO	Women's Education, Development, Productivity and Research Organization
WISEThailand	Women in Science and Engineering in Thailand
WLN	Women Leaders Network
WTO	World Trade Organization
WWW	Women Working Worldwide

Preface

The Genesis and Journey of This Volume

In May 1999, the co-editors attended a one-day round table organized by the Canadian Centre for Foreign Policy Development (CCFPD) for academics, graduate students, and policy-makers at the Department of Foreign Affairs and International Trade (DFAIT). The afternoon discussions ended at 3 o'clock, leaving the participants with a break of several hours before dinner. As some of the very few women present at the round table, we decided to get together to share a more private drink, which eventually became dinner in the Byward Market in Ottawa. Though our paths had crossed previously at various academic conferences, the round table solidified our friendships, in part through our common experience of it. Throughout the day, the three of us had made comments and asked questions relating to gender, most often to find silence the only response. We agreed that more—indeed, that something—needed to be said. Over dinner we discussed the possibility of writing this book, all the while exchanging stories of how we came to realize the importance of feminism and gender analysis to our research and lives. What would Canadian foreign policy be about if we took gender seriously, we wondered.

During that summer, we drafted and redrafted a short synopsis of what we thought the book could look like. We approached colleagues who had done previous work in Canadian foreign policy and who might, we thought, be interested in trying to do feminist analysis of their areas of expertise. We were heartened by the response: almost all the women we approached said yes right away. During the following months we confirmed commitments, filled in the gaps by finding new contacts, and developed a funding proposal for the John Holmes fund of the CCFPD.

In May 2000, with funding in hand from the CCFPD, Deborah Stienstra hosted a round table on gender and Canadian foreign policy, attended by many of the authors, in Winnipeg. We shared our drafts, talked about common themes, and enjoyed good food and each other's company. We also worked with students who were excited by our project and the possibility of meeting the authors they had studied. Participants from the Winnipeg women's community shared their comments and insights on our project. In late July 2000, the Canadian Political Science Association held its annual meeting in Quebec City. We decided to take advantage of the opportunity provided by this conference to get together as authors a second time, and put together a conference panel to share our project and chapter drafts with a broader academic audience. We invited David Black from Dalhousie University to participate on the panel, and to comment on our work. Despite some apprehension, we were surprised by the warmth and support of the responses to our collective endeavour, from David as well as from the audience. In the face of such support, our project continued to gain coherence and momentum. In Quebec City, we also found our publisher, Oxford University Press. We had invited their editor, Laura Macleod, to attend our session in order to see whether Oxford would have any interest in this volume. Her response to our work was 'yes, yes, and yes'. Her support has been an invaluable part of this journey. In March 2002, the authors met together for the presentation of our final chapter drafts, this time at the annual meetings of the International Studies Association in New Orleans, Louisiana. Andrew Cooper of the University of Waterloo and Andrea Brown from Wilfrid Laurier University, offered helpful and insightful comments helping us to make further small adjustments to our arguments. For the authors, however, the opportunity to hear each other's chapters at this final stage of research convinced us all the more about the strength and value of our collective enterprise.

The journey, however, has not always been without its bumps. In keeping with its mandate to foster links between the academic and policy communities, the CCFPD circulated our report on the two round tables on gender and Canadian foreign policy widely throughout the foreign policy community. The report attracted much interest, but also some hostility, from policy makers. The editors weathered some difficult waters in trying to respond to demands from DFAIT officials via CCFPD. The community of chapter authors provided support and advice throughout this episode. In the end, CCFPD accepted our suggestion that they hold an open and constructive dialogue about gender and Canadian foreign policy, rather than allow some officials to engage in personal attacks, and thus created a short-term list serve, open to all and moderated by CCFPD, on which these issues could be debated. If ours was a skeptical undertaking from the start, the experience of sharply critical reactions made us realize that some might greet our work with more than a good dose of skepticism.

In many ways, the journey leading to the production of this book has been about writing at the right time and with the right people. But it has also demonstrated the possibility of creating a diverse and respectful community of learning, while challenging some of the ways in which we have done things in the past. We have all been enriched in different ways by the opportunity to share the experience.

The success of any journey depends on the support offered by others, and we are thankful to those who have so unfailingly supported us. Rachel Kelly and Lindsey Troschuk, both students at the University of Winnipeg, provided logistical support and acted as conference rapporteurs during our meeting in Winnipeg. Lindsey subsequently helped us compile the bibliography for the volume, a tedious task at best. The Canadian Centre for Foreign Policy Development provided the financial support which made our first meeting in Winnipeg possible, and we are indebted to them for their role in fostering reflection on Canadian foreign policy among a broader Canadian community—even when the perspectives adopted might not always respond to the perceived requirements of policy makers. We are grateful to the University of Winnipeg, which also provided financial and logistical support for the Winnipeg conference.

We owe an enormous debt of gratitude to Laura Macleod, Senior Acquisitions Editor of Oxford University Press, as well as to Mark Piel, Assistant Editor, for their unwavering commitment to, and enthusiasm for, our project. We are also thankful for the comments and critiques of three reviewers selected by Oxford University Press. Their comments helped us strengthen the manuscript in important ways. One of the reviewers chose not to remain anonymous to us, and for the time and energy she devoted to going through our manuscript, and the insights she shared with us, we owe Claire Cutler of the University of Victoria a special acknowledgement for her support. Phyllis Wilson, Managing Editor at Oxford University Press, was patient above and beyond the call of duty during a lengthy copy-editing process, and we are particularly grateful to her for accepting the time constraints imposed by our overly busy academic lives. Freya Godard, the manuscript editor, helped sharpen our often cumbersome prose; the book is certainly more readable as a result of her diligent review.

The book would not be what it is without the support and enthusiasm of our authors, who began as a community of scholars and ended as a community of friends. As scholars, many explored new avenues of research, previously unexplored by themselves or others. The authors are now an integral part of the remapping and redefining of Canadian foreign policy. As friends, we laughed and sometimes cried. We are stronger for the journey.

Finally, people in each of our lives provided the support needed to bring to fruition this project.

Claire: I owe thanks first and foremost to the support of my colleagues in the Department of Political Science and in the Faculty of Social Sciences at the University of Ottawa, and in particular to Caroline Andrew, whose contribution to improving the lives of her colleagues is inestimable. Words cannot do justice to the strength that comes from a respectful and collaborative university environment, and it is a privilege to be a part of such a world. To Heather and Deborah, my deepest thanks for becoming my friends, and for being there through good and difficult times. May this be but the beginning of many other collaborative ventures! Finally, to my life partner, John, I owe a debt I can never repay. Thank you always for your unfailing support of my work, even when that work has too often taken over our lives.

Deborah: My thanks go to my two academic homes since this project began – the University of Winnipeg and my colleagues in the Politics department, and the Canadian Centre on Disability Studies. Both have provided support in terms of time, funds, and staff to assist with this project. To Claire and Heather, your virtual and real-time hugs, glasses of wine, and words of encouragement have kept me strong through some of the toughest times—thank you. And last, but not least, my love and thanks go to Patrick, my life and research partner, and to our children, Becca and Cailum, who all keep reminding me why this work is so important.

Heather: Thanks to UNBC for financial support for my research and travel related to this project. To Claire and Deb—you inspired me to be a better scholar and a more decent human being. Red rooms rock! To my friends and family—your support keeps me centred. Finally, my contribution to this volume is dedicated to my grandmother, Sara Catherine Ross—a fierce rule breaker in her day. Her strength and passion live on in her daughter, granddaughters, and great-granddaughter—such a legacy from an everyday and extraordinary life!

Chapter 1

Taking Up and Throwing Down the Gauntlet: Feminists, Gender, and Canadian Foreign Policy[1]

Deborah Stienstra, Claire Turenne Sjolander, and Heather A. Smith

What happens when an analysis of Canadian foreign policy starts from a specifically feminist perspective? This volume offers a first attempt by many of the authors to answer that question. Thirteen women—friends, activists, students, and scholars—have turned to their own areas of expertise and considered how feminists write (or rewrite) Canadian foreign policy. The results are unique and ground breaking for the study of Canadian foreign policy specifically, but they are also significant for foreign policy analysis and the study of international relations more generally. Not only does this collection shine a light into the corners of Canadian foreign policy where women and men exist, but it also shows that what we in universities have been calling Canadian foreign policy is much more complex than much of the previous literature has suggested.

This book presents diverse perspectives both on foreign policy and feminist approaches. Each author was asked to reflect on her work and reply to the question: How does your chapter question the fundamental nature and orientation of Canadian foreign policy in order to include gender, women, and feminist analysis? Each of the chapters challenges what constitutes legitimate knowledge in foreign policy analysis, and in the discussion that follows, we draw out some of the common themes. In examining how knowledge is seen as legitimate, however, we are also compelled to redefine what we mean by foreign policy and to expose some of its multiple sites, for our different feminist approaches can no longer be content with traditional definitions. We illustrate the scope of differing feminist analyses and their contributions to the study of Canadian foreign policy. Having taken this first step, we are left to ponder the possible future directions for feminist research in Canadian foreign policy.

What Constitutes Legitimate Knowledge?

A collection on feminism and Canadian foreign policy is at its very core a skeptical undertaking. We wondered, as readers and as scholars, what the contributions of feminism to the study of Canadian foreign policy might be and whether the study of Canadian foreign policy has anything to offer to us as feminists or to feminists more generally. Indeed, the creative voyage of the volume has been one of running a gauntlet of daunting criticism or challenges from both sides. Feminism and Canadian foreign policy are seemingly quite disparate subjects, and any attempt to bring them together will elicit words of caution.

Many of the social sciences have replied to feminist critiques over the past twenty years. Even international relations, which some consider the parent discipline of Canadian foreign policy, has become more open to feminist concerns, although feminists continue to face resistance in that field (Marchand 1998; Murphy 1996; Tickner 1997, 1998). Given the current of change in the social sciences, we began by asking ourselves why there might still be reluctance to integrate feminist critiques and to address gendered analysis in the analysis of Canadian foreign policy and foreign policy more generally.

Building on the insights of Robert Cox (1986) on the relationships between problem solving and critical theory, Stienstra argues that 'most foreign policy analysts use the problem-solving approach. They take the existing system of foreign policy making for granted. The role of the analyst is to explain how policies have been made and how the organization or decision-making processes could be strengthened' (2001: 61). From this perspective, legitimate knowledge is what is found in the existing policy-making frameworks. In Canadian foreign policy, this includes the state apparatus (particularly the Minister of Foreign Affairs and the Department of Foreign Affairs and International Trade (DFAIT), Cabinet, Parliament, and the provinces. Some analyses also examine the context or setting for foreign policy making, including the influences of Canada's international location, power, ideas about foreign policy, and civil society (see Nossal 1997). In most analyses, foreign policy is considered to be separate from domestic policy, although there are signs that this is beginning to change (see Cooper 1997).

How do we—as an academic community—learn about what exists in foreign-policy making frameworks? Many of us examine ministerial statements on foreign policy, or public descriptions of foreign policy, such as those on the DFAIT website. We may examine major reviews of foreign policy conducted by parliamentary committees, such as the 1994 *Report of the Special Joint Committee Reviewing Canadian Foreign Policy*. We may use other primary sources, including the published diaries of, or interviews with, policy makers. These are all examples of what we consider legitimate knowledge in foreign policy, but they all begin by examining the existing policy system, the state, or responses to what the state does. For example, when discussing the work of civil society, we may examine briefs submitted by interest groups to parliamentary committees, or alternative civil society actions, such as the 1992 Citizens' Inquiry into Peace and Security Commission organized by unions and peace and Aboriginal organizations. What is crucial is that we take the state as the starting point, and that we rarely question what the state does within a broader context.

Many of the chapters in this collection use these same methods to examine feminist analyses of Canadian foreign policy. Whitworth examines the transcripts of the Commission of Inquiry into the Deployment of Canadian Forces to Somalia in 1997. Turenne Sjolander analyses the analogies from competitive sports used in speeches about the global economy by various ministers responsible for foreign affairs and international trade. Tiessen describes the international and domestic commitments made by Canada on sustainable development. Riddell-Dixon highlights the relationships between Status of Women Canada and DFAIT in the development of foreign policy related to women's equality. In spite of using traditional academic methods, however, these authors do not take the position of the state as a given. Rather, they seek to uncover fundamental discrepancies in the state's actions and policy pronouncements—discontinuities that traditional analyses (including those which do not adopt a feminist lens) do not uncover.

But this book also challenges the concepts of where legitimate knowledge can be found and in so doing, ask questions about our roles in relation to that knowledge. Much of Canadian foreign policy has separated what Canada does within its own boundaries from its activities in the international arena, arguing that only the latter is relevant to foreign policy. Using a feminist lens illustrates the serious implications this has for women and men in Canada and around the world, as well as for foreign policy. It leads in part to the separation of Canada's domestic economic policies and commitments from its foreign policy. Day outlines the separation that has occurred between commitments made to pursuing human rights on the one hand, and the formulation and pursuit of economic policy on the other. 'Governments have placed economic policy in a watertight compartment that is separated from human rights completely. They assert that economic policy is apolitical and gender-neutral and has nothing to do with human rights.' Day, Stienstra, and Healy all illustrate the consequences for women of this separation.

The separation of domestic and foreign policy also means that we do not necessarily look at the implications inside Canada when we evaluate our foreign policy. Keeble and Ralston argue that although Canada speaks eloquently in international meetings on trafficking for the protection of women against gender-based exploitation and violence, it fails to take action on internal trafficking situations that result from its immigration policies. Stienstra illustrates the gap between the domestic commitment to gender-based analysis, and the failure of DFAIT to adopt gender-based analysis in its own programs, not just as a recommendation for international audiences. Healy shows how the Canadian Women's March Committee uses international commitments to gender equality made by the Canadian government to evaluate domestic policies relevant to women in Canada.

The authors in this volume also illustrate that we rewrite Canadian foreign policy when, as Smith suggests, 'we put the voices of outsiders in the foreground as opposed to ignoring them or rendering them illegitimate'. Her chapter shows how different legitimate knowledge about foreign policy is when we use the point of view of Chinese migrants or Aboriginal peoples in Canada. Crosby suggests that Canadian defence policy looks very different when we begin from the vantage point of women's peace activists like the Canadian Voice of Women for Peace. Stienstra and Healy begin from the writings of Canadian women's groups that are related to foreign policy, although not often defined as foreign policy.

Determining what constitutes legitimate knowledge in Canadian foreign policy also entails making our status as researchers and authors more complex. This book raises questions about who can write authoritatively about foreign policy. We include tenured professors, graduate students, and activists, and we argue that all have relevant comments to make about Canadian foreign policy. We also make the relationships between what we write and ourselves more complex. While it is not the norm, it has not been uncommon for academics and policy makers to go back and forth between universities and government, aided in large part by the problem-solving orientation of much of Canadian foreign policy research. Lloyd Axworthy, who is one of the more notable recent examples, left his post as Minister of Foreign Affairs to head the Liu Centre for the Study of Global Issues at the University of British Columbia. It has been common for Foreign Affairs and other government departments to solicit advice from academics about particular aspects of Canadian foreign policy, a practice that further reinforces the problem-solving orientation of much research. This book illustrates at least two tensions for researchers that result from their feminist analysis of Canadian foreign policy, and from the relationship between research and practice.

For some, using a feminist analysis has meant facing conflict between their commitment to feminist processes and theories, which advocate policy change, and the commitment to existing policies by government funders or policy makers. Academic support for social science research is at an all-time low, and government support for research—particularly from a particular government program or department—is a welcome, and often necessary, part of a researcher's life. What happens, however, when the objectives of a research-funding department or program conflict with the research objectives of the scholar? Often such a conflict is very subtle and only becomes apparent as a research project progresses. Keeble and Ralston, for example, describe their experience of confronting the attempt by the Canadian International Development Agency (CIDA) to incorporate the issue of prostitution into its policy of poverty alleviation and their commitment to addressing prostitution in a rights-based discourse emphasizing women's sexual exploitation.

Several authors also describe the tension they face in their dual role as activist and researcher. This tension comes about because in working from a feminist perspective, they consider it their work not only to create knowledge, but also to use that knowledge in advocating and working for political change. The position of the objective researcher who is separate from the research is rejected by some (though not all) feminists and by other critical theorists engaged in emancipatory research (see Neufeld 1995, for example). Stienstra, in the appendix to her chapter, makes explicit the tensions she faced and frames some of the questions feminist researchers may face when they also engage in advocacy work in the same area. Keeble and Ralston describe how their attempts to use feminist practices, for example through participatory videos, caused tensions for their academic work. Researchers are often at once insiders and outsiders in both communities.

This volume reframes the way in which we decide what is legitimate knowledge in Canadian foreign policy and who can research it. Using feminist perspectives also changes how we define foreign policy—that is, how we look at the object of our inquiry.

What Is Foreign Policy?

There may be some irony in the fact that we ask oursel Nossal (1997) did in the first chapter of his seminal wo policy, and that we ask it in the same way. This suggests, p the question we are asking is truly transcendental, or that scholars of foreign policy, whatever their orientation or theoretical lens, are equally puzzled by the subject they are investigating. Though Nossal goes on in his first chapter to argue that the term 'foreign policy' is multifaceted and that we must be conscious of the complexity of the phrase, he does draw one 'line in the sand'. 'Foreign policy, properly speaking, is concerned with explaining the behaviour of those who have the capability to exercise supreme political authority over a given set of issue areas, for a given people in a given territory' (Nossal 1997: 4). As we have noted above, our approaches hardly preclude an examination of the actions and policies of the Canadian state; we do not try to make such a leading actor invisible. We do, however, ask whether or not the state is always the necessary *starting* point of foreign policy, and in this way, we raise serious questions as to the way foreign policy has been defined.

These chapters together ask how the concept of foreign policy in general, and Canadian foreign policy in particular, narrows our scope for inquiry. Smith, for example, clearly asks the question 'what is Canada, and what is Canadian?' when we speak of Canadian foreign policy. Who speaks for Canada?[2] In examining the experiences of the First Nations and indigenous peoples in Canada, and that of the Chinese migrants arriving in British Columbia in 1999, she problematizes the notion of who is part of Canada and who is not. Both she and Day also raise questions about the discrepancy between the image that Canada wishes to project on the international scene, and political practice within its borders. Baines's chapter raises similar points in looking at the assumption by the Canadian state of a leadership position internationally in its promotion of women's rights under refugee determination processes, and yet its failure to protect women in Canada from domestic violence. Whitworth's examination of the Somalia inquiry clearly signals the discrepancy between the reputation as a peacekeeper that Canada promotes abroad and the Canada that arrived in Somalia to protect the peace. The problematization of 'Canada' when we are investigating Canadian foreign policy points us to the disparity between official actions and political realities.

It might be argued that other critical scholars are quite able to recognize the discrepancy between the Canadian state's public statements and its actions—much good investigative journalism concerns the same paradox. Feminist approaches, however, lead us to ask about the gender, ethnic, racial, and class positions that are privileged in the articulation of Canadian foreign policy by the representatives of the state, and to ask the potentially transformative question: what foreign policy would look like if it were defined in an alternative site? Feminist analyses also allow us to illustrate some of the bases for fundamental disjunctures; Turenne Sjolander reveals the way in which the analogies from male sports that are used to explain the global economy have effectively blinded the Canadian state to the gendered nature of globalization and its consequences. Even for scholars who do not share our feminist perspectives, questions da?' would seem particularly critical at a time when the tate is being challenged by the processes of globalization ntrifugal forces within the country on the other. We tate as a central actor in the foreign-policy process for nproblematized.

rive us to ask 'what is foreign?' We have already spoken of the artificial distinction between domestic and foreign policy, a point not lost (at least, rhetorically) on most of the discipline of international relations, although foreign policy analysts still remain, by and large, forced by their emphasis on the foreign policy bureaucracy to think in terms of a nearly clean divide. Particularly in an era of globalization, not only of the economy but of a multiplicity of human activities, the problematization of 'foreign' is critical. Macdonald's examination of women's groups, both inside and outside Canada, that together challenge international trade agreements, such as the NAFTA, is a case in point. Problematizing the concept of 'foreign' in this case allows us to ask where the boundaries are between Canada and the world outside. Are transnational coalitions 'domestic' or 'foreign'? Are international trade agreements 'domestic', or are they 'foreign'? More pointedly again, we can ask: 'What is the meaning of sovereignty in an era of globalization'? How do we distinguish between what is necessarily 'outside' and what is necessarily 'inside' Canada?

Problematizing 'foreign' not only requires us to think about the blurring of the distinction between what is inside and what is outside Canada. Our analyses also ask us to think about how the Canadian state makes 'foreign' that which is domestic. Smith does so when looking at First Nations peoples or at the Chinese migrants applying for refugee status. She also does so, as does Tiessen, when looking at the way in which the environment has been made 'foreign'. Using different analytical tools, both authors demonstrate how the environment is defined as an autonomous sphere in Canadian foreign policy and is made 'foreign' by other preoccupations. Tiessen, for example, demonstrates how DFAIT's sustainable development strategy has erased all notions of holism from the challenge of responding to the environment, and has made the environment foreign even to itself by incorporating an environmental strategy within a logic dictated by international economic competitiveness. Keeble and Ralston raise serious questions for scholars and activists as to the demarcation between national (Western) and 'foreign' values and social structures, and point to the inherent ambiguities in separating what is 'foreign' from what is not. In each of these chapters, 'foreign' is constructed rather than given, implying that a proper and necessary focus of Canadian foreign policy analysis is to be found in the examination of the way in which such constructions of the 'foreign' take place.

Finally, and in some respects, most contentiously for more traditional analyses of Canadian foreign-policy, our analyses drive us to problematize 'policy'. Nossal is quite correct when he argues that 'the word "policy" connotes the actions, goals, and decisions of authoritative political actors—or, more commonly, governments' (1997: 4). Yet, the word 'policy' also has an etymological connection with the word 'politics', and all too often, policy is about many things—but not about politics. Feminist analyses require us to ask questions about politics, and in so doing, we find

that the sources of policy are myriad and, most often, fi
reason for being and caring outside the halls of DFAIT's Pea
Drive in Ottawa. Riddell-Dixon, for example, examines th
groups learned about the policy process by taking part in
consultations, and thereby learned how to confront the go

Stienstra, Healy, Crosby, Day, and Macdonald focus on v
women's movement, and we find here critiques of government policy and attempts to engage the state on the need to change policy (a process which has much more in common with politics than the bureaucratic games often played inside government bureaucracies). Such examinations also reveal the origins of many policies, which are showcased by Canadian governments as 'innovative' and 'new'. Crosby, for example, details how Canada's human security agenda was articulated first by Voice of Women in the early 1960s. Through explicitly political practices, such as the March of Women (discussed in Healy's chapter), women's groups challenge policy and create new spaces for the articulation of politics. In an explicitly political chapter, Stienstra—as both scholar and activist—holds Canadian government policies to account by comparing the government's record with the alternative policies proposed by women activists in Canada. Such comparisons, which appear in many of the chapters, demonstrate the political engagement of the authors in this volume, and are in themselves political acts. Feminist analysts of Canadian foreign policy, therefore, are not content to assess policy as the actions of authoritative political actors, but rather drive us to think about politics and the means by which political change can be brought about. Whatever differences exist between the feminist approaches taken by the different authors in this volume, a feminist writing (or rewriting) of Canadian foreign policy can be no other than an emancipatory political project.

What Is Gender or Feminist Analysis?

For those unfamiliar with feminist literature, this collection may come as a bit of a surprise. The chapters illustrate a range of approaches to feminist analysis, reflecting the diversity of feminisms in the broader feminist literature. The collection suggests by its example that there is no one way to do feminist research, nor one path to feminist 'truths'. Indeed, one of the strengths of this volume is the variety of perspectives that challenge our thinking and stimulate debate among the chapters as well as with those outside the volume.

Many of the chapters begin from the implicit question: what happens when we start from the vantage point of women in Canadian foreign policy? Others begin by exploring what gender has to do with foreign policy and don't ask at all about women's experiences. These questions reflect the number of different feminist theories developing within international relations. Different approaches have been called variously 'feminist empiricism' or the 'adding women and stirring' approach, 'feminist standpoint', 'feminist critical theory', and 'feminist postmodernism.' For those unfamiliar with the theoretical discussions in feminist international relations, they are summarized here.

Feminist empiricism is perhaps the oldest approach in international relations. As Stienstra suggests, 'feminist empiricism argues that we can correct gender disparities in research by including women in already existing research programs. Thus, our task in Canadian foreign policy would be to examine where women are or are not present and provide some explanation for their absence or presence' (1994–5: 110). Keeble and Smith take this a little farther:

> According to feminist empiricism, women have been absent, missing, excluded or very few in number (and the latter is only observable very recently) because of social biases against women. The problem is not with the tools that we use to investigate reality (science) but with society: the scientific method has simply been used incorrectly by those in society (namely men) with androcentric biases. If we used science accurately, not only would women be 'added' to our reality, but these biases would also be corrected. (1999: 14)

The claims of feminist empiricism have, at times, led some authors to assume that biological differences between females and males will necessarily lead to policy differences. Yet feminist empiricism is more complicated than this. Spike Peterson suggests that adding women 'to existing frameworks exposes taken-for-granted assumptions embedded in those frameworks' (1992c: 8). Feminist empiricism therefore, can constitute an important 'take' on foreign policy, as the attempt to find the women reveals unstated assumptions about the nature of that policy, and can lead us to ask 'foreign policy for whom?'

Feminist standpoint offers a further critique to feminist empiricism. Standpoint feminism asks not just where the women are, but begins the analysis from the experiences of women, including the multiple experiences of women of different races, cultures, abilities, and classes. It thus challenges the masculinist biases inherent in much of international relations theory. Keeble and Smith suggest that 'international reality is fundamentally gendered and the tools we use to uncover that, to 'find the women', are not grounded in Western scientific thinking'(1999: 16). This challenges not only our sense of how to look for women, but also how to consider Canadian foreign policy. 'From this perspective, our sense of place and identity is understood not in terms of rigid separation between "inside" and "outside", "domestic" and "foreign", but in terms of interconnections' (Steans 1998: 170).

Feminist standpoint has been criticized by proponents of feminist critical theory and feminist postmodernism, who have questioned whether the complexity of gender is revealed when we use only the experiences of women. Rather, both in different ways have pointed to the need to examine the constructed nature of gender, which finds its constitutive basis in social relations. Feminist critical theory insists 'that power cannot be understood as an instrument of policy but that it extends to social relations' (Steans 1998, 173). Feminist critical theorists look at the emancipatory potential of social movements, including feminism, to bring about change in the dominant power relations. Feminist postmodernism, which focuses on the complexities in identities,

> rejects the notion of fixed identity as a starting point for feminist praxis, but also the notion that race or class, for example, can be 'added' to gender, because they are, rather, constitutive of it. Gender relations, then, have to be viewed in the context of the nuances and complexities of social relations, culture and power. . . . It is necessary, therefore, to examine what women do in particular societies and how, for example, their access to resources is limited within specific definitions of femininity. (Steans 1998: 177)

Each of these approaches is complex, and there is much overlapping between them. It is an on-going and dynamic dialogue about ways of understanding women/gender/feminism in our world.

The authors of this volume use many of these ideas to explore areas of Canadian foreign policy. Some ask implicitly what happens when we begin from the vantage point of women in Canadian foreign policy, and they offer complicated answers. Riddell-Dixon, Stienstra, Healy, Day, Keeble and Ralston, Crosby, and Macdonald all suggest that our answer can in part be found by looking at what women's groups, and in many cases, feminist groups, identify as Canadian foreign policy. This emphasis on the experiences and analyses of women's groups is quite different from much of the literature of Canadian foreign policy. Few scholars in this field, with the notable exception of Cranford Pratt and Mark Neufeld, place civil society actors anywhere other than on the fringes of Canadian foreign policy. Yet, as Stienstra (1994–5) argues, part of the gendered nature of foreign policy is the marginalization of women's experiences as other, as outside the 'real' Canadian foreign policy.

For other authors, their analysis is not simply an argument that what women do collectively is important and worthy of note, but that when women act collectively using feminist analysis, they reframe Canadian foreign policy. As an example, Stienstra offers a rendering of the integrated feminist analysis used by the Canadian Feminist Alliance for International Action (FAFIA). Healy uses the tools of feminist post-colonial discourses to examine the statements by the Canadian committee of the World March of Women and the ways in which they analyze Canadian foreign policy.

Feminist analysis also offers tools to analyze gender, or the social constructions of what it is to be a man or a woman and what is masculine and feminine in our society. As postmodern and post-colonial feminists remind us, there are numerous ways of being a man or a woman depending on one's culture, class, race, ethnicity, and disability status. There are also different kinds of masculinity and femininity. Authors in this volume also assist in developing these questions in relation to Canadian foreign policy. Whitworth highlights the ways in which masculinity has been militarized in peacekeeping. Tiessen sees gender as a tool for identifying strategic silences in sustainable development policy. Smith takes gender to its conceptual boundaries by arguing that the gendering of internationalism constructs different groups in society, including Aboriginal peoples and Chinese migrants, as 'others'. Turenne Sjolander highlights the links between masculinities of sport and attempts by the Canadian government to define policies to support 'women in international trade.'

The variety of feminist perspectives taken in this volume use existing feminist theories to illuminate the unlit spaces of Canadian foreign policy. By illustrating the ragged edges of seemingly coherent analytical and operational categories, the authors in this volume render Canadian foreign policy both more complex and more gendered.

Where Do We Go from Here?

So what comes next? This volume has taken up the gauntlet thrown down by Stienstra, and Keeble and Smith, as well as that inadvertently thrown down through their silence by our (mostly male) colleagues at the first annual CCFPD academic round table in May 1999. In so doing, however, it has created a community of scholars and activists who together have explored questions and approach which, until very recently, have been marginalized in the study of Canadian foreign policy. In taking up the gauntlet, the volume also throws a new one down.

The chapters in this volume offer insights and suggestions for future innovative and compelling feminist research in Canadian foreign policy. The analysis of the construction of foreign policy discourse leads to the conclusion that much is constructed in foreign policy, rather than given. What happens when, as Stienstra, Day, Healy, Macdonald, Riddell-Dixon, and Crosby do, we begin our analysis of foreign policy in sites other than the state? Not only do issues come to the fore that are not usually thought of in 'foreign policy' terms (domestic human rights commitments, for example), but we begin to see how it might be possible to create real possibilities for political change. What happens when, as Whitworth, Baines, Tiessen, Keeble and Ralston, and Turenne Sjolander do, we begin to problematize the gendered assumption underlying government discourse and policy? In understanding the gendered nature of the state, we begin to see the limits to current policy choices. The problem-solving analytical mode of much of foreign policy research is made more open to challenge, since it tends to reinforce policy avenues revealed as far more complex and unsustainable over the long term than they might otherwise have seemed. What happens when, as Smith, we begin to ask questions about the construction of 'foreign', and find that foreign policy operates as much to make things 'foreign' as it does to emphasize the distinction between 'Canada' and the world 'out there'? Our different approaches to feminism and to Canadian foreign policy do many things, but they all point to the need to shine a spotlight into the corners of the black box of foreign policy in order to find the women (and men) hiding in the corners. They all point to the need to understand Canadian foreign politics, as well as foreign policy. We need to hear different voices, and identify the different sites of foreign policy, the different ways foreign policy creates that which becomes 'foreign', the different policies which reveal the gendered assumptions of foreign policy. In these investigations, we would be well advised to draw on diverse methodologies and different bodies of 'knowledge'. By challenging status quo methodological approaches, for example, we introduce the voices of Mary John (Chapter 3) and Shelagh Day (Chapter 9). There are so many more stories to be told, from so many diverse perspectives. There are so many lives and experiences trapped in the theory and practice of Canadian foreign policy. This volume only begins the process of discovering what is inside.

We hope that this volume will expand dialogue and debate about Canadian foreign policy, and encourage our colleagues to seek out and become familiar (if not comfortable) with alternative voices, and to think of foreign policy in broader terms. We hope it will encourage policy makers to examine the biases of existing policy, and to try to think of gender as something more fundamental than counting the number of senior women who work in their offices (not that this is an unimportant part of the political project of many feminisms). We hope it will encourage activists to continue to push the barriers of interpretation and understanding, and to challenge policy makers and scholars to think less in terms of policy, and more in terms of creating the spaces for real exchange—the spaces for politics. We hope it will encourage us to see our writing as a political act, which speaks in favour of emancipation and transformation, and help us to break down the pretence of 'scholarly neutrality', which too often makes our thinking irrelevant to most. Finally, we hope it will encourage our students to ask questions, and thus to become our teachers, and to never, never accept the received wisdom of ages without first launching the challenge: 'but what about gender?'

Notes

1. Our thanks to Gary Annable and *Brewer's Dictionary of Phrases and Fables* for showing us the potential of this metaphor.
2. The problematization of each of the components of the phrase 'Canadian foreign policy' draws in part upon the discussion in Chapter 1 of David Black, W. Andy Knight, and Claire Turenne Sjolander, *Beyond the State: A Critical Re-evaluation of Canadian Foreign Policy* (Broadview Press, forthcoming).

Chapter 2

Engaging the Possibilities of Magic: Feminist Pedagogy and Canadian Foreign Policy

HEATHER A. SMITH, DEBORAH STIENSTRA, AND CLAIRE TURENNE SJOLANDER

> Words can be gifts, words can be weapons, words can be magic; words can be prayer, poetry, or song.
>
> *–Lama Surya Das 1997: 172*

> The classroom, with all of its limitations, remains a location of possibility.
>
> *–bell hooks 1994: 207*

This chapter began as a three-page single-spaced outline that we wrote in Claire's office at the University of Ottawa in late October 2000. The outline almost wrote itself, and the experience of the three of us sharing stories and insights about teaching was powerful and empowering. Our thoughts and experiences coalesced around a single question, spoken from different locations: 'How do we, in our classrooms, include feminist pedagogy to problematize what we teach, who we teach, and how we teach; as well as what we learn, who learns, and how we learn?' (Stienstra, 2000). We begin by describing our understandings of feminist pedagogy and how it can be applied to Canadian foreign policy. We end by talking about some of our experiences as feminist teachers and using the tools we describe.

What Is Feminist Pedagogy?

Definitions of feminist pedagogy may be as numerous as feminist teachers. Feminist pedagogy involves learning which is based on the students' desires rather than a standard outline, thereby making the authority in the classrooms more equitable or exposing students to a literature outside of a recognized canon. Luke suggests that the focus in most feminist pedagogy has been 'to valorize emancipatory teaching, reading and writing as a politics of consciousness-raising and, by extension, of self-enabling and social transformation' (Luke 1996: 292). Shrewsbury describes feminist pedagogy as

> engaged teaching/learning—engaged with self in a continuing reflective process; engaged actively with the material being studied; engaged with others in a struggle to get beyond our sexism and racism and classism and homophobia and other destructive hatreds and to work together to enhance our knowledge; engaged with

> the community, with traditional organizations, and with movements of social change. (Shrewsbury 1993: 166)

At the heart of the various definitions is an emancipatory and critical project. Our aim is to create a transformative environment, reaching for the host of possibilities suggested in bell hooks' words above. As feminist teachers, when we enter the classroom we can seek to create a community or we can act in ways that reinforce traditional structures of authority. We can be part of the learning process or distant, detached, and immune from the process. We can encourage students to find their own answers, or we can tell them the answers. We can recognize that students come to our classes as diverse individuals, influenced by their own experiences, culture, and biophysical realities, or we can treat them as non-gendered 'homogeneous globule[s] of desire', to borrow from Thornstein Veblen's pointed shorthand description of the rational economic man (1993: 138). We opt for the inclusive, holistic, and community-based options. We want to unseat, unsettle, and disturb the power relations between the teacher and the student. We are not the all-knowing voices of authority. We too are learners. We seek to create spaces that are inclusive, respectful, and safe. This means we encourage students to find their own voices, identify their needs in the learning structure, and claim their right to learn. We seek to build classrooms where the students are more than consumers of 'givens' and 'canons'.

The creation of a safe, inclusive, and creative learning space means that we draw on different tools, tools that are sometimes strange to traditional teaching, but tools that offer students the ability to claim their learning. The key to these tools is student-centred learning. The tools include the creation of a learning contract between student and professor; group work; non-traditional expression of learning and research; and a choice of learning structures and means of evaluation. We will speak about these tools throughout the chapter as we describe some of our experiences in the classroom.

What We Teach, What We Learn

Canadian foreign policy (CFP) is one of the few branches of international relations that has a canon, at least a canon of well-known and influential authors. The contemporary CFP literature includes, at minimum, the work of Kim Richard Nossal, Andrew F. Cooper, Tom Keating, and Denis Stairs, as well as the authors showcased in the pages of the annual Carleton University publication *Canada Among Nations* and, in more recent times, in the pages of the journal *Canadian Foreign Policy*. The names of these authors and publications are familiar to students and teachers of Canadian foreign policy because they represent the dominant voices in the field. Nossal, Cooper, and Keating have all written important books (Nossal is in its third edition; Keating's in its second edition), and these are the texts that are often adopted in CFP courses (with a significant number of additional readings coming from *Canada Among Nations* or *Canadian Foreign Policy*). This canon, while not without its external critics or its internal debates, has tended to shape the boundaries of the study of Canadian foreign policy.

When using a phrase such as 'canon' , we do not mean [illegible] works we cite. In practice, the scholars who have helped to d[illegible] particularly in more recent years, sought to encourage dissent an[illegible] stimulate a flourishing intellectual environment. Cooper's book ackno[illegible] growing disagreement in the study of CFP and tries to present the notion o[illegible] peting points of view in his analysis. Keating's work, which focuses on multilateralism, is in part inspired by the concept of world order that he draws from Robert Cox. Nossal acknowledges the opening for discussion of CFP and gender created by Stienstra's article in 1995 but is careful to state that his work cannot do justice to such an alternative perspective, which would 'require a (re)construction of the project *de novo*' (Nossal 1997: xv). Stairs has been a effective critic of the practice of Canadian foreign policy, eloquently chiding policy-makers for their inconsistencies, contradictions, and ill-conceived initiatives. Beyond the leading texts in the field, many key volumes of case studies, as noted by Keeble and Smith (1999), are quite limited in their presentation of alternative visions of Canadian foreign policy. While the number of views and theoretical perspectives has increased among scholars of CFP since Molot (1990) and Black and Smith (1993) wrote their reviews of the state of the field, much of the study of CFP remains statist and elitist, in that it concentrates on the actions of bureaucrats and politicians as they formulate foreign policy, and of civil society groups in as much as they respond to state actions. Much of the field has tended to focus on 'the facts', where these are narrowly defined as the principal actors in the formulation of state policy.

Yet, as Sjolander (1998) has argued, it is essential to ask about the world we are representing to our students. If the main texts in the field are our prism, what is Canadian foreign policy about? The answer is straightforward and elegant in its simplicity: CFP is about prime ministers, foreign ministers, and bureaucrats—and on occasion, it necessitates a discussion of contributions by someone not employed by the federal government. The important questions are about role and status, the measurement of domestic or external variables, and which department or province or person really has the 'power'. Power is understood to be power over power to control and power over outcome. Students often learn about Canadian exploits abroad, without problematizing the state. 'Canada' becomes a nearly homogeneous entity (except in lectures on bureaucratic politics, which might illustrate bureaucratic in-fighting over policy outcomes). If the professor is using a case study approach, the students will 'learn' about the Suez Crisis, or the Third Option, or Canadian participation in the Gulf War. Students taught about the latest debates will be given information about human security, landmine bans, democratization, and peace building. Canadian foreign policy appears to be about a world that is 'out there' and irrelevant to the daily lives of our students as students (rather than as aspiring foreign service officers). Facts, dates, and names combine with patterns and generalizations and produce that most holy of grails: 'policy-relevant' knowledge. But is that knowledge personally relevant? And for whom is it relevant?

The question of personal relevance may seem silly to some. The point of a course on Canadian foreign policy, surely, is to teach foreign policy as it really 'is'. In defining 'reality' as only being about the world of bureaucracies, and social activists (and only these when they limit the st or confront state policies in vocal ways), we lose the abilit as individuals in a 'here and now' community. Ultimately, retaries of state for external affairs have no bearing on the our classes, apart from the need to pass the final examination. This is not to suggest that an understanding of our foreign policy history is not important to us as Canadians—but it needs to be just that: important to all of us as Canadians. Teaching and learning must be about more than the recitation of a series of facts to be quickly forgotten once in the exam is over—if teaching 'facts' contributes to the training of a new citizenry, then our students must see themselves as empowered citizens who can make use of the 'facts' we present. In sticking only with the 'facts' of the field, we lose the whole world of foreign policy that exists in the lives of our students but that is not included in the discipline's core texts. This world reveals itself when we unsettle the mainstream and problematize foreign policy—when we ask questions about what we teach and what is learned.

If the answer to the question of why we would want to unsettle the mainstream is to be found in the desire to engage our students as students in the here and now, the next question we need to pose is 'how': how do we unsettle the mainstream? As a start, teachers and students can draw on the growing body of critically informed literature that is specific to Canadian foreign policy. From rather humble beginnings in the mid-1990s, that list has grown to include texts by an impressive collection of authors. Nossal provides a cursory review of these emerging perspectives when he writes: 'We have seen the emergence of scholars who teach IR [and Canadian foreign policy] from numerous perspectives that would be considered non-mainstream . . . : international political economy (for example, the contributors to Stubbs and Underhill 2000), feminist perspectives of different kinds (for example, Stienstra 1994–5; Whitworth 1995; Keeble and Smith 1999) and post-positivism (for example, Neufeld 1995; Black and Sjolander 1996)' (2000: 12). The incorporation of different theoretical perspectives into the study of CFP is a welcome departure from the state of the discipline a decade ago (when Cranford Pratt was one of the few critics crying in the wilderness), but not welcome for its own sake. The aim is not to create a new canon—a process which Nossal suggests may well be underway (2000: 16). These texts, and the many others which are beginning to be published, are useful starting points for getting students—and teachers—to think about alternatives, and to present work, not as a series of 'facts' to learn, but as a number of interpretations of 'facts' to be debated after serious reflection and research.

To disrupt the notion of what we learn, we need to ask, as we did in the introduction to this volume: what is foreign policy? The literature above opens some doors in our thinking through its answers to this question, but we can further problematize foreign policy by including the voices of people—non-academics—who might otherwise be labelled non-experts. By breaking out of the tyranny of expertise that comes from academic credentials, we show how individuals from all walks of life are affected by and affect foreign policy. What about the Canadian doctors who work for Doctors Without Borders? Or women, like Shelagh Day in this volume, who have spend years on the advocacy of women's human rights? Or our neighbours who have lost jobs that have been relocated to the southern United States or to northern Mexico? Or our grandmothers or grandfathers who fought in the various wars in which the Canadian state engaged? Surely, the view of a peacekeeper on the ground is different from the detached discussions of peacekeeping in our academic journals and texts. Foreign policy is not just something for educated elites. It affects and is affected by the lives of everyday Canadians, and there are many rich stories to be told. The stories about Canadian foreign policy are also not just told by Canadians, but also come from people around the world, as the chapter by Heather Smith in this volume argues.

Beyond including the views of 'non-experts' we can go further and recognize the multitude of issues that are often excluded from our discussions of CFP. There are a host of issues related to foreign policy that appear only in the background in many analyses. For example, what role does the Department of Finance have in foreign policy? Time and time again issues related to globalization arise and yet the link to the Department of Finance is rarely discussed. Further investigation of environmental issues, such as the use of genetically modified foods, points to the fact that the food we eat is very much part of foreign policy, although it is rarely included in the traditional parameters of the discipline. Similarly, the voice of the First Nations is virtually silent in the mainstream. Foreign policy analysis also includes instances where we treat people differently—particularly if we try to answer seriously the [illegible] For example, why do women who immigrate under the Live-in [illegible]am not receive permanent resident status until much after other [illegible] though they bring urgently needed skills to our country? Why are [illegible]bilities excluded from the pool of acceptable immigrants?

[illegible] how we understand Canadian foreign policy, we need to rely on a [illegible]s, including those from other disciplines or from interdisciplinary [illegible] need to read critiques of immigration policy from disability studies [illegible]ies. We may need to draw on the work of Aboriginal scholars and [illegible]lings of the world that evolved over centuries of nationhood. We [illegible]n from biologists or chemists and their knowledge of biotechnol[illegible]s. In short, we need to go beyond 'Canadian foreign policy' texts—[illegible] part of the canon or the growing list of alternatives.

There are costs to attempting to bring Canadian foreign policy home and make it relevant to our students as citizens in the here and now. Planning a course from an alternative perspective can be time-consuming and difficult. It takes a long time to find alternative texts and articles that are not part of the canon. It is certainly easier to adopt a course book and have the students read only, or primarily, chapters from that text. One way to turn the constraints of time into an opportunity is to use the construction of a new course on Canadian foreign policy as a means of familiarizing oneself with the work of colleagues and people in the community. Again, we—the instructors—can learn from the process. The difficulty in constructing such as course also comes from our own resistance to new ways of teaching and learning. We can get stuck in certain types of knowledge construction and production and therefore feel obliged to teach according to 'the norm', even if it is only 'our' norm. A truly alternative course syllabus (which does not necessarily reject the texts of the canon, but which sets them in a different context) entails taking a risk pedagogically. It is easy to feel that there is no institutional encouragement for taking such a risk, since institutions may not value the time spent in preparing such a new course. It is possible, however, to start slowly by including some alternative sources and incorporating different teaching tools into a course. The results will speak for themselves and will encourage both students and instructors to continue along this path.

Whom Do We Teach? Who Learns?

The feminist teacher, recognizing that we are all learners, seeks to build a learning community. To accept this premise we must be prepared to be more humble in our approach to the classroom. The people sitting in those desks or at those tables have had experiences that can contribute to the learning community. Each person in the community has value. They are not simply student numbers or majors. We, the instructors, can learn from them, the students. The concept of a learning community challenges the traditional power dynamics of who teaches and who learns, for all the individuals in the classroom become part of a larger process. Hierarchy is undermined and unsettled as we all find our voices.

This approach has other implications, some of which are exceedingly positive. The creation of a learning community can empower students and encourage them to express their views in a safe environment. Consequently, many more women become engaged in the process as their fear of being silenced and ignored is reduced. As the student body becomes more international, those who are marginalized begin to take your course because the student grapevine informs other students of the inclusiveness in your class. And if the classroom is safe it also enables men to ask questions about gender and allows the 'dominant whites' to investigate race.

This approach will also increase the divisions between those who want to learn traditionally and those who want to take risks. Those who want to learn traditionally often become more intransigent, and this can result in a backlash against the professor. As we challenge traditional learning styles, some students become unsettled, for the critically engaged classroom can pose challenges that they have never had to face. Students may accuse the professor of 'not telling the truth' and they want the 'truth'. They want to know what will be on the exam and what they have to 'know' in order to pass the course with a good grade. Students may respond negatively to these methods in their course evaluations. Students can have difficulties accepting the complexities of the classroom when they are used to more traditional teaching and learning. We, both student and instructors alike, however have to recognize the multiple experiences in the classroom.

Once the students become engaged and feel safe with the pedagogy, they will demand more time from the instructor and will demand more control of their class. They will not be passive consumers but will want to engage you both inside and outside the classroom.

How Do We Teach? How Do We Learn?

How we understand critically engaged pedagogy is evident in how we teach and how we learn. We all learn by receiving information from our different senses. Unfortunately, as Luke points out, traditional teaching has privileged learning that we hear or read. 'Enlightenment pedagogy is fundamentally occularcentric: learning by looking at the printed word, rather than learning by doing, and importantly, looking at the teacher to access mind and knowledge' (Luke 1996: 288). When we consider critically how we teach and learn, we recognize that this style of teaching gives precedence to learners whose brains or bodies work effectively that way. But there are other forms of learning. Some learn by speaking, some learn by doing. When we reframe our classes, we can ensure that a variety of ways of learning are recognized. We may also choose to address two senses at a time to ensure that more than one style of learning is engaged. By adopting different kinds of teaching and learning tools, we optimize the experience for the different kinds of students in the classroom. Different tools can be used for different learning styles.

For learning by doing, we can use role playing. Students are assigned different roles and have to act them out in a debate or presentation or even a skit. The roles are as varied as the individuals touched by Canadian foreign policy and therefore can range from bureaucrats representing different departments to community members to individuals in states affected by our foreign policy. One of the great advantages of this method is that shy students will often excel at the acting because they feel safe behind the label of the role and are able to discuss all sorts of topics in an energetic manner because they do not feel that 'they' are under scrutiny.

For those who learn by speaking but may be shy about speaking in public, Internet discussion groups are a great tool. Many universities have course communications packages that can be used to create a closed discussion group. These can be used as a debate or simply a threaded discussion. The Internet is a safe space for students—often women and other marginalized students—who would not otherwise feel safe enough to share their views in the classroom. It also allows students who have learning disabilities or are deaf to communicate. The anonymity of the Internet aids some students in finding their full expression. The instructor can moderate the discussion or simply help set the terms of the debate.

For students who learn best together, a third strategy is group work. Often students groan when a professor suggests group work, but the beauty of this strategy is that it can be completely student-driven and can let students provide leadership. Students can work on developing a set of pertinent questions or issues related to the course, or they can work together on debates or their role playing. Often group work can be used to facilitate the application of knowledge, which usually results in more 'learning' than the standard lecture. There are many options for group work. The instructor can act as a resource person or moderator as the group work progresses. The environment allows students to become comfortable with each other, and again, because it removes the authority figure, quiet students will be more likely to participate.

Perhaps the essential element to how we teach is to bring ourselves into the classroom. We humanize ourselves to our students, and this allows them to humanize themselves to us. We disrupt our position as 'the professor'. We can share our narratives that relate to the subject and share our stories. We encourage them to share their knowledge and acknowledge their knowledge as legitimate. In this way we help our students to see what they already know. It is in the recognition of the value of all of our knowledge that we build the learning community.

We also bring out the humanness of our colleagues and can work to demystify the academic world to them. When we introduce a book or article, we can say what we know of the author and our experiences with them. This reminds the students that the written words exist because the author wrote them and because of who the author is. More generally, our teaching can help our students make sense of the academic world. This can be done by telling them how we write (and rewrite and are edited, and so on), what our paths were to our current careers, and how decisions are made in universities, as well as providing opportunities for students to participate in our work. All of these are the work of mentoring students and being mentored by them.

AUTHORS' REFLECTIONS ON PEDAGOGY

Our discussions in Ottawa came to a close by asking: does it matter? Does it matter how we teach, what we teach, and who learns? We believe that it does matter—not only from our political commitments to feminist pedagogy and what it implies, but because we have seen the results, the effects on different students. Students have become more empowered, and they do claim their own learning. We have to listen to that and acknowledge their right to learn. But we truly need to recognize that we too are learners and that much can be taught to us by the amazing people who sit in front of us in our classrooms.

To conclude, we would like to share some snapshots that illustrate how feminist pedagogy has changed how we teach Canadian foreign policy.

Heather: One year I had a CFP class that started at 8:30 on Friday mornings. Yet, it was somehow one of the most enjoyable classes I've ever had. There were a couple of students in the class who were exceedingly well-read, and they contributed daily but also in a manner that was respectful of other students. This allowed for some disruption of my authority and made the other students feel safer with their own views. This class also did group work that resulted in presentations, which at times included colouring images of Canada and Jeopardy style games. The students fully expected that I would participate in one of the groups rather than function on the outside. The laugher was as infectious as the learning. There was a joy in learning in this classroom that was quite amazing, and attendance was exceptional given the hour.

An upper-division CFP class I taught last year was quite small and composed of almost all women. It was run in a seminar style where the students ran the discussions, and they were not shy about asking very pointed questions of me, from time to time. As we sat around the table, the traditional deference to the professor evaporated as we all eagerly engaged in the discussions. The freedom to think for themselves was liberating, and the work that was done in this class was outstanding. The disruption of authority does not have to mean that there is chaos in the classroom; rather it empowers the students, they take more responsibility for their learning, and their work is often quite striking.

I also try to adopt a critically engaged position in all my classes and include gender in all of them, as well. There are ripple effects that my colleagues do not always appreciate. I've known students to leave my classes, having investigated gender or race or any number of issues from a critical perspective, and then ask for the same in other classes. They seek to claim their learning elsewhere.

Deborah: In every course, I try to include activities—role playing, simulations, or group research. In one class, I ask the students to take what they have learned about what is happening around the globe to their own communities, however they are defined. One year a group of students chose to explore the links between Canada's foreign policy and garment workers in Winnipeg. Another looked at the links between Canada's defence policy and the manufacture of components of arms in Winnipeg. Each of these brought Canadian foreign policy to where we all live.

I am using the Internet more in class as a separate place for class discussions. At the beginning of the year I put weekly questions on for discussion. As the year progresses, the students generate more and more of the questions and discussion. At one point in a recent year, in response to a general comment about human rights, a student asked specifically about how to deal with a recent experience with racism. The class was wonderfully supportive. They created a place online where this and other experiences of and responses to discrimination could be discussed frankly.

Once I let go of the need to be in complete control of the course agenda, I have found that the course is more dynamic and I am learning much more with my students. Students in third- and fourth-year classes have the option of presenting their research in a traditional research essay or in an alternative medium that we discuss and agree upon. Several students have created games that the class can play in the final days of the course. Others have chosen to present their work through an artistic medium. I have seen quilts of the capitalist world economy, plays about women's rights, and felt hangings about community economic development. My understanding of how research can be done has changed as a result.

Claire: I've found that the most difficult thing I've had to learn—and am still learning—is that teaching does not mean that I have to control everything that goes on in my classroom. That has been a tough struggle for someone whose natural inclinations are much more those of a control freak than of a more laid-back personality. I've had to learn to really trust my students, and not to simply pay lip service to trusting them. I have found that when I really trust my students to want to learn, to want to question, to want to work to gain their education, I feel more comfortable turning over part of the class time to them. I've done this in a variety of ways: open-ended simulations of the UN system or of the negotiations leading to the adoption of the International Convention banning anti-personnel mines is but one example. I ask students to work in teams to research the positions that they will be defending in the class simulation rather than provide them with the specifics of any national, or NGO, negotiating position. My trust has always been rewarded by students who become completely captivated by the learning process, even to the point of arriving at class on simulation day with carefully sewn national flags identifying their team and wearing doctors' lab coats if they were representing Médecins sans frontières, or Red Cross arm bands if they were speaking for the International Committee of the Red Cross. It is, however, the breadth and detail of their research which always strikes me and, if truth be told, surprises me still. They become the groups they are 'representing' in ways which are beyond anything that traditional pedagogy would suggest.

I think that the most significant part of feminist pedagogy for me is trying to create an environment that is supportive of student learning and that encourages students (I more naturally say 'class participants', and include myself in that group) to ask questions they otherwise might not ask. As a student, I was reluctant to take part in class discussions. As a professor, I constantly ask myself why, recognizing that I missed some of the most stimulating aspects of my education through my self-imposed silence. Though I still have not figured out how to create a supportive environment in a class of 75 or 100 (not to mention 200!), I do seek out the more timid students in my smaller classes and seminars to ask them if there are things I can do to make them feel more comfortable in my classroom and to make it easier for them to participate to the extent they might want. This does not always work, and there is always the chance that the student will try to tell you (in the most polite way, of course) that they are not participating because they are not interested in the subject matter that you are teaching and find the class a bore—but I have found that some of my 'quiet' students (mostly women) become active participants who bring an enormous amount to class discussion if I only take the time to find out how I can make the experience of class a more comfortable, and safer, one for them.

It's not all easy, though, and the demands of involved teaching are heavy. The real challenge now, for me and for my students, is one of time—wanting to hear all voices can inadvertently silence those who assume I'll be too busy, and who don't even try to see me any more as a result. Feminist pedagogy is about listening more than it is about speaking, and I continue to hope that I will be able to hear those who don't speak loudly, or who have chosen not to speak at all.

* * *

As bell hooks notes, the classroom is a location of possibility. We as instructors need to remember that while some say that teaching is a gift, we receive many gifts from the people in our classrooms. It is not a one-way street. Without a doubt some of the greatest satisfaction in our careers comes from knowing that these amazing people let us, even briefly, into their lives. None of us remain untouched from the experience. Words are magic, especially when we explore them together.

Part I

Internationalism and Globalization

Chapter 3

Disrupting Internationalism and Finding the Others

HEATHER A. SMITH

> All countries have national interests, but Canada has defined its national interest more broadly, less selfishly, than many others.
>
> –*Former Minister of External Affairs, Joe Clark (1997: 541)*

> Putting people first is a foreign policy approach suited to Canadians experiences, needs, interests and capacities. It is also an approach that is entirely suited to the realities of the world we live in, and in particular to the new dynamic of global peace and security.
>
> –*Former Minister of Foreign Affairs, Lloyd Axworthy (2000: 1)*

INTRODUCTION

To the uninitiated, the statements above may inspire a sense of pride in Canada's place in the world. We are less selfish! We are putting people first! We support global peace and security! The political discourse, as articulated above, suggests that Canada is a country committed to the global common good and the promotion of some vision of an international community. We understood Canada to be a moral state that seeks to build a more humane world.

Though the government rhetoric would be accepted wholeheartedly by few citizens or scholars, it perpetuates a myth of the good internationalist. Not only does this myth serve the political purpose of providing the government with a legacy of good works, but it masks the nature of Canadian foreign policy. Simply put, there is a gap between discourse and practice and discourse serves a purpose.

The various permutations of internationalism have been widely discussed by authors such as Kim Nossal (1997), Mark Neufeld (1999), Cranford Pratt (1990), and Michael Tucker (1980). This chapter problematizes the concept of internationalism by asking questions about otherness and difference. In doing so, it shows that a concept apparently based on inclusiveness actually creates others and promotes difference in the interest of the state. The analysis reveals that the inside/we and outside/them is a fluid construction. As Roxanne Doty (1996: 126) argues, 'the identity of the "we" is a flexible political resource, adaptable to changing circumstances and new crises'. In spite of the fluidity, the outside is inevitably manipulated, marginalized, and silenced, and those who are made to be others most often consist of women and the feminine, people of colour, and nature.

The chapter begins with a discussion of the concept of internationalism. Adopting a definition of internationalism offered by Kim Nossal (1998–9), we can identify, a government discourse infused with the precepts of internationalism. Turning to the analysis, I begin with an argument made by this author and Edna Keeble (Keeble and Smith 1999) in *(Re)Defining Traditions: Gender and Canadian Foreign Policy*. In that book, we focus on the gender dichotomies throughout the Canadian foreign-policy debate on role and status. We argue that internationalism is 'gendered' as the feminine as a means by which to promote difference. This 'gendering', however, masks the nature of internationalism and locks us into a binary analysis that needs to be made more complicated. Thus, this chapter extends the analysis to identify the multiple types of 'othering' that are embedded in the concept of internationalism and that are observable in the practice of Canadian foreign policy. The chapter proceeds to identify three examples of othering. First, the treatment of indigenous peoples in Canada shows us that in order to accept the legacy of internationalism we need to forget others inside the black box of the Canadian state. Second, the response to Chinese migrants in British Columbia reveals that the openness of internationalism is conditional on 'others' staying outside. Third, drawing on the case of climate change, we see that internationalism becomes bound to the interests of the state when 'genuine' state interests are challenged; this case also shows how the natural environment becomes the other. The penultimate section of the chapter attempts to bring the voices of the others back into Canadian foreign policy. This practice inevitably disrupts the mainstream understanding of the discipline but shows us a different vision when we bring the voices of the outside into the foreground as opposed to ignoring them or rendering them illegitimate.

Defining Internationalism

There is a certain irony in attempting to define internationalism with the aim of ultimately problematizing the concept; and yet we must have a starting point, and that starting point is a framework offered by Kim Nossal (1998–9). The Canadian variant of internationalism, according to Nossal, has four characteristics. The first is a commitment to multilateralism. Second, 'internationalism is, at bottom, directed toward creating, maintaining, and managing community at a global level' (Nossal 1998–9: 98). The third is good international citizenship, of which Nossal (1998–9: 99) says: 'while the phrase carries with it some ambiguities and unexplored assumptions, it nonetheless suggests that a country's diplomacy is directed toward ameliorating the common weal by taking actions explicitly designed to achieve that end'. Examples of good international citizenship include peacekeeping, military spending to support an alliance, and organizing support for a global ban on landmines (1998–9: 99–100). Nossal also argues that good international citizenship is marked not only by actions designed to change the external environment but 'rather, it is to convince others to alter their behavior and join in what ideally becomes a bandwagon effect, where the costs to recalcitrants go up sharply.

In other words, the demonstration effect of one's good international citizenship is as important as its instrumental impact' (1998–9: 100). Finally, 'internationalism is fundamentally a voluntaristic form of diplomacy; it is an entirely optional form of statecraft' (1998–9: 100). You act because you believe that 'contributing to a rules-based order will be in the general interest' (1998–9: 102).

Nossal does not consider that the present government is practising the kind of internationalism described above. Rather, he regards those characteristics noted above as the internationalism of the past. His argument, and dismay, are consistent with the views of scholars from across the ideological spectrum. Mark Neufeld (1995a: 22) argues that in the mid-1980s Canada began to adopt a 'limitationist conception of middle power'. This is 'a call to abandon exactly the kind of progressive action entailed by the definition of middle power proffered by the counter consensus, in favor of an orientation more in keeping with the existing power and privilege in Canadian society and in the global order' (Neufeld 1995a: 22). Jean-François Rioux and Robin Hay (1998–9: 57–8) describe Canada as 'practicing selective internationalism', which is driven by economic criteria with the end of promoting a narrowly constructed self-interest. It is not altogether clear what they view as internationalism and what they suggest Canada has moved away from. This said, the concluding paragraphs seem to imply that internationalism, as it used to be practised, was rooted in a sense of 'duties beyond border' and in interests that were not defined simply in economic terms (Rioux and Hay 1998–9: 74). Like Rioux and Hay, Nossal sees a change in Canada's international orientation. 'In particular, although the government remains concerned about community at the global level, there is no longer any great enthusiasm for voluntary acts of good international citizenship' (Nossal 1998–9: 103).

While I am completely sympathetic to the academic dismay at the gap between rhetoric and reality, what is crucial here is that the government's discourse suggests that internationalism is alive and well. The term 'internationalism' is used infrequently in the government's discourse as human security, and the promotion thereof, is undoubtedly the favoured term in the present government's foreign policy lexicon. Yet, internationalism underscores human security, and it functions as the dominant idea (Nossal 1997: 138–43) in which human security is nested. To flesh out this argument, we return to Nossal's (1998–9) fourfold definition to show how it correlates with government statements.

First, multilateralism is viewed as an essential component of Canadian foreign policy. One of the preferred options for multilateral foreign policy is the building of coalitions of like-minded states. In the case of the landmines ban it has been said that the Ottawa Process 'was carried forward by a coalition of the willing seeking a solution to an international humanitarian crisis that ignores national boundaries' (Axworthy and Taylor 1998: 193). Second, community is understood very broadly. The international community is all-inclusive, involving states, non-governmental organizations, the private sector, and—most important—human beings. It is a global community, not just a state based community. In a statement by the Department of Foreign Affairs and International Trade Statement (DFAIT), the introduction by Lloyd Axworthy quotes a statement by Vaclav Havel that seems to suggest Canada's vision of community in the new global order: 'the sovereignty of the community, the region, the nation, the state . . . makes sense only if it is derived from the one genuine sovereignty that is, from the sovereignty of the human being' (DFAIT 2000a). Central to Canada's role in the creation, maintenance, and management of community at the global level is the promotion of new norms. For example, Canada appears to be an avid supporter of the concept of democratic peace. 'The absence of inclusive and responsive institutions may contribute to political and social exclusion and discontent, destabilization and, in some cases, violent conflict. By contrast, democratic political institutions entail structures of governance that promote and ensure political access, responsiveness and accountability' (DFAIT 2000a: 10). Another norm that Canada is actively promoting is freedom of opinion and expression: 'Respect for freedom of opinion and expression, including freedom of the press and access to information, is a cornerstone of a free and democratic society' (DFAIT 2000a: 9). Particularly important to Canada is the promotion of people's safety, which must be seen as a central element of global peace and security (DFAIT 2000a: 13). Putting people at the centre 'reminds us that sovereignty as a concept has no defensible meaning unless it is grounded in the state's responsibility and accountability to its people' (DFAIT 2000a: 13). The reason that Canada is able to promote new norms in the international arena is that we have assets, including 'attractive values, a reputation as an honest broker, a democratic tradition of openness, and a willingness to work closely with civil society' (Axworthy and Taylor 1998: 193). Good international citizenship is viewed as a moral imperative in an era of rapid change. In our capacity as good international citizen, Canada recognizes the need for new kinds of diplomacy, leadership in setting agendas, and the need to promote human security. For Canada, the emphasis is now on the protection of people from the threat of violence, and thus five priorities have been identified: the protection of civilians, peace-support operations, prevention of conflict, governance and accountability, and public safety (DFAIT 2000a: 4). Finally, voluntarism also informs the government discourse. There is a clear sense that the security of Canadians is contingent on the broader global security, but the promotion of the International Criminal Court, for example, is in the greater interest and not motivated by a particular Canadian national bias. Canada's goal of ensuring that 'people can live in freedom from fear' (DFAIT 2000a: 2) can further be interpreted as representing an optional form of statecraft.

In spite of the acknowledged existence of the gap between discourse and practice, consideration of the discourse remains an important task because internationalism is gendered. It is used rhetorically to soften the hard edges of what is otherwise realist behaviour—behaviour that contributes to the perpetuation of others. There is power in discourse that must be acknowledged and examined. As Deborah Stienstra (1994–5: 123–4) notes, the words and ideas that are the language of Canadian foreign policy affect human activities, define what is legitimate and illegitimate, and thus have a role in silencing and marginalizing certain voices.

Problematizing Internationalism

In the third chapter of *(Re)Defining Traditions: Gender and Canadian Foreign Policy* (Keeble and Smith 1999), we examine the role and status debate from the standpoint feminist approach. We begin by asking: 'are there countries that exhibit feminine characteristics and behavior' (Neack, Hay, and Haney 1995: 168). Feminine characteristics are understood to include 'pacificity, passivity, cooperative-problem solving and mediation', in contrast to masculine characteristics such as 'belligerence, fierce independence, self-interested actions over community interests' (Neack, Hay, and Haney 1995: 168). The chapter surveys the role and status debate while rereading the middle power, principal power, and satellite debate. Of particular interest here is the analysis of internationalism.

We showed that the academic debates about internationalism assume a gender neutrality. We also recognized the universalizing tendencies inherent in internationalism. These tendencies are readily apparent when one considers the assumption that Canada is promoting norms and values that it deems attractive. Canada is working with like-minded states to promote a world order that seems like an attempt to tame other civilizations in our own image. These tendencies are obvious in current practice, but they are not new to this government, for the civilizing thrust of Canadian foreign policy has historical roots (see Keeble and Smith 1999: 54).

What we found particularly intriguing was that some strains of internationalism valorized the feminine. For example, Michael Tucker (1980) and Peter Dobell (1972) identified an idealist impulse in Canadian foreign policy. This impulse softened the hard edges of realism. This idealist impulse was the basis for claims that Canada was somehow being more moral and less selfish than other countries, as suggested in the quotations at the beginning of the chapter. Internationalism is painted with a 'feminine' brush if Canada acts for the global good as opposed to nationalistic self-interest, promotes co-operation rather than conflict, and seeks to mediate and solve problems rather than to engage in belligerent autonomy. We argued that one can describe the construction of Canada as 'feminine' state in such a way as to make Canada appear 'better'.

We concluded that 'the feminine gender stereotype was used in Canadian foreign policy to lay claim to a unique foreign policy, not to create fundamental change in the international system. For the purposes of the Canadian state, the "feminine" is used to infuse internationalism with a sense of difference or uniqueness' (Keeble and Smith 1999: 56). In this instance, the 'other' is presented as masculine, while Canada, as the 'we', is feminine.

We do not accept that Canada is a feminine state. This construction completely obfuscates the reality of Canadian practice and would lead us to accept, uncritically, the pronouncements of the Canadian government. Moreover, to accept the construction of Canada as feminine would make us complicit in the denial of the way the discourse functions. Ultimately, we argue that a critical feminist perspective is needed because it asks us to inquire 'for whom that construction is' and 'what purpose it serves'.

These questions are the basis for the analysis here. They move us beyond an assessment of the contrivance of the feminine state and lead us to a richer analysis of the concept of internationalism. We are reminded that internationalism is far more complicated than the rhetoric would suggest. We find that internationalism serves the Canadian state, not the global community, and in the service to the state, many voices are silenced.

Internationalism is a multi-dimensional concept. Cecilia Lynch (1999), for example, has identified four types of internationalism, and although her analysis draws on the American experience, some parts of her typology are applicable to the Canadian case. First, she identifies democratic peace internationalism, which is committed to promoting 'the cosmopolitan project on a world wide scale' (Lynch 1999: 94). We can observe this in Canada in its promotion of global governance. Second, and primarily linked to the work of non-governmental organizations, is the promotion of humanitarian internationalism, which according to Lynch (1999: 94), 'attempts to relieve suffering in the midst of civil and nationalist strife'. In the Canadian case we may make links to humanitarian intervention. Third, there is market internationalism, which is rooted in the assumption that 'economic globalization is both inevitable and the best means of improving economic welfare' (Lynch 1999: 96). This type of internationalism dominates Canadian practice as evinced in niche diplomacy. Finally, there is anti-market globalization that promotes 'a measure of economic egalitarianism while providing a frontal challenge to economic globalization' (Lynch 1999: 96). One is hard pressed to find evidence of this practice by the Canadian state, but it is evident in civil society activities, discussed elsewhere in this volume.

Drawing from the democratic peace internationalism, Canada's internationalism is marked by a liberal rights ethic that extends the equity principle while at the same time functioning in a manner that is assimilationist and colonizing (Dunne 1997: 315). Second, liberal internationalism itself, and especially the market internationalism manifested in current government practice, is driven by 'notions of competition, individuality, and rational economic man [that have] meant prosperity for the few and exploitation of the many' (Ashworth and Swatuk 1998: 87).

Finally, by thinking critically about the manipulation of the feminine by the Canadian state, we are reminded that internationalism is integral to Canadian nationalism. This is important because internationalism functions as a rhetorical device in the service of the state. It veils, albeit thinly, the actual practices of the state, which are ultimately designed to reinforce and protect the state. This manipulation of the feminine to serve the national interest and promote the state is not unique to Canada.

Internationalism may be described as anti-statist, or as denoting 'a cosmopolitan non parochial stance toward obligation beyond borders' (Lynch 1999: 83), but it is limited by the essentials of nationalism. The national interest 'is in essence about the preservation of the political expression of the nation, the sovereign state, and defense of the nation from "foreigners" who threaten its political and territorial integrity and its distinctive identity' (Steans 1998: 63). While former Minister of Foreign Affairs Lloyd Axworthy envisions a world of more than sovereign states, in fact Canadian practice does not suggest a promotion of global community but rather the reinforcement of difference. Our practice preserves the integrity of the inside outside dichotomy, and 'renders invisible the multiplicity of identities which co-exist within this particular political space and the transnational dimensions of political identification' (Steans 1998: 76). In its Canadian manifestation, internationalism cannot escape its nationalist bias and does little to challenge the 'inside/outside' problematique of sovereignty in the global order (Lynch 1999: 83).

Three examples that illustrate the 'othering' that takes place in Canadian foreign policy are the treatment of First Nations and indigenous peoples in Canada, the treatment of Chinese migrants who arrived in British Columbia in 1999, and Canadian policy on climate change. It will be seen that there are many others created by Canadian practice as the 'we' is defined in terms that exclude others inside, try to keep others outside, and forget that in some ways we are part of a greater we. These examples also expose the realist face of the Canadian state and contradict the foreign policy rhetoric.

Internationalism must be understood as the Canadian face to the outside. The domestic sources of Canadian foreign policy have been considered by scholars (Nossal 1983–4; Pratt 1983–4), and while we promote our values to the world (DFAIT 1995a: 34–9), the inside of the state is rarely problematized. Thus, the discussion of human security, governance, and peacemaking and the promotion of soft power is what 'we' show others while at the same time strategically ignoring some of the contradictions that exist inside the black box. It is assumed that Canada speaks with one voice as we express a homogenized set of values. What happens if we rip open the black box? We find a country that is unquestionably privileged but also a country whose history has moments of shame, moments that disrupt the legacy of internationalism.

The genesis of internationalism as a dominant idea is generally associated with the 'Golden Era' of foreign policy in the late 1940s and the 1950s. It is rarely mentioned that during this time the Canadian state was actively involved in the relocation of Inuit peoples in the Eastern Arctic (Tester and Kulchyski 1994). Canada was, at the same time, maintaining a reserve system for First Nations peoples that has been described as 'coercive tutelage' (Dyck 1991: 3). The horrid conditions of the reservations have been described by Bridget Moran, author of *Stoney Creek Woman: The Story of Mary John*. She describes her first visit to the Stoney Creek reserve in northern British Columbia:

> Within minutes, when the residents of Stoney Creek recognized the car as a government vehicle, they surrounded me, crying for help. Almost all the pleaders were women. Many of them had rags wrapped around their feet; their clothes were pitiful to see and their faces were lined and haggard. I was ashamed then, and I am ashamed to this day, that I could do nothing for them. (Moran 1988: 14–15)

While Canada was promoting internationalism to the outside, it was maintaining a reserve system on the inside akin to that of the South African townships. Boundaries were constructed to keep First Nations and Inuit peoples in their place. These peoples were viewed as inferior. Noel Dyck (1991: 25–6) writes: 'The entire exercise is founded upon not only the moral devaluation of Indians and Indianness, but also on the creation of an ideal and privileged image of Euro-Canadian values and virtues. At this level of discourse the notions of Indianness and Whiteness cannot be dealt with in isolation from one another.' These boundaries were defined by racism, but it was racism masked by the human face of the liberal welfare state.

> In the case of First Nations and aboriginal peoples, the racism inherent in the welfare state takes an assimilationist form but has been couched, historically in liberal humanitarian language. Thus, those developing and delivering services within the precepts of welfare liberalism argued, as was consistent with the liberal discourse on rights, that they were committed to extending the privilege of citizenship developed by the Canadian state to all Canadians. This discourse is also about nation building—about creating a country of shared values, in the belief that the end result would be social harmony, as well as proficiency and efficiency in the capitalist development of Canada's economic base. (Tester and Kulchyski 1994: xi–xii)

The example of the treatment of First Nations and aboriginal peoples is food for thought about how internationalism selectively forgets this part of the country's past as it is buried in the black box. The Canadian government has asserted that 'Canadians by and large are not seen as encumbered by colonial or imperial baggage; as a result, we do not face an initial wall of suspicion when we work with another country or culture' (DFAIT 1999f: 2). A member of a First Nation would differ on that point. Internal colonization is still colonization, but it is strategically forgotten when we promote our values internationally. If we open up the black box we challenge the assumption of exemplarity that is embedded in the universalizing pronouncements (Doty 1996: 135) of internationalism. If we looked even more closely, what would we find? Who is at the margins of society and who is on the bottom rungs (Enloe 1996)? Lines are drawn in such a way as to discourage that kind of investigation of the black box because we find 'others' on the inside that contradict the vision that 'we' seek to promote.

Not only does the horrid treatment of First Nations peoples contradict the image of Canada projected during the Golden Era, but it reminds us of the assimilationist tendencies of the liberal humanitarian ethic that is promoted to this day. 'Canadian values' were imposed on the First Nations with the assumption that social harmony would follow, as noted by Tester and Kulchyski. Are we not doing exactly the same thing through the promotion of democratic peace? If internationalism is about creating and maintaining a global community, as suggested by Nossal in the previous section, should we not ask: whose community? Whose norms should dominate the international arena? The language of internationalism assumes that the community would be created in our own likeness, thus exposing the embedded exemplarity. In this instance, we are trying to make 'them' more like 'us'.

As noted earlier, however, there are many forms of othering. Around the world developed states are trying to grapple with the growing flow of people fleeing their countries because of war, famine, repression, and poverty. Most developed countries try to keep the migrants out, especially the poor and unskilled. Those with skills and money are generally more welcome. While not unique in its position, Canada is expelling migrants who have arrived in Canada as part of the growing trade in people.

Illegal Chinese migrants began to arrive in boatloads off the coast of British Columbia the summer of 1999 (see also Chapter 11, this volume). Reflective of worldwide human smuggling operations worth about $9 billion US [$15 billion Cdn] a year, these migrants were coming to find a better life, although they were probably headed for restaurants, sweatshops, and in the case of the women, prostitution. Their reception in British Columbia was chilly: they were greeted in Port Hardy by some local residents holding signs that said 'feed our people first' and 'go home' (CBC News 1999a). In September of 1999, the Reform Party of Canada stated that the migrants should simply be deported more quickly, casting the migrants as tuberculosis-ridden 'others' who wanted to live off Canada's generous social programs (CBC News 1999b). Many of the migrants were transported to northern British Columbia to be housed in an old prison in the city of Prince George. They were to be detained until they had gone through the refugee process. Almost all failed to meet the criteria for refugee status.

In May 2000, the first group of migrants was deported to China. According to one official, the transfer went well. 'Apart from some tears from one or two of the migrants who did not want to leave, there were no problems' (Miller 2000: 1). 'Most of the individuals were very happy to be going back to China', stated an immigration official (*Prince George Citizen* 2000a: 6). Refugee advocates, however, tell a slightly different story. They speak of the three women who tried to commit suicide before the deportation, of a man who packed a razor blade so that he could kill himself en route, and of SWAT teams and police officers guarding against the escape of the shackled deportees, who were terrified of the implications of their return (*Prince George Citizen* 2000a: 6). Meanwhile, other migrants were escaping from the Prince George prison. All were captured. The last of a group of seven escapees was captured in the first week of June after he appeared at the door of a local citizen 'wearing white overalls and bundled in brown industrial paper' (*Prince George Citizen* 2000b: 1) and asking for help or food. The citizen called the police. Local officials have told the citizens of Prince George that the migrants are not 'considered dangerous or criminals in the traditional sense of the word' (*Prince George Citizen* 2000b: 1) but that 'because of the security risk, migrants are no longer being offered work in the less secure areas of the jail' (*Prince George Citizen* 2000b: 1).

The response of some of the citizens of Prince George was similar to the sign wavers in Port Hardy. While not representative of the views of all the citizens, the 'Letters to the Editor' section of the Prince George newspaper included statements such as the following: 'Is it any wonder that there is apparently no funds to provide adequate health care when our money is being spent on those illegal immigrants who have no business being here in the first place' (*Prince George Citizen* 2000c: 4). Another letter appears under the headline 'Migrants: Our Health Risk'. The writer asks: 'Just because we have this old jail sitting here, do we have to take in all the illegal immigrants? Since no one is complaining, what's the next step, after they get out of jail? Finding them jobs and housing in Prince George? We don't have jobs for our own young people, let alone taking in China's' (*Prince George Citizen* 2000d: 4). The letter goes on to link the migrants with tuberculosis, hepatitis, malaria, and criminal activity. What little can be discovered about the migrants suggests that rather than criminals they are farmers and factory workers often making as little as $6 a day (CBC News 2000a).

This case is important for several reasons. It tells us a lot about what 'internationalism' does. First, internationalism as is understood in Canadian foreign policy does not encourage us to look within, and consequently, the migrants are nameless and faceless. They are not people, they are 'migrants' who have chosen of their own will to come to Canada, illegally. And though they are part of a global phenomenon of human smuggling, they are not given a human face when they infringe on our security. And in presenting the migrants as the other, we absolve ourselves of complicity in fostering a global system that impels desperate people to board leaky boats and try to get into Canada 'illegally'.

Second, the case of the migrants shows the complicated and often arbitrary nature of citizenship. The migrants have few rights in Canada. Indeed, by virtue of the *Singh et al. v. Minister of Employment and Immigration* case heard by the Supreme Court of Canada in 1985, inland claimants, as in the case of the migrants, were entitled to a full oral hearing before the Immigration and Refugee Board (Ontario, Attorney General 2002, 1). Yet the state retains the right to detain people 'who arrive illegally and claim refugee status if the person's identity cannot be determined, if it is feared the person might disappear before the refugee hearing, or if he or she is thought to be potentially dangerous to society' (CBC News 1999c). The Chinese migrants were deemed both 'illegal' and 'dangerous'. It is particularly interesting to note, however, that these illegal and dangerous migrants could have been given landed-immigrant status if they testified against the smugglers (CBC News 1999d, 1). Did they suddenly become 'legal' and 'safe' when they put themselves at greater risk in the Canadian state's pursuit of the snakeheads?

Though the issue is certainly too complicted to be presented in a few pages, it illustrates the double edge of internationalism. The actions of the Canadian government and some Canadian citizens do not reflect the values of humanitarianism; rather the state and citizens are protected from the foreigners, from the 'others' who in some way threaten our well-being (see also Chapter 11, this volume). We may promote community internationally, but it seems that our 'community' is defined on our terms by our state for fear that snakeheads will deliver boatloads of poor Chinese migrants to the shores of Vancouver Island. One must wonder if rather than community, Canada is in fact promoting 'global apartheid' (Richmond 1994). Global apartheid hardly sits well with the language of 'good international citizenship'.

This case also encourages us to think about race. As Randolph Persaud argues (1997: 183), 'race is likely to overlap with the marginalisation generated by globalisation, and with the new national security of the West. The proximate concerns about too many migrants (and refugees), combined with the larger fears of civilization erosion, have already given rise to a siege mentality type of politics in the West'. This attitude toward refugees and migrants or groups of citizens considered to be 'others' is not new to Canada: one needs only to think of the Japanese interned during the Second World War. Historically, the Canadian state had rules for refugees and immigrants that were racist and discriminatory, and though one may wish to argue that this is a thing of the past, the work of the Canadian Council of Refugees (2000) suggests otherwise. For example, in 1995, the federal government imposed a Right of Landing fee of $975 on every new immigrant and refugee. Canada was the only country in the world to charge such a fee. This fee has just recently been rescinded (Citizenship and Immigration Canada 2000b), but regulations concerning immigration and refugees have tightened since the events of 11 September 2001.

Finally, this case reveals that an enthusiasm among Canadian citizens for duties beyond our borders should not be assumed as it is in the pronouncements of DFAIT. The values of Canadians are far more complicated than the discourse suggests. We are not encouraged to examine the underbelly of the state or of the Canadian psyche. To excuse the behaviour of some citizens and claim they are conditioned by the state would deny the power of individual citizens. The actions of the state are legitimized and reinforced by the everyday actions of individual Canadians. The community of 'we' is one made up of Canadian citizens, and that which is sovereign is the Canadian state, which in this instance has the power to undermine the security of individuals. It is a far cry from the rhetoric of internationalism.

Finally, we turn to a third example of 'othering' that exists in Canadian foreign policy: the case of climate change. Here the 'we' becomes the Canadian state working in tandem with other Northern countries. The 'other' is both the environment and developing countries and ultimately, the citizens of developing states. Like the other examples, the story of climate change is one of state defined interests where 'good international citizenship' seems scarce. Canada's behaviour is driven by market internationalism, as described previously.

Theoretically, the issue of climate change centres on competing assumptions about our connection to nature, contested constructions of progress, and clashing philosophies of justice. In practice, it has been an extremely difficult problem to combat because the primary culprit is carbon dioxide, and carbon dioxide is a product of the everyday activities of almost every individual. The largest emissions, historically, are those produced by the activities of the Western developed states, although it is predicted that the emissions of developing states such as China and India will outpace those of the West in the future. The contentious nature of the issue is clear when one observes that recent international negotiations on climate change broke down, interestingly enough, over divisions between the European Union and an American-led alliance over, among other things, the means by which emissions should be reduced.

For Canada, the main concern is competitiveness and therefore the need to get international rules right that ensure that Canadian economic well-being is protected. It is a position shared with a coalition of like-minded countries, including the United States, Japan, and Australia. The 'other' then becomes the developing states. Inherent in this construction is a question of equity, but as seen by Canada, the issue is one of fairness to Canadian companies. This issue of equity

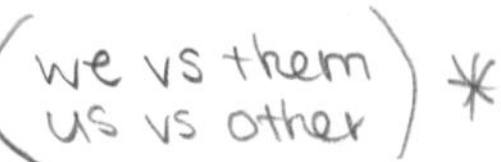

> has traditionally been the most divisive of all issues within the Convention, pitting developing countries (who advocate a formula based on historical contributions to atmospheric CO_2 or per capita emissions) against developed countries concerned with carbon leakage, international competitiveness and general economic well being. (Federal/Provincial/Territorial Ministers of Energy and Environment 2000: 27)

States such as Canada, the United States, and Australia are reluctant to accept their historic responsibilities because it could result in expectations for significant reductions on their part.

Climate change is generally recognized to be a global issue, at least in the government rhetoric. The Canadian position is that all states should take some action, and Canada is willing to help facilitate change in the behaviour of other states. And while it is a global issue, and is presented as a global issue when Canada hopes to encourage the participation of the developing states, the Canadian position is defined by the interests of the state when the economy appears threatened. In the words of one Canadian government document, Canada, Australia, and the United States are 'concerned with the fact that only Annex I countries have adopted emission reduction commitments, as they believe that this represents an unfair trade advantage for developing countries (many of whom compete with Annex I countries for trade markets' (Federal/Provincial/Territorial Ministers of Energy and Environment 2000: 22).

In the midst of all of this the environment is marginalized (see also Chapter 8, this volume). The climate change discourse has become one about competitiveness, and value is accorded to gross domestic product in an era when 'more is better'. True to realist precepts the interests of the state are protected. The integrity of the environment, while perhaps underpinning international concern, is not a driving force in the discourse of most states. The marginal position of the environment is consistent with the eco-feminist argument that the 'so called advancements in human civilization led to the worldwide subordination of all things "other" than white, Western males, including women, non-white humans, non human life and the natural environment' (Hallock Johnson 1999: 222). One does not have to be an eco-feminist to acknowledge that the environment is being treated as less important then immediate concerns of the industrialized world. It should not be difficult to accept that the environment is victimized by human behaviour.

So, one may ask, how does this relate to internationalism? First, it is an example of multilateralism that will perpetuate inequality and unsustainable behaviour. Without the environment on the agenda, the climate change talks are nothing but economic negotiations. Canada's behavior can be regarded as a evidence of the dominance of market internationalism. Second, the notions of community articulated in internationalism must again be questioned. At this time, Canada and other Western states have defined climate change and other global environmental issues as problems, but they are problems to be addressed on their terms, by the others. As Georoid O Tuathail (1996: 253) argues: 'questions of ozone depletion, rainforest cover, biodiversity, global warming and production using environmentally hazardous materials are the subjects of new environmentalist mappings of global contemporary acts of geo-power that triangulate global space around the fears and fantasies of the already affluent'. The climate change discourse is universalizing and can be regarded as new type of imperialism: eco-imperialism. Third, for all of the talk about people being put in the centre of our foreign policy, one cannot help but ask: which people? Canadian negotiators and political leaders might suggest that they are working on our behalf. But what about our children or the children of a woman living in Mexico? One could suggest that the Canadian state is working on behalf of the oil and gas industry. Internationalism seems short on any intergenerational norms in spite of its claims to be so forward thinking. Finally, if the environment is left out of the equation in practice, we can yet again observe another gap between discourse and practice. More significantly, we are reminded of the general tendency to view the environment as something to dominate and master, as opposed to something that sustains us.

The three cases examined in this section show us that while the government discourse may suggest that internationalism is alive and well, we are well advised to be skeptical. Skepticism is important because there is a gap between discourse and practice. Canadian practice has not reflected norms of openness and community but rather the opposite. Practice reveals that we have forgotten those inside who have not and did not fit with the dominant vision of the Canadian citizen. Practice reveals the Chinese migrants are a threat as they run through the woods wrapped in brown paper. Practice reveals that we are reluctant to protect the environment for fear of undermining economic development. And, practice reveals that the integrity of the environment is a secondary concern. There are many 'others' often without a voice or a face. Recognizing the need to give a voice to the others, the next section disrupts Canadian foreign policy by asking about everyday practice.

Canadian Foreign Policy and Everyday Practice

Christine Sylvester (1996: 262) has raised the issue of 'everyday forms of feminist theorizing', which is understood to encompass 'everyday forms of resistance and struggle [which] issue from activities of average people'. She suggests that we look at people in their everyday places of action—places that would not usually attract the attention of scholars of International Relations or Canadian foreign policy scholars. 'To suggest bringing such people into international relations is earth-shaking for a field that admits only official decision-makers, soldiers, statesmen, terrorists, kings, and the occasional "crazed" religious group to the fold' (Sylvester 1996: 264). It is equally bizarre in the context of CFP where, with few exceptions, the individual and personal are virtually non-existent, as the everyday is otherwise insignificant.

The work of Cynthia Enloe, who links the personal and the international, affirms the value of this approach. In her assessments of the lives of women she reveals the fiction of 'the state' and shows how much power is needed to keep people silent and marginalized.

> It is only by delving deeper into any political system, listening more attentively at the margins, that one can accurately estimate the powers it has taken to provide the state with the apparent stability that has permitted its elite to speak on behalf of a coherent whole. Only with this explicit political accounting can we explain why the evolving international system takes the turn it does today (Enloe 1996: 200).

This approach challenges the academic tradition of Canadian foreign policy. It could include the stories of women in Canada and make links to those affected by Canadian foreign policies. A human face could be revealed. Mary John, the Carrier woman on the Stoney Creek reserve, offers us a story of her life. Through her story we are able to see the racism that is inherent in the Canadian system and that is obvious to those who are being oppressed while denied by those doing the oppressing. 'Many times I have wondered why the church and the government got together years ago and almost destroyed our culture. I guess they thought they had to do that to convert the Native people, the savages, as they called us' (Moran 1988: 124). But the story of Mary John is also one of everyday resistance as she teaches her people the language and songs of their culture. And in the end, her hope is for the kind of human security inside that Canada seems willing to offer the rest of the world: 'We must keep our language, our culture, and our land so that, even in Canada, we can still feel that we have our own country. And while we preserve these things, it is my hope that some day we will also have reserves where the young can be educated, where there is employment for all and where my people will choose to live, and work, and finally, to die and rest in peace' (Moran 1988: 159).

Imagine, if you will, if we more closely examined the case of the three Chinese migrant women who tried to commit suicide. She, trying to escape poverty, is drawn to the 'Golden Mountain' of North America. It is a land of privilege and wealth where perhaps a better life can be found. She is subsequently detained in a prison and faced with deportation back to a state that is a well-known violator of human rights. She does not get refugee status. She lacks the skills and money to be considered an immigrant. She tries to kill herself. She is removed from the prison under the darkness of the northern British Columbian night, put on a bus, and driven south. Surrounded by police officers, she and her fellow migrants are loaded on to a plane and sent back to China. One can only wonder, and that is the most that those of us living in Canada can do, what life will be like for her back in China. And, what would our response be if it was someone we loved, someone from our family, our community, someone who was not seen as the other?

What would the environment say? Anthropogenic constructions of security and masculinist visions of the separation of man and nature do not offer us a 'natural' face. In some way perhaps, the environment speaks to us as snowstorms ravage cities unexpectedly, diseases migrate northwards, and land that has had all the nutrients sucked out of it refuses any longer to grow crops. But what if the environment had a voice that spoke in words, not just in natural processes that we seem willing to ignore? What then would the environment say, not as a she or a he, but as an entity that supports our existence? Maybe the environment would simply say that it was tired of all the abuse. Surely it would mock the liberal notions of progress that delude many into thinking that a new car is something we all must have. Maybe the environment would simply weep.

And what of those who become others in the climate change debate because they happened to have been born in developing states? How does a person in Kenya or Madagascar, for example, respond to the views of Canada and other developed states that the growth of the developing countries is a threat to the developed economies? Some may say that they have the right to develop in the manner similar to the North. Still others may simply note that all the commotion about climate change is irrelevant when they cannot feed their children. Henry Shue (1999: 543) argues:

> If wealthy states are content to allow radical inequalities to persist and worsen, it is difficult to see why the poor states should divert their attention from their own worst problems in order to help out with problems that for them are far less immediate and deadly. It is as if I am starving to death, and you want me to agree to stop searching for food and instead to help repair a leak in the roof of your house without promising me any food.

Everyday practice is an approach that would change the way we do and understand Canadian foreign policy. To some it may be nothing more than telling stories, but the stories that would be told would reveal to us the real human face, the face that is homogenized in the construction of human security. We would have a greater understanding of how we as citizens are complicit in the making of foreign policy or how we can offer resistance. Perhaps we would have a greater understanding of those 'others' that foreign policy affects.

As feminist scholars and teachers, everyday practice would affect *us*. If the personal is the international, if we are part of the process and affected by the process, surely we have stories to tell that will help us to understand the power relations that try to keep women, the poor, people of colour, gays and lesbians, and all other 'others' in their place. Random and structural threats of violence, institutionalized obstacles, implicit criteria of legitimate and illegitimate all shape our lives. And surely we can identify how in our everyday lives we resist those forces—non-heroic everyday practice. Perhaps this approach is beyond the acceptance of what constitutes Canadian foreign policy, perhaps it is not scientific or generalizable, however, if the front lines are everywhere, where are our front lines?

Concluding Reflections

This chapter challenges the traditions of Canadian foreign policy in a variety of ways. It asks questions about internationalism in such a way that we can observe the others that are hidden in the concept or the others that are created by the actions of the state. We are reminded of the treatment of First Nations and indigenous peoples in this country, a theme that is rarely addressed in traditional foreign policy analysis. These peoples are strategically forgotten when we consider internationalism. This chapter also considers the case of the Chinese migrants in British

Columbia, a case that reveals the ugly underbelly of so-called Canadian values, values that are rarely questioned. The migrants are presented as a threat and they become 'others' without a voice. By including the environment in the analysis we draw on eco-feminist work while at the same time reminding readers that it is not only non-white people, but also nature, that is pushed to the side in the name of the rational economic man.

This chapter also tells us about the discipline of Canadian foreign policy. Just as we are well advised to be skeptical of the rhetoric, we must be skeptical of using the tools of the discipline. We must not assign a naturalness to internationalism and its component parts. We must question concepts such a good international citizenship. We need to think critically about the ways in which the construction of internationalism translates itself into the management of who is part of a community. We must challenge the implied benevolence of Canadian behaviour at home and abroad. We must ask further questions about silences in the discipline. Where are First Nations peoples in our analysis? Where is the analysis of race and sexual preference? The practice of Canadian foreign policy has been portrayed (at least implicitly) as exemplary. There is also an accepted homogenization in how and what we study. The strangeness of the preceding section is testimony to the power of the discipline to legitimate certain voices and marginalize others. Not only does the practice of foreign policy privilege the state; so too does much of the scholarship. Rarely are people's voices heard as we seek patterns and identify explanatory variables. In the end, however, there is hope. The hope comes from recognizing the proliferation of others, because in this recognition we acknowledge the power relations that support the construction of the state and Canadian foreign policy. Hope also comes from the possibility of including a human voice. This project has only begun, but it a project well worth continuing. Perhaps by listening to the real human voices we can come together to resist the making of multiple others.

Chapter 4

Gender and Canadian Trade Policy: Women's Strategies for Access and Transformation[1]

LAURA MACDONALD

INTRODUCTION

One of the most important changes in Canadian foreign policy in the past ten to fifteen years has been the dramatic transformation of Canadian policy, in which the Canadian state turned away from a more protectionist policy that shielded domestic industry from some of the harsher effects of foreign competition, to a much more open and liberalized policy. This shift is so profound that Canadian trade policy expert Gilbert Winham describes it as a 'revolution' in Canadian trade policy. Not only does this revolution affect trade regulations, but it has important implications for Canadian society, including employment, social policies, the environment, human rights, democracy, and state-society relations. During the period of this trade revolution, public concerns about the social implications of trade agreements have been brought to the fore by debates and protests about trade agreements like the Canada–US free trade agreement (FTA) of 1988, the 1999 World Trade Organization (WTO) talks in Seattle. and the Free Trade Area of the Americas (FTAA) in Quebec City in 2000. The Canadian government has made several efforts to allay these concerns, for example by signing the side accords on labour and the environment in the North American Free Trade Agreement (NAFTA), and by arguing for mechanisms for civil society consultation as part of the talks leading up to the FTAA agreement.

The Canadian government has thus begun a debate with representatives of Canadian civil society about the broader social implications of trade liberalization, moving beyond the impasse that arose during the debate over the FTA (see Macdonald 2000). However, changes in trade regimes also have important implications for gender relations. Nevertheless, up to the present, no constructive dialogue has occurred over the gender implications of trade liberalization between the Department of Foreign Affairs and International Trade (DFAIT) and women's organizations. DFAIT has remained silent about, and seemingly oblivious to, these implications, despite the strong criticism that women's organizations have levelled at Canadian trade policies, dating back to the FTA of 1988, and despite increased recent concern on the part of Status of Women Canada concerning trade issues. Nor, despite Canada's commitments made at the Beijing UN Conference on

Women in 1995, has the department provided any systematic evaluation of the impact of Canadian trade policies on Canadian women, although they have tried to respond to the challenges of women entrepreneurs in the global economy (see Chapter 5, this volume).

This chapter contributes to a gendered critique of Canadian foreign policy in two ways. First, I examine the reasons for the 'gender blindness' in Canadian policy, and indicate how this policy ignores ways in which women (both within and outside Canada) are affected differently than men by changes in trade regulations, as a result of pre-existing differences in access to power and resources. Second, I provide an overview of some of the different ways in which Canadian women have become active in contesting the gendered impact of trade agreements. Canadian women activists and analysts have adopted at least two different strategies in response to the diverse impact of trade on women. Diane Elson refers to the two strategies: one that focuses on *access*, and one that focuses on *transformation*. The strategy for access concentrates on 'removing barriers to women's access to markets, to credit, to land, to training, and to better employment opportunities' (Elson 1994: 8). As well, strategies of access tend to emphasize the number of employment opportunities. This strategy may focus on national policies but also may work for the incorporation of women's voices within official trade negotiations and forums.

In contrast, a strategy of transformation 'considers the social framework and quality of those employment opportunities—whether they are the kind of employment opportunities that deplete human resources or the kinds of employment opportunities that enable us to use our capacities in more fruitful ways' (Elson 1994: 9). This strategy tends to draw out the broader context in which changes in trade and employment occur, and, as we will see in the discussion below of the coalitions opposed to NAFTA, the Asia Pacific Economic Cooperation forum (APEC), and the WTO, it may work more from outside the multilateral trade bodies than from inside. Nevertheless, as Elson suggests, it is possible that 'we need a two-pronged strategy where we think both in terms of access to, and also in terms of transformation of the productive strategies' (1994: 9). Although the changes in trade that have taken place in both regional trading blocs and the implementation of the new WTO create new threats to some women, they also create some new opportunities. In particular, the new trade arrangements, by making the effects of trade more visible, may provide opportunities for unprecedented forms of opposition by women to the terms of trade, as seen in all the cases of women's organizing described below. The previous invisibility of the links between gender and Canadian trade policy, however, mean that much more research is needed on how different groups of women will be affected by changes in world trade, on similarities as well as differences, and on the implications of successful strategies for addressing gender imbalances in the Canadian trade agenda.

In the first part of the chapter I will discuss two major theoretical approaches to understanding the gendered character of Canadian trade policy: liberal feminism and socialist feminism. In the second part, I outline some of the factors that need to be taken into account in order to problematize Canadian trade policy to include a gender analysis, including changes in employment, agriculture, migration, and services and policy convergence. In the third part, I will discuss various ways in which Canadian women's organizations have responded to the new trade agreements. Women are not passive victims of changes in trade, but have begun to organize to resist the harmful effects of globalization. In doing so, they often establish new links between Canadian women and women elsewhere who are also seeing their lives change because of trade liberalization. New forms of international alliances are emerging, based upon the recognition of shared interests. These alliances are inevitably fraught with tension, though, because of the remaining underlying differences between the women involved (Gabriel and Macdonald 1995). I will explore some of the ways in which women are developing common strategies by looking at three specific examples of Canadian women's organizing: responses to the North American Free Trade Agreement and the Free Trade Area of the Americas and the APEC agreement. Finally, in the concluding section of the chapter I briefly discuss various ways in which women can make sure their concerns are on the international trade agenda.

Linking Gender and Trade

How do we explain the lack of attention to the links between gender and trade in Canadian foreign policy? Jill Krause suggests that gender relations are invisible in international political economy (IPE) because of the way in which 'economic' and 'political' activity have been defined. Because of the centrality of the market in conceptions of economic activity in capitalist economies, participation in the labour force and contribution to the national economy are defined on the basis of connection to the market, or the performance of work for profit:

> Unremunerated work is not and the person performing it (usually a woman) is not included because it is not part of the market of paid exchanges for goods or services and so is not viewed as economically significant. This is based on a 'common sense' view of what constitutes 'economic' activity. IPE has also explored particular kinds of power relationships which underpin economic activity, but the measure of 'power' and what may be construed as 'political' has not been expanded to include areas outside of what is conventionally defined as the 'public sphere'. (Krause 1994: 3)

Developing a more gender-sensitive approach to trade policy thus requires looking beyond balance of payments and trade statistics to discover ways in which the political and the economic interconnect, and in which 'private' forms of power and inequality underpin the seemingly neutral mechanisms of the market. Marina Fe B. Durano summarizes the implications for studying trade policy:

> Trade policies have different consequences on women and men because women and men differ in their economic and social status. Women and men respond differently to economic and trade policies because they have different sets of private resources and levels of access to public ones. Status and control over resources are intricately woven into the sexual division of labor, the assignment of productive

> and reproductive roles. Thus, [to analyze the] economic impact of trade policy on the genders [one] must look at price and quantity effects as they relate to the differential status of men and women and their different sets of resources. Meanwhile, the social and human development impact of trade policy must look at how choice sets have been altered and how alterations have affected women and men. Both kinds of impact analysis, in turn, help determine the changes in the welfare of both genders. (1999: 76)

The links between gender and trade are very complex, and the implications of recent changes in trade for both men and women are far from obvious, especially given the lack of research in this area. There is no single feminist or woman-centred reading of the links between gender and trade. Broadly, however, we can delineate two main ways of looking at those links and at the strategies women should adopt to advance their interests and mitigate the negative effects of trade.

On the one hand, some analysts and women's groups draw on liberal feminist tradition in their approach to gender and trade issues. Liberal feminists generally accept the reality of trade liberalization, and look for ways to make trade more 'women-friendly'. For example, the US-based Women's Environment and Development Organization (WEDO) argues, 'We cannot and should not attempt to halt the expansion of world trade and economic growth' (cited in Blacklock 2000: 8). Women looking at trade from this perspective view trade liberalization as generally positive for most women, given that the growth of world trade has led to greater participation by women in the paid labour force, which is assumed by liberals to be necessary for an improvement in women's status. Susan Joekes and Ann Weston (1994: 34) thus argue that 'the jobs created within an export-oriented development pattern have been disproportionately taken up by women. Exporting industries have a much higher proportion of women workers than other sectors.' The prospects for women to benefit from trade liberalization are relatively strong in the short to medium term, they claim, although they recognize that there will be losers as well as winners among groups of women, and that the implications for the longer-term participation of women in the labour market on terms equitable to those of men are less assured. Although writers from this perspective do recognize some of the negative implications of trade liberalization for women, they argue that women must seize the current opportunity for 'advocating women's rights in the trade arena' and also promote 'compensatory policies' to help the workers whose jobs are eliminated as the result of new competition (Joekes and Weston 1994).[2]

Advocates of this approach thus adopt what Elson referred to above as the 'access' strategy, in which emphasis is put on increasing women's capacity to influence trade policy (that is, obtain access to the centres of power in the public sphere). While this emphasis is important, this approach reproduces the distinction made between the public and the private domains in classical liberal thought, focusing on the gains made by women in the public sphere as the sign of progress, such as improvements in levels of employment in the formal economy or the presence of women at the bargaining tables when trade deals are negotiated. But in order to appreciate the effects of of trade liberalization on women, it is necessary to examine the ways in which changes in the global economy affect the public/private divide. As we will see below, changes in the global economy have promoted changes in national policy that shift responsibility away from the public sphere toward the private sphere; this increases the burden on women, who generally bear the ultimate responsibility for the care work that takes place in the household.

Some of these concerns are addressed from another perspective on gender and trade, which we might characterize as socialist feminist. Individuals and groups that adopt this approach present a broader critique of the nature of globalization than liberal feminists. Socialist feminists tend to argue that the benefits to women from new employment emerging from trade (when it occurs) are few, and that the costs are extremely high. Increased access to paid employment does not necessarily improve women's welfare, since women often enter the workforce only as a means of surviving increased poverty (Bakker 1997: 9). Thus, activists in the Vancouver Status of Women group, preparing for the November 1987 APEC meeting in that city, argued that what they call 'corporate globalization' has had a devastating effect on the lives of millions of women by increasing poverty all over the world.

> Despite significant gains by women's movements, the mechanisms of corporate globalization have . . . further strengthened the already tight grip of patriarchal control on our world. The radical restructuring of economies has deepened existing inequalities of gender, class, race, caste, ability, religion, sexual orientation and age. (Vancouver Status of Women 1997: 10)

From this more critical perspective, attempts to introduce gender concerns into trade negotiations are probably futile. Socialist feminists would suggest that trade agreements fail to recognize the needs of most women not merely because governments lack adequate information about the effect of liberalized trade on women, because of some careless oversight or because there are not enough female trade negotiators[3], but because of the nature of power in the global political economy. As the quotation from Jill Krause at the beginning of this section indicates, women's work, particularly unpaid work, is not taken into account in conventional analyses of the global political economy because it takes place in the so-called private sphere. Strategies of 'access' fail to challenge power disparities in the private realm of the household. Another important reason is the way in which power is linked to knowledge. The fields of international trade law and economics are highly technical and abstract, and defenders of trade liberalization base their arguments on claims to knowledge of objective truths of the economy. Alternative forms of knowledge, particularly those dominated by women, receive short shrift in this field. It is thus extremely difficult for women's groups to develop arguments that will pierce the epistemological shield of the proponents of trade liberalization. As a result, a socialist feminist perspective would suggest that mere tinkering with trade agreements to include women is not sufficient. Women's movements must therefore mobilize globally to oppose the expansion of the neo-liberal trade agenda; they must, in Diane Elson's terms, adopt a strategy of transformation.

Despite their differences, both perspectives agree on two counts: first, that trade has a differential impact on men and women, and second, that most women are among the most vulnerable of the world's population, and that the conditions in which they work, whether in the home, in the informal sector, or in the paid workforce, are highly inequitable. As indicated above, further research is needed in order to judge the probable impact of trade liberalization on women's status. The effects of changes in the trade regime will vary dramatically between groups of women across the global economy. It is important to recognize that Canadian policy must be analyzed for its effect both on women abroad and on Canadian women, and those effects may well be different, given the relatively privileged position most Canadian women occupy in the global economy.

Analyzing the Effects of Trade on Women[4]

The above discussion suggests some of the analytical difficulties of calculating the effects of changes in trade regimes on women, since what is involved is not just quantitative changes in the open economy, but also changes in the nature of power in the economy that have implications in the rather opaque domain of the private sphere. As well, quantitative analysis using the usual tools of econometric analysis is difficult because sex-disaggregated data are not widely available (Blacklock, 2000: 10). Moreover, as indicated above, not all women are affected the same way by trade liberalization—the effects will vary by age, race, ethnicity, class, and geographic location. Nevertheless, some analysis of this question has been done.

Employment

The earliest studies of gender and trade in Canada, which came out during the debate over the Canada-US FTA, focused heavily on the implications of free trade for women's employment. Indeed, most analysts agree that one of the most obvious results of liberalization of trade and restructuring of production relations worldwide has been the 'feminization of the workforce', that is, increased participation of women in paid jobs formerly usually occupied by men, particularly in the developing world (Standing 1989). Feminists frequently argue that one of the causes of globalization is the recognition by corporations that they can lower wages and increase their control of the labour force in an increasingly competitive international environment by taking advantage of traditional patriarchal controls over women around the world. Particularly in the manufacturing sector, many corporations have relocated labour-intensive processes to 'world market factories' in Export Processing Zones (EPZs) mostly located in the South. In these factories, women workers are preferred because it is thought that they have greater manual dexterity, bear the tedium of routine tasks better than men, and are less likely to cause trouble by joining labour unions. Because women are discriminated against all over the world, they are accustomed to working as hard as or harder than men for lower pay. In Mexico, although women may have greater opportunities for paid work because of Mexico's entry into NAFTA, the jobs they get in the *maquiladoras* (labour-intensive assembly plants) are usually poorly paid compared to male manufacturing positions, and highly insecure. Women workers in the EPZs are also often subject to sexual harassment and unsafe working conditions, and their labour rights are not protected. Women workers also suffer from the lack of affordable housing and day care, and usually have to cope with the so-called 'double day' of domestic responsibilities in addition to their paid job.

In Canada, during the early stage of debate on the Canada-US FTA, feminist critics of free trade feared, however, that women, particularly women of colour, would be among the most vulnerable workers in the Canadian population, since they were most likely to work in the low-skilled manufacturing jobs that were likely to shift to lower-wage economies like the southern United States or Mexico as a result of free trade (Cohen 1987). While there has been a shift in women's employment away from manufacturing to service jobs, it is difficult to directly attribute these changes to the FTA, since they may be part of a broader process of economic restructuring that would have occurred with or without the FTA. However, since the FTA, more Canadian women have entered paid employment because of economic restructuring, although their jobs are likely to be part-time and insecure (CLC 1997). Job gains in export industries also have to be measured against job losses in areas such as public sector employment, where in the past women often enjoyed relatively high-status jobs with good working conditions (Women Working Worldwide n.d.: 7).

Feminization of the workforce is the result not only of the expansion of EPZs, but, more importantly, the growth of informal sector employment since the early 1980s. The informal sector covers a wide range of enterprises, ranging from individual street merchants to small industries sub-contracting to multinational corporations. In general, compared with the formal sector, informal sector enterprises are small, labour intensive, operate on the margins of legality, and possess relatively low productivity, employing unorganized and low-paid labour, and operate outside government regulation (Sen 1991: 2).

Women make up a large and apparently growing proportion of the informal sector both in Canada and in the Third World, but most of them either work for low wages in small enterprises or are self-employed individuals 'eking out an existence with minimal capital, skills or access to other resources' (Sen 1991: 5). Studies show that the wages of women working in the informal sector fall not only below minimum wage, but also significantly below male earnings, with greater income differentials than in the formal sector (Sen 1991: 6; Tokman 1989). Since these jobs exist largely because of the opportunity to employ labour at lower costs than in the formal sector, other vulnerable groups like ethnic minorities and children are also disproportionately employed in this sector.

From a liberal perspective, it might be expected that since liberalization of international trade seems to lead to the growth of the informal sector, in which women predominate, that women will therefore benefit from trade promotion, particularly if policies can be designed to help women entrepreneurs take advantage of these new opportunities. This analysis reveals an incomplete understanding of the relationship between the informal sector and international trade. Female dominated informal sector enterprises tend to be small, fragile, and unlikely to engage in production for export. The more dynamic component of the informal sector are those export-oriented industries which have benefited from the shift toward more 'flexible' production strategies of multinational corporations, involving the contracting out of many segments of the work to medium-sized local industries. While this segment of the informal sector may indeed benefit from the liberalization of trade and investment rules, it is likely that the benefits will accrue to the largely male owners, rather than to super-exploited female workers. This conclusion applies equally to women, particularly women of colour, in Canada, where large corporations have responded to new competitive pressures by outputting labour-intensive processes to home workers, who often earn substantially less than the minimum wage and receive few or no benefits (Gabriel and Macdonald 1994). Given the disadvantages women entrepreneurs face in terms of access to credit, marketing, and lack of economies of scale, etc., it is unlikely that they will benefit from trade expansion unless they are given significant support (see Beneria and Lind 1995: 6).

Food and Agriculture

Another important aspect of recent trade agreements is the increased liberalization of agricultural trade. The extent to which specific countries will benefit from increased export opportunities in agriculture will vary dramatically depending upon resource base (Joekes and Weston 1994: 35). Within countries, however, there are clear gender differentials which affect who will benefit and who will lose from increased agricultural exports. In sub-Saharan Africa, for example, women provide the majority of the labour in agricultural production, but men reap most of the benefits. Women are more likely to be farming for family subsistence or for sale in local markets (Beneria and Lind 1995: 5). In joint household small farms, men generally keep the profits from the sale of exported crops, without paying women for their extra work. The result may be a reduction in women's and girl's nutritional status, or a drop in the number of girls going to school enrolment (Joekes 1995: 88; Bakker 1997: 20).[5] Even when there are large numbers of female heads of households who farm, their plots are so small and their production so marginal that they are much less likely than male farmers to gain access to export markets (Joekes and Weston 1994: 54–5).

Liberalization of agricultural trade also affects women working (either on a paid or unpaid basis) in vulnerable sectors of Canadian agriculture. Some Canadian women are also concerned about Canadian government support for the application of WTO rules such as the Agreement on the Application of Sanitary and Phytosanitary Measures that would promote Canadian exports of 'biotech' or genetically modified food products. As the main food preparers for most Canadian families, Canadian women want to be sure that the food they are providing is safe and nutritious, and free of hidden allergens, and they are often concerned about the genetically engineered foods. On the other hand, Canadian women have benefited from the lower food prices and greater availability of fruits and vegetables that have resulted from agricultural liberalization. Both the benefits and the costs of agricultural liberalization need to be more carefully evaluated.

Migration

A less-studied result of globalization and the new trading system is their implications for increased levels of migration. Economic restructuring has resulted in the geographic shift in economic opportunities, leading to both internal and external migration of poor people in search of jobs. Increased foreign investment tends to locate in cities, ports and border areas, intensifying existing tendencies for the poor to migrate to these areas as traditional economies are undermined (Keller-Herzog 1996: 22). Economic crises in the South also leads to increased attempts to migrate North, but such attempts are often thwarted by the intensification of controls over labour migration by countries like Canada. These controls have been harmonized within trading blocs in both Europe and North America (Pellerin 1996). New trade agreements like NAFTA and the General Agreement on Trade in Services (GATS) also contain provisions on services that allow the migration of certain categories of highly educated, well-paid professionals (usually men) while restricting the movement of other categories of workers (Gabriel and Macdonald 2002).

This process, too, is not gender neutral. Traditionally, most migrants were men, but new migrant populations are in some cases increasingly female, partly because of the new demands for female labour both in the EPZs and for domestic workers in the North (Riley and Mejia 1996: 6–7). When it is mostly men who migrate, women are left with an increasing share of the work in household labour and rural production (Gutierrez 1995). Migration may provide new opportunities for women to escape traditional patriarchal controls, but it also opens up new kinds of exploitation, particularly for foreign domestic workers subject to high levels of control both by the host state and by employers. The case of foreign domestic workers also illustrates the accentuation of divisions between groups of women in the new global economy, for upper-middle and upper-class white women in Canada often take advantage of the vulnerability of domestic workers, who are often women of colour (see Bakkan and Stasiulis 1997).

Gender, Consumption, and Unpaid Labour

As we have seen above, the analysis of the links between gender and trade has tended to concentrate on the changes in women's role in production (particularly in the EPZs). An important insight of feminist economics, however, is the importance of women's unpaid reproductive work in the household. Further research is needed on how changes in trade affect women's role in reproduction, including their role as the family members most responsible for consumption decisions (see Durano 1999).

Theoretically, trade liberalization should improve women's lives by bringing down prices of imports, as discussed above. However, this theoretical tendency cannot be abstracted from other changes going on in the economy. For example, as the European Union and the United States are forced to cut subsidies to agricultural exports under the Uruguay Round agreement, food prices are likely to rise in many countries that have become dependent on cheap imported food (Joekes and Weston 1994: 17)—often encouraged to do so by the International Monetary Fund, which views basic grains production by Third World peasant farmers for the local market as inefficient. Moreover, when trade liberalization occurs in the context of the devaluation of local currencies imposed under structural adjustment, import prices rise, and imports become available only to a small elite. As Isabella Bakker (1997: 9) notes, the combination of cuts in public services such as education and health and cuts in subsidies to basic needs like food, transportation, and electricity have an important impact at the micro level:

> The need to stretch the pay cheque in order to meet basic needs and the anxiety and conflicts about which items to cut from diets and household consumption often means more domestic work: more cooking, changes in shopping habits, and so on.

Export promotion strategies may thus sap women's energies both in the sphere of production (where they are forced to enter the labour force to supplement family income or as the main income earner), and of reproduction (where they are forced to economize by cutting back on the family's basic purchases). It is possible, though, that this is yet another area where trade liberalization is accentuating the divisions between groups of women, both domestically and internationally, for price reductions on imports may favour women in the North who have not seen their currencies decline in the same way as many Southern women. The objective of international alliances among women around trade issues must be, therefore, to make women in the North more aware of these growing contradictions, and to find ways of reducing them.

Services and Policy Convergence

Finally, with recent changes in regional trade blocs and the WTO, feminist concerns are shifting away from changes in employment patterns (which may have more or less stabilized) toward the more indirect effect on women of changes in the regulation of services, investment, and property rights. Trade policy is not isolated from other macroeconomic policies. WTO and other trade regime rules tend to define most social and environmental regulation as 'trade barriers'. As a result, they may encourage (either through compulsion or through informal coordination), changes in domestic labour legislation, social insurance programs and policies, and other areas that affect the duties and obligations of states to their citizens, particularly their female citizens (Women's EDGE 1999: 5). In this respect, a Status of Women Canada staff person says

> What's really getting our attention is the area of services because international trade agreements are now moving toward domestic regulation and it will have a real impact on sectors that women's organizations are saying those things are important to us—we're looking at health, education, immigration perhaps, also intellectual property. (Interview, Ottawa, 9 June 2000)

The main Canadian women's organization, the National Action Committee on the Status of Women (NAC), also expresses concern about changes in a number of social policies over the last ten years that they view as connected with globalization. For example, changes in the Unemployment Insurance system and the

Child Tax Benefit and transfers for health care and education affect women more than men, and may have a particularly severe impact on women of colour or disabled women. NAC argues: 'The shrinking role of states in social programming is part of a broader trend to allow the market to provide services; this means increased privatisation, decreased protections for workers and individuals and ultimately, less democracy' (NAC 2000: 5). Here again, the private world of the household intersects with the public world of the workplace, the state and the economy, resulting in new forms of power.

Women's Resistance to the New Trade Agenda

To this point, I have provided a brief overview of some of the many factors that must be taken into account in order to provide a gender sensitive reading of the impact of changes in the international trade regime. However, it must be emphasized that women cannot be viewed merely as economic agents—women are not just workers and consumers, but also citizens with rights to democratic participation in the decisions that shape their lives. In this respect, one of the most worrying aspects of recent trade agreements (as well as earlier agreements) is the undemocratic nature of the bodies that carry out negotiations, as well as those that adjudicate decisions under the new rules. This 'democratic deficit' of the increasingly powerful international trade institutions affects all but a small minority of the world's peoples, but it has special implications for women, who, as noted above, are virtually unrepresented among the individuals and groups that do have a voice. The following section describes different efforts by groups of women (and some men) to alleviate the gender biases of various trade arrangements.

Trade Agreements in the Americas

Much of the advocacy by Canadian women's organizations concerning trade issues has concentrated on regional trade agreements in the Americas. Women's groups, particularly NAC, participated actively in mobilizing opposition to the form of economic integration represented by first the Canada-US FTA, and later NAFTA, which came into force in 1994. NAC is now active in a hemispheric coalition of women's groups disputing the gender blindness of the Free Trade Area of the Americas (FTAA) initiative. During the debate over the FTA, NAC played a leading role in the Action Canada Network (ACN—formerly the Pro Canada Network), a coalition of labour groups, women, students, farmers, and others, opposed to further Canadian economic integration with the United States. NAC's status as a unified national women's movement with a large membership gave it greater weight in the Canadian coalition than more fractured women's groups in the United States and Mexico. As was pointed out above, NAC's participation was based upon the argument that women would bear the brunt of continental restructuring under the FTA. However, even though NAC had a similar critique of NAFTA, women were less active in the fight against NAFTA than the FTA, partly reflecting the fact that the public generally saw further integration with Mexico, with which Canada had few economic links, as less of a threat than with the giant United States economy

(Gabriel and Macdonald 1994). Moreover, however, NAC's lesser involvement in the fight against NAFTA was due to the cuts in government funding to NAC under the Mulroney government. As well, growing divisions within the organization left Canadian women without a strong and cohesive voice on international trade issues.

As Deborah Stienstra outlines in her chapter in this volume, the Canadian Feminist Alliance for International Action (FAFIA) has taken up Canada's international economic policies, including trade policies, as one of its areas of emphasis. There are also important grassroots organizations devoted to trade issues. One example is the Maquila Solidarity Network (MSN), a Canadian network based in Toronto which promotes solidarity 'with groups in Mexico, Central America, and Asia organizing in *maquiladora* factories and export processing zones to improve conditions and win a living wage'. The group's web site quotes Carmen Valadez, from Casa de la Mujer in Tijuana, Mexico: 'Our starting point is the recognition that women maquila workers have the ability to organize themselves. What we do is promote solidarity between the workers and their struggles.'[6] The MSN builds solidarity through corporate campaigns, like recent 'Stop Sweatshop' campaigns targeting companies like the Gap, Woolworth, Nike, Mattel, and Wal-Mart, through government lobbying, popular education, and international links.

The public opposition to NAFTA did not succeed in preventing the agreement from being signed, but coalitions in the United States were successful in persuading the US Congress to include side agreements on labour rights and the environment. These side agreements are often criticized as ineffective, and they are not gender-sensitive, but they may created new opportunities for promoting women's rights. For example, in 1997 the National Association of Democratic Lawyers in Mexico and the International Rights Fund and Human Rights Watch of the United States launched a joint challenge to the Mexican government under the NAFTA labour side agreement (Prah 1997). The groups accuse the Mexican government of failing to enforce anti-discrimination laws, particularly in the maquiladoras, using as examples the pregnancy testing required of female employees by many multinationals in the region, including Zenith, W.R. Grace, and Sanyo (see Human Rights Watch 1996). According to one of the lawyers in the National Association of Democratic Lawyers, pregnancy testing violates not only Mexican labour law but also international human rights conventions signed by Mexico (Prah 1997).

More recently, women's groups in the Americas, including Canada, have been organizing to develop a gendered critique of the FTAA, which is scheduled to be completed in 2005, with the objective of creating a free trade zone for all of the countries of the Americas, excluding Cuba. Canada was host to the Third Summit of the Americas in Quebec City in April 2001, and a parallel summit was held, hosted by the Hemispheric Social Alliance (HSA), an alliance of social movements from all over the Americas concerned about the FTAA. Since the primary member of the HSA has been the labour movement, it is perhaps not surprising that the HSA was somewhat slow to address gender issues. However, women's groups have organized to push the HSA to incorporate a gender perspective in their critique of the FTAA. At the Quebec's People's Summit, the Women's Committee of the HSA, along with the World March of Women and the Fédération des Femmes du

Québec, organized a day long Women's Forum and a 'Council of Wise Women'. The Women's Committee has also developed a chapter on gender and the FTAA, and has suggested revisions to the *Alternatives for the Americas* document written by the HSA, to incorporate women's concerns. Gender is included as one of the topics (albeit the last) covered in an HSA document called 'Competing Visions for the Hemisphere' that lays out in schematic form the differences between the official FTAA draft and the alternatives proposed by the HSA (HSA 2001).

Asia Pacific Economic Cooperation Forum (APEC)

APEC is another regional grouping, made up of eighteen 'member economies', but unlike NAFTA, APEC is a consultative forum that cannot make legally binding decisions. Also in contrast with the organizing that has taken place in the Americas, where women have organized almost exclusively from outside of official circles, the case of APEC shows two simultaneous strategies adopted by different women's groups, reflecting the two broad approaches to gender and trade outlined above. On the one hand, a more liberal approach is adopted by more elite women involved in the Women Leaders' Network (WLN) in APEC Economies, a group designed to promote the integration of gender perspectives into APECs work. At the same time, organizations representing women in the popular sectors have been vocal in their opposition to APEC from a socialist feminist perspective.

The WLN is 'an informal network of women in business, government, academe and civil society from the countries that comprise APEC' (Gibb 1997: 2). The network first met in Manila in 1996, a few weeks before the annual APEC Ministerial Meeting in the Philippines; the second meeting took place in Ottawa and Hull in September, before the Vancouver APEC meeting in November. The WLN has received support from the United Nations Development Fund for Women (UNIFEM) and the Canadian International Development Agency (CIDA), as well as from national women's groups like the National Commission on the Role of Filipino Women, the international division of the Women in Science and Engineering in Thailand (WISEThailand), based in the Ministry of Science, Technology and Environment, and in the Canadian case, the Interdepartmental Sub-committee on Gender in APEC, co-chaired by Status of Women Canada and the Department of Foreign Affairs and International Trade. Although the network is officially non-governmental, its membership thus overlaps substantially with governmental bodies. The Canadian meeting also received considerable support from corporations like the Royal Bank of Canada, IBM Canada, Northern Telecom, and ManuLife Financial.

At the first meeting, the WLN presented a Call to Action to that year's APEC Chair, President Fidel Ramos, who subsequently urged APEC leaders to recognize and integrate gender considerations in APEC (Gibb 1997: 37). The second meeting called for an acceleration of this process at both national and international levels. According to Rosario Manalo (1997: 6–7), Philippine Undersecretary of Foreign Affairs, an ASEAN Dialogue meeting in Bangkok in preparation for the 1997 meeting in Hull proposed that APEC adopt the following responses to discrimination against women:

1. build women's capacity for global competitiveness;
2. promote participation of organized businesswomen in appropriate APEC structures and fora, like in the APEC Business Advisory Council;
3. promote gender-sensitive, community-based micro-enterprises through institutionalized support services and facilities;
4. promote access to credit for micro-cottage and small and medium enterprises;
5. develop a database on women in business and sex-disaggregate national economy level as well as APEC level databases;
6. provide business services, such as business matching and participation in trade promotion, for women;
7. and advocate women's concerns as a cross-cutting theme in APEC.

In keeping with its liberal orientation, the Network places particular emphasis on the role of women in small and medium-sized enterprises (the informal sector). As a result of the WLN's lobbying, a meeting of ministers whose responsibilities include women's issues was held in the Philippines in 1998, to discuss ways that APEC can address women's concerns more effectively (WLN 1997b: 2).

A more critical view of APEC was presented by groups participating in the Second International Women's Conference against APEC, held in November 1997 in Vancouver. The first meeting was held in Manila in November 1996. The conference was an 'issue forum' of the 1997 People's Summit on APEC, convened by non-governmental, labour, and popular-sector organizations, designed to 'discuss, debate and build opposing and alternative visions'. However, the women's conference was funded independently and organized by a coalition of women's groups in British Columbia, and, unlike the People's Summit, from the outset it adopted an explicitly anti-APEC position (Vancouver Status of Women 1997).

The division among women's organizing around APEC thus illustrates vividly both the divergent views of the prospects that trade liberalization will improve women's lot, and the way in which changes in trade are contributing to new divisions among the world's women, divisions that are etched in lines of class, race, and geography. The APEC example is also an interesting one because it is the only case of recent trade arrangements to explicitly address gender concerns at the official level (although so far in only a very limited way, since APEC leaders, like leaders of other trade arrangements, tend to see social issues as peripheral to its main, economic, agenda) (Grandea 1997: 7).

Conclusion

As we have seen above, trade does indeed have a female face. The gender division of labour within the family and the wider society thus means that women are affected differently than men by changes in the global economy. These effects are not straightforward, however, but depend also on race, ethnicity, location, nationality, age, sector, and other factors. Nonetheless, sufficient commonalities exist to create the basis for common strategies for women within and between nations.

Notes

1. This chapter was written with the financial support of the Social Sciences and Humanities Research Council of Canada. I thank Cathy Blacklock, Isabella Bakker, Sheila Katz, Heather Gibb, and Pamela Sparr for helping me with my research, and the editors of this volume and anonymous reviewers for their helpful comments.
2. For a similar approach, see Marsden, 1992.
3. Indeed, while trade policy is predominantly a male field, there have been some notable trade negotiators like Carla Hills in the US or Pat Carney who was the Canadian Minister of Trade when the Canada-US FTA was negotiated. Observers of the trade negotiation process have noted that it is a macho affair; women who participate thus have been heavily socialized in the norms and assumptions that underlie conventional trade policy. Interestingly, as well, Pat Carney publicly complained that her important role in the negotiation of the FTA went unrecognized because she was a woman, and that she was undermined at the time by macho-style Canadian negotiator Simon Reisman.
4. This section draws heavily on Macdonald, 'Trade with a Female Face . . .'
5. Nona Grandea (1997: 5) notes a similar tendency in the Asia-Pacific region.
6. <http://www.maquilasolidarity.org/aboutus.htm>, p. 1. Accessed 19 Dec. 2000.

Chapter 5

Of Playing Fields, Competitiveness, and the Will to Win: Representations of Gender and Globalization

CLAIRE TURENNE SJOLANDER

> As Canada enters a new millennium, the role of international trade has reached an unprecedented level of importance in the strengthening of our economy. . . . For the first time, particular attention is being placed on the unique challenges faced by women owners of export-oriented small- and medium-sized businesses (SMEs). . . . [This] report serves as a flag . . . that the barriers to trade confronting women-owned SMEs are often distinctive. At the same time it applauds the professionalism and dedication of a rapidly growing number of women entrepreneurs that are overcoming these hurdles daily in the international marketplace. (Rayman 1999: 2)

By the mid-1990s, Canadian policymakers had begun to recognize that women entrepreneurs were a significant feature of the changing Canadian economy. Almost as many businesses were being started by women as by men. The start-up rate of women-owned businesses had become nearly equal to that of men (Marchi 1999b), and had grown at a rate of twice the national average (Eggleton 1997). These businesses led by women were creating jobs at four times the national average (Marchi 1999b; Eggleton 1997). By the end of the 1990s, 30 per cent of all businesses in Canada were owned or operated by women, and they provided 1.7 million jobs—more than Canada's top 100 companies combined (Marchi 1999b). As former Trade Minister Sergio Marchi noted when he addressed the Canada–USA Businesswomen's Trade Summit in May 1999: 'Quite simply, women are fuelling the growth in small and medium-sized enterprises . . . in this country and contributing both to our balance of trade and to our national prosperity. And in this era of globalization and interdependence, Canada's national prosperity is increasingly linked to our success in international markets' (Marchi 1999b). As the Minister had said in an earlier speech, 'Clearly, the world of business is no longer just a man's world' (Marchi 1997).

Nevertheless, in many respects (indeed, in most), the Minister was wrong. As Marianne Marchand has written, gender operates on at least three interconnected levels: the individual (through the social construction of physical male and female bodies), the collective (through the interactions among and between men and women structured in terms of gender roles and expectations), and the ideational or ideological (through the gendered representations of different social spheres, processes and practices, and the relative value placed on each) (Marchand 2000:

223; 226, n. 4). For the Minister, the physical presence of a growing number of women entrepreneurs signalled the end to the maxim that business is a man's world and changed a preconception as to the gender-exclusive nature of business.[1] Whether or not international trade is a man's world, however, depends not only on the number of women who operate export industries, but also on the social practices in the business of international trade, and most significantly for this chapter, about the representation—or the discursive construction—of international trade. This representation of international trade confirms that while women entrepreneurs may be involved in business in greater numbers, the way in which business is represented has not changed. The business of international trade remains a gendered world, even if it is no longer the exclusive preserve of men.

This chapter examines the ways in which globalization, in particular, international trade, has been constructed, or represented, in Canadian foreign policy. It argues that this construction has been founded on a number of analogies centred on the jungle and competitive sports. These analogies begin with the premise that globalization is a jungle 'out there', which necessitates negotiation of multilateral trade and investment laws (to tame the jungle). These multilateral laws become the 'rules of the game', and international trade is transformed imperfectly into a 'competitive game' which countries, firms, and individuals play to 'win'. However, the sports analogies which prevail in the construction of globalization and international trade define the terrain of trade in very masculine terms. Sports analogies are gendered, and this has implications for policy—particularly at a time when some of the efforts of the Department of Foreign Affairs and International Trade (DFAIT) to respond to the challenges of globalization have led to the formulation of policies designed to encourage the participation of women entrepreneurs in international trade.

As many contributors to this book demonstrate (see the chapters by Macdonald, Stienstra, Healy, and Day), globalization is a gendered series of processes—it functions in a gendered manner and has gendered consequences. The discursive construction of international trade, however, has effectively limited the capacity of the Canadian government to see globalization in gendered terms; to use Marchand's typology, it has been unable to respond to issues of gender at an ideational or ideological level (given that it participates in the construction of the gendered trade world at the ideational level), and rather, responds to gender at the individual level—with some acknowledgement of a collective concern. As a result, issues of gender and international trade are translated into the observation that while women entrepreneurs have become an engine of growth for an often stagnant Canadian economy, they remain under-represented in international trade (Marchi 1997). The Canadian government, concerned about Canada's capacity to compete in a globalizing economy, became determined to change that. The 'man's world' of international trade was to be opened up to 'the incredible dynamism of women entrepreneurs' (Marchi 1997).

Globalization, Multilateralism, and the 'Rules' of the 'Game'

The restructuring of the global marketplace has been a central theme in Canadian foreign policy for at least two decades. First given tangible expression in the negotiation of the Canada-US free trade agreement, the apparently immutable reality of a globalizing world has surfaced repeatedly as an imperative force that is driving, and to a large extent defining, Canada's foreign policy. Globalization has been invoked as the unquestioned and unquestionable justification for economic and financial deregulation, the liberalization of trade and investment, and deficit and debt reduction—and the consequences for spending on social and other programs has often been hastily dismissed as part of this 'new' reality. Paying close attention to discourse, however, reveals that globalization can be, and has been, constructed as many things, and thus it is imperative to understand the way in which the term has been and is defined as a backdrop for the expression of Canadian foreign policy. What becomes clear through an examination of ministerial speeches and policy pronouncements is that globalization has been presented as a series of expansive processes taking place 'out there' which limit state action. These processes are often threatening, or at least potentially so, and the international marketplace conceals the unknown dangers of a global jungle. Such a representation of globalization and of trade, however, has particular consequences for our capacity to imagine alternative foreign policies, consequences which are seen strikingly in attempts to respond to issues relating to gender and the global economy.

One of the most compelling—and revealing—assessments of the nature and significance of globalization was offered by International Trade Minister Pierre Pettigrew in a speech before the Global Forum 2000. Reflecting upon the implications of citizen unrest during the December 1999 World Trade Organization (WTO) meetings in Seattle, Washington, Pettigrew painted a sombre picture of globalization: Globalization, he argued, 'is the result of technological advances, trade liberalization and deregulation'; it leads to a world where 'corporations can decide to carry out a given industrial function in a given geographic region for economic reasons, notwithstanding any political considerations.' Globalization 'ignores political borders and merges economic spaces'. It is best described as 'a stateless power' defined in the horizontal processes and structures of the marketplace, 'at once intoxicating and fearsome to watch as it gradually replaces the vertical power of the state' (Pettigrew 2000b). In Pettigrew's interpretation, globalization is a force outside the state, with which states are confronted and threatened. Globalization produces an international marketplace where the 'law of the jungle' often prevails (Pettigrew 2000a; Marchi 1999c), and the Canadian government, and Canadian exporters, are confronted by the perils that hide within it.

The portrayal of globalization existing outside the state, a force 'out there', is reminiscent of early realist writings, where the space inside the state was controlled by rules and laws, while the space outside the state was anarchic—a Hobbesian state of nature—where the rules of the jungle, and might equals right, prevailed. As in these early writings, Pettigrew's portrayal of globalization is possible because the state and the market are each assigned their own spheres, the one independent of the other. In this way, Pettigrew is able to argue that in an earlier era, a 'too exclusively' *political state* committed blunders because of its inherent inability to read the market's signals, whereas globalization has witnessed the emergence of a 'too exclu-

sively' *economic market*, equally incapable of reading the state's signals (Pettigrew 2000b). The state and the market are distinct, but the fundamental restructuring of the economic marketplace brought about by globalization has in turn led to a change, if not a diminution, in the role and capacity of the state.

Pettigrew's analysis, though fuelled by the protests in Seattle, is not in itself new. In January 1995, the then Trade Minister, Roy MacLaren, was musing about how globalization was 'somehow circumventing and diminishing the influence of national governments.' The restructuring of the global economy was not mainly a by-product of state regulation or even deregulation; rather, 'trade liberalization is following as much as leading the underlying economic trends'. For MacLaren, quoting Marx (of all economists!), 'technology shapes the course of history', and information technology as an autonomous force was leading the processes of globalization to which states were then compelled to react (MacLaren 1995). Trade Minister Sergio Marchi also invoked globalization as a force 'out there' to which the state must respond or suffer the consequences of its refusal to do so, when he asked whether 'Canadians [are] prepared to accept the decline in our standard of living that would be sure to result from trying to hide from globalization?' (Marchi 1998; see also Axworthy 1999d). The jungle which is globalization envelops us all, and the brave must confront it. Failure to do so inexorably leads to marginalization and defeat.

Seen from this perspective, globalization becomes a significant and potentially determining factor in foreign policy. The state is not a principal architect of the processes underway; rather, it is confronted by the global economic restructuring brought about by revolutionary technological change, and it must adapt to the best of its abilities. The state is not part of globalization *per se*, but it cannot escape its exigencies. Globalization, in a sense, is the antithesis of the state; the anarchic realist international system it reinforces in the economic sphere—the globalization jungle—is the antithesis of the rule of law of the Western, liberal state. Trade Minister Pettigrew expressed this viewpoint most succinctly when he reported an encounter with protestors at the WTO meetings in Seattle. 'They said, "We hate globalization." I looked at them and said, "I am a member of a government. It is far more difficult for me to accept globalization because globalization is threatening us. You are globalization"' (Pettigrew 2000b). Globalization, even as manifested in the uneven capacity of protestors to use information technology to co-ordinate transnational political action, is beyond the control of the territorial state, and the state is at its mercy, trying its best to respond.

Of course, this picture of globalization belies the extent to which the entire post-war economic order has been constructed by states and the international organizations as they have given voice to their interests at a global level. This is not to suggest that there is no reciprocal relationship between states, transnational corporations, and the technological changes that have facilitated processes of economic restructuring, nor is it to suggest that states bear exclusive responsibility for the fundamental economic changes underway. But to diminish the extent to which states and the international financial and economic institutions have been key players in orchestrating trade, financial, and investment liberalization and deregulation is to be more than somewhat disingenuous. To the extent that globalization has become the jungle out there, states and international organizations have fostered its development. The portrayal of globalization as a jungle, however, conditions the kind of foreign economic-policy responses chosen by states. Jungles can never be fully tamed; those who flourish in the face of its perils are individuals of skill and cunning, often possessing special expertise and daring. To face the jungle of globalization, governments must facilitate the activities of national Tarzans. Those sectors of the economy that hope to succeed in the jungle must be 'hardened', having been fully tempered by exposure to international competition. As Marchand notes in the case of a similar discussion of the Dutch economy, the notion that export sectors must be tough or hard in the face of the perils of globalization 'evokes elements associated with contemporary hegemonic masculinity: facing tough competition, taking on responsibilities and the use of new technologies.' (2000:222)[2] The Tarzans of globalization are constructed as men.

Paradoxically, Canada's role in the international financial and economic institutions is not one which political leaders seek to disavow, even in their discussions of the challenges posed by globalization. Rather, Canadian participation in the structuring of the post-war economic order is heralded as an attempt to devise a response to the externally imposed restructuring processes known as globalization. Canadians, we are reminded, have been 'team players' and active members in—at times, architects of—a wide variety of multilateral economic forums, including the General Agreement on Tariffs and Trade (GATT, now the World Trade Organization, or WTO), the International Monetary Fund, the World Bank, and the G-7 (now the G-8).

In keeping with Canadian traditions, the maintenance and strengthening of multilateral institutions is presented as the key to the challenges—the jungle—posed by globalization; while the state may be overwhelmed by global economic restructuring and may find that its capacity is limited by the exigencies of economic change, answers are to be found in the structures already in place. In some respects, this is an interesting sleight of hand; the very states and institutions which played a crucial role in setting the liberalization of the global economy in motion are seen as those most likely to control the genie, if not to put him back in the bottle. Former Finance Minister Paul Martin, testifying before the Standing Committee on Foreign Affairs and International Trade, explained the current situation as follows: 'Globalization poses new and difficult questions that no single government can resolve by itself. This means if we're going to address the challenges that are posed by modern globalization, we're going to have to find ways to promote cooperative solutions', solutions which, for Martin, are to be found in the reform of the Bretton Woods institutions (Martin 2000).

Such a commitment to working collectively resonates well with the traditional Canadian commitment to multilateral practices and negotiations. While it might be a little strong to suggest, as did Sergio Marchi, that 'multilateralism is part of the Canadian DNA' (Marchi 1998), the Canadian propensity to seek out collective forums for the discussion of international problems is well documented and serves as a pillar of Canadian foreign policy (see also Chapter 3 of this volume). The Chrétien government's foreign policy statement, *Canada in the World*, underscored this historical commitment when it emphasized the importance of the multilateral economic system for Canada: 'The system has, on the whole, worked well for us and has demonstrated an impressive capacity to adjust to changing times and pressures. Moreover, Canada has worked hard to protect and promote our interests through the international economic system, a system that we have shaped to a very significant extent' (DFAIT 1995b). The newly appointed foreign affairs minister, John Manley, was already pointing to this tradition within days of assuming his new responsibilities: 'Canada has a strong multilateralist tradition. . . . We must reaffirm our commitment to multilateralism and focus on updating international institutions in order to ensure their continuing relevance in the face of new global realities' (Manley 2000).

In the era of globalization, the need for multilateral solutions framed within the context of international financial or economic institutions is defended because these alone can define the 'rules of the game' that are badly needed to tame the jungle out there. The analogy is pervasive; the new global economy needs rules and referees, and multilateral solutions are the only ones that might work to the advantage of states, including (and perhaps especially) Canada. Canada is committed to a 'rules- and order-based system' (Manley 2000), and such a system will only emerge from a renewed effort to strengthen multilateral institutions. The need for rules is a profound motivator for Canadian foreign policy; over and over again, the Canadian government, through the speeches of its ministers and its policy statements, reiterates this observation. Multilateral rules are the only way to guarantee that Canada has a chance to compete successfully in the global marketplace. The multilateral rules are necessary to guarantee that the workings of the global economy will be fair and that, by extension, Canadians will have a reasonable shot at success. Pierre Pettigrew has underscored this relationship between multilateral rules and fairness on a number of occasions, though never more strongly than when he argued, 'We needed—and we still need—to have a system of international trade governed by the rule of law, not the law of the jungle; a system where disputes are settled based not on the size of your economy or the strength of your military but according to a predictable set of agreed multilateral rules that determine the rights and obligations of the parties. A system that levels the playing field.' (Pettigrew 2000a) The anarchic realist jungle must be tamed by laws and rules.

What becomes clear in the discourse of a rules-based regime governing international economic restructuring is that the rules are intended as the framework for a competitive global economic game—on a playing field that cannot be level without the clear elaboration of rules and of mechanisms to enforce them. The promotion and negotiation of multilateral rules ensuring a more 'level playing field' and the flourishing of fair competition thus becomes a central pillar of Canadian foreign policy. The rules of the game are the only mechanism that can bring the jungle of globalization under control, and Canadian foreign policy must ensure that the rules are fair. This games or sports analogy is a constant in speeches dealing with the multilateral economic and financial institutions, although some statements carry the analogy much further than others. Two examples serve to illustrate this point. In his speech to the Ottawa-based Centre for Trade Policy and Law in 1998, Sergio

Marchi bemoaned the growing opposition to the negotiations for Multilateral Agreement on Investment (MAI). He justified the need to participate in this multilateral process by making reference to the sports world of many Canadian children. 'You know, anyone who played hockey as a kid or who has children playing hockey now will remember what every good coach drills into young players: "You can't score if you don't shoot." The same is true of international trade negotiations: You can't score a good deal if you don't take your best shot at negotiating it' (Marchi 1998). In the same vein, Former Finance Minister Paul Martin commented before the House of Commons Standing Committee on Foreign Affairs and International Trade: 'Hockey, Mr Chairman, is a wonderful game. It's fast paced, free wheeling, and sometimes risky. It's the players that make the game, not the referees. But that being said, hockey without rules and referees wouldn't be hockey. It would be high-speed, high-risk, high-stakes anarchy. Unfortunately, without rules and referees, that is what the international financial system all too often resembles' (Martin 2000).[3] Whether or not the international financial or economic system is truly comparable to a game of hockey, the point is clear. The globalized economic order is a competitive one (a jungle), taking place on a playing field that is only at times level, and in need of multilateral rules and international referees, without which smaller players (like Canada) confront unfair, and therefore unacceptable, risks. Without referees, hockey is not hockey—it is the anarchy and the peril conveyed by the jungle imagery. Rules and referees turn the jungle into a playing field, where competitors are able to display their skill, protected, at least in part, from the perils of the untamed jungle.

The use of sports imagery as a shorthand for the global economy does not end with the discussion of the multilateral economic order. The name Team Canada for the Chrétien government's policy response to the challenges confronting small- and medium-sized firms attempting to participate in the global economy further emphasizes the image of sports. It is not necessarily bad to thinking in terms of a team; much can be said that is positive about team work and collaboration. However, the imagery of a team also signals competition, battle, and victory or defeat. There are winners and there are losers in the globalized economy, and one way to enhance one's chances of victory is to make certain that you are playing for the best possible team. The speeches of federal ministers are therefore also filled with statistics supporting the claim that the Canadian team is one of the best: *Time* magazine describes Canada as an 'exporting superhero' (Marchi 1999c); a 'leading US magazine' refers to the 'Maple Leaf Miracle', and *The Economist* calls Canada a 'fiscal virtuoso' (Marchi 1999a). In a speech to the Ireland-Canada Business Association, Sergio Marchi went so far as to congratulate the two winning teams of the global economy—the 'Celtic Tigers' and the 'Maple Leaf Miracle'—encouraging them to 'form the partnerships that will allow both of our nations to prosper in new and exciting markets' (Marchi 1999a). Images of on-field camaraderie and locker-room celebrations are evoked; even picturing the team jerseys does not require much imagination.

So what does this all mean? After all, it is not difficult to make the claim that the global economy is an arena of increasing competition, that states have lost (by choice or otherwise) some of their capacity to soften the blow of international competition, and that the multilateral system might provide the best guarantee for smaller states that they too will have a place in the global marketplace, that they will be able to find their way in the jungle. If discources coloured by the analogy of sports, with its playing fields, fierce competitions, and victory celebrations for the best teams, conveys the reality of the global economy, what is the objection? The answer is twofold. First, as we will see, sport in modern western society remains a fundamentally gendered expression of those societies, and sports analogies perpetuate this gendered experience of the modern Western world. Second, and more important, this image of the global economy both camouflages important truths about the structure and functioning of that economy in the era of globalization and makes the state less able to imagine policies that might mitigate the gendered nature of globalization. In important respects, the articulation of Canadian foreign policy alternatives in response to some of the challenges of globalization has become a prisoner to the gendered logic of a sports analogy.

SPORT AND GENDER

Understanding gender requires an appreciation of the fact that 'gender is socially constructed, producing subjective identities through which we see and know the world; and . . . that the world is pervasively shaped by gendered meanings. That is, we do not experience or "know" the world as abstract "humans" but as embodied, gendered beings' (Peterson 1992c: 9). Such an understanding of gender as a social construct inevitably leads us to an analysis of social relations and of the ways in which the world (and in this case, international trade policy more specifically) is characterized by particular and often persistent rules and discursive practices. These rules and practices are not simply neutral abstractions that facilitate international life, but rather are themselves gendered, 'construct[ing] and reproduc[ing] notions of masculinity and femininity and associated power differentials' (Prügl and Meyer 1999: 5).

Foreign policy in general is not a field of study in which analyses of gender are prevalent, and Canadian foreign policy is no exception. The place of and for women is often secondary, if it exists at all, in foreign policy statements and policies. The international system is a place where the histories of diplomats, soldiers, and heads of state prevail, and these histories, and the discources that represent them, are predominantly those of men. It is within this context that the sport analogy that is prevalent in Canadian discourses on discussions of multilateralism and the global economy assumes its significance, for sport is part of a social and political culture, and its symbols reinforce a particular understanding of social order. That order is neither trivial nor neutral; rather, the culture of sport 'generates, reworks, and affirms an elitist, masculine account of power and social order' (Burstyn 1999: 4).[4]

The masculine bias of sport is quite clear. Despite some progress over the past three decades, male sports are still much better funded than female sports, they receive far more media attention, and they enjoy far greater public support. 'Athletics have long been the province of men. In the Western world, not only have men dominated the playing fields, but athletic qualities such as aggression, competitiveness, strength, speed, power, and teamwork have been associated with masculinity. For many men sport has provided an arena in which to cultivate masculinity and achieve manhood' (Cahn 1994:3). Burstyn puts it more bluntly: 'While many girls and women are athletic, women are not organized in and through sport such that it serves as an economic, cultural, and associational backbone for their gender interests. These are functions sport plays with respect to men as a gender, indeed as a gender class' (Burstyn 1999: 8). Thus the symbolism of sport and the role sport plays in defining a gendered order speak to women in very different ways than to men.

Acknowledging that sport is a gendered construct in modern societies does not necessarily tell us very much about the implications of that gendered construct, or why it is a problem. The answer is to be found in some of the 'athletic qualities' identified above, and the way in which they organize society and are celebrated in particular patterns of order.

> The problem—if the myriad difficulties of modern sport can be connected in one phrase—is that sport . . . divides people in ways that are often destructive and antisocial. Sport divides people against themselves. It separates children from children, men from women, men from men, and community from community. Sport models and exacerbates social conflict and encourages antisocial and undemocratic values. And it does this most centrally through its inflection of gender, particularly its offering of ideal types and behaviours for men. (Burstyn 1999: 27)

Sports divides people; it encourages individualist behaviour, competition, and coercion—and these 'athletic qualities' are a gendered expression of what is important to success. 'The athletic world of power, speed, and pain is an expression of the masculine ideals of our culture' (Pronger 1990, as cited in Burnstyn 1999: 8) In this respect, the analogy of sport 'fits' particularly well with the logic of globalization, for 'the rhetoric of competition has been tied up with the rhetoric of the market since Adam Smith proposed his invisible hand' (Burstyn 1999: 43). Competition is central to sport, it is central to the processes considered intrinsic to globalization, and it is central to the discourses about the global economy and Canada's place within it.

As we have seen above, the sports analogy closes the circle between globalization and competition—Canada must be able to compete, and to win, on a level playing field, defined by clear, 'sporting' rules. Tarzan must be able to demonstrate his skills, cunning, and superiority in an ordered jungle. As a model for social order or for the global economy, however, competition has its problems.

> Competition, often praised as one of the most important lessons sport teaches, is at bottom a hostile dynamic based in a mentality of scarcity. It can be seen as rationalized hostility because it is based on a zero-sum equation . . . The victory of one party entails loss by the other. The competitive relation, embodying hostility, is rehearsed over and over again through the rituals of childhood and youth sport.

> It is . . . celebrated by culture and the mass media. The message is simple: doing one's best is measured in doing *better* than others and in getting more (love, respect, stuff) as a reward. In the core men's sports, doing better usually means being more physically aggressive. Children's empathetic and cooperative impulses are thwarted through the culture of physical competition, and their narcissism and aggression rewarded. (Burstyn 1999: 43)

In the global economy, winning comes at someone else's expense. Winning must mean doing better than others because the global economy is a zero-sum game defined by scarcity—the jungle may be tamed by rules, but it remains a jungle nonetheless. Helping Canadians to win internationally must be a foreign policy goal of government, for losing is unthinkable. The analogy is problematic in at least two ways. First, the notion of competitiveness as a value in and for itself obscures the nature of the global economy, in particular the interests that reside there. 'Where the idea of competition once represented the aspirations of bonded individuals against a fixed feudal order, today it cloaks the interests of huge transnational corporations, many times more powerful than the old monarchies and aristocracies. As the mechanism seen to guide the market, the idealization of competition by sport has approached sanctification' (Burstyn 1999: 43). The 'individuals' who are successful in the competitive game are very often huge transnational firms, whose advantages far outweigh the individual skills and talents of the individual competitor. Second, in concealing the nature of the interests residing in the global economy through this insistence on individual preparation, skill, and achievement, the sports analogy of competition also conceals the extent to which the operation of the global economy is in itself gendered and reproduces the gendered social order. The celebration of competition and sport is also a celebration of socially constructed men; it is men who are the warriors, men who are the entrepreneurs, men who are the competitors, and men who are the risk-takers. It is men who define the 'game' of the globalized economy, and masculine values prevail; '[m]others should take care of nappies, clothes and food; fathers are for money, sport and punishment' (*The Economist* 1996, as cited in Burstyn 1999: 44).

The focus on competition, even within a set of defined rules (although the rules are never perfect, and an element of risk—the perils of the jungle—prevails), drives analysis of the global economy to the level of the individual, whether it be an individual person, firm, or even country. As in sport, the competitive basis of the global economy drives players who wish to be successful to train—to acquire the *individual* skills and assets required in order to extract the biggest pay-off from playing the game. As in any game, the assumption is clear: identify your skills and talents, practise hard, and invest the effort required in order to perfect those areas where you are lacking, seek mentors who can point out your weaknesses and suggest remedies, work hard, and you will succeed. While the portrayal of the competitive game is inherently gendered, its representation as such reduces policy responses to globalization to the level of the individual players in the game and to the strengthening of individual teams. Failure is a failing of the individual (person, firm, or country), who has not been daring enough, cunning enough, knowledgeable enough, dedicated enough, or tough enough. Nowhere does this discursive construction of international trade and the global economy allow policy makers or even critics to ask whether this game is itself being played with a stacked deck that requires the labour of the non-competitive marginalized 'losers' in order to guarantee the success of the entrepreneurial 'winners', as we will see below.

The gendered nature of the global economy, however, is well-documented (for some of the discussion of concrete ways in which globalization has had a differential, and largely negative, impact on women, see in particular the Chapters 4, 9, 12, and 14). Cynthia Enloe's groundbreaking work, *Bananas, Beaches and Bases*, documents the way in which the exigencies of the global economy (whether in the growth of export-processing zones or in the austerity programs promoted by the International Monetary Fund) not only have a greater impact on women than on men, but are dependent upon the willingness of women to adapt to them. For example, the adoption of IMF austerity measures depends on the capacity of women to respond to those measures:

> A government's ability to maintain its legitimacy [after IMF austerity measures have been adopted] depends at least in part on the capacity of families to tolerate those measures, specifically on the capacity of women to stretch their budgets, to continue to feed, clothe, and care for their families. . . . A dynamic is [thus] set up around ideas about what women will and will not do, the actual material conditions of their lives, and the policies produced by international organizations and foreign governments. This dynamic both sustains and is dependent on assumptions about what are considered the appropriate roles and qualities of women, and women of particular races, in specific times and places. (Whitworth 2000: 96)

The 'hard-edged' policies associated with the IMF austerity measures, the notion of 'getting one's financial house in order' so that a national economy may be able to compete better in the global economy (and thus to raise export revenues), conceal the gendered reality of the impact of such policies as they deploy gendered representations of that reality.

In a similar vein, the celebration of the new world of global finance evokes—as Marianne Marchand has written eloquently—'images of adventurous, risk-taking, fast-paced, globetrotting young men' (2000: 223). The new risk-taking warriors of the global economy are the most potent symbols of globalization, and yet the image projected by global finance conceals the gendered nature of this industry:

> What is often overlooked, however, is that this same global financial community cannot function without the existence of an internationalized service economy in both the private and public spheres: for instance, large groups of migrant women (and men) are employed in the global financial centres of London, New York, and Hong Kong as domestic help, nannies, gardeners, etc.; alternatively, migrant women (and men) may find themselves cleaning the offices of Chase Manhattan and similar banks at night; and increasingly, it is also possible for women to find work in the Philippines or India as data-entry clerks for large companies abroad. (2000: 223)

Global finance rests on the emergence of this feminized internationalized service economy, and yet the representation or discursive construction of this apex of globalization conceals the reality underpiniing its operation. As a symbol of this economy, George Soros is the picture of the victorious male warrior who has succeeded through his daring, skill, and competitive edge—the jungle's new Tarzan. The women (and men) who provide the services that make his success possible are invisible, as are the gendered power relationships enshrined therein—and yet, these are critical to the global financial economy. The logic inherent in the competitive sports analogy would suggest that domestic workers, for example, need only work harder, work longer hours, and hone their competitive skills in order to succeed in the international marketplace; in fact, however, the international marketplace could not function without such domestic workers.

DFAIT and Women Entrepreneurs

As other chapters in this volume have documented, the Canadian government, in particular the Department of Foreign Affairs and International Trade, has been largely unable, and often unwilling, to consider the ways in which the global economy has a fundamentally gendered nature, and that global economic restructuring has a consequential gendered impact. From the perspective of the discursive representations of the global economy echoed by Canadian policy makers, however, a failure to grasp this reality within a policy context is unsurprising. In fact, the sports analogy which drives the discursive construction—and therefore conceptual understanding—that characterizes almost all discussion of the global economy makes it all but impossible to understand globalization in broader structural terms. Calls to pay attention to the gendered nature of globalization and to the gendered consequences of global economic restructuring are inevitably answered with the question of 'what do (individual) women need to help them to perform more effectively in the global marketplace?'. The gendered reality of globalization is obscured by the logic of competition, winners and losers, and the rules of the game, which reinforces the bias toward the analysis of individual circumstance at the expense of the whole—of an analysis of globalization as a series of processes that depend upon gender to function. This is not to say, of course, that there is no worth in attempting to understand how individual women have confronted the jungle of the global economy. Such a response, however, does not address questions of gender and globalization, but rather, focuses attention on (individual) women in international trade. To return to Marchand's typology, the gendered ideational or ideological level of understanding of globalization defined in a sports analogy of competition fosters a gendered individual—and to some extent, narrowly collective—response.

In April 1997, the Organisation for Economic Co-operation and Development (OECD) held a conference called 'Women Entrepreneurs in Small and Medium Enterprises: A Major Force in Innovation and Job Creation'. The OECD was motivated in large part by the same observations as those made by Canadian trade ministers, namely, that 'women-owned SMEs . . . are growing at a faster rate than the economy as a whole', yet, that despite this, 'the economic potential of women entrepreneurs remains partly untapped' (OECD 1997). The purpose of the conference was to assess the problems confronting women entrepreneurs and to facilitate the growth and development of the SMEs that they head. Billed as a 'true world economic summit on women entrepreneurs in SMEs' (OECD 1997), the conference was the most significant international event to that point to focus on the specific issues and problems confronting women entrepreneurs in business, and in international trade.[5] This OECD conference initiative, motivated in part by the emerging reality of women's greater entrepreneurial participation in the Canadian market, also coincided with a series of measures by the Canadian government to facilitate women entrepreneurs' access to international markets.

These Canadian initiatives took a variety of forms. The trade commissioner's staff at the Canadian Embassy in Washington inaugurated the Canadian Women's International Business Initiative to provide women entrepreneurs with information and business contacts needed in order for them to pursue export opportunities in the mid-Atlantic states of the United States (Eggleton 1997). The centrepiece of this enterprise was the first ever Canadian Women's Trade Mission to Washington in November 1997 (Marchi 1999b)—a women-only 'Team Canada'. Following upon this Team Canada mission, Minister Marchi announced the establishment of a public-private-sector consortium of individuals and organizations, the Trade Research Coalition (TRC), whose mandate was to 'gather information which clarifies the degree and type of participation by Canadian businesswomen in the trade environment, particularly in the US market; and to propose recommendations, policies, measures and activities to promote export development by businesswomen' (Trade Commissioner Service 1997). Significantly, the TRC was also to report on the 'barriers which may have limited' the 'success' of women entrepreneurs in gaining access to the US and international markets.

The new women-focused activities of DFAIT did not end there, however. In June 1998, International Trade Minister Sergio Marchi introduced 'Businesswomen in Trade', the first website created especially for Canadian women exporters (DFAIT 1998c)[6], which offered electronic access to a broad range of business information in Canada and internationally. The website was also designed to facilitate networking between the businesswomen. The first women-only Team Canada mission spawned several others, including the Canadian Women's Mission to the World Bank and the Inter-American Development Bank in Washington in March 1998, the Businesswomen's Mission to Chicago in January 1999, the Businesswomen's Mission to Los Angeles in March 1999, and the Women's Information Technology Mission to the Federal Office Systems Exhibition in Washington in April 1999 (Marchi 1999b). In March 1999, the TRC published its report *Beyond Borders: Canadian Businesswomen in International Trade* (DFAIT 1999d, Orser et al. 1999a); a parallel study of US businesswomen was being published in the United States—*A Snapshot of Selected U.S. Women Owned Exporting Firms* (Marchi 1999b). Both reports profiled the experiences of businesswomen in international trade, and both served as the basis for discussion at the first Canada-USA Businesswomen's Trade Summit held in Toronto in May 1999. The recommendations of that summit on the opportunities for, and barriers to, enhanced participation by women in interna-

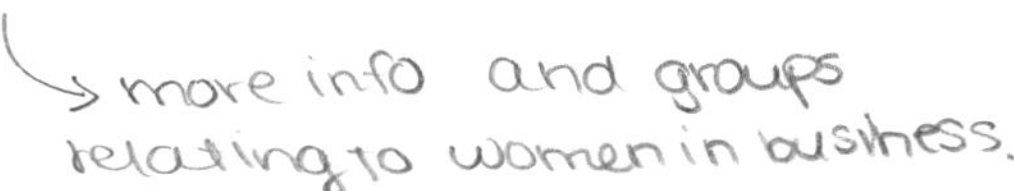
more info and groups
relating to women in business.

tional markets formed part of the basis for discussion at the 'Women Entrepreneurs in SMEs: Realising the Benefits of Globalisation and the Knowledge-based Economy', the OECD conference held in Paris in November 2000. The OECD made it clear that although women's entrepreneurship was generally growing in the OECD countries, the impetus for the OECD's attention to the issue came from North America: 'In some countries, *for example the United States and Canada*, women-owned businesses are increasing at a very rapid pace.' (OECD 2000; italics added). The OECD went on to note, 'In an era of global economic integration, this significant economic and social development is of growing interest to practitioners and policy makers worldwide' (OECD 2000).

In order to assess more carefully the nature and significance of these initiatives, it is worthwhile to turn our attention to the *Beyond Borders* report published by the Trade Research Coalition.[7] In many respects, *Beyond Borders* details the assumptions about women in international trade that have motivated Canadian government policy. As mentioned earlier, the TRC was a private- and public-sector consortium made up of individuals representing various interests, although three-quarters of the members were drawn from different government departments (including DFAIT, Status of Women Canada, and Industry Canada). This consortium's activities were sponsored by a number of private- and public-sector organizations, including DFAIT, the Royal Bank of Canada, the Export Development Corporation, the Canadian Institute of Chartered Accountants, Status of Women Canada, Industry Canada, the Certified General Accountants of Canada, Lever Enterprises (a firm specializing in international commercial development and finance), and the Women Entrepreneurs of Canada (a national association for established women business owners, founded in 1992).

The study began with two related premises: that exports, which constitute 40 per cent of Canadian gross domestic product, are a leading source of new jobs, and that the 1990s witnessed an unprecedented increase in the number of women becoming business owners. Taken together, and given the need identified by the Canadian government in the establishment of its Team Canada initiative to stimulate export activity among small- and medium-sized businesses, the report sought to identify the 'conditions that assist the development of export business; [the] major impediments to the development of export business for women business owners in Canada; [the] strategies and tactics used by Canadian development of trade relationships, and [the] awareness of and satisfaction with existing public and private sector initiatives that related to export promotion' (Orser et al. 1999b).[8]

The study presents a profile of women entrepreneurs involved in export activities. The majority were born in Canada (75 per cent), did not describe themselves as a member of a minority group (93 per cent), were highly educated (28 per cent had a graduate degree, 43 per cent have a college diploma or university degree, 18 per cent had some college or university education), had founded their own firm (88 per cent), were living with a spouse or partner (69 per cent)[9], were unilingual (60 per cent), had never worked outside of Canada (62 per cent), and sold products rather than services (64 per cent) (Orser et al. 1999c). It is clear, and hardly surprising, that the profile of these women does not suggest the average Canadian woman. The atypical profile of these women, mostly white and highly educated, underlines the individualist bias of the government response which stems quite naturally from the understanding of globalization as a competitive game. Canada's best potential players must be sought out in order to strengthen the team. It is the activities of *some* women in international trade that are being examined, and not the relationship between women and international trade in any broader sense. When asked about the nature of the challenges facing women entrepreneurs in engaging in international trade, the respondents pointed to the cost of developing such markets, the difficulties in setting up distribution channels, in finding local partners, obtaining information about foreign markets, and in complying with the regulations of foreign governments (Orser et al. 1999d). These challenges were not framed by the respondents in gendered terms; it is as likely that SMEs headed by men would confront the same difficulties.

The survey did, however, did push respondents to identify ask about specific gender challenges relating to exporting. Roughly three-quarters of the participants did report on some gender-specific aspects to the business challenges they faced. These were primarily defined in terms of cultural and interpersonal differences, focusing in particular on the attitudes of the people the exporter dealt with. The comments of respondents referred to: 'a perceived lack of respect by male business owners; businessmen who explicitly refuse to do business with a woman; bravado, physical gestures and chauvinism; clients who verify the female business owner's decision through a male member of staff; perceived gender discrimination by Canadian lending institutions; the assumption that the business is owned by a man; differences in management experience and style of doing business; and different or more limited professional networks' (Orser et al. 1999e). Businesswomen also complained of not being taken seriously, or of having their ability, experience, and background minimized because of their gender. Family issues were also identified as a gender-specific challenge, including the logistical hurdles posed by family responsibilities and the potential limitations on travel for mothers of young children (Orser et al. 1999e). What is perhaps most telling about the discussion of gender-specific challenges, however, are the recommendations for responding to them—the shared 'tricks of the trade' offered as assistance to other businesswomen in similar situations. The report presents a list of these 'hints' for handling gender-specific problems: avoiding personal or phone contact in certain countries through the exclusive use of e-mail; ignoring slights; insisting that customers must deal with them if they want to do business; building their own credibility; avoiding social events if the purpose of the event might be misconstrued; having a male employee handle certain firms or customers; changing business cards to clarify ownership of the firm; working with Canadian trade commissioners as interlocutors; and consciously hiring male employees and subcontractors (Orser et al. 1999e).

These gender-specific challenges, and the solutions to which they give rise, are undoubtedly perfectly accurate and reasonable assessments of the situation for women entrepreneurs as they engage, or attempt to engage, in international trade. They are also the stories of *individual* women, and of their strategies as *individuals* for overcoming some of the gendered consequences of their business participation, consequences which are largely understood to be the result of the collective, rather than ideational, level at which gender can be constructed. As these women reflected on the ways in which the construction of gender in the interactions between men and women affected them—women perceived to be less competent, less credible, and less worthy than their male colleagues—the ideational or ideological context in which they find themselves remains unexplored. The 'game' of international trade, with its rules of competition and winning, is their mantra as well. *Beyond Borders* paints a picture of a community of women business owners prepared to share their expertise and experience in order to help others to 'train', or to practise, in order to win at the game of international business. As one of the respondents noted, in her experience: '[w]omen have a problem with the concept of making money. . . . And with selling themselves and thinking as a business. . . . So it's making that transition . . . that you're . . . selling a service and you're developing a quality service but it's all right to charge for it. It's all right to market it. It's all right to hustle' (quoted in Orser et al. 1999e). It's all right to play the competitive game to win. The role of government, and thus the consequent objective of Canadian policy, is to become a better coach or personal trainer, in order to enhance the performance of its winning athletes. From websites to women-only Team Canada missions, the way to address gender and globalization is to respond to the requirements of individual women and women-led firms so that they might be more successful in the export game. The individualist logic of a gendered competitive sports analogy drives the government response in that direction; when globalization is seen as a competitive game, it is inconceivable that its gendered nature and consequences would be uncovered.

The extent to which trade, and women's places as exporters, become defined in terms of this competitive sports analogy is reinforced by the publication of the *Beyond Borders* summary document (Rayman 1999). Here, the academic prose and carefully crafted research results are translated into a glossier publication that highlights the main findings of the study. What is striking, and in many respects disturbing, is the addition of illustrations designed to enhance the portrayal of women in international trade. Of the seven women portrayed in the publication, only one is engaged in what might be considered a business activity: she is talking on her cell phone. The other six images are engaged in various sporting activities: speed skating, volleyball, running hurdles, a foot race on an athletic track, a soccer match, and a celebration of an athletic team victory. These women are all competing, displaying in their determined faces and in their athleticism that they too possess the qualities such as aggressiveness, competitiveness, strength, speed, power, and teamwork that have been associated with masculinity, and which are deemed to be necessary for success in the globalization jungle—even if that jungle has been tamed by international rules. One woman, the head of a freight forwarding company in Toronto, commented in the summary report that, given the lack of women in the transportation industry, 'I found some of the people were negative about me in business. I knew I could do it and that's what I did. . . . Now they accept me because they see that I know what I am doing and I can be just like one of them' (Arlene Singroy, quoted in Rayman 1999: 19). The quite logical response to the gendered representation of globalization is to learn the rules of the game and to play as well as possible—to be a skilled, cunning and knowledgeable Tarzan, just like one of them.

Conclusion

The identification of globalization as a perilous condition existing 'out there' to which governments are subject builds a conceptual prism for the Canadian government. The jungle of globalization must be tamed in order to ensure that those who venture forth into the wild can survive, and taming the jungle becomes a pressing need because withdrawal and hiding from it are not options. The means for doing this taming are multilateral rules (despite the fact that some of these rules fostered the growth of the jungle in the first instance), and these rules turn the jungle into a competitive game. Without rules and referees, there can be no game, just as, to return to Paul Martin's analysis, without the rules and referees of hockey, there is only anarchy, not hockey. Faced with the jungle that they have partly created, states and international financial and economic organizations create the rules to ensure fairness, but the jungle remains an arena for competition and for the survival of the most talented, cunning, and skilled.

The study of Canadian foreign policy has not been characterized by attention to the gendered construction of the key concepts that dominate the foreign policy discourse and agenda. Sensitivity to the gendered construction of discourse, however, allows us to interpret Canadian foreign policy in a different light—and allows us to ask how the conceptualization of globalization as a competition defined by certain multilateral rules drives policy in a particular direction. If globalization is a game, then the policy responses to it are almost naturally to be found in assisting the players to succeed, and in so doing, strengthening the team. What this analysis allows us to see, however, is the way that conception of the global economy discourse conceals its underlying gendered nature, and thereby privileges responses that target individual women rather than seek to address its foundations. In deploying a discourse that conceals the nature of globalization, links between foreign policy and issues of labour standards, human rights, and welfare support are never made. The consequences for foreign policy of seeing globalization as gendered are potentially transformative: women working in sweatshops in developing countries, or immigrants doing piece work for desperation-level wages in Toronto, become part of globalization. Human rights policies become part of international trade. Labour standards become part of international trade. And international trade becomes something other than sport.

These sports analogies, however, are neither trivial nor neutral. Sports and sport culture celebrate the masculine values of individual skill, power, aggression, and speed, just as the contemporary global economy celebrates the victories of its most successful entrepreneurs. Microsoft becomes Bill Gates rather than a multi-billion dollar corporate empire, and it is he who is celebrated for having been tougher and stronger than his rivals in business and trade, whatever rules of fair play may have been broken along the way. Such an analogy brings with it its own logic, however: the individualistic focus on competition conceals the power of today's largest corporations, as well as the fundamentally gendered nature of the global economy. Using such a pervasive analogy to define globalization, the Canadian state is reduced to devising strategies to help Canadians, including women entrepreneurs, win on the global playing field. Trying to respond to more fundamental challenges posed by globalization is inconceivable because globalization has been defined as an incontrovertible reality 'out there', to be faced by only the most skilled players. This observation should neither be construed as a critique of the government's trade policy *per se*, nor as a dismissal of the possible benefits of helping women become more proficient exporters. Nor is this observation in any way a criticism of women exporters themselves, for they, like others, have learned to succeed in a harsh and competitive environment. Rather, this analysis suggests that the government's deaf ear that has often greeted women's groups when they raise issues of the gendered nature of the global economy is unlikely to change, because at least from the government's perspective, the state is doing everything it can and should do. When globalization is seen as a competitive game, those who complain about its effects simply are not aggressive enough, or have not worked or trained nearly hard enough. Only a broader perspective on gender and international trade moves us beyond the individualistic competitive game, and makes it possible to appreciate the long-term unsustainability of continuing to play hockey in the jungle.[10]

Notes

1. It is important to note that the existence of women in business-ownership activities in no way tells us whether they had chosen to become entrepreneurs, or were had been driven to seek self-employment as their only option during the massive restructuring of the Canadian economy, with its particular impact on women.
2. For a similar argument analysis of finance and credit, see Marieke de Goede (2000).
3. It is interesting that Martin emphasizes the need for referees and rules for the game to be considered hockey. Referees create a particular kind of order and enforce rules which in themselves are hardly neutral—the construction of 'playing fields', and the extent to which they are 'level', depends upon the rules and the enforcement mechanisms put into place. Martin could just as easily have promoted the image of shinny as the 'real hockey' representative of international finance and the global political economy, but had he done so, he would have denied the existence of a space for political action in taming the hockey 'jungle'.
4. In the way in which sport is being discussed in this chapter, sport is much more than the athletic competition itself; it is much more than a 'game' for those who play, and 'entertainment' for those who do not. Sport is not somehow separate from society, nor does it transcend or have '"nothing to do with" politics and social conflict.' (Allison 1993b: 5). Sport is not reducible to the 'physical activities and game forms that have promoted personal well-being, community coalescence, and social equality' (Burstyn 1999: 4); rather, through the power of its symbols, it plays a significant role in shaping our understanding of modern society.
5. This is not to say that the 1995 Beijing World Conference on Women did not address issues of the global economy or of women's place within it. The 1997 OECD Conference represented the first major international discussion among *economic* bureaucracies focused exclusively on the issues relating to women as entrepreneurs.

6. The URL for DFAIT's 'Businesswomen in Trade' website is <http://www.inforexport.gc.ca/businesswomen/menu-e.asp>.
7. The research for *Beyond Borders* was conducted by a team of academics, led by Barbara Orser, President of Equinox Management Consultants Ltd (Ottawa) and Adjunct Professor of Business at Carleton University, and including Eileen Fischer (York University), Rebecca Reuber (University of Toronto), Sue Hooper (Asia Pacific Foundation), and Allan Riding (Carleton University).
8. The study's results were compiled using rigorous social-science methodologies. Criteria were established in order to select appropriate participants for the study, including firms employing fewer than 500 full-time employees, actively involved in exporting, or planning to become actively involved, which were owned or partially owned by a woman who had equity capital at risk in the venture, was responsible for the strategic direction of the business, and has the authority to make decisions, including export decisions. From a list of more than 1,000 contacts, 735 firms met the screening criteria for eligibility. Data were obtained from 254 faxed survey responses, 54 in-depth telephone interviews, focus group sessions with experienced women entrepreneurs and telephone consultations. A total of 67 women business owners were involved in the focus group sessions and telephone consultations (Orser et al. 1999b).
9. Although 69 per cent of the women reported living with a spouse or partner, only 17 per cent of women business owners reported having to pay for daycare services for children, or for elderly or disabled relatives (Orser et al. 1999d).
10. I am indebted to Ann Denholm Crosby for pointing this out.

Part II

Human Security

Chapter 6

Militarized Masculinities and the Politics of Peacekeeping: The Canadian Case[1]

SANDRA WHITWORTH

> The image of a Canadian soldier wearing his blue beret, standing watch at some lonely outpost in a strife torn foreign land, is part of the modern Canadian mosaic, and a proud tradition.
>
> –*General Paul Manson (1998)*

> Arone lapsed in and out of consciousness during the beating. When he was conscious, he was heard to scream 'Canada, Canada', on several occasions. . . .
>
> –*Murder of Shidane Arone by Canadian soldiers, 16 March 1993*
> *(Somalia Inquiry 1997a, General Court Martial*
> *Transcripts of Private Brocklebank, Vol. 3, entry 19.)*

The image of Canada as peacekeeper, so aptly described above by former Chief of the Defence Staff General Paul Manson, has long served as one of the 'core myths' (Francis 1997: 10) of Canada's 'imagined community' (Anderson 1991: 6). In that myth Canada is an altruistic and benign middle power, acting with a kind of moral purity not normally exhibited by contemporary states (see Stairs 1998b; Neufeld and Whitworth 1996; Neufeld 1999, also Smith this volume). Thus when, in March 1993, two Canadian soldiers beat a Somali teenager, Shidane Abukar Arone, to death, with their fists, their boots, a baton, a metal rod and cigarettes, the myth was reasserted at the very moment it began to disintegrate. Arone's only words in English that night were the name 'Canada, Canada', which he repeated throughout his ordeal. The myth had been sold so well that even a sixteen-year-old Somali shepherd, murdered by those who were supposed to be its exemplars, apparently believed in it.

Arone's tragic death, and the shooting several weeks earlier of two Somali men by Canadian soldiers, sparked a series of courts martial and eventually prompted the Canadian government to set up a commission of inquiry to investigate the activities of its forces in Somalia. Intended in part to resuscitate the image of Canada's military forces and Canada's reputation internationally, many of those investigations emphasized the problem of 'a few bad apples' or otherwise lamented a decline of traditional military values. Only rarely were the events of Somalia associated with the problems of militarized masculinity and the use in peace operations of soldiers trained to destroy other human beings by force. However, the dramatic expansion of peacekeeping missions since the Cold War demands such an analysis.[2] The events in Somalia, in short, revealed not only some of the contradictions of one of Canada's 'core myths', but underscored as well the pervasiveness, and effects of, militarized masculinity within issues of Canadian foreign policy.

This chapter illustrates the ways in which a feminist analysis disrupts traditional interpretations of Canadian foreign policy. While the policy implications of particular peacekeeping missions have been questioned with considerable regularity, rarely does an analysis of 'masculinity' figure in those studies. Indeed, part of the argument of this chapter is that the 'representational practices' (Doty 1997: 10–11) associated with peacekeeping are in many ways as important as the peacekeeping missions themselves. This is so because the two are integrally related: Canadian representations of nation and military depend upon the benign and altruistic image of Canada as peacekeeper, images which come to form the 'background knowledge that is taken to be true' (Doty 1997: 10) about peacekeeping. But at the same time, those images are fundamentally at odds with the duties that soldiers are expected, and indeed were *created* to perform. As feminist and other critical analysts point out, soldiers are not born; rather they are made, through training, institutional expectations, psychological conditioning and a variety of material and ideological rewards. What has been particularly revealing in the Canadian case has been the dangerous behaviour that erupts when soldiers trained 'to engage in wanton destruction and to slip the bonds of civilized behaviour' (Bercuson 1996: 29) have been limited to mere peacekeeping duty. The Airborne, when it was chosen to go to Somalia as one of Canada's elite units, expected a traditional peacekeeping mission. By the time it arrived, it had been given licence, unprecedented in some forty years, to actually act like soldiers. And the events that resulted shocked people both in Canada and around the world. Canada's image as the liberal internationalist state and neutral arbiter of conflicts was built in part on the myth of a benign and altruistic military force. What Somalia demonstrated was how precarious these various myths really were.

Masculinities and Peacekeeping

Since the end of the Cold War, it has become commonplace to note that there has been a proliferation of peacekeeping missions: the United Nations (UN) launched fifteen between 1956 and 1989, and a further twenty-two between 1989 and 1995 alone (Sens 1997: 22). The proliferation of missions has led also to a proliferation of peacekeepers around the world: in 1991 the UN deployed some 11,000 blue helmets, and by 1994 the number of peacekeepers in the field numbered well over 75,000 (Coulon 1998: ix). Those missions also have become much more complex, departing from the traditional interposing of neutral forces between belligerent groups to include, for example, military and police functions, the monitoring of human rights, the conducting of elections, the delivery of humanitarian aid, the repatriation of refugees, the creation and operation of state administrative structures, and so on (Heininger 1994: 26).

Peacekeeping, and peace operations generally, became the way in which the UN asserted its visibility internationally, and many referred to peacekeeping as 'perhaps the major instrument of diplomacy available to the United Nations for insuring peace and international security' (Rubinstein 1993: 548). That instrument, however, continues to depend primarily on the use of soldiers as peacekeepers. Nobody knows better than the military itself what is involved in the creation of a soldier. As Major R.W.J. Wenek wrote in 1984: 'The defining role of any military force is the management of violence by violence, so that individual aggressiveness is, or should be, a fundamental characteristic of occupational fitness in combat units' (Wenek 1984: 46). These are the kinds of qualities that feminist scholars point to when they note the way in which most militaries promote a particular kind of masculinity, one premised on violence and aggression, but also institutional unity and hierarchy, 'aggressive heterosexism and homophobia', as well as misogyny and racism.[3]

The argument of this chapter is that peacekeeping may have resolved what was a crisis of legitimation for post–Cold War militaries, but it did so in a way that is not fully or properly, militaristic. The restrictions on firing except in self-defence and a sometimes multilateral chain of command disrupt the prevailing notions of military purpose and structure. In traditional military culture, peacekeeping and peace operations are often ridiculed and demeaned: while they have become increasingly important since the Cold War, there is not much prestige associated with a 'blue beret fight' for the (mostly) young men trained to do battle whom we send on these missions. The resolution of the military's legitimation crisis becomes to some extent a crisis of masculinity. The strains which emerge, and their sometimes horrifying consequences, are made clear by examining the Canadian case.

Canada and Peacekeeping

As has been suggested, peacekeeping is highly regarded in Canada. It was assessed favourably in the most recent reviews of both foreign and defence policy as a central and primary element in Canadian foreign and security policies. As the 1994 Special Joint Committee on Canada's Defence Policy noted:

> In virtually every one of these [successful peacekeeping] cases, Canada has played a constructive and often leading role. Canadians are rightly proud of what their country their military has done in this regard. Indeed, the demand for our services, and arguably the need, is growing. Since 1988, the United Nations has undertaken more peacekeeping missions than in the previous thirty-five years, and Canada has been a key participant in almost every one of them. (Canada, Special Joint Committee on Canada's Defence Policy, 1994: 12)

The Standing Committee on National Defence and Veterans Affairs (1993: 7) affirmed Canada's commitment to peacekeeping, and noted in 1993: 'Canadians have always seen peacekeeping as an important element of their identity and of their country's position on the international stage, even when peacekeeping meant little to much of the international community'. Likewise, as Janice Stein reported to the Special Joint Committee Reviewing Canada's Foreign Policy in 1994, 'the overwhelming sense [is] that this is an area of comparative advantage for Canadians' (Canada, Special Joint Committee Reviewing Canadian Foreign Policy 1994: 16). Canadian government documents reveal an assumption not only that Canadians are experienced and committed peacekeepers, but that peacekeeping is a clear extension of Canadian values on the international stage (Cox and Sjolander, 1998). As the 1995 government statement, *Canada in the World* noted:

> Canadians are confident in their values and in the contribution these values make to the international community. . . . Our principles and values, our culture are rooted in a commitment to tolerance; to democracy, equity and human rights; to the peaceful resolution of differences; to the opportunities and challenges of the marketplace; to social justice; to sustainable development; and to easing poverty. (DFAIT 1995a: 8)

Or as Stéphane Dion, President of the Privy Council and Minister of Intergovernmental Affairs, commented enthusiastically: 'Canada is a good global citizen, projecting beyond our borders our values of generosity, tolerance and an unswerving commitment to peace and democracy (Dion: quoted in Cox and Sjolander, 1998).

Such widespread government support does not mean that there are not disagreements within the Canadian government about peacekeeping. The Department of National Defence's enthusiasm for peacekeeping is tempered somewhat by the disadvantages associated with the popularity of an activity that does not require nearly as much capital expenditure as the geo-strategic defence of Canada and its allies. As the Defence White paper stated repeatedly, there is more to defence than peacekeeping, and Major General (retired) Glen Younghusband pointed out to the Special Joint Committee Reviewing Canada's defence policy in 1994, 'To believe that Canada will never require a greater military capability than peacekeeping is wishful thinking, and a defence policy based on wishful thinking would be dangerous indeed' (Canada, Special Joint Committee on Canada's Defence Policy 1994: 14). More recently, concerns have been raised about spreading the Forces too thin and taking on too many peacekeeping duties. But in general, the advantages of peacekeeping are widely accepted, and defence department anxieties notwithstanding, its popularity has been central in securing a certain amount of financial support for the Canadian military, a major challenge in the relatively threat free environment of the post–Cold War world (Dale 1993).

There is also considerable support for peacekeeping in the general population. In a 1995 study, Pierre Martin and Michel Fortmann note that peacekeeping has enjoyed a relatively high level of public support in Canada throughout its history, often receiving in public opinion polls higher support than any other role for the Canadian Armed Forces (Martin and Fortmann 1995: 379). As Martin and Fortmann write, the generally positive image of the military in Canadian society is in considerable measure due to its participation in UN peacekeeping forces. Also in 1995, women's groups that appeared before the Joint Committee reviewing foreign policy made a number of important criticisms of peacekeeping, but most of the groups were quite supportive and viewed it as an element of defence which should be expanded (Whitworth 1995). Peace groups also frequently argue that the emphasis in the Canadian military should be shifted from 'combat to peacekeeping' (Project Ploughshares 1996). In 1992, even the Citizens' Inquiry into Peace and Security (an 'alternative' foreign and defence review organized by the Canadian Peace Alliance and funded by a number of largely peace, native and labour NGOs) found that support for peacekeeping activities was 'virtually unanimous' (Citizens' Inquiry into Peace and Security 1992: 23).

The image of Canada as peacekeeper has also served a variety of important political goals of the Canadian government. Not only do visual images of Canadian peacekeepers figure prominently during national unity debates, but as Joseph T. Jockel notes, 'Canada's reputation as a good international 'citizen', a reputation acquired partially through extensive peacekeeping, may have strengthened its position in the UN across a wide range of issues on the world agenda' (Jockel 1994: 15). It was certainly helpful in Canada's successful bid for a Security Council seat in 1998 and Jockel notes that in the post-Cold War period:

> Canada was the peacekeeping country *par excellence*, having contributed to virtually all UN peacekeeping operations. . . . [Its] peacekeeping experience, coupled with its well-recognized commitment to the UN, appeared to have left it especially suited to play if not a leading role, then at least a significant one in the building of the new world order. (Jockel 1994: 1)

Indeed, as numerous commentators have noted, it has been Canada's involvement in peacekeeping and its 'history of altruism, compassion, fairness, and of doing things irrespective of our own national interest' which gives it influence internationally far out of proportion to its military or economic power (quoted in Cooper 1997: 20).

Canada's commitment to peacekeeping is also, in no small measure, intended to contrast with the far more ambivalent position on peacekeeping found in the United States, where peacekeeping does not appear to receive the same widespread public support as in Canada and where peace operations generally are regarded with considerable caution, and sometimes outright hostility. It is difficult to imagine the Canadian state falling into arrears to the UN for peacekeeping contributions, as the United States has done consistently; and it is equally unthinkable that a Canadian soldier would be lauded by some political elites for refusing to serve under UN command, as occurred in the United States in 1995 (Sokolsky 1995; 'US soldier discharged for refusing to serve UN'). As the Somalia Commission later wrote:

> Canada's foreign policy with respect to peacekeeping has been consistent since Canadians embraced peacekeeping in the late 1950s. Peacekeeping has become a characteristic Canadian metier, a function distinguishing us from Americans and reinforcing our sovereignty and independence. Americans were seen to fight wars, but Canadians pictured themselves as working for peace. (Somalia Inquiry 1997b, Vol. 1: 198; quoted in Razack 1996: 156)

Or, as Sherene Razack notes: 'Peacekeeping as a national vocation, and as the dream of a middle power that exists next door to the United States, neatly enables Canada to tell a story of national goodness and to mark itself as distinct from the United States' (Razack 1996: 134). Through its policy decisions and the activities of its people sent abroad, Canada was depicted as the 'helpful fixer' to the international stage (Neufeld and Whitworth 1996).

The Reputation Tarnished: Canadian Peacekeepers in Somalia

The very favourable image of Canadian peacekeeping was shaken to its foundations when reports emerged from Belet Huen, Somalia, of the shooting of two Somali men and then the subsequent torture and murder of Arone by members of Canada's elite Airborne Regiment (Whitworth 1998). The two men who were shot, it was learned later, had been lured into the Canadian compound with food and water left out as bait (Somalia Inquiry 1997a, Vol. 146: 29777; Vol. 124: 24994; Vol. 32: 6120). Both were shot in the back, and one, Ahmed Aruush, died. Although an initial investigation concluded that the Airborne soldiers involved in the shooting had acted properly, a Canadian military doctor later reported that the dead man had been shot once in the back and then 'someone had finished him off with a lethal shot to the head' (Armstrong 1997). The doctor reported, moreover, that he had been pressured to destroy his medical records concerning the alleged murder (Pugliese 1995: A6).

Shidane Arone was captured two weeks later, on the first evening after the platoon commanders received orders that it was permissible to 'abuse' infiltrators who resisted capture (Worthington and Brown 1997: 112–13). The two soldiers who were guarding Arone beat and tortured him for several hours. As many as seventeen other soldiers visited the bunker in which he was held and occasionally took part in the beating themselves; still others could hear Arone's screams from their nearby tents, the sentry post, and even the command post. Sixteen-year-old Shidane Abukar Arone died shortly after midnight. In the sanitized language of the Somalia inquiry's final report: 'Death was preceded by prolonged and severe pain and suffering' (Somalia Inquiry 1997b: 324). Canada's peacekeeping reputation was shaken even more when, at court martial proceedings, it was revealed that Shidane Arone's torturers had photographed his ordeal. The pictures, described as 'trophy photos', depicted two soldiers, Master Corporal Clayton Matchee and Private Elvin Kyle Brown, striking various poses with the bloodied Arone, one of which showed Matchee holding a loaded pistol to Arone's head and another in which Matchee was forcing Arone's mouth open with a riot baton.

The first reaction by mainstream observers of peacekeeping in Canada to the Arone murder was to dismiss it as the act of a few 'bad apples' (Somalia Inquiry 1997b; Desbarats 1997; Whitworth 1997), most likely the result of years of underfunding, which had led to the deployment of a unit not ready for duty (Jockel 1994: 33). The bad-apple theory was undermined when, some months after the Inquiry was called into the events in Somalia, a number of videos were released to the Canadian media. The first, which was a video from the Somalia mission taken by

Canadian soldiers on duty there as a personal record, showed Airborne soldiers describing the mission as 'Operation Snatch Niggers' and lamented that they had not 'shot enough niggers yet.' In the second video, which showed one of the hazing rituals of Airborne's Commando Unit, soldiers were seen vomiting or eating vomit, being smeared with faeces, and, in the case of the single black soldier in the regiment, being forced to walk around on all fours with the phrase 'I love the KKK' written on his back (Dornan 1995; Somalia Inquiry 1997a, Exhibit P-53). The problem, it would appear from the videos, was far more pervasive than could be blamed on 'a few bad apples'.

The courts martials eventually found one of the men involved in Arone's murder, Elvin Kyle Brown, guilty of torture and manslaughter, sentenced him to five years in prison (of which he served just under two years) and dismissed him in disgrace. Clayton Matchee tried to commit suicide after being arrested in Somalia, suffered brain damage, and was found unfit to stand trial at his subsequent courts martial. Other soldiers who had heard but not stopped the beating and murder were found guilty of lesser charges, and after the release of the hazing videos, the Airborne Regiment itself was disbanded.

The government inquiry that had been called to investigate the events in Somalia was halted before it could actually examine the murder of Arone. The inquiry had exceeded the time allowed for its investigation, and the Canadian government refused any further extensions. This was the first time in Canadian history that a commission of inquiry of this magnitude was brought to a halt before its completion. But the commissioners did hear extensive evidence on pre-deployment issues as well as the shooting on 4 March 1993. Its five-volume report, entitled *Dishonoured Legacy*, while critical of the military in a number of important respects, picked up on the theme that had already been emphasized by military apologists: the problem was not one of the military itself, but rather one of a military gone wrong:

> It is the sharp contrast between [the events in Somalia] and the accustomed performance of our military that elicited reactions of alarm, outrage, and sadness among Canadians. In the end, we are hopeful that our Inquiry will yield corrective measures to help restore the Canadian Forces to the position of honour they have held for so long. (Somalia Inquiry 1997b, Executive Summary: ES-5)

The events in Somalia, the final report argued, were a result of poor training and even poorer leadership. In David Bercuson's opinion, the Canadian military had become stifled by budget cuts, was over-bureaucratized and staffed by career-minded 'cover your ass' officers who have replaced the disciplined and honourable leaders of the past (Bercuson 1996: vi). The problem, in short, was a failure of traditional military values.

Feminist and Critical Questions

Feminists and critical theorists, however, might ask instead whether the problem was not in fact the result of military values themselves. Theorists of both militarism and of masculinity have long argued that there is an intimate connection between military organizations and hegemonic representations of masculinity. As David Morgan writes:

> Of all the sites where masculinities are constructed, reproduced, and deployed, those associated with war and the military are some of the most direct. Despite far-reaching political, social, and technological changes, the warrior still seems to be a key symbol of masculinity. In statues, heroic paintings, comic books, and popular films the gendered connotations are inescapable. The stance, the facial expressions, and the weapons clearly connote aggression, courage, a capacity for violence, and, sometimes, a willingness for sacrifice. The uniform absorbs individualities into a generalized and timeless masculinity while also connoting a control of emotion and a subordination to a larger rationality. (Morgan 1994: 165)

And this is as true of Canada's ostensibly benign and altruistic peacekeepers as it is of soldiers elsewhere.

Although the two videotapes (the first from Somalia and the second from 1 Commando's hazing rituals) were perhaps the most obvious indications of racism in the Airborne and apparently shocked many Canadians, officials at the Department of Defence may not have been surprised at all. It was learned within the first week of the Somalia Inquiry's hearings that the Department had been investigating the presence of racist skinhead organizations and neo-Nazi activities in the Canadian Forces, and had described the entire CFB Petawawa (home of the Airborne Regiment) as 'one of the several areas where right-wing activities are centred' (Commission of Inquiry 1995: 13). Military officials, in other words, had allowed members of the Airborne Regiment who were either known to be members of racist skinhead organizations or who were under investigation for suspected skinhead and neo-Nazi activity to be sent to Somalia.

The military's apologists were greatly relieved and quick to point out that none of the suspected skinheads in the Airborne Regiment were actually charged in Arone's murder. Whether or not the racism exhibited by Airborne soldiers was 'organized', much of the evidence from interviews, testimonies, photographs, diaries, and letters home from Canadian soldiers reveals the ways in which racism pervaded the Airborne. From posing in front of the Confederate flag (which is often used by white supremacist groups in the United States), through tattooing themselves with swastikas, to calling Somalis by any number of pejorative names ('smufty', 'smoofties', 'moolie', 'flip-flop', 'nig nog', 'nigger', and 'gimmes'[4]) (Winslow 1997: 252), Canadian soldiers demonstrated the ways in which many of them viewed the Somali people as both different and inferior to Canadians.

Many of the soldiers assumed that the desperate poverty they witnessed in Somalia was the result of a backward and lazy culture. As paratrooper Robert Prouse reported in his diary from the mission, fellow soldiers said that Somalia should be used 'as a nuclear dump, it's worthless' and others asked: 'F_____g tar monkeys, why should we help them? If they haven't improved in the last thousand years, they won't improve now. They're so backwards, why bother?' (Prouse 2000:

A6). As Prouse commented, 'The majority of our people hate the Somalis and the country' (Prouse 2000: A6). Many also considered Somalis a people with little respect for human life, who had different standards, and different expectations about death and violence (Winslow 1997: 235). Kyle Brown reported that in Somalia, '[Violence is a] part of their culture, and a language they understand' (Worthington and Brown: 123). If nothing else, one soldier complained, it was hard to distinguish between the 'good guys' and the 'bad guys': 'They're all Black, who's who? They all look alike' (Winslow 1997: 249).

Race and racism often figure in hazing and initiation rituals, and hazing normally involves tests of loyalty. As Joel Newman writes of the socialization in the Philippine military:

> The Honor System and the hazing process are essential to the process of assimilation of a new identity. Enduring bonds of social solidarity are formed through the cadet's adherence to the strict precepts of the all-encompassing Honor Code and the almost overwhelming hazing process. (cited from McCoy 1995: 695)

The hazing itself, as Alfred McCoy describes it, is usually brutal and normally aims at 'breaking down a cadet's civilian identity creating what one study called a "remarkable unity"' (McCoy 1995: 695). Race is often emphasized, and this certainly was true of the hazing videos released to the Canadian media. Indeed, Corporal Christopher Robin's testimony at the inquiry was revealing for what it illustrated about unity and loyalty to his regiment. He was asked whether writing 'I love the KKK' on his back and other acts depicted in the video (he was also tied to a tree and fellow soldiers poured white powder on him) were 'racist': he said that they were. When asked if he had ever experienced 'racism' in the Airborne, he said that he had not; rather, these incidents showed 'what you can take under adverse conditions.' He said also that no matter what people now thought, he was very proud of the regiment of which he was a part and that he 'would do everything [he] could to protect 'its good name' (Robin 1995).

Race was apparently a factor also in Kyle Brown and Clayton Matchee's hazing, especially upon entering the Airborne. Matchee is full Cree and Brown part Cree, and reports indicate that in Matchee's case in particular, his 'Cree heritage became a focus' of his hazing when he arrived at Canadian Forces Base Petawawa to join the Airborne. Matchee, in turn, became one of Brown's 'most feared hazers' when the latter arrived at Petawawa (Cheney 1994: F1). Alfred McCoy has argued that soldiers subjected to brutal hazing as cadets repeat that behaviour later in their careers (McCoy 1997). Thus as Matchee was beating Arone, he told his fellow soldiers, 'The white man fears the Indian and so will the black man.' When asked the next day about the murder he boasted, 'Indians: two, White man; nothing' (MacDonald 1997; Brockelbank 1996).

Hazing, and militarized masculinity generally, also tend to be associated with misogynist practices and sometimes outright violence against women. Early questioning at the inquiry by the Canadian Jewish Congress alleged that members of the Airborne held a celebratory dinner to honour Marc Lepine, the man who massacred fourteen women at the Université de Montréal in 1989. A former member of the Airborne, who confirmed that the dinner had taken place, commented, 'It would have been the same as having an Adolf Hitler party on his birthday. . . . It's just the shock value' (*Ottawa Citizen* 1995).

Similar evidence emerged in the Hewson Report, which was one of the first documents tabled at the inquiry. It confirmed what feminists have long argued, namely, that there is a disproportionate amount of violence against women in militaries, and this is true also of the Canadian military.[5] The Hewson Report was a 1985 inquiry into infractions and antisocial behaviour in the Mobile Command, with particular reference to the Special Service Force and the Canadian Airborne Regiment. In essence, Major General Hewson had been charged with investigating whether there was a higher rate of criminal behaviour in the Canadian forces than in Canada more generally. The report was requested after a series of media stories covering crimes by Airborne members, one of which involved the murder of a civilian with a machete (Commission of Inquiry 1995: 15).

Hewson reported that there was no higher incidence of crime in the Canadian forces, with two exceptions: first, there appeared to be a higher frequency of sexual offences, and second, that there was a higher incidence of violent crime in the Canadian Airborne Regiment (Commission of Inquiry 1995: 17). Further analysis of these two 'exceptions' is needed, however. Hewson recommended that the higher level of sexual offences be studied further, though he did not include that recommendation in his *Main Summary of Recommendations* At the same time, he did not say how much more frequent sexual offences were, but indicated that one piece of evidence in the report, an appendix outlining 'crime case synopses' for 1984/85, 'does not, statistically, reveal any significant or alarming trends'(20–1). This was far from the case. The synopsis of crime cases , in fact, reveals that the incidence of sexual crimes was dramatic. If one includes in the category of sexual assaults all assaults in which the victim is a woman, more than half of the 141 crimes listed were either sexual assaults or physical assaults against women: 76 out of 141 cases, or 54 per cent (Annex G). Hardly a figure that could be described as insignificant.

Hewson's explanation for the higher incidence of violent crime in the Airborne Regiment is also illustrative of the extent to which he relied on gendered explanations. The analysis he offered to explain this incidence of higher violent crime was that 'local girls' tended to be attracted to the 'young single soldier with his new "sporty" car, regular and higher pay and job security.' The outcome of this, he argued, was disputes between local males and soldiers over girls. The local male population was described as 'robust and tough', and there simply were not enough girls to go around (19). It was recommended (in the *Main Summary of Recommendations*) that the 'long term impact of employing a large population of single soldiers in a semi-isolated location' be studied further.

What emerged also, in both the inquiry and analyses made of the murders in Somalia, was the extent to which soldiers involved in peacekeeping duties see themselves performing 'less than' soldierly functions. David Bercuson has noted that armies are created first and foremost to wage wars, and though they may become involved in other functions, those are not their prime task. 'Prolonged peace,' he notes, is a 'time of trial for any military.' And it is Canada's long-standing commitment to peacekeeping which is at the heart of the problem in Somalia:

> [The solution to the crisis in the Canadian army] entails the restoration of preparation for war fighting and combat at the centre of the army's existence. Any other mission is peripheral. If that is done, the warriors, the real professional soldiers, will regain control. When that happens, the old-fashioned, but necessary, virtues of honour, integrity, professionalism, dedication to the military as a vocation, and acceptance of the unlimited liability of soldiers will once again form the core values of the Canadian army. (Bercuson 1996: 242)

Evidence given at the Somalia Inquiry might paint a truer picture of what will happen when we privilege the war-fighting activities of armies over all other duties. The soldiers in Canada's Airborne regiment were excited to be going to Somalia, especially as it became clear that it might become a Chapter 7 mission.[6] Elvin Kyle Brown, like many of his fellow soldiers, was 'delighted' (Worthington and Brown 1997: 69–70). The Airborne had been chosen to go while Somalia was still designated a 'blue beret mission', but according to Major-General (retired) Lewis MacKenzie, it was evident from the media coverage that this mission would be upgraded to a Chapter 7, and this would mean real soldiering (MacKenzie 1996, 1996). The mission indeed was changed in early December of 1992, just before the Airborne took up their duties. One soldier commented, 'I think the men were glad when the mission changed from peacekeeping to peace making. . . this was more real. We're training for war all our lives, and the guys all want to know what it is like. That's why they join the army, to soldier' (Winslow 1997: 198). Or as Peter Worthington notes: 'The change of mandate held promise of more challenge, more excitement, more responsibility, even action. They might even have to fight' (Worthington and Brown 1997: 69).

The Airborne soldiers were apparently so excited by the prospect of real soldiering that a number of them allegedly torched an officer's car and others went into a provincial park and fired their weapons in a small shooting spree. Asked at the inquiry whether this might have signaled discipline problems in the Airborne, Mackenzie's response was revealing: while it didn't excuse what the soldiers did, he said, these incidents could be explained by the fact that there had been few Chapter 7 missions in UN history to that point and the soldiers were all 'psyched up'. Somalia had become 'a non-blue beret fight', and though 'some of this is macho stuff', there was 'more prestige' for Airborne soldiers in a Chapter 7 mission than a Chapter 6. The greater prestige resulted, he said, from the fact that soldiers on a Chapter 7 mission can take 'premeditated' action if they need to. They are no longer restricted, in short, to firing in self-defence (Mackenzie 1996; Somalia Inquiry 1997a, Hearings Transcripts, Volume 43: 8422).

The change of mission was important for the soldiers, but it meant everything to the defenders of the Airborne who came later. The Canadian public, the inquiry Commissioners and the media were reminded regularly that the mission to Somalia was not peacekeeping. A mission that was not, strictly speaking, peacekeeping, could not be judged by peacekeeping standards:

> When the incidents of violence came to light, it became a fact of considerable importance that the mission was characterized as one not of peacekeeping, per se, but of peace enforcement. What this meant to those making the distinction was that the troops operated within a warlike and dangerous context. (Razack 1995: 137)

And in war, ugly things happen. One soldier commented, 'The fact that it was peace making and not peacekeeping played a large role in what happened I think. The Airborne went in to expect the worst' (Winslow 1997: 200).

But after their training, their preparation, and perhaps most important, their anticipation of real soldiering, the Airborne discovered that the war had moved on from Belet Huen. The country was hot, dusty, dry, and full of scorpions, which provided a certain amount of danger during otherwise boring daily routines but little in the way of exciting military action. Life in Somalia was unpleasant, but Belet Huen was not a war zone. One soldier remarked, 'When we got there, there was no war. The war had gone by. Probably for some guys that was a disappointment' (Winslow 1997: 231). Winslow notes, 'Once the Canadians concluded that they were "wasting their time" in Somalia came the brutal realization that one could die "for nothing"' (Winslow 1997: 231). That realization, joined with a pervasive attitude that depicted the Somalis as different and inferior, made violence almost inevitable. As Razack argues, it 'is a short step from cultural difference to naturalized violence', (Razack 1995: 146) and this was certainly in evidence in Somalia.

Conclusions

An analysis of Canada's reputation as a country committed to the ideals of peacekeeping, and the way in which many features of that reputation were seriously challenged by the murders of Somali citizens by Canadian soldiers, leads to questions about the creation and effects of militarized masculinity. The evidence shows that it is constituted through norms of masculinity that privilege violence, racism, aggression, and hatred towards women. And its effects were shown dramatically in Somalia. What this means is that a change of 'mission' does not by itself transform the years of training and socialization that have gone into the creation of a soldier. Ominously, and in an observation which might have served as a prediction of the murders in Somalia some ten years later, Major R.W.J. Wenek wrote in 1984:

> Particularly in [elite units such as commandos, paratroopers, and special service forces], but also in other combat units, behaviour which may be considered verging on the sociopathic in peacetime becomes a prerequisite for survival in war. Aggressiveness must be selected for in military organizations and must be reinforced during military training, but it may be extremely difficult to make fine distinctions between those individuals who can be counted on to act in an appropriately aggressive way and those likely at some time to display inappropriate aggression. *To some extent, the risk of erring on the side of excess may be a necessary*

> *one in an organization whose existence is premised on the instrumental value of aggression and violence* [emphasis added]. (Wenek 1984: 13)

Or, as a paratrooper in the newly recreated Light Infantry Battalion at Petawawa noted: 'People worry we're too aggressive. But that's what soldiers are supposed to be. You don't go out and give the enemy a kiss. You kill them' (Pugliese 1996: A1).

What this suggests, quite dramatically, is that the skills of war are often entirely at odds with those required for peace operations. Some of the Airborne's loudest and most consistent defenders underline the ways in which the peoples of Belet Huen were grateful for the efforts of the Canadian military there. But ironically, it was the Airborne's *non-military* contributions for which they are best remembered: helping to re-open the local school, stocking it with pens, pencils, chalk, and paper sent by their families in Canada; re-opening the local hospital, building bridges, trying to purify local water supplies, and the like (Mackenzie 2000: A6). In other places they have built parks for children and served as mediators in difficult situations. But none of these skills are unique to soldiering. This means that we need to acknowledge that soldiers don't always make the best peacekeepers; sometimes it is carpenters, mediators, and doctors who best perform that function, and who best contribute to a people's sense of a meaningful security. It means also that when we do send soldiers on peace operations, they need to be soldiers who have been trained and encouraged to understand that properly masculine behaviour need not be dependent on misogyny, racism, or violence (Enloe). It means they have to be trained in ways that do not privilege militarized notions of masculinity. Keeping the peace positively demands it.

Notes

1. This chapter is reprinted with permission, in slightly modified form, from Ken Booth, ed. (2001), *Security, Community, Emancipation* (Boulder: Lynne Rienner). The author is grateful for financial support received from the Social Science and Humanities Research Council of Canada.
2. This chapter focuses on a series of incidents that occurred in Somalia. Problems of physical and sexual violence have been reported in other peacekeeping missions, some which included Canadian soldiers. These incidents include sexual assaults and the dramatic increase of prostitution as well as allegations in Cambodia, the former Yugoslavia, and Kosovo that peacekeepers have been involved in actually running brothels to for the military forces. (See Whitworth 1998 and Whitworth forthcoming; Off 2000; Kien 1995)
3. Militarized masculinity, like all masculinities, is not the same at all times and in all places. See for example Morgan, Enloe, and Hooper. It is important to note also that militarized masculinity is both complex and at many times, contradictory. Whitworth (forthcoming) examines in more detail than is possible here some of the complexities of militarized masculinities.
4. The latter was intended to refer to the constant begging by Somalis, and Winslow reports that the Canadians also purchased a 'commemorative T-shirt with an outstretched Somali hand and the word "gimme" on it.'
5. Much, though not all, of this violence is directed at the women (and children) in military families. A 1994 US study indicated that the rate of domestic violence in American

army families was twice that of comparable civilian families. (See Harrison and Laliberté 1994: 189.)

6. Though peacekeeping is not defined in the UN Charter, peacekeeping missions are normally deemed to fall under Chapter 6, or 'Pacific Settlement of Disputes'. Chapter 7, 'Action with Respect to Threats to the Peace', allows the Security Council to take such actions 'as may be necessary to maintain or restore international peace and security' and is generally described as the peace enforcement mechanism of the UN Charter.

Chapter 7

Myths of Canada's Human Security Pursuits: Tales of Tool Boxes, Toy Chests, and Tickle Trunks

Ann Denholm Crosby

> The Voice of Women is a fine example of a bunch of hens running around with their heads cut off.
>
> There was something pathetically foolish about the appearance at the Parliament Buildings in Ottawa the other day of a group of matrons styling themselves with the pompous and absurdly unappealing title of the Voice of Women.
>
> The world must pity this nation's fall so low with a government bedeviled by wailing women and afflicted with indecision.
>
> –*Media Reports, 1962 (NFB 1992)*

In 1997 Minister of Foreign Affairs, Lloyd Axworthy claimed that human security 'includes security against economic privation, an acceptable quality of life, and a guarantee of fundamental human rights' and that these ends were to be realized through 'the rule of law, good governance, sustainable development and social equity' (1997: 84). Axworthy has argued further that human security pursuits are particularly suited to the exercise of soft power, that is, to 'negotiation rather than coercion, powerful ideas rather than powerful weapons, public diplomacy rather than backroom bargaining.' In promoting this agenda, Axworthy wrote, 'Our basic unit of analysis in security matters has shrunk from the state to the individual' (1998a).

These are precisely the ideas held by the Voice of Women (VOW), that 'group of matrons' and 'wailing women' of the above quotations. The similar discourses, however, are embedded in very different understandings of security. The VOW perspective was, and is still, rooted in an understanding of the gendered nature of power relations and how these support a range of power hierarchies involving gender, class, race, and culture that make some peoples secure at the expense of others. The perspective supported by the Department of Foreign Affairs and International Trade (DFAIT) under Axworthy's tutelage, on the other hand, masks the Canadian government's understanding that security is dependent upon global market forces and belongs to those who comply with those forces, and particularly to those who ply the forces. Lost in the government's rationale for pursuing human security initiatives within the context of market forces is a historical analysis of the ways in which that market, and its promotion, creates or exacerbates insecurities for the non-elites of the world, both at home and abroad. Retained in the rationale, however, is the gendered nature of security policy decision making as described by the VOW.

The debates about human, as opposed to state-centred, security practices that, in the past decade, have exercised politicians and bureaucrats from both DFAIT and the Department of National Defence (DND), as well as a range of interested observers and academics, are essentially about means rather than ends. They can be reduced to whether the Canadian state, in its pursuit of prosperity and employment, should tackle the related security issues with instruments from DFAIT's tool box of soft-power resources or with DND's toy chest of military technologies. Either way, the debate is implicitly about how to address with one hand the ills produced with the other, and it serves to disguise the fact that this is what is being done. Soft and hard power advocates are equally implicated in this act of prestidigitation, and in furtherance of the charade, both dip into the tickle trunk of disguises to dress their discourse and practice of human security in the garb of humanitarianism. Hence, although the disguise gives the appearance of security having taken on a human face, it remains the face of power acting in its own interests behind the mask.

The following exploration of DFAIT's human security agenda in the context of its primary foreign policy interests, and the debates about the relative merits of hard versus soft power, is set within the theoretical context of 'conditioning frameworks' as described by Ricardo Grinspun and Robert Kreklewich (1994), and against the backdrop of the Voice of Women's human security discourse and practice. The former allows for a Gramscian explanation of the disciplinary nature of neo-liberal forces, including how they reinforce the gendered nature of security policy; the latter provides an example of how alternative ideas about security arise from within civil society as a result of particular experiences of power relations, as well as an example of feminist critical thinking about security that anticipated contemporary writings on the subject.

The Voice of Women: A Civil Society Conception of Human Security[1]

The VOW was founded in 1960 when, as Kay Macpherson, a founding member, wrote, 'one of those far-off summit conferences between the US and the USSR . . . had failed; Khrushchev banged his shoe on the desk at the UN; an American U2 spy plane was shot down over the USSR; [and] the Cold War was rapidly getting hotter . . . (1994: 89). At home, the Canadian government was 'afflicted with indecision' (NFB 1992) over whether to accept US nuclear weapons on Canadian soil for use by Canadian forces in the East/West relations of nuclear deterrence. It was the gathering of 400 VOW members in Ottawa to petition the government not to accept the weapons that earned them the criticisms quoted above.

Anticipating the works of post–Cold War critical-security theorists,[2] the organization mounted a critique of Cold War state-centred security practices. The VOW perspective understood the state to be a part of the security problem in that not only were women disadvantaged within the institutions and structures of the state and thus less secure than men in both the public and private state realms, but the promotion of state interests through the use of military means created further insecurities, and not just for women. Vast sums of money were being spent on nuclear weapons that exposed all peoples to the possibility of a nuclear war and annihilation; the testing of these weapons exposed peoples to the health hazards of radioactive fallout; and the legitimation of the use of violence by the state in pursuit of state interests conditioned peoples to accept violence was an inevitable characteristic of relations between states. Their bottom line, however, was that the use of state violence through military means aggravated rather than addressed the conflicts among the world's peoples. Instead, the VOW held that negotiation, compromise, conciliation, and the building of trust among peoples and their governments, in other words, the tools of soft power, should be the means of choice for pursuing peaceful relations of global cohabitation.

Since its founding, the VOW has embarked on numerous campaigns which reflect their human security perspective. Throughout the Cold War, the organization consistently lobbied the government against military build-up and reliance on the use of force; its argument was that force, whether used or threatened, intensified and prolonged East-West tensions and mistrust. To demonstrate that the testing of nuclear weapons was a health hazard, the organization collected over 5,500 baby teeth from across the country and had them tested at the University of Toronto for the effects of radioactive fallout. As the Cold War raged in the 1960s, VOW hosted Russian women in Canada and visited the USSR on a number of occasions in efforts to build transnational channels of communication and trust. During the Vietnam War, the organization brought Vietnamese and American women together in Canada to discuss the war, its effects on both Americans and Vietnamese, and possible ways to bring it to an end. VOW has also worked against the use of nuclear power since the 1960s; lobbied representatives of NATO, the Warsaw Treaty Organization, and a range of international disarmament fora; and organized and attended numerous conferences throughout the world on peace, development, refugee, and health issues, building bridges with similarly inclined women in the process. In this way, the VOW's efforts to address Cold War security issues evolved, over the ensuing years, into attempts to also address inequities rooted in gender, class, race, and cultural hierarchies of power.

Representatives of the VOW were vilified in Ottawa in 1962, however, not only for their ideas and activism, for like those of the peace movement in general, these tended to be dismissed by the media as the noise of the 'frighteningly muddled', 'emotional', 'malinformed and misinformed', and representative of 'an unholy mixture of greedy opportunism, naive idealism and pious hypocrisy' (Denholm Crosby 1998a: 169–70). Rather, VOW members were vilified primarily for stepping outside their prescribed gender roles and behaviour, and thus flouting the public and private authority of men. As one member of the Ottawa delegation put it, 'men didn't let their wives go out like that, especially not to challenge government policy' (NFB 1992). By publicly censuring these women for breeching gender norms and rules, the media both reinforced those norms and rules, and demonstrated the barriers to women's social, economic, and political mobility, as well as to their freedom of speech, association, and movement. The public ridicule demonstrated the gendered nature of power in Canada at the time, and the extent to which women's lives were compromised by the structures and relations of gender.

The VOW took up the challenges of the Cold War on their understanding that men and women in general had different ways of doing things, had different knowledge, and that these were derived from their differing experiences of, and roles within, the public and private realms of the state. Some VOW members held to the radical feminist belief that gender differences were biologically determined; others believed that they were learned. All, however, felt that they had a better understanding than men in public office of what constituted security and how it could be realized. Although they gave voice to and embodied the liberal feminist belief that a larger number of women in public office would lead to progressive change, the kind of egalitarian change that the VOW has struggled to establish in the organization and through its national and international activities, implies a critical feminist understanding of the socially constructed nature of gender relations and the links between gender, race, class, and cultural hierarchies of power.

This perspective, since articulated and nuanced by a number of feminist scholars working in the area of critical security studies,[3] holds that the societal norms, rules, traditions, and laws that have established women as nurturers, conciliators, compromisers, and the purveyors of subjective forms of knowing and being within the private realm of the state, and as secondary to men, have also assigned to men the characteristics of aggressiveness, competitiveness, individualism, and rational objectivity, the attributes thought to be required for the management of the public spheres of business, politics, and national security, the spheres that were understood to be appropriately populated by men. Within this gender construct, neither men nor women are able to explore, without social constraints, the spectrum of human characteristics and attributes in order to develop those expressions of being human with which they feel most comfortable; by the same token, neither the public nor private realms of the state is shaped by the range of human possibilities.

Thus, for VOW members it was not an inevitability of human nature that the realist perspective dominated the security ideas and practices of the Cold War era. Men had defined and shaped the security interests and relations of states and had done so from their gendered perspective which understood the dominant human characteristics to be those of themselves, of gendered males. States, run by statesmen, were therefore seen to embody the characteristics of the gendered male, and as such were understood as sovereign, unitary actors, pursuing self-interest competitively and aggressively, particularly in the anarchical international environment which they inhabited. Given these characteristics, a self-interested state's security depended on its ability to defend its interests and territory from the self-interested encroachment of other states. Although accommodation, negotiation, and conciliation were tools of the state, they were considered the tools of second-order human activities, as more appropriately women's way of doing things. Force and violence were the tools of the first, or dominant, order of human activity, and military means were therefore the ultimate guarantor of state security.

This perspective is self-perpetuating because it creates state relations of competitive self-interest dependent upon the use of force and violence, and practising these relations over time leads to the belief that they are the 'natural' relations among states.[4] The ideas and practices of state-centred security pursuits are further reinforced because they are also functional for the interests sustained by the use of force and power, the interests that thrive on the pursuit of wealth and power within global cultural, political, and economic structures.[5] Hence, making states and their political, economic, and cultural interests secure, ultimately through the use of military force, is seen as tantamount to making people as citizens of states secure. Not incidently in the practice of this understanding of security, gendered hierarchies of power are sustained, reinforced, and reproduced, as they in turn sustain, reinforce, and reproduce the relations of hierarchical power that privilege some peoples are the expense of others.

Despite the VOW's long history of attempting to redefine who security should be for, what it could consist of, and how it might be achieved, DFAIT claims that the government's efforts to promote a human security agenda are rooted in international institutions and documents: the International Committee of the Red Cross, the UN Charter, the Universal Declaration of Human Rights, the Geneva Conventions, and the 1994 UNDP Human Development Project (DFAIT 1999c). In this way, the Canadian government demonstrates how women's contributions to the making of a society's history are lost. In this case, however, the lack of recognition is a blessing in disguise for, from a VOW perspective and from that of a number of feminist critical-security scholars, the government has the concept wrong anyway. The difference in the two perspectives becomes apparent when the government's version of human security is viewed in relation to its dominant foreign policy interests.

DFAIT's Human Security Agenda

Since the Liberal government's 1994 Foreign Policy Review, Canadian foreign policy has been broadly defined by three objectives: 'the promotion of prosperity and employment; the protection of our security within a stable global framework; and the projection of Canadian values and culture.'[6] Although presented as the 'three pillars' of Canadian foreign policy, the security and cultural pillars are little more than flying buttresses to the economic pillar. According to *Canada in the World*, the government's still relevant response to the foreign policy review, both domestic and international stability are rooted in the processes that 'reinforce' global prosperity, while Canada's role in promoting that prosperity is facilitated by the projection of Canadian values—'respect for human rights, democracy, the rule of law, and the environment. . . . After all, the document notes, 'More prosperous people are able to maintain more mature and mutually beneficial economic partnerships with Canada, becoming increasingly open to our values and thus more active partners in building the international system.' Accordingly, the main thrust of Canadian foreign policy, which the document describes in considerable detail, is the promotion of rules-based forms of economic multilateralism at all levels and in all institutions of global governance. In keeping with this policy position, the Canadian government is active in the World Trade Organization, the International Monetary Fund, the World Bank, APEC, the OECD, and in the temporarily suspended MAI negotiations. In addition, DFAIT has pursued bilateral trade and investment arrangements on its own initiative and through its Team Canada partnerships with Canadian business.

Since from DFAIT's perspective, the security of the world's peoples is dependent upon the prosperity and stability provided by global market forces, it follows that the pursuit of prosperity for Canadians by promoting those global market forces is tantamount to pursuing prosperity, and hence security, for all peoples. This logic allows DFAIT to state quite simply that 'the promotion of prosperity and employment is at the heart of the Government's agenda.' Hence, one foreign policy pillar and two flying buttresses, and hence also, the Canadian version of the Western panacea for global ills—liberal democratic practices and neo-liberal markets.

Much has been written, however, about the ways in which global neo-liberal economic forces create insecurity for vast numbers of the world's peoples. As Susan Strange argues, for example, global market forces are largely responsible for the distribution of the world's goods, for determining who gets how much of the world's political, economic, social, and cultural resources and under what conditions (1996: 3–15). This, she claims, constitutes a shift in power from states to markets, a shift that has eroded the state's ability to perform a number of its traditional functions, including its ability to shape or stabilize its domestic economy, to set taxation standards, to impose wage and price controls, to determine trade policy, to control foreign investment, and to stabilize its currency. These constraints have created a widening economic gap within states between those who benefit from market-driven deregulation and those who do not. The state is caught, therefore, in a double bind. Not only is it restricted in its ability to manage its domestic economy and distribute resources on a stabilizing and equitable basis, but its pursuit of 'prosperity and employment' for Canadians within the global economy strengthens the very forces that tie its hands domestically.

At the same time, Strange holds that whatever power less or non-industrialized states have enjoyed in the past is shifting upwards to the industrialized states, with the latter, although limited in their ability to influence global market forces, still better positioned than the former to realize their economic and political interests within that market. Thus, there are growing gaps in wealth and privilege amongst states and peoples in the international realm. Strange also argues that, because of these two market-induced shifts in power, there are now places where no power at all is being exercised, as evidenced by the contraction or absence of social, health, educational, and environmental programs.

According to a number of international political economy theorists (Strange 1996: 44–65; Cox 1999; Lipshutz 1992), these market-induced shifts of power and authority are directly responsible for producing or exacerbating a range of insecurities for peoples, including those rooted in poverty, environmental degradation, resource depletion, and the inequitable distribution of political, economic, and social resources. In turn these insecurities produce others, including population movements, human rights abuses, conflicts between states, crime, prostitution, child soldiering, and arms trafficking. Axworthy has called this range of market-induced insecurities the 'dark side of globalization' (1999c). It is, however, precisely these insecurities that DFAIT's human security agenda is intended to address.

In essence, the government is attempting to address with one hand the ills it is causing with the other. In other words, DFAIT's human security agenda is meant to address the range of insecurities produced or exacerbated by global market forces even as the government's main foreign policy interest, the pursuit of prosperity and employment for Canadians through the global economy, serves to reinforce those forces. In this context, the best that the government can hope to accomplish with its human security policy is an easing of the symptoms of insecurity, not the root causes. However, because the state is constrained by market forces in implementing domestic remedial policies or circumscribing market interests, even its ability to ease the manifestations of market-induced insecurities is limited.

Human Security as a Conditioning Framework

Rather than constituting an alternative practice of security as imagined by the VOW and critical security theorists, the discourse and practice of human security as plied by DFAIT serve, in a manner similar to that described by Ricardo Grinspun and Robert Kreklewich, as a 'conditioning framework' for business as usual (Grinspun and Kreklewich 1994: 34–7). Borrowing from Robert Cox, Grinspun and Kreklewich employ the concept of conditioning frameworks in relation to neo-liberal economic processes, specifically free trade agreements. It is their contention that such agreements 'impose and lock-in neoliberal reforms' by promoting 'what Cox has defined as the "internationalization of the state".' This, is a 'global process whereby national policies and practices have been adjusted to the exigencies of the world economy of international production.' This process is 'largely elite-driven and rarely mandated by popular "free choice".' Although there may appear to be 'free choice', the choices are restricted to policies that represent the interests of global market practices, and it becomes almost impossible to imagine any alternatives. Hence the reproduction of hegemonic neo-liberal ideas and practices. Inasmuch as global economic structures, like political structures, are gendered, as argued earlier, this too is reproduced through neo-liberal conditioning frameworks. Grinspun and Kreklewich further argue that conditioning frameworks can be formal or informal 'depending on whether or not the terms are prescribed in a legal agreement.' Informal frameworks do not involve legal agreements, and their 'effects are invisible (i.e., not spelled out explicitly to the public), although they are clearly observable.'

In this way, DFAIT's discourse and practice of human security can be understood as an informal conditioning framework for the pursuit of neo-liberal economic interests and processes in that human security is about security *within the context* of global market forces and the on-going efforts by the state to reinforce them. Market-induced insecurities are represented either as time-bound aberrations of that system rather than endemic to it, or as phenomena caused by 'failed or rogue states' or to ethno-nationalist programs rooted in historical hatreds, that is, to disorientations unrelated to the history and effects of the growing reach of Western political and economic interests. Moreover, by focusing on the plight of the individual in any of its various environments of insecurity, the government's human security perspective further conditions both itself and its citizens to see situations of insecurity in isolation from their causes. At the same time, both governments and individuals enjoy a sense of moral rectitude for trying to alleviate suffering instead of feeling responsible for having created or aggravated these insecurities. DFAIT's human security agenda, then, is a *restricted* set of policy choices adjusted to the exigencies of the world economy of international production and finance; and practising human security facilitates the on-going practice of market interests.

A range of what the Canadian government considers to be human security initiatives demonstrates this dynamic. Recognizing a need to bring 'greater "coherence" to [its] capacity to solve these interlinked and increasingly prominent [human security] issues' (Malone 1999: 197), the government established a Global and Human Issues Bureau in 1995. Its responsibilities cover a range of 'functional issues' which sweepingly include 'the environment, human rights, children's questions (e.g., child labour, children in war, sexual exploitation of children) gender issues, youth, humanitarian policy, conflict prevention and peace building, terrorism, crime and drugs, health, population, migration and refugees, as well as circumpolar and Aboriginal issues' (Malone 1999: 197). The Canadian International Development Agency (CIDA), the funding agency for the Human Issues Bureau, also deals with many of these matters in its development assistance programs. Sixty per cent of CIDA's funding is from the Overseas Development Assistance (ODA) program, and the ODA budget was consistently cut throughout the 1990s; funding was increasingly targeted for the more developed of the developing countries and often tied to the World Bank's structural adjustment programs. 'Indeed, government policy towards developing countries since 1994 has focused almost exclusively on bilateral and multilateral trade and investment initiatives, meeting the primary foreign policy goal of *Canada in the World* of strengthening Canada's economic prosperity' (Draimin and Tomlinson 1998: 145; 150–7).

The conclusion that most analysts reach after examining Canada's ODA and CIDA programs is that 'pressures from the private sector, the Prime Minister's Office and DFAIT continue to ensure that much Canadian aid is deployed to advance Canadian trade interests' (Pratt 1998: 13). Similarly, Cranford Pratt argues that efforts to create new funding programs that might favour the Human Issues Bureau over CIDA 'could easily prove to be activities to promote Canadian trade rather than efforts to augment global human security' (1998: 12).

Nor has Canada been able to maintain its rhetorical commitment to human security concerns related to environmental degradation, as evidenced by its failure to meet the targets for reducing greenhouse gas emissions that it set for itself at the Kyoto Summit in 1997. Moreover, it has adopted the US position that 'developing nations . . . should bear the costs of transition to more environmentally friendly industrial technology' (Draimin and Tomlinson 1998: 159). Again, trade and investment interests are the primary determinants of environmental policy. As Linda Reif concludes (1998: 281), 'The formation, content, and implementation of Canada's international commitments on environmental protection are, in the majority of sectors, being influenced by the economic interests of both government and civil society actors, the latter primarily in the commercial and industrial sectors.'

To the extent that the federal government has domestic human security concerns, these are not well served either by cuts in federal funding to education, health, and a variety of social programs. These cuts serve to further deprive the already underprivileged in Canadian society while safeguarding the interests of the privileged. In other words, as the government's security focus has, in Axworthy's word, 'shrunk' from the state to the individual, so has the funding for domestic human security initiatives.

Whereas the VOW's understanding of human security depended upon the deconstruction of class, gender, and racial hierarchies of power, DFAIT's version reinforces all three, for it works to the advantage of those in control of global market forces, those being predominantly privileged white men from the industrialized West. At the same time, because those characteristics that have been constructed as stereotypically male are functional for the management of globalized political and economic processes, the system attracts people who have honed those characteristics and thus it remains gendered even as women enter the systems in increasing numbers and increasingly in positions of authority. When assuming positions of power under these conditions, women do not, for the most part, bring with them alternative understandings of security. Moreover, although their presence in positions of power indicates a weakening, particularly in the West, of the barriers to women's participation in public life, this does not translate into a weakening of gendered hierarchies of power in the globalized political economy. As Cynthia Enloe has documented so well (1993), women continue to be economically disadvantaged as compared to men, and this is especially so in industrializing or non-industrialized states. When doing business in these countries, western transnational corporations, carrying western understandings of gender construction, and supported by political and economic institutions dominated by western values, deem it appropriate to disproportionately disadvantage women simply because they are women.

In as much, then, as DFAIT's human security perspective *disciplines* both government and civil society to an understanding of security as dependent upon market forces, it simultaneously *disciplines* both to reinforcing gendered structures of power. In this way, DFAIT's version of human security acts as a conditioning framework for both market forces and for hierarchical relations of power rooted in an unequal valuing of peoples according to gender, race, class and/or culture.

Finally, DFAIT's human security perspective also fails to address the concerns of both the VOW and critical-security scholars concerning the efficacy and ethos of military means for addressing conflicts among states. As examples of its success in pursuing human security initiatives, DFAIT cites the Ottawa Process that produced the Convention to Ban the Use of Anti-Personnel Landmines, which was signed by 122 countries in December 1996; as well as Canada's role in establishing the framework for the International Criminal Court, its on-going efforts to control the trade in and use of small arms and light weapons, and its involvement in the issue of child soldiers. As Robin Jeffrey Hay points out, however (1999: 229), 'Save for the International Criminal Court, one would be hard pressed to point to any one of these issues that addresses the root causes of human insecurity.' Indeed, the flagship initiative, the convention to ban land mines, was successful in large part because it stigmatized a weapon rather than its users. States were applauded, and applauded themselves, for banning anti-personnel land mines when it was primarily states themselves that had produced, transferred, sold, stockpiled, and implanted them throughout vast regions of the world. Yet the ethos of state military practices emerged unscathed from the landmine campaign. What changed was the relegation of one weapon of questionable military utility to the junk heap of obsolescent military means. What did not change was the perception of the appropriateness of killing, and threatening to kill, others as a means of addressing problems (De Larrinaga and Sjolander 1998; Beier and Denholm Crosby 1998).

Still, when the Secretary-General of NATO spoke in Toronto in 1989 'about cooperation being better than confrontation,' some VOW members took this as a sign that new ideas had 'penetrated the obsolete and inappropriate thinking of those in so-called high places' (Macpherson 1994: 137), ideas about the advantages of soft power over hard power. This conclusion only holds if the ends to which soft power are applied are significantly different than the ends pursued by hard power.

DFAIT's Tool Box of Soft Power Means

As Minister of Foreign Affairs, Lloyd Axworthy argued that 'in the conduct of international relations in a globalized, integrated world, . . . traditional military and economic might, while still important, do not have the over-whelming pre-eminence they once did.' Instead, he proposed, 'Skills in communication, negotiating, mobilizing opinion, working within multilateral bodies, and promoting international initiatives are increasingly effective ways to achieve international outcomes.' These are the tools, or methods, of 'soft power' and are, according to Axworthy, particularly suited to the problems of human security, the kinds of security issues that 'do not pit one state against another, but rather a group of states against various transnational challenges' (1998b: 192).

In the same article, however, Axworthy went on to cite Joseph Nye's definition of soft power as 'the power to co-opt, rather than to coerce, others to your agenda and goals,' and in another venue he added that the soft power means to these ends are, 'negotiation rather than coercion, powerful ideas rather than powerful weapons, public diplomacy rather than backroom bargaining' (1998a). In the language of peace research and feminist writings on the subject, this translates into bringing 'others to your agenda and goals' through structural, as opposed to direct, violence.[7] From Axworthy's perspective, then, the ends to which both hard and soft power are turned are the same and since for DFAIT, human security is to be found within the western forms of liberal democracy and the globalized market system, the promotion of both are the ends to which soft power is applied. Negotiation, powerful ideas, and public diplomacy are not tools for discovering and pursuing common definitions of what it means to be secure, but rather for bringing others to DFAIT's understanding of what constitutes security.

Moreover, Axworthy has noted that a soft power focus does not negate the need for hard power 'when conditions warrant' (DFAIT 1999c). Soft and hard power are understood as the flip sides of the same coin, the latter providing the muscle for the former when necessary. Thus, Axworthy was able to argue that the NATO bombings of both Bosnia and Kosovo were human security initiatives; 'concrete expression(s) of this human security dynamic at work.' In particular, the Kosovo initiative 'should serve to dispel the misconception that military force and the human security agenda are mutually exclusive' (Axworthy 1999b). Again, neither what constitutes security for others, nor the efficacy of bombing peoples into submission, is seen as a problem (Cox and Axworthy 2000). Instead, the questions about the ethics of humanitarian interventions are settled in favour of those states with the power to intervene on the basis of their own understandings of security (Pasic and Weiss 1997; Smith 1998). Those states are also free to decide when soft power means have run their course, if they choose to employ them, and when and how to escalate their intervention to the use of military power.

Yet, despite this, soft power *still appears* to represent a more conciliatory, democratic, and egalitarian method of conducting relations amongst states and peoples and this *appearance* is supported by a number of DFAIT's soft power tools. One of these tools is fashioned out of a selective understanding of Canadian history and culture.

Canadians tend to imagine themselves as being particularly adept at plying the methods of soft power in support of human security pursuits. Aiding the destitute, diseased, displaced, and disoriented peoples of the world fits the image Canadians hold of themselves as 'helpful fixers' and a morally conscientious people. According to Cranford Pratt, there has been a consensus, at least since the 1970s, in the Canadian public domain 'that industrialized states have ethical obligations relating to global poverty'(1994b: 334). It is these images and beliefs that the government reflects when presenting its rationale for pursuing human security initiatives. 'Canada's history as a non-colonizing power, champion of constructive multilateralism and effective international mediator,' states *Canada World View* (DFAIT 1998a: Executive Summary 1), ideally situates the country for 'an important and distinctive role among nations as they seek to build a new and better order.' Moreover, and in explicit reference to human security, the document declares that 'the concerns of Canadians about security issues are broader than those of self-interest. The desire to help others to build peace reflects some of the most deeply-held and widely-shared Canadian values' (DFAIT 1998a, Section IV, 1). Indeed, Axworthy and Taylor assert that Canada's history is one of 'attractive values, a reputation as an honest broker, skills at networking, a democratic tradition, and a willingness to work closely with civil society' (1998: 193).

Forgotten in this history, however, is the one Laura Macdonald (1995) describes of Canada as a colonizer by proxy in its political support of Britain's empire-building efforts, and its enjoyment of the fruits of colonialism through its Most Favoured Nation trade status with England. Forgotten too is the history of Canada's culturally insensitive missionary zeal at home and abroad, as well as the country's legacies of genocidal practices with respect to the First Nations peoples, of racism during and after the Second World War towards Jewish and Japanese people, and its history of endemic sexism and homophobia.[8]

Through this selective historical memory, Canadians are conditioned and condition themselves to support a human security agenda because it feels both right and

Canadian from every angle: political, economic, social, and moral. In this way, attention is diverted from considerations of what it means to pursue a human security agenda *within* the context of global market forces. In this way too, the means of hard and soft power become separated in the national imagination. Traditionally, hard power, that is, military means, has been used in support of state-centred security pursuits, but when the government promotes the use of soft power in pursuit of human security, with both the tools and the agenda supposedly reflecting quintessentially non-aggressive Canadian values and culture, then the assumption is that new understandings of what constitutes security and for whom are coming into play. The government displays this assumption itself when it indulges in self-congratulation for its moral and sensitive human security discourse and practices. But the ends to which both soft and hard power are directed are the same.

There is also an array of international institutions that provide legitimacy for Canada's human security agenda and in doing so prevent a deeper investigation of the ends that are being pursued. As mentioned earlier, DFAIT locates the origins of its human security policies in the International Committee of the Red Cross, the UN Charter, the Universal Declaration of Human Rights, the Geneva Conventions, and the 1994 UNDP Human Development Project. Variously, these, as well as Boutros Boutros-Ghali's *Agenda for Peace* and the UN's *Agenda 21* report, which emerged from the Rio de Janeiro conference on Environment and Development, cite environmental degradation, economic development, and human rights abuses as security issues; locate security as residing with the individual as well as the state; and call for partnerships between government and civil society in the pursuit of human security. Despite the controversial nature of the UN's humanitarian interventions in places such as Somalia, Haiti, Rwanda, and the former Yugoslavia, and whatever the *intent* of the UN documents, the international human security discourse legitimizes the Canadian government's particular human security understandings, including its efforts to inculcate with the same understandings, the range of multilateral bodies with which it is involved. Two examples of the latter are the government's efforts to use its seat on the Security Council in 1999/2000 as a forum for 'advancing Canada's agenda, especially integrating the human dimension—human security—into the council's work' (Axworthy 1999a); and the government's role in 1998 in negotiating the Lysoen Declaration with Norway, which is designed to serve as the basis for building a human security network amongst 'like-minded countries and partners from civil society to promote respect for human rights and humanitarian law' on the understanding that 'a humane world is a safe world' (Axworthy and Vollebaek 1998).

Finally DFAIT's partnerships with NGOs and activists working in issue areas involving aspects of human security also make it *appear* that the government has embarked on a new way to define and address security issues. Whereas the state tends to act behind closed doors in traditional security pursuits involving the military and issues of 'national interest,' in human security pursuits it works in co-operation with NGOs and concerned citizens through both traditional and non-traditional diplomatic and civil society channels and fora.

Here, the anti-personnel landmine campaign is again informative as to the nature and limits of the state/civil society relationship. Because the goal of the lead NGOs in the Ottawa Process, the International Committee to Ban Landmines, and the International Committee of the Red Cross, was to remove anti-personnel land mines from military arsenals and use worldwide, they were not interested in mounting a critique of military practices in general.[9] The NGOs associated with the campaign that had a deeper understanding of the causes and contexts of human insecurity, and a related critique of military means in general, shelved those concerns in order to help achieve a landmine ban.[10] In this way, and by promoting the Convention as a humanitarian initiative, the *appearance* of systemic change was achieved while the power structures and ethos of military means remained unchallenged, and indeed were reinforced under the guise of humanitarianism.

Not surprisingly, the NGOs that *do not* challenge basic state interests are the ones that governments tend to consult, or more accurately, hear.[11] Consequently, both openness and a democratic consideration of the range of civil society concerns in human security issues are compromised and the wielding of soft power is not then all that it purports to be. Ironically, however, what human security and the exercise of soft power do purport to be can be used as a tool by those NGOs with a deeper critique of government activities. They can hold the government accountable to its own rhetoric on poverty alleviation, environmental integrity, and the full range of justice concerns, and in this way there is a potential for change.

While DFAIT's tool box of soft power means, then, support a rhetorical reframing of security issues, there is no substantive change in the ends being pursued. Soft-power means do not challenge the underlying government understanding that human security is security within the context of global market forces, and that military means are the ultimate guarantor of security as it is defined by the state according to state interests. Ultimately, it is not that the government's pursuit of economic prosperity has trumped its human security concerns, but rather that DFAIT's human security discourse and practice are cut from the same cloth of intentions as the government's economic pursuits. Using soft power means to alleviate human insecurities that are produced and reproduced by those pursuits does nothing to ameliorate the root causes of a vast array of human insecurities; rather it reinforces them, while at the same time rendering invisible the role Canada plays in exacerbating them.

Still, proponents of military means are not convinced of the efficacy of soft power, and the contest between hard and soft power proponents is another element in the framework that serves to condition Canadians and the security-policy-making community to a new way of conducting old-style security pursuits.

DND's Toy Chest of Military Means

Advocates of military means are quite clear that the ends sought by both soft and hard power proponents are similar. David Haglund (1999: 176) argues that Canada's security interests are designed to support its trade and investment interests, while most who have joined the hard/soft power debate in favour of strengthening the former, are explicit about their concern for securing both states and peoples from non-traditional, as well as traditional, security threats and within the changing global environment of political, economic, cultural, and social relations.

Despite this agreement on ends, the attack by hard power proponents on the Axworthy Doctrine, as it is often described, is virulent. It has been referred to, in derogatory tones, as pulpit diplomacy, moral multilateralism, nickel diplomacy, Canada's Methodist phase of foreign policy, quasi-pacifism, boy scout imperialism, and foreign policy for wimps. This is name-calling, not argumentation, and is a sign that something more personal is at stake in the debate, that being the professionalism of the practitioners of military means, and by extension, the professionalism of their promoters. Since the government's budget for security programs is finite, the most direct challenge to military professionalism is financial, for a strengthening of DFAIT's soft power tools can impinge upon DND's ability to maintain, let alone strengthen its toy chest of military means. But the military is also being constrained in its professional role for a number of other reasons.

As one hard power proponent put it, 'profoundly unwise decisions over the past three years to "restructure" the military for what politicians and policy-makers in Ottawa foolishly believe will be a comparatively benign post-Cold War era . . . have done grave damage to Canadian power, position and influence over the "high" political issues on the global agenda' (Ross 1996–7: 2). These 'unwise' decisions, according to Douglas Ross, include budget cuts to DND and decisions not to replace aging military equipment, and both have compromised the Canadian forces' ability to participate in high-risk peacekeeping on land, in the air and at sea, to undertake anti-submarine warfare, to effectively control Canadian waters, and to monitor and impede foreign traffic in the Arctic archipelago. In short, 'Canada has no credible military instrument to apply to international crises when they arise' (Ross 1996–7: 4).

The Canadian military has also suffered from what some hard power proponents refer to as a series of 'public relations disasters' in relation to 'assorted misdeeds of Canadian military personnel' (Ross 1996–7: 2 n. 1) which Denis Stairs (1998a: 548–9) lists as including:

> Soldiers viciously torturing their prisoners. Soldiers and sailors crudely hazing their new recruits. Officers failing to enforce discipline and making exploitive use of their own expense accounts. Officers covering up. Officers and enlisted personnel alike abusing—even raping—their female colleagues and showing signs of racism and other forms of illiberal and intolerant disposition. The establishment as a whole failing to maintain the incomes of its personnel, and even the living quarters of its families, at a standard reasonable for our time. And so on.

Stairs is quick to argue that although these are all serious matters, they 'are *not* about "defence policy" or "security policy"' (emphasis in the original). Rather they are about the 'internal affairs' of the military and 'the behavior, treatment, and circumstances of individuals.' They are 'human interest' issues and examples of 'simple sinning'. The problem, he asserts, is that because the media have chosen to sensationalize them, the military fears it will lose respect in the public mind and therefore be disadvantaged in its competition for its share of the budget. 'The Art Eggletons of the world thus lose out to the Lloyd Axworthys of the world' (Stairs 1998a: 549–50).

In the zero-sum game of security budgets, then, the debate is about winning the means for the means, not the ends. With a bad press, aging and obsolescent equipment, the government making 'profoundly unwise' assessments of the global security environment, and the high profile of soft power means, the cards appear stacked against the military. To compound matters, the military's source of alliance toys is also drying up. Canadian troops have been removed from permanent deployment in Europe under the NATO command, and their access to US military means depends on the government's decision whether to participate in the American National Missile Defense program. Should Canada not participate, the Canadian military's role within NORAD, if not NORAD itself, will be seriously jeopardized. This would be a monumental blow to the military, for it is through the joint Canada–US command that Canadian military personnel are able to participate in the planning and manning of the systems that project US power and interests worldwide (Crosby 1998b).

Hence the vitriol on the part of the beleaguered hard power proponents. But more to the point, the debate contributes to the framework that conditions both the Canadian public and policy makers to the government's human security agenda. It does this in two ways. First, the debate about which means to use in combatting the fallout from the 'dark forces of globalization' treats the 'fallout', and therefore the market itself, as a given, thus rendering invisible the ways in which the market has been constructed out of specific interests, and the ways in which the government's security programs are designed to address the insecurities which that same government helps to create by supporting market forces. Hence it is possible for Canadians to believe that the government's foreign policy is solving, rather than creating, security problems both for themselves and others.

Second, the arguments in support of hard power means are, for the most part, so doctrinaire as to entrench the thinking of soft power advocates and to attract the uncommitted to their camp by default. In both instances, a deeper analysis of the security problem is bypassed. Describing, for example, acts of racism, rape, torture, murder, and cover-up performed by military personnel as 'simple sins' having no bearing on defence or security policy is fundamentally at odds with the perspective of a number of military analysts and critical feminist theorists who convincingly argue otherwise.

Since the end of the Cold War, some military analysts have noted the direction that military strategies have taken under the contemporary dual influences of arms-length, or stand-off, warfare and zero-tolerance, at least amongst the militaries of Western industrialized states, for 'friendly casualties'.[12] These analysts have argued that, as a result of both influences, military conflicts can no longer be defined as struggles of soldiers against soldiers, but rather as a 'struggle between one side's military might and the other side's civilian population,' and that, accordingly, soldiers are now being trained, not as warriors but as killers. As a case in point they cite NATO's high-altitude bombings of Kosovo by pilots who flew high enough to avoid anti-aircraft fire but too high to distinguish between civilian and military targets. This, according to Gwynne Dyer, was 'a coward's strategy' and clearly representative of what a former US army officer has described as efforts to conduct a 'bloodless techno-war.'[13]

Similarly, the 'simple sins' of racism, rape, torture, and murder committed by members of the Canadian military were all acts of cowardice in that they were perpetrated by the relatively powerful, the victims being prisoners, women, youth, recruits, or members of racial minorities. As cowardly acts, they reflect the ethos of contemporary military training as described by Dyer and others. More generally, they substantiate the military ethos of the appropriateness of pursuing the interests of the powerful at the expense of the less so; the appropriateness, in other words, of the strong victimizing the weak. As such, and in contradiction to Stairs conclusions, the acts of 'simple sinning' are quintessentially about 'defence policy' and 'security policy', for it is this ethos that is at work when the government mobilizes the military. This is precisely the point of the critical feminist scholars mentioned earlier. Mobilizing a military is also the mobilization of its ethos, and when that ethos is socially constructed out of gendered practices that deem it appropriate to secure some at the expense of others, then mobilizing that ethos is reflective of the state's understanding of what constitutes security and who it can be for. Mobilizing that ethos also reinforces the gendered understandings that support it.

In terms of the doctrinaire arguments employed by the proponents of hard power in support of their case, most treatises on the subject list the traditional threats to state security that are presently in existence and conclude, therefore, that traditional military means are required to address them, as though this were self-evident (Hampson and Oliver 1998: 382–5; Stairs 1999: 386–91; Ross 1996–7: 8–19). It is not self-evident, however, to a growing number of security analysts, including some former realists.[14] Moreover, as proof of their arguments, hard power advocates cite the 'successes' of military undertakings in Bosnia, Kosovo, and the Persian Gulf, as though these too are self-evident 'successes', and as though 'success' is to be measured only in terms of the immediate interests of those with the preponderance of military means; this is another realist tenet that is being contested in the literature on the subject of what constitutes security, for whom, and by what means (Cox and Axworthy 2000).

Rooted as they are in traditional realist thinking, and what perhaps can be called the super-realism of bloodless techno-war strategic thinking, these arguments not only fail to reveal the range of insecurities produced by the exercise of contemporary military means, but they also divert attention from the root causes of conflict and how these might be attacked by other than direct or structural force.

By contrast, the government's soft power arguments tend to explore alternative forms of conflict resolution, and that provides an opportunity for progressive change of the kind envisaged by VOW and critical feminist theorists.

HUMAN SECURITY PROSPECTS

In its pursuit of economic prosperity and employment for Canadians through trade and investment initiatives and the promotion of rules-based forums of political and economic multilateralism, the Canadian government reinforces the political, economic, and cultural forces of the global market. In so doing, it also reinforces the market related forces that create or exacerbate a wide range of insecurities for both states and peoples, at home and abroad, including all manner of inter- and intra-state conflicts rooted in the inequitable distribution of the world's resources, resource depletion, and environmental degradation. The government then attempts to correct these insecurities as though they were aberrations of the system and not endemic to it, thus distancing itself from its role in producing them, and further doing so by dressing its security practices in the discourses of human security, soft power, and humanitarianism.

Freed from the constraining influences of the Cold War relations of nuclear deterrence, these discourses are represented as quintessentially Canadian, reflecting the country's history, culture, and internationalist interests, with the 'successes' of human security initiatives taken to date cited as proof. The ideological content of the Canadian government's promotion of soft power means, the range of tools available and used in its practice, and the debate between hard and soft power proponents, all serve to deflect both vision and analysis from the causes of the insecurities that the government seeks to address, and its own role in producing them, as they also serve to condition Canadians to the view that new, meaningful, and moral *choices* are being made with regard to our role in global security relations. However, the ends of both soft power and hard power pursuits are similar. Both means are exercised in support of Canada's foreign policy agenda and goals, the former through processes of structural co-optation, the latter through practices of direct coercion.

This is not to argue that it matters little whether the government chooses to dress its security interests in the suits of diplomacy or the battle fatigues of the military, for it does matter. As compared to the VOW understanding of human security, the government has it all wrong in that neither its discourse nor its practice substantively challenge gender, racial, class, or cultural hierarchies of power within which relative insecurities reside. For a number of reasons, however, even having it wrong opens spaces for change.

When the Canadian government's security interests are dressed in the character of soft power, not only are a wider range of policy tools available for addressing conflicts, but they are taken seriously, as compared to the often dismissive attitude of hard power proponents towards the use of soft power instruments. A soft power approach also includes more actors, many of whom are in civil society. This extends the range, density, and quality of the transmission of ideas and practices, increasing the range of alternatives and the opportunities for their serious consideration. By comparison, hard power approaches are generally limited to hard power players employed by the state, to a highly specialized set of hard power tools, and to closed-door decision making.

Furthermore, while hard-power tends to be exercised at arm's length, soft power means tend to be hands-on in terms of addressing security issues and thus actors are more likely to be brought into contact with the origins of insecurities, making it more difficult to ignore the root causes, and Canada's role in fostering them. In this way, spaces are opened for transformative change, for addressing the causes of insecurities rather than only the manifestations. Without intending to, DFAIT under the leadership of Lloyd Axworthy has opened spaces for these kinds of changes.

Should both the discourse and practice of DFAIT's version of human security fall into decline, as now seems to be the case after September 11, one of the tragedies would be in the closing of these spaces.

NOTES

1. Throughout, information about the VOW is taken from the National Film Board documentary (1992); Kay Macpherson (1994) especially pp. 89–149; and from my own 25-year involvement in the organization.
2. For non-feminist works of this ilk see Walker (1990); Paul (1999); Booth (1991); George and Campbell (1990).
3. See for instance Tickner (1992b); Peterson (1992); and Stienstra (1994–5). For a discussion of the distinctions among various feminist perspectives, see Whitworth (1994) and Keeble and Smith (1999).
4. For discussions of the socially constructed nature of the realist perspective, see Murphy (1996); Rosenberg (1994); and Wendt (1992).
5. For discussions of the historical relationship between state security and economic interests, see Miller (1990); and Ruggie (1993)
6. All quotations in this and the following paragraph are from Canada, Department of Foreign Affairs and International Trade, *Canada World View*, 20 October 1998, Executive Summary, 1–2. This is a slightly edited update of *Canada in the World*, indicating the continuing relevance of that 1995 document. Details of DFAIT's economic and trade policy are in Section III of the document, 'The Promotion of Prosperity and Employment'.
7. In the peace research literature, see for example Galtung (1971). In the feminist literature see Peterson (1992); Enloe (1993); Reardon (1985).
8. See also Stienstra (1994–5); and Whitworth (1995).
9. For the position of the ICBL, see Beier and Denholm Crosby (1998: 276–8). The ICRC is constitutionally unable to be involved in the politics of conflict and war, and although some members have voiced criticisms of military means, the organization's publication *Anti-personnel Landmines: Friend or Foe?* (1996) was a key resource document for the movement to ban land mines. It contains a chapter on military alternatives to landmines thus indicating ICRC's unwillingness to critique military means as part of the land-mine initiative.
10. These were mainly NGOs working on 'development' issues in mined communities. For references to their concerns see reports on various mine action forums in *An Agenda for Mine Action* (DFAIT 1997b).
11. See Raustiala (1997) for a discussion of this phenomenon as it also applies to environmental issues which are heavily populated by NGOs.
12. For the most recent, and extensive, Canadian writing on this topic see Ignatieff (2000).
13. For these arguments and their proponents, see Robinson (1999), particularly p. 673. Hampson and Oliver (1998: 385) also attest to the penchant for targeting civilians, particularly women and children, in contemporary military initiatives operations.
14. A former realist who has had a change of mind, for example, is Booth (1991).

Chapter 8

Masculinities, Femininities, and Sustainable Development: A Gender Analysis of DFAIT's Sustainable Development Strategy

REBECCA TIESSEN

INTRODUCTION

According to the Department of Foreign Affairs and International Trade (DFAIT), sustainable development is a cornerstone of Canadian foreign policy: 'Canada is working towards a world that is more secure, more prosperous, and more sustainable' (DFAIT 1997a), and DFAIT plans to achieve this through 'peace building measures, economic arrangements and agreements, development assistance programs, and global environmental partnerships' (DFAIT 1997a).

An examination of DFAIT's sustainable development strategy (SDS), however, reveals a narrow interpretation of sustainable development. A gender analysis is used in this chapter to expose the masculinities and femininities in the sustainable development strategy adopted by DFAIT. This analysis, which is informed by a growing body of literature examining gender dynamics in international relations and foreign policy, shows the assumptions about masculinity and femininity that infuse foreign policy and foreign policy making. Two important observations are uncovered in this analysis. The first is the strategic silence on gender issues in DFAIT's SDS. Second, DFAIT lacks the political will to incorporate the core principles and components of sustainable development into Canadian foreign policy matters. Some progress has been made in fostering Canadian commitments to address gender inequality, the environment, and sustainable development; however, a number of challenges to translating these commitments into action plans remain. The challenges range from the relatively small number of women working in DFAIT to the institutional cultures in which inequalities flourish. In this chapter, I focus on the latter challenge.

SUSTAINABLE DEVELOPMENT STRATEGIES

The Department of Foreign Affairs and International Trade, along with twenty-eight other departments, tabled its first sustainable development strategy in Parliament in 1997. The initiative emerged from Canada's broader commitments to promoting sustainable development nationally and internationally. In particular, the sustainable development strategies are evidence of Canada's support for the adoption of *Agenda 21*, one of the important documents to emerge from the United Nations Conference on Environment and Development (UNCED) held in Brazil in 1992. Since UNCED, Canada has continued to report to the United Nations Commission on Sustainable Development (CSD). The CSD was established to evaluate the progress countries have made in the implementation of *Agenda 21* and to make recommendations for further sustainable development activities. The CSD, which meets each year, provides a forum for countries to present their national sustainable development strategies.

Canada embarked on a national sustainable development strategy in December 1995 when the *Auditor General Act* offered a number of changes, including the establishment of the position of Commissioner of the Environment and Sustainable Development (CESD) within the Office of the Auditor General of Canada. The Act further required ministers to table sustainable development strategies in the House of Commons by 15 December 1997 and to update them every three years (Office of the Auditor General 1997). The federal sustainable development strategies are evaluated by the Commissioner of the Environment and Sustainable Development. The first CESD, Brian Emmett, was appointed to the position in June 1996. In August 2000, the Auditor General announced the appointment of Johanne Gélinas as the second Commissioner of the Environment and Sustainable Development. She began her duties in September 2000 (Office of the Auditor General 2000). The responsibilities of the commissioner include monitoring sustainable development strategies, conducting audits and special studies, receiving public petitions, and providing green reports to the House of Commons.

DFAIT's SDS is one example of the federal government's obligation to adopt the principles set out at UNCED. DFAIT's SDS is entitled *Agenda 2000*, a name that bears a striking resemblance to that of the United Nations document (*Agenda 21*) that is meant to guide it. However, the two documents are strikingly different. DFAIT's SDS is strategically silent on issues pertaining to major groups, gender equality, indigenous peoples' rights, consumption, poverty, and other important issues carefully addressed in *Agenda 21*. In particular, DFAIT's SDS does not incorporate the issues surrounding gender equity despite references to gender issues throughout *Agenda 21* and an entire chapter (24) devoted to gender equity.

That chapter, 'Global Action for Women towards Sustainable and Equitable Development', is a result of a series of local, national, regional, and international meetings of women's groups, such as the Global Assembly of Women and Environment: Partners in Life and the World Women's Congress for a Healthy Planet (WEDO 1999). Women from around the world were able to reach agreement on some important ideas about what sustainable development should be and how gender equality is central to sustainable development, and to present that information to the politicians at Rio (MacDonald 1996). After UNCED, the federal government continued to support research into an analysis of Canada's commitments to gender and sustainable development. One example is a report entitled *Women and Sustainable Development: Canadian Perspective*, which includes some draft policy statements written in 1994. A second example is the work of Projet de Société, which is a set of Canadian responses to *Agenda 21* designed to 'capture the essence of *Agenda 21*; identify Canadian policies and positions with respect to Earth Summit objectives; and identify what Canadians are doing, or are planning to do, which is consistent with those objectives' (Projet de Société 1995).

Canada's commitments to gender equality are further evidenced in Canadian legislation, policies, and programs and are subject to the Canadian *Charter of Rights and Freedoms*. Promoting gender equality in Canada builds on the belief that 'equal rights for women are an essential component of progress on human rights and democratic development; and that sustainable and equitable development will only be achieved if women are able to participate as equal decision makers in and beneficiaries of that development' (Status of Women Canada 1999). At the Fourth World Conference on Women in Beijing, the Government of Canada presented a national plan entitled *Setting the Stage for the Next Century: The Federal Plan for Gender Equality (1995–2000)*. In this plan there is a special section on women and the environment. The plan further notes that 'Canada is committed to including women's perspectives on achieving sustainable development' (Status of Women Canada 1999). Canada recommended that a gender perspective be integrated into the international agreements on sustainable development and requested a review and assessment of the Rio Summit and the recommendations of the Commission on Sustainable Development (Status of Women Canada 1999).

Additional Canadian commitments to gender, the environment, and sustainable development include DFAIT's financial and policy support for the participation of Canadian indigenous women at a biodiversity convention working group meeting and at the Madrid Workshop on UN Biodiversity Convention/Traditional Knowledge. Canada's commitment to promoting sustainable development in the circumpolar countries was further evidenced when the government ensured that Canadian indigenous women were represented at the Northern Lives Conference in 1997. One of Canada's six priorities for overseas development assistance (ODA) is to 'strengthen the full participation of women as equal partners in the sustainable development of their societies by supporting initiatives within and among developing countries to increase women's participation in decision making processes, improve women's income levels and economic conditions, [and] improve women's access to basic health' (CIDA 1999).

The Canadian International Development Agency (CIDA) is involved in a number of projects around the world that are geared to women's involvement in sustainable development projects. For example, in India a woman's organization is reclaiming unproductive land and engaging in sustainable agriculture and development. Other examples of Canada's international support for women include contributions made through CIDA's support for a United Nations Fund for Women (UNIFEM) project in Mali. This project trains women and provides them with credit in order to establish a waste-disposal business in Bamako, Mali. Reports on this project point to a high degree of success. The project now offers garbage removal to 18,000 residents (Status of Women Canada 1999).

Despite these commitments, the low representation of women in decision-making positions is a challenge to the implementation of gender equitable sustainable development strategies. At the United Nations Conference on Environment and Development (UNCED) in 1992, only 15 per cent of the official delegates and advisers were women (Kettel 1996). And of the heads of state represented at UNCED, only three out of 118 were women (Kettel 1996). Women play important roles as environmental managers in their communities and as activists in environmental movements, but they are seldom the heads of environmental departments and rarely the leaders of national or international environmental non-governmental organizations (Kettel 1996).

Overall, the representation of women in professional environmental careers is also low. In Canada, women's employment in resource-management careers is 'substantially less than men' (census data cited in Nesmith and Wright 1995: 85). Furthermore, less than 16 per cent of the workforce, including clerical positions, in the traditional resource-management fields (forestry, fisheries, mining, and trapping) consists of women (Nesmith and Wright 1995). Women 'occupy less than 11 per cent of the professional, semi-professional and technical positions' (Nesmith and Wright 1995: 85) in environmental work. Therefore, women have fewer opportunities than men to effect environmental changes through decision making and participation in international decision making and in national legislative processes (Kettel 1996). However, the Government of Canada continues to adopt policies that promote the increased participation of women in decision making.

The Government of Canada made a commitment at the 1995 Fourth World Conference on Women (FWCW) to offer more than 3,000 federal commitments to promote women's equality. These commitments are based on the critical areas of concern in the *Beijing Platform for Action*. As noted above, Canada's Auditor General recently appointed a woman as the Commissioner of the Environment and Sustainable Development (CESD), Johanne Gélinas. This new appointment is one increase in the representation of women in senior environmental decision-making positions.

The limited representation of women in environmental careers can be partially explained by the professionalization of environmental jobs. When jobs are considered professional they take on masculine characteristics. Thus, environmental professions can be characterized as risk-taking (such as tree felling), labour intensive (such as mining), entrepreneurial (such as small environmental engineering companies), and scientific (such as soil-sample analysis).

The professionalization of environmental work reinforces the argument that 'flexibility in job descriptions and career paths is being reinterpreted as "masculine" risk-taking and entrepreneurialism' (Hooper 1998: 40). Hooper cites an example of computers, which 'have lost their feminine associations with keyboard skills and are now marketed as macho power machines' (Hooper 1998: 40). As environmental issues have gained prominence in international circles, environmental careers have achieved elevated status. The masculinization of environmental careers offers reasons for women's marginal representation in the decision making processes of environmental planning. The prevalence of men in environmental policy making positions offers a partial explanation of the ways in which masculinities are reinforced in environment and sustainable development work.

However, gender inequality in environment and sustainable development issues is also deeply entrenched in policy documents, organizational practices, and institutional norms. The masculinities and femininities that characterize gender relations are institutionalized in policy-making procedures and organizations.

Gender, Masculinities, and Femininities in International Relations and Foreign Policy

In 1988, a feminist writer, Sarah Brown, noted that 'international relations has failed to theorize on gender, and that, theoretically and substantively, women need to be brought into the discipline' (1988: 461–2). Brown's critique further reveals how gender is silenced in international relations even though 'issues of gender are already embedded in the theory and practice of international relations' (464).

Feminist contributions to international relations and foreign policy have shed light on gendered norms and how 'socially constructed notions of masculinity and femininity help to oil and turn the wheels of international politics' (Smith 1995: 25). Much of this feminist literature has focused on the public/private analytical framework to explore gendered institutions. The public/private model can tell us a great deal about how attitudes, behaviour, and norms surrounding responsibilities and work for men and women are shaped by the separation of public and private spaces. While the simplistic division between public and private spheres does not accurately depict the world we live in, it does tell us something about how people form opinions about what is appropriate behaviour and actions for men and women.

Different feminist perspectives have brought diverse contributions to the public/private model. For example, liberal feminism does not question the division between public and private domains; 'rather, it disputes the relegation of women to the latter as the irrational expropriation of women's political power' (Brown 1988: 463). The central concern for the liberal feminists is women's lack of participation in public life and decision-making positions. However, critical and postmodern feminists have offered a more profound analysis of gender inequality.

As a core concept in feminist literature, gender is frequently used to describe the social and cultural roles that are assigned to males and females. These roles are classified as masculine or feminine and are learned through socialization. Masculine and feminine also describe responsibilities, characteristics, kinds of behaviour, and symbols that correspond to the sex of an individual. Women are symbolically associated with the feminine and the private sphere (the home); men are symbolically associated with the masculine and the public sphere (the office, factory, or official workplace). These associations vary from culture to culture. Women are further symbolically associated with nature by virtue of their ability to give birth. Through socialization, these stereotypes are reinforced and meanings are embodied by individuals.

More specifically, masculine and feminine are categories used to describe and reinforce the 'processes and relationships through which men and women conduct gendered lives' (Connell 1995: 71). Masculinity and femininity are places in gender relations, practices that negotiate and situate men and women in gendered spaces, and positions in relation to access to, and control of, resources and decision making. While actions and roles have contributed to our understanding of masculine and feminine, meanings and words can also be designated masculine and feminine. Society's understanding of the roles and characteristics of masculine and feminine, and the hierarchy implicit in these terms, will determine individual and collective actions.

What is analytically significant about the divisions between masculinity and femininity is that masculine activities, characteristics, and identities are more highly valued than feminine activities, characteristics, and identities (Peterson and Runyan 1993). Thus power is central to the social construction of gender relations. The result is that 'many of the most serious global issues facing humankind and the planet today are caused, in part, by the practices, processes, and structures of gender hierarchy (the power system that privileges maleness over femaleness)' (Peterson and Runyan 1993: 40). Gender divisions that result from the hierarchical ordering of masculinity over femininity further reveal who has access to and control over resources. From the perspective of environmental degradation, these divisions and differences demonstrate 'who suffers most from environmental degradation, and how gender stereotypes relate to irresponsible resource use' (Peterson and Runyan 1993: 40).

Binary opposites such as masculine/feminine, public/private, or modern/traditional are false and simplistic representations of the world used to perpetuate artificial divisions. However, these binary frameworks continue to be used by policy makers to reinforce institutionalized privilege and patterns of inequality. Binaries reinforce and legitimate each other and are purposefully used to reinforce and legitimate specific interests. For example, 'dichotomies are crucial to the maintenance, legitimation and perpetuation of the guiding principles and discursive practices of Canadian foreign policy.

'Dichotomies maintain the idea of internationalism by allowing the Canadian state to appear to be kinder, gentler, softer, and more feminine, and thus appear to be less threatening and less self-interested. This appearance serves to legitimize the uniqueness of the Canadian state' (Keeble and Smith 1999: 86–7). Domestic politics and international politics are also expressed as binary opposites that legitimate political practices. A nation is composed of both a feminine domestic side and a masculine international side. The domestic side is equated with the private sphere while the international side 'refers to the projection of this domestic identity into the public sphere of relations among states' (Weber 1998: 155).

The domestic/feminine/private and the international/masculine/public reinforce each other, but 'the feminine (domestic) makes the masculine (international) possible' (Weber 1998: 155). The equating of public with international and of private with domestic is not a natural reflection of international relations and foreign policy. However, the private/public divide has gone unchallenged, thereby rendering masculinities invisible by failing 'to recognize the interconnections between the international and the private world of personhood' (Hooper 1998: 38). It is possible to expose the socially embedded dichotomies of masculinities and femininities in international relations and foreign policy through a gender analysis. Critical and postmodern feminist analyses have made possible the exposure of these artificial, but nonetheless, frequently employed, frameworks of analysis.

Another false division promoted in international relations can be found between national security and human security. National security has traditionally involved notions of military strength, aggression in world politics, and state coercion. Human security, on the other hand, has gained popularity in the past decade for its emphasis on peace and people-centred security. In 1994 United Nations Development Program (UNDP), in its *Human Development Report*, the UNDP extended global security to all humans, noting that the concept of security needs to change from a focus on national security to people's security.

Additional changes have included a shift from security through armaments and territorial security to human development, food, employment, and environmental security (UNDP 1994). Since the publication of the *Human Development Report*, politicians such as Lloyd Axworthy (former minister of foreign affairs) have incorporated the concept of human security into foreign policy documents. Axworthy's understanding of human security is one in which 'human rights and fundamental freedoms, the rule of law, good governance and social equity are as important to global peace as are arms control and disarmament' (DFAIT 1999a).

Human security 'means freedom from pervasive threats to people's rights, their safety or even their lives. The concept of human security has become both a new measure of global security and a new agenda for global action' (DFAIT 1999a). The requirements for human security, Axworthy goes on to note, include 'promoting sustainable human development, through the alleviation of absolute poverty, providing basic social services for all, and pursuing the goals of people-centred development' (DFAIT 1999a). As Axworthy said in a speech at the University of British Columbia in 1997, human security and sustainable development are closely linked. 'They are based on the recognition that what happens in our own backyard can have global implications and conversely, that global trends can affect our everyday lives' (DFAIT 1999a).

Since society considers peace, co-operation, and nurturing to be feminine qualities, then human security can be understood as a feminine concept. This does not necessarily mean that human security advocates gender equality or promotes women's security interests. On the contrary, definitions and discussions of human security have neglected women's security interests and gender-related issues and ignored the fact 'that women's security interests are often different than men's nor have they highlighted women's empowerment as a priority' (Woroniuk 1999: 4).

As a feminine concept, however, human security promotes those characteristics socially deemed feminine. The failure to address gender issues explicitly in discussions about both human security and sustainable development is problematic. The notion that gender equality is implicit in these definitions does not provide opportunities to address the challenges to sustainable development and human security faced by women (Woroniuk 1999:4).

Unlike gender issues, environment and sustainable development have been discussed in both the human security and national security literature. One example of how the environment is a national security issue is resource scarcity. As more and more people seek access to fewer and fewer resources, the state is required to step in to regulate access to and control of resources within national boundaries. Environmental security is important because national security concerns can also be found in day-to-day experiences in sustainable development work. An example of the latter surfaced during a Sustainable Livelihoods meeting sponsored by the United Nations Development Program (UNDP) in Malawi in 1997. At this meeting, a group of people met to discuss sustainable development strategies for the various Malawian government departments. One government representative provided a detailed summary of the difficulties of wildlife management in Malawi. Poachers of natural resources (such as timber) pose a threat to government workers because the poachers have bigger and better guns than the government staff who are mandated to protect these resources by preventing stealing and apprehending the poachers.

This example demonstrates that the environment is a national security concern. Nature conservation areas have become place where groups fight for access to, and control of, resources. Preserving the environment and maintaining order in the environmental sector requires knowledgeable environmental actors (good soldiers) with advanced technology (big guns) to keep the resource-poor (enemy) at bay. Environmental security concerns in international politics are now a rich source of masculinities which reveal power relations that privilege scientific knowledge, advanced technology, environmental management, professional male policy makers, and good soldiers over indigenous and local knowledge, environmental conservation, and day-to-day providers of household environmental resource needs (primarily women).

Homer-Dixon's work demonstrates how security concerns are related to environmental threats. His analysis highlights the impact of environmental changes as the environmental resources needed for survival, such as water, soil, and a stable climate, become scarce. Canada, he says, should be concerned with environmental security because Canada's peacekeepers will be needed to deal with the growing conflicts over scarce resources in other parts of the world. Furthermore, the increase in regional conflicts and the use of weapons of mass destruction as a result of these growing conflicts over scarce resources will challenge Canada's national security interests (Homer-Dixon 1994).

Homer-Dixon goes on to identify the potential for mass migrations of poor people seeking opportunities in resource-rich countries and regions (such as Canada, which is home to 10 per cent of the world's fresh water). The problems of sustainable development from a national environmental security perspective, are thus a result of population growth, ozone depletion, global climate change, and pollution of the earth's water, soil and air. The centrepiece of many international environmental policies has been the fight to end over-population in the South rather than over-consumption in the North. The binary argument used in this example makes it possible to distract attention from responsibility in the North to responsibility in the South.

Environmental security, as a national security matter, encompasses the link between environmental degradation, resource competition, and war (Thakur 1999). However, 'environmental factors, whether rooted in scarcity or degradation, do not generally cause wars directly; rather, they are catalysts to war. Scarce or strategic resources can be causes, tools or targets of warfare' (Thakur 1999: 53). While the correlation between war and resource scarcity is clear, the relationship needs to be understood in the broader social, political, and economic context.

Environmental conflicts can be intensified or reduced by other factors, including the ability to adapt to change, to the provision of alternative resources, a fair distribution of resources, and the political will to find solutions. Environmental security matters also needs to be understood in relation to the potential for sustainable development. Sustainable development and environmental policies are therefore urgent and important national and international strategies for rectifying the pressing issues surrounding environmental degradation and insecurity. The *Convention to Combat Desertification* (CCD) is one example of an international environmental policy designed to mitigate the effects of desertification, and therefore to prevent conflict over scarce, and increasingly scarcer, resources. The Canadian government strongly supports the CCD and has described it as an important international initiative in support of global sustainable development in Canada's foreign policy statement *Canada in the World* (DFAIT 1995a).

Canada continues to promote national environmental security interests while at the same time misleadingly promoting sustainable development strategies at home and abroad. The lip service paid to sustainable development allows Canada to project the image of sustainability abroad and fosters fallacies about Canadian foreign policy priorities and concerns.

Wolfgang Sachs (1999) provides numerous examples of how more developed countries of North America and Western Europe have projected an image of sustainability abroad. One of the examples he offers is the production of the highly toxic microchips in factories in less developed countries. Globalization has facilitated the production of environmentally destructive products in some parts of the world so that the more developed, powerful countries are able to cultivate knowledge-based economies that promote the perception of environmentally conscious development strategies.

One of the reasons that DFAIT has failed to adopt all the principles of *Agenda 21* is a lack of political will among politicians to implement these conference recommendations. 'This lack of will is central to political stability, to the resistance of political systems to change in the status quo' (MacDonald 1996: 191). In addition to the lack of political will to implement these policies is the purposeful omission of gender issues.

Strategies for sustainable development require co-operation in order to prevent conflict over scarce resources. Sustainable development also entails the fair distribution of resources to all groups over a period of time as the commonly cited definition, meeting the needs of current generations without jeopardizing the needs of future generations, suggests. However, the Canadian federal government consistently places competition, consumption, and confrontation (masculine characteristics) ahead of gender equity, co-operation, and participation of marginalized groups  (feminine characteristics). This is particularly evident in DFAIT's SDS where gender equality, co-operation, and participation are strategically silenced concerns.

Adopting the masculine language of economic efficiency and international competition gives the SDS greater urgency and prominence than a document framed around the concept of co-operation.

A Gendered Analysis of Agenda 21 and DFAIT's Sustainable Development Strategy

Agenda 21 is an important document that offers a global within which Canadian strategies can be assessed. As a comprehensive document, *Agenda 21* embodies multiple activities. One set of activities supports scientific, objective, environmental research and policy attention (i.e., greenhouse gas emissions, ozone depletion, hazardous waste management, and trade liberalization). An additional set of activities described in *Agenda 21* includes the participation of women, indigenous peoples, minority groups, human and reproductive health, social equality and the eradication of poverty. *Agenda 21* is a holistic document that brings multiple concerns together in a comprehensive policy framework.

What makes the sustainable development literature and policies different from other environmental policies and approaches is its emphasis on equity between more developed and less developed countries, gender equity, participation of major groups, and attention to human health. These are traditionally matters of domestic or local politics and tend to be undervalued in international policy making because they are couched as feminine characteristics in a masculine/feminine binary framework. These contributions to *Agenda 21* highlight femininities that have been brought to the international level where masculinities permeate decision making. However, to serve DFAIT's purposes, the feminine elements of sustainable development (such as environmental and human security, gender equity, social justice, poverty alleviation, and human health) are appropriated into a masculine agenda.

The sustainable development strategies that are meant to mirror *Agenda 21* are arenas for new battles that reveal masculinities in new forms of conflict and struggle. DFAIT's SDS in particular draws on the specific masculinities in *Agenda 21*, leaving out those principles characterized in foreign policy as feminine and thus perpetuating masculinities in Canadian foreign policy and international relations.

In his discussion of the masculinities learned by military sons, Craig Murphy makes reference to the gendered social construction of military work as men's work whereby boys are raised in military families to be good soldiers (Murphy 1998). The good-soldier example also applies outside the military. Battles are lost and won in policy circles and boardrooms, during trade negotiations and through financial assistance packages. Winning in international politics depends on more than who has access to military personnel and resources. It also depends on the preservation and reinforcement of masculinities.

Masculinities are reinforced internationally through the masculine traits of state making and war making (Pettman 1998). However, they are not confined to these two international activities, for 'similar observations could be made of global capitalists in the world market (the heroic entrepreneur doing battle for greater profit or market share)' (Pettman 1998: 174–5). International politics comprises multiple battlefields where access to and control over natural resources, like military resources, are venerated as opportunities for decision making and masculinities.

The global political economy is also characterized by masculinities, control, rationality, self-reliance, and risk taking (Ashworth and Swatuk 1998). On the other side of the coin, we find ideas, institutions, and material conditions that 'objectify and commodify women and entrench them as states to be protected, as natural resources to be exploited, as 'other' markets to be captured, and as producers of and primary caregivers to the next generation of labor' (Ashworth and Swatuk 1998: 76). The global political economy therefore has winners and losers. The decision-making arenas are battlefields where these winners and losers get sorted out.

Sustainable development policies are no exception to these new and emerging battlefields. The sustainable development strategy that has emerged from DFAIT embodies masculinities in Canadian foreign policy and international decision making with its emphasis on increased economic growth, security, western values, and 'green' decision making which is tacked onto existing practices and procedures.

Sustainable and equitable development were formerly undervalued but are now valued just as peacekeeping and peace building were undervalued in the past but are now part of the human security discourse (Keeble and Smith 1999). It is an 'appropriation of a feminine discourse by masculinist ideas and assumptions' (Keeble and Smith 1999: 82). The appropriation of feminine discourse reinforces what Niva (1998) argues is the tough but tender masculinity, which, Parpart explains, 'leaves male power intact . . . it allows masculinity to absorb feminist challenges without questioning the association between manliness and power' (Parpart 1998: 206).

By appropriating femininities, sustainable development disguises the underlying masculinities of international policy making. This appropriation of sustainable development concepts and meanings (as feminine concepts and meanings) in masculine forums has perpetuated the status quo that undervalues femininities in relation to masculinities. This can be further compared to Canada's security policy, which perpetuates the existing world order through its commitments to human security and peace building (Keeble and Smith 1999).

An examination of the meanings of sustainable development in the context of international and domestic politics highlights a number of important relationships. Weber argues that 'sustainable development is inherently an international concept' not a domestic concept (international = masculine versus domestic = feminine)' (Weber 1998: 51–5). Thus projecting sustainable development ideas and policies onto the international level actually masculinizes it and recodes sustainable development as masculine. These revelations and debates surrounding masculinities and femininities in sustainable development policies reinforce dualisms and problematize dichotomies by demonstrating the fluidity and complexity of masculinities and femininities in sustainable development. For example, people are encouraged to learn new, modern conservation techniques while at the same time being encouraged to increase the trade in, and export of, cash crops that are a drain on the soil nutrients, water supplies, time, and financial and labour resources. However, actors and institutions secure these binary divisions by perpetuating their interconnectedness and relational power dynamics. Environmental and sustainable development policies reinforce dichotomies such as the modern environmental practices versus traditional environmental practices.

How can we truly understand multiple masculinities and the ways in which previously feminine meanings have been appropriated to fulfill masculinist agendas? It is essential to understanding the powerful forms of masculinity at play. The fracturing of a holistic document such as *Agenda 21* has resulted in parts of the document being appropriated for certain purposes and other sections ignored. The SDS cannot be complete or whole if it is only reflecting some of the sustainable development concepts and components. Without a comprehensive approach to sustainable development, the SDS becomes a narrow, self-serving interpretation of sustainable development that reinforces divisions between masculinities and femininities and disperses them in parochial practices and policies.

The language of DFAIT's SDS does not even make mention of some of the core concepts of the sustainable development literature (such as participation and gender equity). The language of the SDS is thus a narrow adaptation of sustainable development ideas which reflects masculinities and reinforces a polarized world. In so doing, some ideas are exported and reinforced while others are submerged or marginalized. On the surface, the SDS gives an illusion of feminine meanings, soft politics or gender-equitable development. The strategic silence on issues such as participation and gender equity ensures that the status quo is maintained. Exposing these complex relationships and nuances is a useful starting point in revealing ways in which masculinities and femininities are reinforced and encoded in international policy making and how, as a result, international policy making is gendered.

The common use of sustainable development as a concept and *Agenda 21* incorporate both masculinities and femininities and symbolically reflect both in multiple ways as the above examples demonstrate. But by encompassing everything, *Agenda 21* leaves countries, organizations, institutions, and policy makers free to choose those concepts and strategies deemed worthy of addressing in specific action plans. For DFAIT those concepts and strategies include increased trade, exporting Canadian values, and peace building and security. These strategies are indeed part of *Agenda 21*, but they do not represent the comprehensive nature of this document and the important achievements set out in it.

A recasting of the SDS proposed by DFAIT could elaborate on some of the trade-related goals and actions by discussing the need for reforms to trade negotiations. These reforms would allow for environmental and social costs to be built into the commodities that are traded as well as in the production and transporting of these goods. Also, governments need to ensure social equity and diversity by bringing major groups, including women, the poor, minorities, and others into the decision making. Decision making within international organizations needs to be democratic and dedicated to the public interest, and needs to ensure that trade commitments and aid represent the public interest (Projet de Société 1995). A less imperialist version of the DFAIT SDS would eliminate goals such as the 'projection abroad of Canadian values and culture that support sustainable social development' which supports the observation made by Pettman of the 'promulgation of statewide nationalism' (Pettman 1998: 174).

A further masculinity in DFAIT's SDS is the avoidance of the word co-operation—unlike, for example, Chapter 2 of *Agenda 21,* which is called 'International Cooperation'. Instead DFAIT's SDS refers to cooperative international action on issues of global concern (DFAIT 1997a). The operative word or goal changing from co-operation(a characteristic that can be deemed feminine) to action (masculine meaning). In reference to building peace and security (objective number two in DFAIT's SDS), the document again avoids the use of the word co-operation referring instead to 'cooperative efforts'. Efforts are means to an end, whereas co-operation denotes an end in itself. This language is less committal, less binding, and more obscure and leaves the document open to greater interpretation.

The new battles in environmental policy making are battles over resources in an increasingly insecure global environment where population growth threatens to alter the status quo as more and more people compete for fewer and fewer resources. These concerns are clearly identified in the Minister's message regarding Environment Canada's SDS. The challenge of sustainable development is a result of the gap between the people's demands on the environment and the environment's capacity to meet those demands. 'Each day brings fresh evidence of that gap: on the one hand, further growth in the world's population and in patterns of consumption; on the other, an overall downward trend in the quantity and quality of much of the earth's natural resources' (Environment Canada 1997). The securitization of environmental concerns emerges again as the fear of resource scarcity is highlighted.

An additional battle illustrated in DFAIT's SDS is an effort to win the war against barriers to free trade. The document promotes the idea that barriers to free trade are our enemies and that free trade will necessarily promote economic growth and therefore economic growth is good for sustainable development. This is in opposition to the argument that 'free trade is fundamentally incompatible with environmental protection and that the operation of the free market and the free movement of capital will result inevitably in the lowering of environmental and other social standards' (Projet de Société 1995). There is a general lack of evidence to support the claim that wealth is a precondition for environmental protection since it does not address the questions about power structures and how resources are distributed.

One battle that is not posed as central to DFAIT's SDS is 'combating poverty', the title of Chapter 3 of *Agenda 21.* Instead, the term used in one of the SDS goals is 'reduction of poverty'. This goal, while laudable, is lumped together with others, such as the rights of indigenous peoples, social equity and diversity, and access to health and education. These goals are part of DFAIT's mandate to 'project abroad . . . Canadian values and culture' (DFAIT 1997a). Nowhere in the document is social equity or diversity described or defined. Furthermore, the social dimensions of this document consist of only three actions (unlike the economic growth and prosperity dimensions, which consist of twenty actions and six action plans). These three social actions involve institutional reform of UN bodies, 'support[ing] international market expansion opportunities for Canada's aboriginal peoples', and 'work[ing] with CIDA in negotiations on the replenishment of the Global Environmental Facility' (DFAIT 1997a). In this section, social equity and diversity are not elaborated on, and there is no discussion of the importance of gender equity or participation of major groups.

The objectives emerging from DFAIT's SDS perpetuate the masculinization of wealth in money (that is, income) and in natural resources providing strategies to increase export earnings and protect natural resources that represent 'more than a quarter of Canada's trade' (DFAIT 1997a). Concentrating on increasing trade to the exclusion of other important sustainable development initiatives upholds 'the national and international masculinization of policy and decision making that has sustained the masculinization of wealth in income and natural resources for the past several decades' (Kettel 1996:172).

The DFAIT SDS discusses only a few of the topics covered in *Agenda 21*; among those it omits are human health and risk management in relation to toxic chemicals and waste. In so doing, the DFAIT SDS is particularly narrow in scope and thus ignores the many facets of the sustainable development approach. Furthermore, in not addressing consumption patterns (Chapter 2 of *Agenda 21*) and the need for changing consumption patterns, the SDS is evading issues surrounding the status quo. Rather than a policy framework that encourages and provides incentives for changing consumption patterns in order to reduce wasteful consumption, DFAIT's SDS notes the need for 'fostering sustainable and equitable economic growth and development' (DFAIT 1997a), but omits any actions for meeting this goal. The actions identify the need to pursue economic growth, reduce debt, and enhance dialogue with developing countries.

The DFAIT SDS identifies some of the causes of unsustainable development, highlighting first the barriers to free trade, international indebtedness, and later in the chapter noting problems such as child labour, meeting basic human needs, and protecting human rights. DFAIT prioritizes these problems in a specific way to call attention to some issues as more relevant and urgent than others. DFAIT also 'works to influence and leverage arrangements with other sovereign nation-states on issues of common interest, on issues as diverse as negotiating rules on sustainable management of forests and marine management practices, and negotiating agreements to ensure a fair and open system of world trade' (DFAIT 1997a). If these are issues of common interest, then it unclear why DFAIT needs to influence and 'leverage' arrangements. It would seem appropriate instead to note that DFAIT co-operates with other sovereign nation-states.

A one-way flow of information is assumed in the document's discussion of trade relations and information sharing. There is a need to 'promote the development, effective transfer and application of innovative sustainable technologies, including technology exchanges and the export of Canadian knowledge, products, expertise and services' (DFAIT 1997a). The specific reference to export with no mention of two-way communication is indicative of a power relationship in which Canada strives to maintain its position as a dominant international force.

A preoccupation with national environmental security pervades the SDS: 'Borders are increasingly open to human, economic and environmental trends affecting our security (examples include the illegal movements of peoples, long range transport of various pollutants, global warming, health risks, drug trafficking and crime, terrorism)' (DFAIT 1997a). Canada's geography poses additional challenges for national environmental security: Canada's 'huge landmass and long coastlines, relatively open borders, small population, and open economy influence and determine the approach Canada takes to such issues as collaboration and cooperation . . .' (DFAIT 1997a). This statement demonstrates Canada's vulnerabilities as a coastal state and explains one of the reasons why Canada is faced with national environmental security concerns. This in turn, reflects the prioritization of national security issues over human security concerns.

Throughout the SDS, there is virtually no mention of gender equity or equality. There is a short reference to social equity in the objective summarized as Canadian values and culture and the goal of projecting Canadian values and culture that support sustainable social development abroad. One of the action milestones is that DFAIT should 'support UN objective of fully integrating women's rights and equality issues into the programs and agendas of international human rights fora, and support the UN Secretariat's objective of gender equality as well as the work of the UN Special Rapporteur on Violence Against Women' (DFAIT 1997a). The indicators of success will be the 'achievement of gender equality within the UN by 2000' (DFAIT 1997a). There is no mention of how these milestones will be reached, how women's rights will be integrated into programs and projects, and what equality issues entail.

The vagueness of this section on gender issues is a clear example of DFAIT's minimal or lack of commitment to gender equality and failure to say exactly how it will achieve these goals. The other reference to gender issues is made among a long list of actions recommended by DFAIT, including encouraging and negotiating agreements on a variety of issues, such as forest management practices, management of hazardous materials and wastes, satisfaction of basic human needs, democratic development, and the rights of women and gender equality.

The neglect of gender in the SDS is consistent with the challenge to mainstream gender into the human security strategies adopted by DFAIT. There are many elements missing in DFAIT's discussions of and policies on sustainable development. These missing dimensions would help address gender inequality in access to and control over resources and gender inequality in power and decision making. Furthermore, highlighting gender issues in DFAIT's SDS would put women's human rights at the centre of sustainable development and point to women as environmental actors rather than merely victims of environmental degradation. It would also help to distinguish between the different sustainable development needs experienced by men and women and reveal how sustainable development and environmental challenges are shaped by masculinities and femininities.

The strategic silences on gender issues can be understood in the context of structures of gender hierarchy that reinforce inequality and power relations between men and women, rich and poor, more developed and less developed countries, and masculinities and femininities. In each case the former is privileged while the latter is depreciated. Dichotomous divisions are used strategically and to maintain the status quo. Binaries do not reflect the reality of day-to-day life since they are artificial divisions that are manufactured to promote the status quo and to maintain power. The dichotomies are therefore relational and hierarchical and are used purposefully to promote certain interests over others. In the specific case of DFAIT's SDS, the binary framework bolsters masculinities while silencing femininities and does this by both appropriating the masculinist pillars of *Agenda 21* and by filtering *Agenda 21's* principles and recommendations through a masculinist lens. By re-reading DFAIT's SDS using a gender analysis, the strategic silence on gender equality is exposed. This analysis also challenges the notion that Canadian foreign policy is gender-neutral. In fact, Canadian foreign policy is deeply entrenched with masculinist meanings and language as the examples cited in this section demonstrate.

Summary

The limitations of DFAIT's SDS provide insights into the strategic silences on issues of increased participation, gender equality, human security, and people-centred and sustainable development. These insights reveal the extent to which DFAIT resists any measures to challenge or alter the status quo. Sustainable development therefore is translated in DFAIT's SDS into sustaining development in its current form so that trade is enhanced. Maintaining the status quo means Canada, as a nation, continues to reap the benefits of trade liberalization and terms of trade that favour those who already have access to, and control of, a disproportionate amount of resources and decision-making positions.

Maintaining the status quo extends beyond favourable trade relations to gender inequality. Some institutions (such as CIDA) have established gender-related programs and adopted the language of gender equality. The extent to which institutions have effectively integrated gender into their programs and activities has provided additional challenges. However, DFAIT is still limited by its failure to address gender inequality explicitly and to write gender into its sustainable development strategy. DFAIT's strategic silence on gender issues in its sustainable development strategy suggests that gender is at the heart of DFAIT's foreign policy in so far as addressing gender issues means reinforcing masculinities in Canadian foreign policy.

This analysis demonstrates how DFAIT's silence on gender issues is in fact a gendered function of state building whereby masculinities are privileged over femininities. The inability of DFAIT to incorporate the core principles and policy objectives of *Agenda 21* into its policy demonstrates the narrow definition of sustainable development adopted by DFAIT. The strategic silences on gender inequality further demonstrate DFAIT's narrow interpretation of *Agenda 21*. The discourse analysis of DFAIT's gendered institutional culture highlighted how masculinities and femininities are translated into policy documents on sustainable development, and by extension, how these gendered norms reinforce the status quo, preventing any real opportunities to address gender inequality.

Part III

Human Rights

Chapter 9

Women's Human Rights: Canada at Home and Abroad

SHELAGH DAY

This chapter consists of transcript of an interview with Shelagh Day conducted by Deborah Stienstra. Shelagh Day is a human rights expert, and the Special Advisor on Human Rights to the National Association of Women and the Law.

Deborah Stienstra: What is the central human rights problem for women in Canada right now?

Shelagh Day: The central problem is that Canadian governments are not implementing rights that Canada has agreed to. Canada is a signatory to a number of international human rights treaties, including the *International Covenant on Civil and Political Rights* (ICCPR, 1966), the *International Covenant on Economic, Social and Cultural Rights* (ICESCR, 1976), the *Convention on the Elimination of All Forms of Discrimination against Women* (CEDAW, 1981), and the *Convention on the Elimination of Racial Discrimination* (CERD, 1966). Being a signatory to these treaties means that Canada has agreed to protect, respect, and fulfill the rights set out in them. The ICCPR provides that everyone has the right to life, liberty, and security of the person; to freedom from slavery; to freedom from torture or cruel, inhuman, or degrading treatment; and to freedom from arbitrary arrest, detention, or exile. It also declares the right of everyone to freedom of thought, conscience, and religion, and freedom of expression, peaceful assembly, and association with others. It sets out the democratic rights to take part in the conduct of public affairs, to vote, and to be elected at genuine periodic elections. The ICESCR obliges state parties to progressively extend economic and social rights, including the following: the right to earn a living by work that is freely chosen; the right to social security, including social insurance; the right to an adequate standard of living, including adequate food, clothing, and housing; the right to the enjoyment of the highest attainable standard of physical and mental health; and the right to education. CEDAW and CERD articulate the rights to be free from all forms of sex and race based discrimination and to racial and sexual equality.

The treaties oblige Canadian governments to ensure that people in Canada enjoy these rights in fact, and to provide effective domestic mechanisms for obtaining remedies when these rights are violated. Each of these treaties contains specific commitments to equality for women. In addition, of course, Canada has adopted a constitutional guarantee of equality, and there are human rights statutes in every jurisdiction that protect women from discrimination in particular areas such as employment, services, and housing.

However, women are faced with a lack of government will to actually fulfill the rights that they have underwritten and enacted. This is specifically a problem with respect to women's economic inequality. That inequality is currently being maintained, if not deepened, by a government policy of downsizing, cutting social programs, privatizing services, and deregulating markets. This neo-liberal economic agenda, which seems to be endorsed by governments globally, is understood by more and more women to have a regressive, not an emancipatory impact. It is being imposed without regard to the commitments that have been made to women's human rights and to women's advancement.

Deborah Stienstra: Are there conceptual problems in the human rights framework that make it easier to ignore women's economic inequality?

Shelagh Day: Yes. As human rights have developed, there has been a division between civil and political rights on the one hand, and economic, social and cultural rights on the other. Civil and political rights have been thought of as real rights, 'hard rights', ones that can be enforced by courts and tribunals. They are considered negative rights, that is, rights that restrain government from violating the liberty of its citizens. In this paradigm, the state is the principal violator of rights.

Economic, social and cultural rights, by contrast, have been considered 'soft rights', not real rights enforceable by courts, but rather expressions of government aspirations. They are also positive rights; that is, they posit the state not as the violator of rights, but as the potential implementer of them. For women, who need equality, this vision of the state is essential. Women need a state that is prepared to intervene on their behalf to ensure that patriarchal forces within the marketplace and the family do not simply perpetuate the subordination of women.

This divided rights thinking is antithetical to the women's equality project. Full equality for women requires both the achievement of women's civil and political equality, and of their economic and social equality. The economic and social dimensions of women's inequality cannot be treated as though they fall into a less important, or less attainable category, that is dependent on the goodwill of governments, rather than on women's entitlement. So, we have a problem when the vision of rights is split in this way, because women's right to equality can be diminished to a kind of procedural equality that does not deal with women's long-standing economic disadvantage.

Despite the split, it has always been said that rights are indivisible and interdependent. Women's lives manifest the importance of that understanding. Women will not achieve equality unless equality is understood to be an encompassing right that is applicable to all the dimensions of women's inequality civil, political, economic, social, and cultural. In addition, it is impossible to separate, in women's real lives, violations of civil and political rights violations from violations of economic, and social rights violations. For example, in the Quebec case called *Gosselin*, which was heard by the Supreme Court of Canada in 2001, the Quebec government was accused of having reduced Louise Gosselin's welfare payments to approximately 170 dollars a month, which was acknowledged to be below subsistence level. In order to survive, Louise Gosselin prostituted herself to get money to buy clothes so that she could search for work, was followed and subjected to attempted rape by a man who was giving her food, lived in a relationship she did not want in order to have food and shelter, was sometimes homeless, and twice tried to commit suicide. The violation of her right to an adequate standard of living was inextricably connected to violations of her rights to personal liberty and security of the person, which are commonly understood as civil and political rights.

To move forward on women's equality, women must establish a common understanding about two things: (1) that economic inequality is an important manifestation of the subordination of women, and (2) that the right to equality is a 'real right', an enforceable right, no matter which kind of inequality is at issue.

In its development, the human rights framework has been male in its understanding and conceptualization of rights. The paradigmatic human rights violation has been torture by the state of a male political dissident. Women have been successful in the last decade in breaking into the male human rights framework by demanding recognition of violence against women as a violation of human rights. This has required a rethinking of the right to freedom from torture so that it can recognize women's experiences of violence and torture, which are often inflicted not by the state, but by intimate male partners.

Women have made an important breakthrough by establishing that violence against women is a violation of human rights. However, women cannot stop here; women's human rights encompass more than freedom from violence and torture. They must also be understood to encompass freedom from economic subordination. Women's poverty and economic inequality are central manifestations of long standing discrimination and subordination.

Deborah Stienstra: So as human rights have developed they have taken account primarily of male experience, not female experience, and in that framework, civil and political rights have been divided from economic and social rights and given first priority in the hierarchy of rights. What have been the effects of this for women, and for women in Canada in particular?

Shelagh Day: Governments have placed economic policy in a watertight compartment that is separated from human rights entirely. They assert that economic policy is apolitical, and gender-neutral, and they operate as though it has nothing to do with human rights. Unfortunately, the dominant (male) thinking about human rights may give them some permission to do this. But the separation of economic policy from women's human rights has a profoundly negative impact on women. Governments are continually designing and reconfiguring economic policy. Economic policies should be designed to be vehicles for fulfilling the human rights commitments; that is, they should be designed in such a way as to ensure that they advance the equality of women. Instead, governments are currently designing and implementing economic policies that, at best, maintain the status quo of women's inequality and, at worst, deepen it.

There are a number of examples in Canada at the moment. The major one of the last decade was the federal government's 1995 *Budget Implementation Act*, which repealed the *Canada Assistance Plan Act*, a cornerstone of Canada's social safety net, and introduced the Canadian Health and Social Transfer. The *Budget Implementation Act* brought structural adjustment to Canada. It repealed crucial rights, including the right of persons in Canada to social assistance when in need; it ended 50/50 cost-sharing of critical social programs and social services; it rolled into one block fund the federal transfer to the provinces of dollars that were previously designated for health, social assistance and social services, and post-secondary education, and removed all conditions on the transfer; and it cut drastically the amount of the transfer drastically. In effect, the federal government took a giant step back from funding and setting standards for Canada's social programs.

This structural adjustment has had a negative impact on women over the last five years. Strong and effective social programs are essential to women, precisely because they shift some of the burden for care giving from the shoulders of individual women to the shoulders of the state. Social programs are emancipatory for women.

When those social programs are cut, significant damage is done to women's freedom and opportunities. Women have lost 'good' jobs (jobs that are unionized, and have benefits and pensions attached to them) in the care-giving sector; their burden of unpaid care giving has increased; and welfare rates have been cut in a number of jurisdictions, deepening the poverty of the poorest women. More women and children are homeless, and more women are staying in violent relationships because the amount of social assistance they can receive now is not sufficient to allow them to adequately support themselves and their children independently (National Association of Women and the Law 1998, and Day and Brodsky 1998).

This restructuring of social programs in 1995 was the most significant change to social policy in Canada of the last thirty years, but it was presented as a budgetary measure, ostensibly to lower a deficit. It was introduced apparently without taking into account, or despite, the entirely predictable harm that it would cause to women, and to the human rights commitments that Canada has made. Governments do not admit that they are dealing with economic and social policy that affects women if the issue is macro-economic policy, trade agreements, tax law, or overall budgets. These are offered as apolitical, gender-neutral, and unconnected to human rights commitments. This is inaccurate; women feel the effects of these larger economic policies, and the implementation of those policies needs to be understood as government conduct to which rights attach.

Flowing from the dominant thinking about human rights is the idea that the social and economic dimensions of women's inequality can be categorized as the kind of rights that are not 'real rights'. Under those circumstances, a government claim of limited resources, even if that claim does not withstand scrutiny, can defeat commitments to women's social and economic equality.

This, however, is not the approach of the United Nations Committee on Economic, Social and Cultural Rights, which monitors the compliance of signatories to the *International Covenant on Economic, Social and Cultural Rights.* When the

National Association of Women and the Law made submissions to that committee in 1998, the committee 'noted with grave concern that the repeal of CAP and cuts in social assistance rates, social services and programs have had a particularly harsh impact on women who are the majority of the poor, the majority of adults receiving social assistance, and the majority among the users of social programs' ('Concluding Observations' 1998, par. 23). The Committee also indicated that it was not persuaded by Canada's assertions regarding the deficit that this damage was necessary. It concluded, 'In addressing budget deficits by slashing social expenditure, the State Party has not paid sufficient attention to the adverse consequences for the enjoyment of economic, social and cultural rights by the Canadian population as a whole, and by vulnerable groups in particular' ('Concluding Observations' 1998, par. 11). The committee recommended that

> a greater proportion of federal, provincial and territorial budgets be directed specifically to measures to address women's poverty and the poverty of their children, affordable day care, and legal aid for family matters. Measures that will establish adequate support for shelters for battered women, care giving services and women's non-governmental organizations should also be implemented. ('Concluding Observations' 1998, par. 54)

In short, the committee was not persuaded that in one of the wealthiest countries in the world, it was necessary to violate the economic and social rights of the most disadvantaged people in order to pay down a budgetary deficit.

The Human Rights Committee, which oversees compliance with the *International Covenant on Economic, Social and Cultural Rights*, was also concerned about the discriminatory impact of the cuts on women. It said in its 1999 'Concluding Observations on Canada':

> The Committee is concerned that many women have been disproportionately affected by poverty. In particular, the very high rate among single mothers leaves their children without the protection to which they are entitled under the Covenant. While the delegation expressed a strong commitment to address these inequalities in Canadian society, the Committee is concerned that many of the program cuts in recent years have exacerbated these inequalities and harmed women and other disadvantaged groups. The Committee recommends a thorough assessment of the impact of recent changes in social programs on women and that action be undertaken to redress any discriminatory effects of these changes. ('Concluding Observations of the Human Rights Committee' 1999, par. 20)

It is clear that in the view of the treaty bodies, there is a discrepancy between Canadian conduct and the obligations that Canada has undertaken to fulfill. Canada is not in compliance with its international human rights obligations, including its obligation to ensure that women enjoy equality in all aspects of their lives.

It would be comforting to believe that governments have acted without comprehending the harsh effects that the restructuring of social programs has on women, and that once having seen that harm, they would be eager to reverse it. Unfortunately, this does not seem to be the case. Former Finance Minister Paul Martin, for example, who was the architect of the 1995 restructuring of Canada's social programs, made it clear in a speech to the International Monetary Fund in 1998 that he understood that structural adjustment programs have a negative impact on women in developing countries, and that policies should be designed from the outset to avoid harming the most vulnerable groups. He said: 'Women and children, who are the most vulnerable, feel the impact of adjustment efforts first and hardest. The social implications [of adjustment programs] have to be recognized up front.'[1] Martin's concern about the negative effects of structural adjustment on women does not appear to extend to women in Canada.[2]

Deborah Stienstra: Is Canada united in its approach to its human rights obligations, or are there jurisdictional tensions?

Shelagh Day: There are certainly problems. When Canada prepares its reports to the United Nations treaty bodies, it's the federal government that takes the lead role because it has responsibility for foreign affairs, but submissions are requested from all the provinces and territories. Consequently, Canada's reports are a compilation of responses from all of Canada's jurisdictions. Under international law, however, Canada is one state party, not a group of mini-states. Canada as a state party has made undertakings to fulfill treaty specified obligations. Problems arise when the federal government says it is not responsible for a failure to comply because a matter falls within the jurisdiction of a provincial or territorial governments. To the UN Committee on Economic, Social and Cultural Rights in 1998, this was evidence of a serious obstacle to implementation of the ICESCR (International Covenant on Civil and Political Rights 1966, par. 12). There is no pan-Canadian mechanism for ensuring compliance with international human rights obligations in all jurisdictions. The Continuing Committee on Human Rights, a federal/provincial/territorial committee of officials, co-ordinates the preparation of Canada's reports, but that committee has no authority when it comes to government decision-making. There is no body, or minister, and no intergovernmental committee that takes responsibility for remedying non-compliance. Before the United Nations Human Rights Committee in the spring of 1999, Minister Fry made a commitment to ensure that a parliamentary committee would hold hearings on issues arising from that committee's observations (Convention on the Elimination of all Forms of Discrimination Against Women 1966, par. 3). No such hearings have been held. The fact is that the concluding observations of treaty bodies fall into a vacuum.

Also, Canada is now increasingly being criticized by treaty bodies for the inadequacy of its domestic mechanisms for providing remedies for violations of human rights violations. Inadequate protections in law for economic and social rights, inadequate enforcement of human rights laws, and regressive positions taken by governments in litigation about the meaning of Charter rights are all matters of concern (*Convention on the Elimination of all Forms of Discrimination Against Women*

1966, par. 14–16).[3] But no government appears to be taking responsibility for correcting these inadequacies.

Deborah Stienstra: Are there any tensions inside the federal government, or do they act with one voice?

Shelagh Day: It would be more accurate to say that there are gaps, or disconnections, inside the federal government. There is little apparent connection between the Ministry of Foreign Affairs, which deals with international human rights matters, and all other parts of government that are responsible for specific aspects of the realization of rights at home. Human rights appears to be a priority in Canada's relations with other countries. But human rights commitments do not appear to be a priority at home; they have not been incorporated into the ordinary workings of government. Particularly in the Ministry of Finance, where budgets are constructed and economic policy is shaped, human rights commitments, both domestic and international, are being ignored. Budgets are not being constructed with women in mind, or with human rights advances in mind.

Deborah Stienstra: Canada has often been perceived at the international level as a leader in human rights. Do you think, first of all, it is an accurate assessment, and secondly, is this leadership evident in how it deals with human rights work within Canada?

Shelagh Day: There are instances in which Canada is out in front on the international scene, and for this it deserves praise. For example, Canada has been a leader in bringing forward issues of violence against women, and in recognizing gender violence in the context of war as a crime against humanity. On the other hand, Canada was a foot-dragger until the late days of the negotiations of the Optional Protocol to CEDAW. The Optional Protocol provides a complaint mechanism that allows residents in ratifying countries to file complaints that will be adjudicated by the CEDAW Committee. Canada for a number of years was not a supportive participant in those negotiations, and took a more positive stance only after the chair of the United Nations Drafting Committee, and other more progressive delegations, began to make it known that they considered Canada an unsupportive player. One of the notable differences between the *Declaration on Violence against Women*, and the Optional Protocol to CEDAW is that the former has no legal force in international law, whereas the latter is a legal instrument that is binding on those countries that ratify it. In other words, one is a statement of principle, while the other is a piece of international law. Canada has not yet ratified the Optional Protocol.

So Canada is sometimes a leader on women's human rights and sometimes is not, depending on its assessment of its own vulnerability to liability or embarrassment.

The second issue is harder. Canada does care about how it is perceived in the international arena on human rights issues, and it does hold itself out as a leader. There are times when women in Canada can be proud of what Canada does at the international level. But for women who are acutely aware of the many ways in which Canada is not living up to its obligations at home, the claim to leadership sits uneasily. This is particularly the case because Canada is one of the countries in the world that could achieve equality for women. It has the wealth and the infrastructure to support real advances.

It is particularly difficult to support the claim to leadership in light of the fact that there has been little change to the women's economic situation of women in Canada since the Royal Commission reported thirty years ago. Monica Townson, in her new *Report Card on Women and Poverty*, says: 'Women remain among the poorest of the poor in Canada. Over the past two decades, the percentage of women living in poverty has been climbing steadily. As Canada enters the twenty-first century, almost 19 per cent of adult women are poor—the highest rate of women's poverty . . . in two decades' (Townson 2000). Comparing the rates of poverty of single women, single mothers, and unattached older women, Townson finds little change between thirty years ago and today. Current rates of poverty for these groups stand at 41 per cent, 56 per cent, and 49 per cent respectively (Townson 2000). There are other groups of women in Canada who also have high rates of poverty. Statistics Canada's new report *Women in Canada* shows the poverty rates for Aboriginal women at 43 per cent, for women of colour at 37 per cent, and for women who immigrated to Canada 10 to 20 years ago at 32 per cent (Statistics Canada 2000: at 259, 232, 206). As Townson says, in her report: 'Addressing women's poverty no longer seems to be a high priority among policy-makers—if indeed it ever was' (*Concluding Observations of the Human Rights Committee: Canada* 1998, 1).

Women's experience of this pattern of poverty and economic inequality is not consistent with Canada's understanding of itself as a leader in the field of human rights. Canada has made commitments to women at every level— internationally, constitutionally, and in statutory human rights legislation. Canada is an enthusiastic signatory to international commitments, and that is an achievement, but it is not living up to those commitments at home, and Canada's domestic mechanisms for actually realizing those commitments are not adequate.

Deborah Stienstra: What kind of openings are there are for women's activism on human rights now?

Shelagh Day: Many different things need to be done. There is work to be done at the theoretical level. Rights do not have fixed meanings. It is always necessary for women to be thinking and writing about how rights need to be interpreted and applied in order to fulfill their purpose. At this time, bringing the economic and social dimensions of women's inequality to the fore is an essential piece of work if women are to advance.

It's useful to appear before UN treaty bodies to highlight Canada's lack of compliance with its obligations and to bring that to public attention. Rights need to be understood better by more people. Canadian women have started to make submissions to UN treaty bodies just in the last five years. More of that work needs to be done.

There is work to be done to make Canada's domestic human rights system work for women and others who are disadvantaged. Currently, it is an ineffective system for addressing the larger patterns of women's social and economic disadvantage. Yet, it was originally conceived of as a system that would have a direct effect on women's economic inequality.

The *Canadian Human Rights Act*, which was first drafted in the 1970s, is badly out of date. There is a new report by a panel appointed to review the *Canadian Human Rights Act*, which discusses amendments that are needed (Canadian Human Rights Act Review Panel 2000). It recommends the addition of 'social condition' as a prohibited ground for discrimination and more direct access to tribunal hearings. The federal government will respond to this report soon. However, intensive lobbying will be necessary to effect substantive change.

As I mentioned earlier, there have been constitutional cases, such as *Gosselin*, coming into the courts that deal directly with economic inequality. Louise Gosselin and some interveners will argue that the rights that Canada is a signatory to internationally, including the right to an adequate standard of living, must be taken into account when reading the rights in the Charter, because the Charter is acknowledged to be one of the vehicles through which international human rights are realized. It will be essential for women to watch these cases, and to be ready to respond in case the Supreme Court decides that the Charter cannot deal with economic manifestations of inequality. Were the court to move in this direction, the Charter would be gutted of its ability to assist women with one of the most serious aspects of their subordination.

Also, women need to intervene in the development of social policy under the Social Union Framework Agreement, which has been in effect for almost three years. This agreement was supposed to provide a public participatory element, some avenue by which for members of the public to could participate in establishing priorities and standards for social programs, and standards for them. Unfortunately, the Social Union Framework Agreement seems to be framework for ministers and officials only. Principally it has resulted in private conversations among governments, but it has produced no programs that address alleviate the poverty of women.

Most important, however, it is essential for women to insist wherever they are engaged that economic and social rights are an essential element of women's equality, and that economic policy and human rights are integrally connected. Women need to resist the disconnection between these two, and insist in every way possible that women's human rights include the right to social and economic equality.

Deborah Stienstra: Finally, what do you think are the implications of the disconnections you describe for Canadian foreign policy more generally?

Shelagh Day: Canadian foreign policy with respect to human rights is concerned with (1) forging agreements among states about human rights standards and (2) intervening when human rights are violated in other countries. But Canada's stance seems unselfconscious, thoughtless, and unreflective about human rights conditions at home. Canada can (rightly) make a diplomatic protest about the flogging of a young single mother in Nigeria for 'fornication outside of marriage', but (wrongly) fail to address the deep poverty of over 90 per cent of young single mothers in Canada (National Council of Welfare 1998: 36 and 53). This betrays a failure to address violations of human rights at home with the same clarity and righteous indignation as those taking place in other countries. It also betrays a failure to recognize as a human rights issue that poverty is also a brutal penalty for single motherhood, which women should be protected from. The main problem with Canadian foreign policy on women's human rights is that it is not reflected in an equivalent political commitment to fulfill women's human rights at home. Genuine leadership in foreign policy depends on a state's ability to show the world an integration between standards of conduct that it holds itself to and standards that it sets for others. A wealthy country like Canada, with its wealth of resources, should be setting the highest standards for itself in the area of women's equality, and showing, by its actions and its economic policies, that it sets a priority on the advancement of women. If it did that, Canada could be a leader.

Notes

1. From the text of a statement delivered by Finance Minister Paul Martin to the International Monetary Fund's development committee in Washington, 5 Oct. 1998, reprinted in *The Globe and Mail*, 6 Oct. 1998.
2. See also, Janet Mosher, 'Managing the Disentitlement of Women: Glorified Markets, the Idealized Family, and the Undeserving Other', in Sheila Neysmith, ed., (2000). *Restructuring Caring Labour* (Toronto: Oxford University Press, 2000), 30. Jane Mosher also concludes that the Harris government's new 'spouse in the house' rules, which have a profoundly discriminatory impact on women, and single mothers in particular, were not enacted in ignorance. These rules are being challenged in *Falkiner et al. vs. Director of Income Maintenance Branch, Ministry of Community and Social Services, and Attorney General of Ontario*, 29 Oct. 1997, Court File No. 810/95 (Ontario Divisional Court), currently on appeal to the Ontario Court of Appeal. Mosher concludes: 'One might hope that this is simply a case of omission; that the state, through some oversight, failed to consider the implications for women when crafting these reforms. I am inclined to think that the situation is far graver. The state actively defended its new definition of 'spouse' in the *Falkiner* case, arguing that neither equality nor security of the person's rights were infringed. More tellingly, it argued that if such rights were infringed, such infringements were justified in order to save money. In other words, the state is prepared to carry out its economic reforms on the backs of women who are already multiply oppressed. This speaks volumes as to the depth of the state's commitment to women's equality and safety.' (p. 98)
3. See also *Convention on the Elimination of All Forms of Racial Discrimination Against Women* (1981) par. 9.

Chapter 10

Discourses and Feminist Dilemmas: Trafficking, Prostitution, and the Sex Trade in the Philippines

EDNA KEEBLE AND MEREDITH RALSTON

INTRODUCTION

Female sexual slavery[1] across national borders has become a prominent issue in the global arena: not only has it received a great deal of attention from the press, but it has also moved the international community to make agreements preventing the sexual exploitation of women and young girls. The trafficking in women and children is a dreadful tale of poverty, deceit, fear, and coercion; and the heart-wrenching stories are becoming all too familiar. Young, rural, relatively uneducated women from one state (the 'source') are lured or sold into prostitution or simply kidnapped. They are often moved through one state (the 'transit') before they reach their journey's end (the 'destination' state). Along the way, they are drugged and raped repeatedly by their procurers and pimps as a means of control. They are forced to have sex with countless clients. Yet they are quickly abandoned by their captors if they are caught by the destination-state authorities and sent home. And even that may not offer any reprieve because sometimes they simply fall prey to traffickers again, and the abuse and exploitation resume. The trafficking in women and children is what many analysts call 'the new slave trade', and 'both women and children are treated as consumer durables to be used and abused repeatedly by clients, and to be passed on from one trafficker or brothel owner to another in what is little more than a modern form of slavery' (Williams 1999b: 148). It is little wonder, then, that battling the transnational criminal organizations which are largely responsible is one of the key elements of Canada's human security agenda (DFAIT 1999e). There is no better example than the trafficking issue of a threat to human security and the need to take 'individual human beings and their communities, rather than states, as the measure of security', because the 'safety and well-being of individuals [is] integral to achieving global peace and security' (Heinbecker 1999).

To make sense of the trafficking issue requires that we deal with the discourses surrounding prostitution and the extent to which international women's groups, such as the Coalition Against the Trafficking of Women and the Global Alliance Against the Traffic in Women, although locating themselves somewhat on opposite sides of the prostitution divide, demand that anti-trafficking efforts be based on the protection of women's rights, and not simply the maintenance of law and order. On the other hand, to make sense of Canada's anti-trafficking efforts demands that we go beyond the policy pronouncements of the Department of Foreign Affairs and International Trade (DFAIT) and its human security agenda. The Canadian state is a complex entity, and its complexity, we argue, offers the sorts of opportunities for feminists to contribute to change. Anti-trafficking efforts are not the sole purview of governments: the work of non-governmental organizations is central. More specifically, when an arm of the Canadian government, namely the Canadian International Development Agency (CIDA), invites and fosters the participation of the academic and non-governmental sectors in both Canada and recipient states, the opportunities become more plain. Accordingly, this chapter draws out the way in which the authors have become part of a CIDA-funded development project in Angeles City, Philippines. Angeles City is the site of the former United States Clark Air Force Base, which closed in 1992, and it is both a magnet for sex tourists and a source of trafficked women. It is a place where we can easily see how Filipino women are not only exploited by local Filipino men, but also 'marketed' to foreigners both in the Philippines and abroad. By discussing the kinds of dilemmas we have encountered in the project from a feminist perspective, we outline the ways in which we are bridging theory and practice as feminist academics become partners in development.

Although trafficking in women is a prime example of the exploitation of women and the kinds of gendered structures that women face, the issue is not straightforward either discursively or practically. That is, there is no one feminist position on either what trafficking means (and thus what exploitation entails) or what to do about it, particularly in term of working with the state. We begin by looking at the discourses surrounding trafficking and prostitution and the current efforts, centring on battling transnational organized crime, made by the international community in its anti-trafficking efforts. Because states, arguably, have taken the lead, pressured as they have been by international non-governmental organizations, in anti-trafficking, we then move to a discussion of some of Canada's anti-trafficking efforts, specifically in its foreign aid policy. This raises the issue of dilemmas faced by feminists in working with the state. While feminist discussions of the state have become more nuanced, theoretically, in the past ten years, women's groups still worry, quite rightly, about being co-opted. Our project on prostitution in the Philippines, dealing specifically with organizations, is directly concerned with bridging the gap between theory and practice. Hence, we discuss the project and why we see 'opportunity spaces' (Waylen 1998: 16) to address the marginalization of women in the sex trade in Angeles City. One of the more innovative ways that we see to address the marginalization of the women is through the use of participatory video in the project. In the final analysis, we argue that the state provides us with some opportunities for subverting its coercive power and for giving space to women to act and make a difference.

Trafficking and Prostitution

The numbers are plainly stated and the consequences are dire. According to the

United Nations, 4 million people are lured, deceived, and exploited by international traffickers, who take over $7 billion US [$11 billion Cdn] in profit from their human cargo (USAID 1999; Caldwell et al. 1999: 42). Those who fall victim to traffickers are primarily women and children. Indeed, the very use of the term, even by itself (i.e., 'trafficking' as opposed to 'trafficking in women and children'), implies that the victims are of a particular gender (or age). As the international community attempts to deal with the issue of trafficking, protocols and agreements have centred on the extent to which those who are the least likely to protect themselves from exploitation (namely, women and children) have been the ones most likely to be targeted. The prime example of this is found in the *United Nations Protocol to Prevent, Suppress and Punish Trafficking in Persons, Especially Women and Children*, supplementing the *United Nations Convention against Transnational Organized Crime*.[2] This protocol, which has been subject to widespread scrutiny by both member states and non-governmental organizations, contains the first international definition of trafficking. In December 2000 the UN Convention against Transnational Organized Crime and the Protocol on Trafficking[3] were opened for signature in Palermo, Italy. Whereas all countries signed the larger convention against transnational organized crime, only eighty states signed the trafficking protocol. Among those that did not sign were China, Japan, Singapore, Thailand, and Vietnam. Throughout the negotiations, Canada was a supporter of both protocols and was a signatory to both.

Feminist groups disagree on the link between trafficking and prostitution. On one side is the Coalition Against the Trafficking of Women (CATW), which has historically stood at the helm of the anti-trafficking movement. Founded by the US activist Kathleen Barry, author of *Female Sexual Slavery*, the CATW sees all acts of prostitution as the sexual exploitation of women, in which women's bodies are treated as commodities to be bought and sold. To oppose trafficking, according to the Coalition, is to oppose prostitution, because exploitation is always involved in the sex trade. Like any commodity that is traded, be it on the open market and sanctioned by governments, or clandestinely and illegally by criminal organizations, a woman's body becomes merely a product, a sex object essentially stripped of human dignity, because prostitution is predicated on the notion that the primary function of women is to serve men's sexual needs. Thus, it is no wonder, according to the Coalition, that the trafficking of women and children is such a lucrative business globally. The CATW has endorsed the 1949 United Nations *Convention for the Suppression of Traffic in Persons and of the Exploitation of Prostitution of Others* because the aim of the convention, by equating trafficking with prostitution, is to abolish prostitution. It is a fundamental human right, according to the Coalition, to be free of sexual exploitation and prostitution is sexual exploitation.[4]

The discourse surrounding the commodification of women's bodies, moved across borders and sold, bought and traded, just like drugs and arms, is extremely compelling. It highlights what Jan Jindy Pettman calls an 'international political economy of sex' (1996: 185–207) which exposes the vulnerability of women, particularly when they are literally 'out of place' as in a foreign land and controlled by globalizing forces and the restructuring of the international political economy.

'Debt, poverty, violence and control' results in 'sex tourism that takes Australian and Japanese men to Thailand and the Philippines, and [sex trafficking] which takes poor racialized women from Southeast Asia to the brothels of Amsterdam, Tokyo or Sydney' (Pettman 1996: 207). But this is not merely a North-South phenomenon, because the movement of women from Burma to Thailand, or from Vietnam to Cambodia, or from Nepal to India for prostitution is no less disturbing. Nor are First World men the only clients in this tale of exploitation, for we see women from Eastern Europe ending up in developing countries like the Philippines, where white prostitutes are a status symbol for upper-class Filipino men. Moreover, the international exploitation of women's bodies does not stop at the brothels or the bars. Women who offer their labour abroad in domestic service, as in the case of Filipino maids in Hong Kong, Singapore, or Saudi Arabia, or who find themselves part of the international trade in wives, as in the case of Filipino 'mail-order brides' in Australia, are also frequently subjected to sexual violence (Pettman 1996: 189–95).

On the other side of the prostitution divide has stood the Global Alliance Against the Traffic in Women (GAATW). No less horrified by the widespread abuse of women, this group has worked to end the link between trafficking and prostitution by redefining trafficking. Primarily established by the Dutch-based Foundation against Trafficking in Women (STV) in 1994, the GAATW has rejected the view that prostitution is inherently a human rights issue. Initially embracing the sex workers' rights movement, the Global Alliance has looked at the problem of domestic laws, social attitudes, and out-dated practices which marginalize the lives of sex workers. It distinguishes between 'voluntary' and 'involuntary' prostitution, recognizing that a woman's right to choose sexual work, like any work, to make a living is one side of the issue. Because the 1949 UN convention was, until recently, the sole international agreement defining trafficking, one of the explicit objectives of the GAATW has been a new definition of trafficking in persons predicated on the element of force or coercion, rather than the nature of labour being performed, in order to bring out the level of human rights violations committed against women in the sex traffic. In particular, for women whom the traffickers lure into prostitution, according to the Global Alliance, the threat of arrest becomes twofold since they may be charged for both prostitution and illegal immigration. Anti-prostitution laws only fuel the activities of organized-crime syndicates because the women are working in an area that is poorly regarded, if not condemned, by law-enforcement officials and society generally. The GAATW has stated that trafficking in women does not consist of the prostitution involved, but the coercion, deception, and abuse surrounding the sex trade. For example, there are women who know that they are migrating for sex work but find themselves in exploitative, if not slavery-like, conditions; or women who think that they will be working in a factory or club but end up in a brothel. The rights of migrant women need to be protected.[5]

Jo Doezema (1999) offers a rich and compelling account of how the discourse of the contemporary anti-trafficking movement bears great similarity to the discourse of the anti-white slavery campaigns at the beginning of the twentieth century. Doezema asserts that the 'narratives of "white slavery" and "trafficking in women" function as cultural myths, constructing particular conceptions of migration for the sex industry', with the specific intent of curtailing the ability of women to move across national borders for work, particularly sex work. Underpinning these myths are both the need to control female sexuality under the guise of protecting women and the image of 'a young and naive innocent lured or deceived by evil traffickers into a life of sordid horror from which escape is nearly impossible'. According to Doezema, both narratives are predicated on the perception of women as victims, particularly victims of sexual exploitation, because no decent or 'innocent' woman who is worthy of protection would freely choose a life of prostitution. She argues that the anti-trafficking movement, like the anti-white slavery campaigns, is not concerned with the protection of women in the sex industry but with the prevention of '"innocent" women from becoming prostitutes, and keeping "dirty" foreign prostitutes from infecting the nation'. Doezema considers the CATW as the principal propagator of the dominant discourse in the anti-trafficking movement.

Although in the last decade or so there has been a movement (or counter-movement) to make a distinction between 'free' and 'forced', 'voluntary' and 'involuntary', 'chosen' and 'coerced' prostitution, as shown in the efforts of the GAATW, Doezema (1998) has argued elsewhere that the distinction between free and forced prostitution has often resulted in the protection of the rights of 'involuntary' prostitutes but not those of 'voluntary' ones. This, in the end, still leaves the rights of sex workers unprotected. Cutting the link between anti-trafficking and anti-prostitution has proved very difficult, as was evident in the negotiations leading up to the final draft on the trafficking protocol, during which both the CATW and GAATW played a part. There was a great deal of discussion and debate about what 'trafficking in persons' means. The final text, contained in Article 3 of the Protocol, states:

> 'Trafficking in Persons' shall mean the recruitment, transportation, transfer, harbouring or receipt of persons, by means of the threat or use of force or other forms of coercion, of abduction, of fraud, of deception, of the abuse of power or of a position of vulnerability or of the giving or receiving of payments or benefits to achieve the consent of a person having control over another person, for the purpose of exploitation. Exploitation shall include, at a minimum, the exploitation of the prostitution of others or other forms of sexual exploitation, forced labour or services, slavery or practices similar to slavery, servitude or the removal of organs.[6]

Both the CATW and the GAATW support the trafficking protocol and encourage all states to be signatories to it. However, in a press release on 18 October 2000, the GAATW, along with its partners calling themselves the Human Rights Caucus, pointed out that there was a 'serious gap' in the protocol, for governments are not required to provide services and protections to undocumented migrants, such as women who fall victim to traffickers. This gap came about in part because of a 'drawn-out and unnecessary debate on the definition of trafficking' in which some states and NGOs 'insisted that the trafficking be defined to include all sex work, whether voluntary or forced'. In the end, a compromise was reached on the definition: the protocol recognizes that victims of trafficking are not 'free' to consent to being sexually exploited, but it is silent as to whether prostitution is sexual exploitation.

Thus, unlike the 1949 *Convention for the Suppression of Traffic in Persons and of the Exploitation of Prostitution of Others*, the trafficking protocol does not come from an abolitionist perspective on prostitution. Canada has never signed the 1949 convention because, theoretically, prostitution is not illegal in Canada, but in practice it is. Canada criminalizes prostitution by prohibiting all forms of public communication for the purpose of prostitution (solicitation); the owning, running, or occupying of a bawdy house; and procuring or living off the avails of prostitution. The Philippines, in contrast, is a signatory to the 1949 convention, and in that country prostitution is illegal. In reality, however, the Philippines has a regulationist system, for women in the sex industry are required to undergo health checks for HIV-AIDS and other sexually transmitted diseases in government-run social-hygiene clinics. That is why women in the sex industry are not officially referred to as prostitutes but as guest-relations officers (GROs), hospitality girls, and (overseas) entertainment artists. At the same time, the differences between the Canadian system of criminalization and the Filipino system of regulation of prostitution may be more apparent than real from an enforcement perspective. Although we have witnessed Filipinos, particularly police officers, during interviews express utter surprise, if not disbelief, at Canada's anti-solicitation laws, which means that charges can be laid against johns (customers) as well as prostitutes, both Canadian and Filipino police officers agree that a prime motivation for them to enforce the prostitution law is the desire of the public to 'get rid of the problem.' The marginalization of prostitutes by the larger community is very much a cross-cultural phenomenon.

At the same time, the trafficking protocol, although recognizing that trafficking exploits and victimizes women, places the exploitation and victimization of women outside of the responsibility of states. The women are being harmed by transnational criminal organizations, and not by governments. States have found common cause in combatting transnational organized crime. The current protocol on trafficking must be placed in proper context: it is attached to a larger international convention against transnational organized crime, and states have found it easier to agree on matters dealing with international 'law and order' and the protection of national boundaries, than on human rights. As states have opened up their borders to trade liberalization and have fostered the mobility of finance and investment, they have at the same time jealously guarded the right to decide who, when, from where, and how many are allowed into their territories. Thus the mobility of people remains highly regulated in the international arena. The trafficking in women and children, according to Williams, 'can be understood as an activity where two distinct but overlapping phenomena come together—organized crime and illegal immigration' (1999b: 146). Because the role in international trafficking of transnational criminal organizations, such as the Chinese *triads*, the Japanese *yakuza* or the Russian *mafiya* (Caldwell et al. 1999; Shannon 1999; Richard 2000) has been well documented, it has made sense to attach a protocol on trafficking to a convention against transnational organized crime.

States, however, are not the sole actors in the international arena. International non-governmental organizations (NGOs) are increasingly playing a greater and greater role, not only in monitoring state actions but also in influencing interna-

tional policy (Hobe 1998). And the language of human rights infuses the work of NGOs involved in anti-trafficking efforts. Groups such as the Global Survival Network, the International Organization for Migration (IOM), the International Movement Against Racism and All Forms of Discrimination (IMADR), and Anti-Slavery International join both the CATW and the GAATW in fighting for the fundamental human rights of victims of trafficking, who are primarily women. The reason why they fight for women is clear. As plainly stated by the GAATW in its 'Human Rights Standards for the Treatment of Trafficked Persons', 'the gendered nature of trafficking derives from the universal and historical presence of laws, customs and practices that justify and promote the discriminatory treatment of women and girls and prevent the application of the entire range of human rights laws to women and girls.'

'Women's rights is about human rights' is a central tenet of the international women's movement, one that has both propelled the advancement of women, from changes in state policies to new agreements reached in the international arena. 'At the practical level, women engage in multifaceted activity [and] across the world, women's organizations have mobilized to manage local resources, to empower women and communities, and to pressure governments and international agencies on behalf of women's rights' (McMichael 2000: 264). In a special session of the United Nations General Assembly, entitled 'Women 2000: Gender Equality, Development and Peace for the Twenty-first Century' in June 2000, women pressured member states to reaffirm and implement their commitment to the Beijing Platform for Action from the 1995 Fourth World Conference on Women. The Beijing Platform takes a rights-based approach to gender equality by asserting that women's rights is about human rights. The elimination of the trafficking in women was a strategic objective as well as a set of actions under violence against women in the 1995 Platform for Action.

Although national and international agencies, particularly intelligence units and police forces, gather information and track the activities of traffickers, NGOs such as those named above have also played a vital role in gathering information and monitoring the activities of traffickers. The Global Survival Network went undercover for two years (1995–7) to examine the connections of the Russian *mafyia* with international sex trafficking (Caldwell et al. 1999), and the International Organization for Migration (1995) has tracked the exploitation of migrant women from Central and Eastern Europe. Both the CATW and the GAATW, too, have undertaken their own research into trafficking patterns, particularly in the Asia Pacific. Despite their differences as to whether opposition to trafficking must necessarily entail opposition to prostitution, NGOs are in complete agreement in helping the women. For as well as undertaking research and advocacy, they offer services, such as the provision of temporary shelter. Not only do NGOs want to stop the traffickers (which arguably is the primary focus of law enforcement agencies), but they also want to aid the victims. NGOs usually hear about the abuses and exploitative practices of organized criminal groups from those who have experienced such abuses and practices first-hand. Fundamentally, NGOs agree that these women are victims and that anti-trafficking efforts must focus on protecting their rights. NGOs point out that women need legal protections, such as witness protection, in order to testify against their captors. Women also need legal status in the country, such as temporary visas, so they do not fear immediate deportation when they report having been abused. Moreover, they need social assistance, such as shelter, food, and clothing, to free them from their dependence on their traffickers and allow them the opportunity to recover from the abuse that they have suffered. NGOs have been instrumental in preventing the international community from focusing simply on criminal prosecution and law enforcement when dealing with the issue of trafficking.[7] However, what has become evident in the trafficking protocol is that governments are encouraged to provide human rights protection to victims of trafficking in their domestic trafficking laws, but they are not mandated to do so.

Trafficking, the State, and Canadian Foreign Aid Policy

As part of its human security agenda, Canada is not only a supporter of both the UN convention against transnational organized crime and the protocol on trafficking, but also an advocate of the human rights protection of victims. Indeed, the Canadian government's Working Group on Transnational Crime distinguishes between 'smuggling' and 'trafficking', despite the common use of the terms interchangeably, in order to bring out the difference in the degree of exploitation, at least in terms of the length of time that individuals are held by their captors. According to the Canadian government, 'trafficked persons remain under the control of the trafficking organization or another organization, through the use of violence, [or] threats of violence against their families or other forms of coercion; smuggled persons are released to their own devices' (Canada, Working Group on Transnational Crime 1999). In other words, smuggling refers only to the illegality of entry by persons and the short-term abuse that they may suffer en route to their destination, but trafficking is long-term: once in the destination country, migrants continue to be abused and victimized by their traffickers in what are often slavery-like conditions.

Although the former foreign affairs minister, Lloyd Axworthy, mentions trafficking in many of his more general speeches on human security, and the DFAIT lists efforts against transnational criminal organizations along with its efforts against land mines in a special edition on human security of *Canada World View* (DFAIT 1999e), the Department of Justice, rather than DFAIT, is taking the lead on the issue of trafficking. This is primarily because the protocol is attached to the larger convention against transnational organized crime. In a speech on women in the criminal justice system in Vienna in April 2000, former justice minister, Anne McLellan (2000), focused on the issue of trafficking: 'In all countries, the message must be clear: no matter what the context—trafficking, slavery, sexual abuse or forced prostitution—violence against women is not acceptable. Both at home and within the

international community, we must continue to ensure that women's rights are recognized as human rights.' The former justice minister also emphasized that criminal justice systems must not only 'adopt strong measures to protect women against

gender-based exploitation and violence', but also ensure that they 'do not result in the further victimization of women.'

The rhetoric is very convincing, and the words are extremely clear: the Canadian government is committed to a rights-based approach in its anti-trafficking efforts. However, the implementation of this commitment is arguably fraught with difficulties, not least of which is the number of federal department and agencies involved. In addition to DFAIT and Justice are Employment and Immigration, Status of Women Canada, Human Resources Development Canada (HRDC), and the Canadian International Development Agency (CIDA). Efforts to address the rights of women who have been brought to Canada by traffickers (i.e., Canada as a 'destination' state) are not as straightforward as they first seem. For example, the police raided sixteen strip clubs in Toronto in April 2000 after it uncovered cases of abuse and exploitation by club owners of foreign women, primarily from Eastern Europe, Latin America, and Asia (Jimenez and Bell 2000). Charging the club owners with pimping and immigration offences and the women with prostitution, the police uncovered what they referred to as Canada's role in global 'sex slave trade'. The police officers recognize, however, that the Immigration Act allows foreign strippers to enter Canada if they have a job offer or contract, and that, law-enforcement officials argue, has led to the exploitation of the women. According to one of the police officers in charge of the investigation, 'Human Resources Development Canada polled bar owners and came to the conclusion that Canada is in desperate need of strippers, an occupation that cannot be filled by Canadians. . . . That's like polling drug dealers to see if we need more addicts' (Detective O'Mara, as quoted in Jimenez and Bell 2000: A2). Similar problems with Canada's immigrations laws are echoed by research reports undertaken for Status of Women Canada. It has funded four research projects, dealing with Filipino mail-order brides, sex-trade workers from Eastern Europe and the former Soviet Union, the legal framework for mail-order marriages and immigrant domestic workers, and a comprehensive profile of women who have fallen prey to traffickers in Canada or on their way to or from Canada. Most notable, recently, has been the release in November 2000 of two reports, 'Migrant Sex Workers from Eastern Europe and the Former Soviet Union: The Canadian Case' conducted by Lynn McDonald, Brooke Moore and Natalya Timoshkina of the University of Toronto's Centre for Applied Social Research, and 'Canada: The New Frontier for Filipino Mail-Order Brides' conducted by the Philippine Women Centre of BC (2000). In the latter report, the researchers argue that Canadian men marry Filipino women only to abuse and exploit them. They point out that the Filipino women's identity in Canada as mail-order bride is slowly displacing that of domestic worker. From the kind of research being done for Status of Women Canada, it may seem obvious that one way to curb the trafficking in women is to impose stricter immigration laws, but this may simply reinforce gendered constraints on migration as women, primarily from developing states, find themselves restricted further in their international movements (Doezema 1999).

Efforts to improve the rights of these women in 'source' states, a number of which are recipients of Canadian foreign aid, may also pose problems. The objectives of Canadian official development assistance (ODA) policy are found in the Liberal government's white paper on Canadian foreign policy (DFAIT 1995a).[8] Although one of the objectives of the government is to promote women in development, efforts to combat trafficking are usually found under the mandate of promoting human rights, democracy, and good governance in recipient states. The promotion of good governance, the government argues, is done through the support of capacity building and human resource development. For example, under CIDA's Southeast Asia Fund for Legal and Institutional Development (SEAFILD), Canada supports forty-seven Southeast Asian and seventeen Canadian partners in building capacity to address governance and human rights challenges in southeast Asia. One project under SEAFILD is the advocacy of regional and national initiatives against the trafficking of women and children. The objective of promoting good governance as Canadian foreign aid policy is, in some ways, problematic. Not only does it appear to be an export of Western political values, predicated as they are now on neo-liberalism, but good governance also focuses on the use of aid monies for 'improving the functioning of government'. For feminist organizations, both in Canada and in recipient states like the Philippines, efforts to strengthen the state raise a number of dilemmas.

In the quite recent past, feminists analyzing the state consistently came down to the questions of: is the state a useful tool for furthering women's rights, or is it an essential element in the development of patriarchy? Should feminists work within the state trying to make change as insiders, or should they concentrate their efforts mainly as critics outside the state? Has the state helped or hindered women in their search for social justice (Craske 1998)? Canadian feminists debated two main dilemmas for women's organizing: strategizing that was seen to be 'mainstreaming', i.e., liberal feminism, and strategies that called for 'disengagement', i.e., radical (or socialist) feminism (Adamson et al. 1988). For mainstreaming, liberal feminists, the state could provide resources for women in a welfare state, legislate equality through affirmative action and reproductive rights for women, and ensure that legal discrimination against women would end. For disengaging, radical feminists, working with the state necessarily meant being co-opted: any perceived short-term benefits would come at great cost to the long-term goals of the women's movement. The state, according to this argument, would only protect the interests of the privileged, white men (or ruling class) it really served and would co-opt any woman or woman's group working within the system.

Though feminist analyses of the state have become more nuanced in recent years, in a project dealing specifically with government organizations and NGOs, these questions are still critical. We argue that while feminist debates have become more complex, the question whether to work within the system or from outside is still front and centre in many feminist organizations and is crucial to our work in the Philippines.

Several recent feminist analyses of the state give us some hope that this debate in women's groups themselves can be de-polarized. Georgina Waylen, writing in 1998, argues that the majority of feminists still steer clear of the state because they erroneously believe that women have little influence in the state, and that there is still a danger felt by feminists about working with the state. Waylen believes that the rigid dichotomy between insider and outsider needs to be done away with and the relationship between 'structure' and 'agency' developed. In a sense, Waylen wants to reassure feminist organizers that the radical feminist view that the state acts only to uphold male interests, and the socialist feminist view that the state is primarily an instrument of the ruling class are too limited. She argues that the state is not homogeneous or unitary and that it is an important site of struggle. The state is complex, and the 'relationship to gender is evolving, dialectic and dynamic' (Waylen 1998: 7). Although the state has acted in some ways to enforce the subordination of women, it has also assisted women, so that the negative effects of the state cannot be assumed or taken for granted. The particular state form of the state must be analyzed and its effects on women debated and deconstructed. Waylen concludes that feminists must find alternative ways of organizing and use counter-strategies to constitute their interests so that 'opportunity spaces' for women's groups can be found (16). These opportunity spaces, according to Waylen, are the gaps and inconsistencies within the state that allow women's groups to create opportunities for their lobbying and organizing and, in the end, to effect change.

A very convincing example of Waylen's strategy for 'opportunity spaces' is Alexandra Dobrowolsky's recent exploration of constitutional organizing by women in Canada. Her case study illustrates that women's organizing made a difference to the constitutional wrangling of the 1980s and early 1990s. She also urges us to move beyond theorizing that treats the state and other structures as 'omnipotent and singularly oppressive' (Dobrowolsky 2000: 11). Otherwise, we leave very little room for women's activism and agency. Her example of constitutional organizing by women shows us that the insider/outsider connections need to be reforged and that women need to be active agents working both within the state and from the outside. We see that our project, discussed below, uses the sorts of opportunities described by Waylen and Dobrowolsky.

Sex Trade in the Philippines

Funded as one of the partnership programs of the Canadian International Development Agency, the University Partnerships in Cooperation and Development (UPCD) program, which is administered by the Association of Universities and Colleges in Canada (AUCC) provides opportunities for Canadian university professors to initiate and direct a development project in their research area. The UPCD program is predicated on the ability of universities to undertake capacity building and human resource development. It provides five-year funding for universities as the institutions holding the grants and is divided into Tier 1 (with total funding of about $5 million) and Tier 2 (with total funding of about $1 million).[9] In 1999, the authors were successful in obtaining Tier 2 funding for our project, entitled 'Sex Trade in the Philippines: A Multi-level Gender-Sensitive Approach to Human Resource Development.'[10] Awarded a total funding of $1.1 million from 1999 to 2004, the project is based in Angeles City, and it formally brings together two Canadian institutional partners, Saint Mary's University and

Mount Saint Vincent University, and five Filipino partners.

The immediate constraints of this type of development project are obvious. NGOs have pointed out the kinds of legal and social assistance needed to help women who have been victims of trafficking. This project, like one of the SEAFILD-funded projects discussed earlier, is predicated on helping women in a 'source' state like the Philippines by working with government organizations and NGOs; thus, meeting the objective of promoting good governance in Canadian foreign aid policy. The need to find opportunities to help the women might best be illustrated by our experience when the successful funding of the project was announced in the Halifax press. Public reactions were not wholly sympathetic to the plight of prostituted women, either in the Philippines or in Canada. For some members of the public, the matter comes down to choice: the women 'chose' to be in the sex trade and (as the logic goes) they must suffer the consequences. Interestingly enough, the response of CIDA to this type of public reaction is to emphasize that our project is also predicated on meeting CIDA's objective of poverty alleviation. Although this is not a project that gives monies directly to prostituted women in Angeles, CIDA has asserted that in attempting to change attitudes the project is helping to create the kind of policy environment that will ultimately help the women who, for reasons of poverty, end up in the sex trade in Angeles. CIDA's reaction also tells us that it likely does not want to engage in rights based discourse that would emphasize that the women are sexually exploited, but we certainly are not prevented from doing so in the project. In fact, one of our partners belongs to the Coalition Against Trafficking of Women-Asia Pacific (CATW-Asia Pacific).

Our first two partners are NGOs, Soroptimist International of Angeles City and the Women's Education, Development, Productivity and Research Organization (WEDPRO). These are clearly two very different kinds of women's groups. Soroptimist International of Angeles City is part of a national and international network of professional, mainly privileged women. Dedicated to the concept of 'women helping women', the Soroptimists are key players in Angeles. Traditionally they have raised funds and given resources to less privileged women in their community. WEDPRO, on the other hand, is a dynamic grassroots organization composed of dedicated activists and survivors of the sex trade. They have worked hard at describing the lives of prostituted women in Angeles City (and elsewhere in the Philippines). Ermelita Valdeavilla, the executive director of the National Commission on the Role of Filipino Women (NCRFW) in the office of the President of the Philippines, in giving her support to the project, specifically remarked that bringing together the Soroptimists and WEDPRO was a challenging but clearly commendable and original part of the project (Interview, Manila, Philippines, 13 December 1999).

Our third and fourth partners are government organizations, namely, the Supreme Court of the Philippines and the Philippine National Police in Angeles City. Both have important roles to play in the treatment of the women—through the enforcement of the law. The final partner is a university, Angeles University. The university is interested in developing its capacity to undertake ethnographic research and research on life-long learning, specifically to aid in its efforts to deliver literacy programs and other outreach activities to women in the sex trade in Angeles. On the Canadian side, we have also brought in additional partners, namely Stepping Stone, a Halifax organization advocating for the rights of prostitutes, and the Halifax Police. In this project, which is primarily focused on institutional capacity building, the goal is to increase the ability of the five Filipino partners to understand and alleviate the problem of prostitution in their city. Although the project is clearly not about the disbursements of aid monies directly to the prostitutes in Angeles City, we are also working directly with the prostituted women through the video project discussed below.

Because our project is based on partnerships between government agencies and NGOs, concerns about working with the state are particularly relevant. All of the women's groups that we work with, Filipino and Canadian, feel the real danger of being co-opted. With the state's increasing reliance on structural adjustment and neo-liberal economic policies generally, governments are promoting community-development projects and partnerships between government and NGOs, according to some activists, to relieve their responsibilities for social welfare and to 'privatize' services that were once provided by the state. And as Gwinnett (1998: 100) convincingly argues in her study of prostitution in Birmingham, England, state actors 'like the police reproduce and reinforce gender inequality' and 'unmask the state's supposed neutrality' in relation to prostitution. While some might believe that in working with the Philippine National Police, we are in danger of legitimizing one of the groups known to benefit from and protect the sex trade in the Philippines, we do not. Working with state actors, like the police and judges, in our assessment is the most realistic means possible to promote change for the women in Angeles. Indeed, one of our principal kindred spirits dedicated to helping prostituted women is the most senior female police officers heading the Women's Desks of the Philippine National Police in Angeles.

In addition, with the withdrawal of state services over the last decade, many Western feminists are re-evaluating their critique of the state as they see the potential and importance of the government in redistributing income to women, as well as in regulating and controlling women (Evans and Wekerle 1997; Gordon 1990). For many feminists, then, the question of whether to engage the state is now moot. 'The state must be engaged and the question now is what are the most effective strategies for empowering women in this engagement. . . . Instead of asking what impact does the state have upon gender, we are now asking how a politics based upon redressing gender power imbalances can make use of the state' (Randall 1998: 200).

How are we making use of the state? What are the opportunities that we have opened up? We are attempting to take the feminist message of WEDPRO to the community of Angeles without alienating it. We hope to train community members who have status and legitimacy within the community to be the messengers. We hope to sensitize the police and judges to the plight of prostituted women and to make them more aware of the problems of gender, generally. We hope to provide training for participatory video, bring prostituted women together, and contribute to participatory communication through the video project.

We recognize that these goals are highly ambitious and fraught with ethical dilemmas. As feminists have often pointed out, there are many such dilemmas in dealing with a state-sponsored, cross-cultural project like this one (Ribbens and Edwards 1998; Wolf 1996; Gluck and Patai 1993). Several of the problems we have encountered already have to do with coalition building, control over the project, appropriation of voice, whose voices should be heard, and informed consent.

The problems of building a coalition have been well documented (Dobrowolsky 2000; Philips 1998; Mohanty, Russo, and Torres 1991; Adamson et al. 1988). Women's groups are particularly prone to conflict because of different ideologies, different goals, and different strategies. In our project we are working with several quite disparate groups: government organizations like the judiciary and police, and NGOs, like the Soroptimists and WEDPRO. We are bringing together groups that have historically, and with good reason, been suspicious of each other. It means working out the problems our grassroots partner has with a government group, i.e., the police, that they feel contributes directly to the problem, and reassuring them that we are not being used by the police for legitimization. On the other hand, it means reassuring the police and judiciary that we are not too radical and that we understand their position as state agencies.

The relations between NGOs are problematic, as well. We are working with very different grassroots groups who come to the project with different class backgrounds, different ideas about prostitution, and different levels of awareness of gender discrimination. We try to acknowledge the differences and pave the way for co-operation between the two groups; at the same time, we see the tensions between them and always ask ourselves: is this alliance helping or making the situation worse? In the end, it is only through collaboration in this and similar projects that the situation of prostituted women will be improved. By working together, we are creating alliances between the women's groups, and they are working together for the first time. The particular strengths and resources of each group are being shared with the others, and consequently, it is possible to overcome the suspicions between groups and the barriers between the classes.

The second main ethical issue that we have encountered is power and control over the project itself. Working within the CIDA guidelines is not always easy or desirable. This particular funding is primarily for training and capacity building for organizations, not for operations or equipment. In a developing nation like the Philippines, this has obvious constraints. NGOs are chronically underfunded, and they scramble from project to project to keep themselves afloat. They would prefer that the money go to pay staff salaries and overheads. Government departments and agencies fare little better. It was tempting, for example, when we saw the condition of the social hygiene clinic in Angeles for the first time, to give the money directly to the clinic for proper equipment, facilities, and medicines. This obviously was not possible.

Although we recognize these problems, we have, wherever possible, tried to circumvent the constraints of the project. For instance, although we are restricted by our funding arrangements in how we spend the money, we recognize that structurally we are supposed to have power over our partners and the distribution of the funds. We have tried to share power with our Filipino partners as much as possible by having a management committee made up of two Canadians and two Filipinos.

We recognize our power as Western academics and have tried to weaken it as much as possible by acknowledging and using the expertise of the members of the groups we are working with, and by giving voice to the most marginalized groups.

Another restriction on the project is that there are supposed to be only limited official benefits to Canadians. Though money cannot be given directly to organizations in Canada, we are including the Canadian women's group that is dealing with prostitution in Halifax in any training we do for the Filipino partners. Stepping Stone will be able to participate in workshops on research methodology, program evaluation, and participatory video. We hope that members of the group will be able to travel to the Philippines as well to observe the Filipino women's organizations at work. We are incorporating the training for Stepping Stone, therefore, as a by-product of the training for WEDPRO.

We have also struggled with the problems of ethnocentrism versus cultural relativism. We are working hard not to impose our values on the project and make judgements about the situation in the Philippines from the point of view of our Western, feminist notions of the oppression of women. Alternatively, we try not to be too uncritical in some cases by letting comments, problems and other situations pass because 'it's the culture.' Other dilemmas include the ethics of appropriation of voice for our own ends. We are in essence appropriating WEDPRO's research work for our project, and even though we support its content and want it to be transmitted in more favourable ways to the community, we are also conscious of the problems for WEDPRO if their message is used against them. Our Canadian grassroots partners also worry about having their messages used in ways that hinder their work, and we try always to be aware of how and to whom the information is being used and transmitted. For example, one of our Canadian organizational partners, after working rather unsuccessfully with the Canadian police on an awareness campaign, found itself referred to in the police public relations literature as a shining example of the police department's community-development work.

In a project of this sort, we also have to be careful not to exploit further the most disadvantaged people in the project—the prostituted women. Though we use the principles of informed consent in talking to the women and in the video project, there is exploitation inherent in the video process and in disclosing the women's identities that go beyond the traditional ethical dilemmas in doing research on human subjects. We will guarantee the women's safety by making sure that they are fully aware of what they are participating in and of the possible consequences of participating, and will ensure that there is a benefit to them. We continue to grapple with these questions and will do so as the project continues.

Finally, we try to subvert our power by attempting to politicize the project. Consciousness raising is a crucial part of this project, and we hope to raise the consciousness of many members of the Angeles community: judges, police, local government, local community groups, and specific women's groups dealing with prostitution in Angeles. Our emphasis on community education will raise these issues in schools, universities, and the media. Our participatory video work, discussed below, will be of particular importance in this process.[11]

Participatory Video

Participatory video was designed over twenty-five years ago as a consciousness-raising and educational tool to allow marginalized people to speak for themselves and help with grassroots organizing (Stuart and Bery 1995: 198–9). The video, which was planned, produced, and used by local people, reflects important community issues back to the community, builds confidence in the participants, and informs outsiders about local issues. It helps to project the viewpoints about social issues of the most disadvantaged citizens in a society. It helps to point out the reasons why the poor or marginalized are in the situation in which they find themselves, and it helps raise people's consciousness.

There are several steps in participatory video (Slocum et al. 1995). In pre-production, the participants learn to operate the equipment in workshops that help them get to know one another and build their confidence. They plan the production and decide what format the video will be, what issues will be addressed, how the message will be delivered, and who the intended audience will be. They decide whether the issues will be dramatized or if an interview format will be used. In the production phase, participants go out into the community and do the actual filming, interviews, or re-enactments. Again, this process builds confidence in their own abilities and creates bonds between the participants.

The post-production work is, in many ways, the most important for organizing work. Seeing themselves and their situations on a video screen changes the perspectives of many participants. It reflects their problems and situations back to them and inspires social change by showing them and others that their problems are not simply individual problems but issues shared by many in a community. From being isolated the participants come to see themselves as a unified group. The participants then show the program to their peers and other members of the community. The playback stimulates discussion, inspires other people to organize to change their situations, and helps participants become good communicators and leaders in their communities (Stuart and Bery 1995).

We hope that the participatory video process in this project will stimulate similar responses in both the participants who made the video, and in the community itself. The prostituted women will gain technical and organizational skills, as well as the chance to describe the problems they have with bar owners, customers, middle-class 'helpers', and each other. We are using elements of the 'theatre of the oppressed', here as well as participatory video in the hope that the process will help the women to come up with explanations and solutions for the problems as they see them (Boal 1979; 1992). The community will benefit by seeing themselves through the eyes of the women they are trying to help or condemn. It is hoped that the community will gain some understanding of the difficulties facing the women and find out exactly how they can be of help. The participatory video will be a crucial part of our educational and consciousness-raising work.

Concluding Comments

This chapter has described the discursive, ideological, and ethical dilemmas faced by feminists, particularly ourselves, in taking an international and foreign policy issue like trafficking and combining it with practical development work involving real people. The Canadian government has taken a stand against the trafficking in people, particularly women and children, but its many departments (DFAIT, Justice, Employment and Immigration, Status of Women, HRDC, and CIDA) sometimes work at cross-purposes or, indeed, not really at all to alleviate, if not eliminate, the victimization of these women, particularly for purposes of prostitution.

The exploitation of women in the sex industry is a very real issue with very real consequences, but exploitation comes in many forms and different degrees: international traffickers are obvious exploiters; states, too, either deliberately or inadvertently, are culprits; and perhaps even do-good Canadian feminist academics are not wholly innocent. CIDA policy has provided an opening for us to become involved in an issue and in a place with committed organizations where the lives of women in the sex trade are only too real. Grounding theory in practice is a staple of feminist theorizing, for the everyday experiences of women should inform the theoretical, but it also raises enormous problems. We are trying to grapple with these problems and bridge the gap between theory and practice. We hope that this project will be an example of simultaneously working within the state and working from outside to effect change and to reclaim women's opportunity spaces. While we recognize the danger of co-optation and are aware that there will always be unintended consequences of working with the state and always the possibility of the 'appearance of change while structures are being reinforced' (Crosby, Chap. 7, this volume), we nevertheless believe that the state provides us with some opportunities for subverting its coercive power and for giving space to women. The openings in Canadian development assistance policy have been created by the funding of overseas partnerships led by Canadian universities, and although in many ways such moves by CIDA can be criticized as the further retrenchment of the state leading to the coopting of groups within society, opportunity spaces are evident. We hope that these 'spaces' will eventually make a difference in the lives of women in the sex trade in Angeles City in the Philippines.

Notes

1. The term would be a familiar one because it is the title of a 'classic' text on prostitution by Kathleen Barry (1979). Barry founded the international Coalition Against the Trafficking of Women, an organization which we discuss later in the chapter.
2. The United Nations is not the only body dealing with this issue. Many regional organizations, both in the Asia Pacific and Europe, have been working on the trafficking problem. Indeed, parts of the analysis and many insights of this paper on trafficking are taken from Edna Keeble's involvement in the meeting of the Working Group on Transnational Crime of the Council on Security and Cooperation in the Asia Pacific (CSCAP) in Sydney, Australia, in November 1999. CSCAP undertakes 'track-two' activities (i.e., at the level of academics, researchers, and policy-makers in their personal capacities) in conjunction with the 'track-one' activities (i.e., undertakings at the gov-

ernment-to-government level) of the ASEAN Regional Forum (ARF). The discussion on trafficking at the Sydney meeting was led by Anne Gallagher, then the UN Trafficking Adviser to the Human Rights High Commissioner, Mary Robinson.

3. There are three protocols supplementing the UN convention against transnational organized crime. In addition to the protocol on trafficking, there are protocols dealing with the smuggling of migrants and with the illicit manufacturing of and trafficking in firearms. Canada drafted the protocol on firearms manufacturing and trafficking which became the basis for negotiations. In December 2000 the larger convention against transnational organized crime and the two protocols on trafficking and smuggling were opened for signatures by states, but the protocol on firearms was still being negotiated.
4. The Coalition Against the Trafficking of Women (CATW) is an important actor in this issue, both in the international arena, particularly in the United Nations, where it has Category II Consultative Status in the Economic and Social Council (ECOSOC), and in regions like the Asia Pacific. Indeed, CATW-Asia Pacific is based in Manila, Philippines; its members are some of the more prominent feminist advocates in the region. We have met with members of the CATW as part of our work in the Philippines. See <www.catwinternational.org>, the home site of the CATW, which contains a library of resources, including research reports, statements, and other documents. For CATW-Asia Pacific, see <www. catw-ap.org>, which also contains a number of publications and papers specific to the region.
5. The Global Alliance Against the Traffic of Women is also an important actor and has allied itself with the International Human Rights Law Group. Based in Bangkok, Thailand, it seeks to place anti-trafficking efforts in the larger context of protecting the human rights of migrant women. See <www.inet.co.th/org/gaatw>, the home site of the GAATW; contained on it are links, updates, and research reports, including its 'Human Rights Standards for the Treatment of Trafficked Persons and Recommendations'. In the last year or two, the GAATW has been less emphatic in its support of sex workers' rights and has been concentrating more on the protection of human rights of migrant women (including those who may migrate for sex work). However, it still subscribes to distinctions between 'free' and 'forced' prostitution, as was evident in its reaction to the final draft of the UN trafficking protocol. As part of the Human Rights Caucus, the GAATW issued a press release, 'UN Trafficking Protocol: Lost Opportunity to Protect the Rights of Trafficked Persons' on 18 October 2000. The press release is found on its site, and we discuss it later in this chapter to bring out the continuing differences in how trafficking is defined by the GAATW and CATW.
6. See *Protocol to Prevent, Suppress and Punish Trafficking in Persons, Especially Women and Children*, Supplementing the United Nations *Convention against Transnational Organized Crime* (2000).
7. Crucial to these efforts, of course, has been the aid of other UN agencies, like the Office of the High Commissioner on Human Rights.
8. As many have argued, one of the principal objectives of the Liberal government in its foreign policy paper was to ensure that Canada's aid policy was subsumed under its foreign policy, and that CIDA was subsumed under DFAIT (see Morrison 1998: 380–424). Clearly, the human security agenda is predicated on many international-development issues.
9. Although AUCC helps to administer the competition for Tier 1 grants, the grant holders report directly to CIDA whereas Tier 2 grant holders report to AUCC.
10. This is by no means an effort we have undertaken alone. We are indebted to the kind of institutional support provided by both Saint Mary's University and Mount Saint Vincent University. In addition, the project manager, Maureen Woodhouse, International Activities at Saint Mary's, is indispensable; as are the rest of our Canadian partners: Dr

Charles Beaupré, Professor Richard Devlin, Justice Donna Hackett, Judge William Grant, Ms Fran MacIntyre, Dr Stephen Perrott, and Dr Veronica Stinson.

11. The importance of video in our project attests to our commitment to producing a work that goes beyond the written word. WEDPRO, one of our Filipino partners, has already been involved in producing videos and plays about global trafficking through a Belgium-funded project. Meredith Ralston has already directed or co-produced two National Film Board films: *Why Women Run*, a film about the 1997 federal election race between Mary Clancy and Alexa McDonough, and *Wendy Lill: Playwright in Parliament*, a film about Wendy Lill, Member of Parliament for Dartmouth.

Chapter 11

The Contradictions of Canadian Commitments to Refugee Women

Erin K. Baines

> Canada is the envy of the Western world when it comes to their refugee determination system. Canada can be proud that they have been a world leader in their recognition of gender persecution. (Kelson 1999)

> The [Canadian] Guidelines on Women Refugee Claimants . . . direct that women forced to flee their countries of origin because they suffered domestic violence . . . can be found to be refugees. . . . These women face violence amounting to persecution because of their particular vulnerability as women in their societies, and because they are not protected by the state. In this area, the Guidelines have taken on an international leadership role.
>
> –*Judge Nurjehan Mawani, Chairperson, Immigration and Refugee Board of Canada, 1995*

> As another woman is murdered by her spouse, women and children agonize and weep across Canada. Gillian Hadley was a mother, a sister, a daughter who tried so hard to ensure safety for her children and herself. Her last courageous effort was to save her baby! This is not an isolated case, in fact this is the all too bizarre truth that has fallen on deaf ears. The murder in Montreal in a women's shelter, the murder of May-Illes, Gillian Hadley's murder, and the countless others, speak volumes about the failure to treat violence against women and children as a priority.
>
> –*National Action Committee on the Status of Women Canada, press release, Toronto, 23 June 2000.*

On International Women's Day in March 1993, the Immigration and Refugee Board (IRB) released the *Guidelines on Women Refugee Claimants Fearing Gender-Related Persecution*, making Canada the first country in the world to formally recognize asylum claims on this basis. The ideas upheld in the Guidelines challenge the historical separation of public and private in the 1951 Refugee Convention, politicize gender-specific forms of persecution that were once thought to be 'personal', and assert the state's responsibility to protect women, or men, in these instances. The Guidelines build upon prior Canadian efforts to protect refugee women, such as the active role Canada has played in promoting gender awareness of protection issues globally, and a special project begun in 1989 to fast track 'women at risk' in refugee camps through the overseas asylum process. Collectively, these efforts represent a noteworthy attempt to recognize the specificity of women's experiences of refuge, which may include domestic abuse, forced abortion, dowry deaths, and sexual violence, including rape. That a significant number of countries, such as the United States, Australia, and South Africa, have since followed the Canadian example indeed lends to the prestigious label of 'world leader' in the recognition of gender-related persecution.

Yet as the opening quotations of this paper reveal, a number of factors belie Canadian efforts to extend protection to refugee women. First, the Canadian government has responded to an escalating worldwide refugee crisis by invoking new policies and practices that restrict access to the Canadian asylum system. As the Canadian government has taken steps to open the door to gender related claims, a series of restrictive measures—such as detention—were adopted during the 1990s to limit refugee access. Second, while specific measures such as the Guidelines and the Women at Risk program seek to manoeuvre individual women through a gender-biased system, the number of women gaining access is minimal. This suggests that while the Guidelines are an important symbol, they do not result in equality of access for refugee women and men. Third, while the Guidelines challenge the division between public and private, they produce new distinctions—between 'refugee-producing' states and 'refugee-receiving' states, between First- and Third-World women; in doing so, they ignore the similarities in their experiences of violence that leads to persecution, as the example of Gillian Hadley reminds us. This leads to a final contradiction: that claims to leadership on gender equality globally are dubious given the relative inability of the Canadian state to protect women from violence and persecution at home.

This chapter applies gender analysis to Canadian refugee policies in the 1990s to make feminist sense of these contradictions, and what they imply for refugee women. It takes as a starting point the global political context in which the seemingly paradoxical liberal pursuit (Gibson 2001) of extending asylum to respect principles of human rights is twinned with the closing of borders to protect national security interests. It then asks why the Canadian government recognized gender persecution when it did, and suggests that an investigation of that question provides important insights into how the Guidelines and complementary Women at Risk program are in fact 'productive' of socio-political relations within Canadian borders and beyond, relations that are at once gendered and class- and race-based. The chapter concludes that, albeit perhaps unintentionally, Canadian approaches to the protection of refugee women may in fact contribute to domestic and global asylum trends compromising the rights of refugees at the onset of the new millennium by (re)producing binaries of 'us' and 'them'. Here, the 'productivity' of the contradictions arising from the Guidelines are discussed, and the pertinence of applying gender analysis to Canadian foreign policy becomes apparent.[1]

International Perspectives: The Changing Nature of Refugee Protection in the Post–Cold War Era

The end of the Cold War led to dramatic new intrastate conflicts and, as a result, mass displacements of people. Indeed, the scale and scope of recent conflicts and refugee movements are startling: of the 22 million people killed in armed conflict since 1945, one-quarter perished between 1990 and1995 alone; and of this number, between 75 and 90 per cent were civilians (Chopra 1998: 1). Mutilation, torture, and rape of civilians are haunting characteristics of 'modern' warfare. And as the scale of atrocities peak, people flee *en masse*: tens of thousands of Kurds fled the scourge of biological warfare in Iraq; millions of Rwandans crossed the border in the wake of a genocide that killed 800,000 people; and, millions more have been displaced by ethnic cleansing in the former Yugoslavia. In the last decade of the twentieth century[2] alone, up to 42 million people were displaced by the scourge of war (Feldman 2000). In short, the movement of people since the late twentieth century has been unprecedented in recent history:

> Large scale movements of refugees and other forced migrants have become a defining characteristic of the contemporary world. At few times in recent history have such large numbers of people in so many parts of the globe been obliged to leave their own countries and communities to seek safety elsewhere. Never before has the issue of mass population displacement gained such a prominent position on the agenda of the United Nations and its member states. (UNHCR 1995: 11)

Western and other 'receiving' states are increasingly inclined to regard population displacements as threats to national, regional, or international security (Hammerstad 2000; Mills 1997). Receiving states have taken a series of restrictive asylum measures to prevent a mass influx of refugees (UNHCR 1997: 68). Direct measures include turning asylum seekers away at border crossings or detaining them once inside the receiving country (Mertus 1998: 337). Western states have placed pressure on international organizations such as the United Nations to prevent displacement from occurring in the first place or, when it does, to encourage repatriation. In the late 1980s, Western states began to invest heavily in international organizations[3] such as the United Nations High Commissioner for Refugees (UNHCR) and non-governmental organizations (NGOs) such as the International Committee of the Red Cross (ICRC) in order to contain refugee flows through a series of measures (Lambert 1997: 12; Mertus 1998: 330).[4] Thus by the mid-1990s, UNHCR had more than doubled its staff and budget (Hyndman 1997: 7).

Donor interests in 'preventative protection'—what Jennifer Hyndman (1997) calls the policy of keeping refugees 'over there'—has expanded UNHCR's mandate significantly (UNHCR 1995: 80 and 153–6; see also Newland and Meyers 1999: 17). Whereas UNHCR once worked only outside of the countries producing refugees, they now increasingly work inside in an effort to prevent forced displacement. Because displacement is very often the strategy of a warring faction, the international community has taken the position that to grant asylum or assist in flight is to assist such a strategy. Thus 'containment' of population displacements, or preventing such displacements from spilling across borders in the first place, shifts the responsibility for protecting refugees to the refugee-producing state. Preventing flight is thus a 'proactive' measure to protecting refugees. Yet as Chimni also notes, 'contemporary international refugee policy ... is principally articulated by developed countries to contain and manage the global refugee problem in the light of their interests' (1993: 443). These interests have involved UNHCR, as well as other humanitarian agencies inside zones of conflict, in an effort to thwart population displacements. This global shift in approach to refugees is manifest in three principle ways.

The first is the creation of protectorate zones inside countries of conflict in which UNHCR's main objective has been to bring 'safety to people, not people to safety' (UNHCR 1995: 30). An earlier example was in Iraq in the late 1980s, when UNHCR entered Northern Iraq to provide assistance to Kurdish refugees in 'safe zones'—zones that were considered to be under the protection of the international community (Mills 1997: 394–6). This strategy was repeated later in Somalia, with the creation of 'safe corridors' to provide assistance to populations caught between warring factions; in Bosnia-Herzegovina, where assistance was airlifted for eighteen months to people in UN declared 'safe zones'; and in Afghanistan, where 'zones of tranquility' were established for returning refugees.

A second manifestation of a containment strategy is the use of 'temporary solutions.' These include short-term camps with restrictions on mobility and employment, created in areas such as Northern Iraq and along the border between Somalia and Kenya. During the Kosovo crisis in 1999, UNHCR assisted in the 'temporary resettlement' of hundreds of thousands to European countries; the majority were expected to return after NATO bombing had ceased.

A third manifestation of the containment strategy is the adoption of a broader definition of persons for which UNHCR is responsible. Increasingly, UNHCR is requested to work with internally displaced persons (IDPs), when there is no international convention exists to protect their rights nor any international organization to assist them (Cohen and Deng 1998). During the Cold War, UNHCR had only limited involvement with IDPs. Today, it works to assist between 20 and 25 per cent of the world's IDPs (Cohen and Deng 1998: 129). Of the 22.3 million people under UNHCR care in January 1999, 7.5 million were IDPs (along with 11.5 million refugees, 1.9 million returnees, and 1.3 million asylum seekers) (UNHCR 2000).

In short, UNHCR's new directions strive to prevent population displacements from occurring in the first place. Furthermore, UNHCR now emphasizes the right to return over the right to asylum. In this sense, 'temporary solutions' are intended to uphold this right, and states producing refugee populations are held responsible for creating 'the conditions which allow refugees to return to their homeland' (UNHCR 1995: 43). The solution now favoured by the UN in the post–Cold War era has shifted decisively from resettlement to repatriation.

This section sets the global stage in which the Canadian government formulates and implements foreign policies on refugee rights. The next section illustrates Canada's position on refugees in general, and refugee women in particular, vis-à-vis global events and evolving norms, manifest in the formulation of refugee policy and in the participation of the Canadian International Development Agency (CIDA), Citizenship and Immigration Canada (CIC), and the Department of Foreign Affairs and International Trade (DFAIT) in international forums and mechanisms such as UNHCR. It details how such government bodies respond to changes in the international and domestic environments that relate to a growing desire to keep refugees 'over there'.

Backlash and Border Security: Restrictive Asylum Policies and Practices in Canada

The Canadian government has long been proud of its humanitarian reputation (see Chapter 3, this volume) for having, among other things, a comparatively generous refugee policy, which resulted in the prestigious award of the Nansen Medal in 1986. However, this generosity has been infused with concern over political legitimacy and security, evidenced in changing foreign policy statements about refugees and security. For instance, DFAIT (2000b) relates forced displacement to Canadian interests in security and stability:

> Concepts of state security have evolved to recognize that human security must include an explicit recognition of global interdependence. In an interdependent world, refugee movements and other mass migrations of people are activities which engage Canada's longstanding humanitarian tradition to assist those in need of protection and asylum. Such movements are also often challenges to regional and global political stability and may well affect Canada's broader security interests.
>
> Migration is an extremely complex phenomenon which involves economic, social, demographic and political factors. Decisions to migrate may be voluntary or involuntary as in the case of refugees. For the latter group, the problem of forced displacement has become more complex and geographically more widespread. Refugee movements and other forms of mass migration have assumed a greater degree of political importance due to their impact upon national and regional stability. As the promotion of global peace as a key to protecting our security remains a central element of Canadian foreign policy, threats to peace involving mass migrations across borders are a concern.

Both DFAIT and CIDA have begun to invest in post-conflict peace building in countries where displacement has been greatest. In 1997 CIDA set up a $10 million annual Peacebuilding Initiative, which funds small-scale projects to promote stability and sustainability of local (including returnee) communities in such countries. In DFAIT, the Peacebuilding and Human Security Unit works to strengthen multilateral institutions after conflicts to reinforce international legal and humanitarian norms, such as the *Convention on the Prohibition of the Use, Stockpiling, Production and Transfer of Anti-personnel Mines and their Destruction*.

This trend in Canadian foreign policy must be read in relation to a backlash against refugees arriving in Canada during the 1990s, and subsequent efforts of the Canadian government to restrict asylum. This backlash is perhaps best symbolized by the experience of several hundred Chinese asylum seekers who arrived at British Columbian ports in August 1999. Their arrival was greeted with anger by a segment of the Canadian public, who opposed their applications for asylum on the grounds that they were false claims. This opposition was in part fuelled by fresh memories of Algerian asylum seekers caught some months before crossing into British Columbia with a carload of explosives. The incident led one US official to call Canada a 'Club Med for terrorists' with the implication that Canada's border control was 'soft' (Wilkinson 2000: 6). In this vein, a small but vocal number of Canadians asserted that the Chinese asylum seekers were 'bogus refugees', 'invading' Canada though the same lax asylum system that let in terrorists (Citizens for Public Justice, 1999). Immigration critic Léon Benoît even went so far as to argue that the refugees posed a physical risk to Canadians because of 'increased health risks from diseases like tuberculosis and AIDS' (quoted in Bradley 1999).

Such sentiments were first expressed by the Reform Party of Canada in Parliament in 1994, kicking off a series of national consultations to investigate the charge and submit changes to legislation. These consultations eventually led to the proposed Immigration and Refugee Protection Act brought before Parliament in 2000 (Bill C-31). The Act under consideration conveniently draws upon the 'image of Third World gatecrashers' to 'fortify immigration barriers, and public opinion, against them' (Mottram and Lague 1999; Wilkinson 2000: 6). Bill C-31 speaks of closing the 'back door to those who would abuse the system' while keeping the front door open to 'deserving' people alone (CIC 2000). Measures to 'close the back door' include severe penalties for people smugglers (such as a million dollar fine and a prison term), up-front security checks of all refugees upon arrival in Canada. and 'crack-downs' on improperly documented travellers. The IRB—considered too liberal by some in the past—have cut acceptance rates significantly in recent years from 75 per cent in the early 1990s to 45 per cent in 2000 (Wilkinson 2000: 9). At the same time, and in one of the first such cases in recent history, Fujian asylum seekers were detained in northern British Columbia. Subsequently a number of these refugee claimants were forcibly returned to China, and UNHCR has investigated the living conditions of those remaining in detention.

In addition to this proposed legislation, Canada has taken a series of steps to limit the movement of refugees into Canada. These include economic penalties for carriers of asylum seekers (ships, airlines, etc.), visa requirements, and greater powers for border guards to turn away suspect asylum seekers (see Hyndman 1996).[5] Bill C-31 affirms the power of overseas border guards to make decisions on asylum claims regarding eligibility, thus bypassing traditional processes of asylum that require 'experts' to review files. CIC has placed immigration officials in certain cities abroad to detect 'bogus' refugees before they leave for Canada. Judith Kumin of UNHCR-Ottawa fears such measures will impose further barriers to refugees trying to enter the asylum system (in Wilkinson 2000: 10).

In 1996, Canada and the United States entertained the idea of establishing a 'safe third' country of asylum system; that is, refugees would be forced to return to their first country of asylum if it was deemed 'safe'. Canada has also attempted to dissuade refugees from arriving at their borders by reducing the social services extended to them here (Mertus 1998: 338). Emphasis has been placed on streamlining the asylum process: for example, the processing time for applicants was cut from 13 months to 9.3 months in 1998, with a stated goal of reduction to six months (Wilkinson 2000: 9). Proposed changes also include moving from multi-person panels for hearing asylum claims to single person panels. Both measures will place greater strain on refugees to prove their case and may compromise their right to a fair hearing.

The gender roles of women create additional barriers in this increasingly restrictive environment. Although women, together with their children, make up 75 to 80 per cent of any given refugee population (Connors 1997: 116–17; Tesfay Musa 1993; UNHCR Statistics)[6], two-thirds of all asylum applicants in Canada are men (CIC 1998). Refugee women may find it more difficult to travel because of unequal access to education and paid work, the demands of caring for children, and the economic costs of entering a country. Moreover in Canada, refugees are obliged to meet a set of eligibility criteria based on public-sphere experiences such as work experience, language, or education. Such criteria overlook private-sphere skills that women may bring to Canada, such as survivor skills or the ability to provide for children and elderly relatives (Boyd 1993). As a result, more women than men enter Canada as 'dependants' of refugees, making men the principal asylum claimant (CIC 1998). For those reasons, the proposed changes in Bill C-36 have a differential impact on men and women that requires urgent attention (NAWL 1999b).

The Canadian backlash against refugees also had the support of anti-feminist refugee advocates who argue that the Guidelines and Women at Risk Program are a form of reverse discrimination, and that they even threaten the security of Canadians. As the Guidelines were debated, segments of the Canadian media described a potential 'flood' of asylum seekers, and claimed that the guidelines were akin to 'Inviting in Two Billion Refugees.' In years to follow, Léon Benoît has accused the Women at Risk (AWR) program of representing a violation of the rights of male asylum seekers: 'As recent events in Kosovo illustrate painfully, it is men who are most likely to be interned, tortured, forced into battle against their will, or killed for no other reason than their sex' (Benoît 1999). It is women, children, and the elderly who fill refugee camps. This position received attention in the national media (Mathias 1999; Jones 1999) when two scholars filed a complaint with the Human Rights Commission. In a bizarre twist of logic, they charged that the current refugee system denied access to men because it was too busy helping women:[7] 'The Immigration and Refugee Board has spent years focusing especially on helping women and is totally ignoring the kind of persecution that men are undergoing around the world.' This argument overlooks the fact that the Convention on Refugees (among other international legal instruments) was designed to protect refugees—men or women—in such instances and that the failure of protection is attributable to states and warring factions that fail to abide by, or enforce, this norm and not to a feminist conspiracy.

Given the increasing hostility to refugees and, especially, to feminism,[8] the following section examines why the Canadian government adopted the Guidelines on Refugee Women in the first place, seemingly to open the door to new asylum seekers and in recognition of women's experiences. It suggests that the evolution of feminist activism and legal critiques of norms on women's rights pressured the Canadian government to adopt this position, and so it first examines the content of feminist claims on the subject.

Canadian Commitments to Refugee Women and Gender-Related Persecution

The specific, gender-related need for protection by refugee women was first acknowledged at a global level in the Copenhagen World Conference on Women in 1980, although this recognition was largely symbolic and led to few changes in practice (Baines 2000). Over the following decade and a half, feminist legal scholars advanced the argument that the *International Convention on Refugees* (1959) was in fact biased in favour of men. The Convention defines a refugee as any person who, 'by reason of a well-founded fear of persecution for reasons of race, religion, nationality, membership in a particular social group or political opinion, is outside the country of the person's nationality and is unable, or by reason of fear, is unwilling to avail himself of the protection of that country' (Immigration Act, RSC 1985, c. I-2, s. 2(1)). Therefore, there are three essential requirements: to demonstrate a well-founded fear of persecution, to connect persecution to one of the five Convention grounds, and to establish a connection to the state's refusal or inability to extend protection.

Feminist critiques of refugee law (Adjin-Tettey 1997; Indra 1987; 1989; Castel 1992; Cipriani 1993; Greatbach 1989; Kelly 1993a and b) argued that the Convention definition is based on 'public sphere' forms of persecution, and as a result, fail to address gender-related forms of persecution traditionally associated with the 'private sphere'. For example, sexual violence and rape are sometimes the cause of flight for refugee women and, where the state is unwilling to protect women against these forms of gender persecution, it is argued that asylum should be extended (Castel 1992). Historically, because of the the public/private divide prevalent in liberal interpretations of the Refugee Convention, gender persecution—often perpetrated by individuals—has been viewed as 'too personal' and therefore not connected to either sufficient grounds or the state. This view has been upheld even in instances where the state is the direct perpetrator—such as soldiers committing rape in times of war or peace.

> First, the motivation for rape is sometimes characterized as 'sexual attraction', which does not fall within any of the five grounds. As such, the crime is understood as 'personal harm'. Second, the phenomenon of mass rape is often characterized as generalized and indiscriminate, such that an individual survivor cannot show that she was 'singled out' for such persecution for a Convention reason. In other words, the persecution is either too 'personal' or not 'personal' enough. (Macklin 1997: 5)

Feminist critiques of refugee law assert that a connection can be made between state complicity and so-called personal forms of violence when a state refuses to protect women from gender-related persecution.

Feminist legal arguments politicize private sphere forms of persecution, 'gendering' the grounds, and highlighting the relationship between the state and domestic sphere. 'Gender related persecution' is a broad term used to encapsulate the dynamics of the Refugee Convention. It involves instances where a woman is persecuted *as* a woman (through vaginal rape, forced sterilization, or forced abortion), in addition to instances when a woman is persecuted *because* she is a woman (such as holding a feminist view or refusing to adhere to a restrictive social norm based on her gender) (Connors 1997: 120–3; Macklin 1997: 2). A woman can be persecuted *as* a woman on any one of the Convention grounds. However, the Convention does not hold gender as a particular ground, and so as historically interpreted, does not adequately provide protection for women fleeing persecution *because* of their gender.[9]

While legal scholars were reconceptualizing the Convention from a gender perspective, advocates worked to raise the awareness of states and international organizations on women's experiences of exile. Transnational advocates working with and on behalf of refugee women (largely relief workers in humanitarian agencies) organized a series of panels and workshops for the World Conference on Women, held in Nairobi, Kenya, in 1985. Testimonials were presented, as was documented information on the plight of women refugees. These activities aroused a great deal of interest among national delegations of non-governmental organizations (NGOs), and national advocacy networks began to form around the issue of refugee women soon after (Spencer-Nimmons 1994a).

In Canada, a number of informal meetings of interested women's groups were held under the umbrella of the National Action Committee on the Status of Women (NAC) and refugee rights organizations associated with the Canadian Council for Refugees (CCR), to discuss concerns raised at the Nairobi Conference (Kuttner 1997). In 1985, a more formal meeting was held in consultation with government officials interested in the issue, out of which a Working Group for Refugee Women was formed. Within the largest Canadian refugee advocacy group, the Canadian Council for Refugees (CCR), an Ad Hoc Working Group was also formed in May 1986 to 'sensitize policy makers at the national and international level to the needs of refugee women' (CCR quoted in Spencer-Nimmons 1994a: 256). A year later, the Working Group joined CCR as an official subgroup of CCR, consolidating campaigns around the issue.

Canadian advocacy groups frequently liaised with sympathetic staff of relevant government bodies.[10] An IRB working group on refugee women was created in 1990, with members from both IRB and the non-governmental community (Liebich and Ramirez 1996: 102). In the same year, the United Nations High Commissioner for Refugees (UNHCR) released a compelling statement on the protection of refugee women, which suggested that equal treatment of men and women may require special actions for women (Executive Committee 1990). Shortly thereafter, UNHCR called upon states to do more to guide refugee women at risk through asylum systems, appealing in particular to Western states such as Canada to take the lead (Mawami 1993a: 65–7).

The emerging partnership between Canadian feminist advocates and key lawyers within IRB culminated on the heels of a public outcry over a controversial IRB decision that had denied asylum to 'Nada', a Saudi Arabian women seeking safe haven. Nada's refusal to adhere to the religious norms expected of women in her country had led to persecution: she refused to wear a veil in public or travel at all times in the company of a man, and for this she was publicly beaten. The initial response of IRB members was to admonish Nada that she would 'do well to comply with the laws of general application she criticizes.' Defending the original decision, the Minister for Immigration, Bernard Valcourt, argued that granting asylum on the basis of gender-related persecution would be akin to imposing Canadian 'values on other countries' and would lead to a flood of applications. He further stated he was not ready to make Canada a leader on this issue (Oziewicz 1993).

Yet public attention and lobbying on behalf of Nada by women's NGOs under the network NAC soon placed the Minister of Immigration in a compromised position. The IRB's decision in Nada's case was so contrary to Canadian 'principles' and commitments to gender equality that it became embarrassing to refuse Nada asylum on this ground. This was particularly so in light of Canadian commitments to women's rights in the Charter of Rights and Freedoms and Canadian efforts at the Vienna Conference on Human Rights to persuade states to recognize violence against women as a human rights issue (Daley, 21 May 1998). Likewise, it contradicted Canada's position in the Executive Committee of the UNHCR until this point, where Canadian delegates had taken a lead in drafting various decisions relating to the protection of refugee women during the 1980s (e-mail exchange with CIC official, 1998). Moreover, Canada had taken several concrete steps to protect the rights of refugee women. For example, the Canadian International Development Agency (CIDA) lobbied for, and eventually funded, the position of Senior Coordinator for Refugee Women in UNHCR (1989).[11] This position was held by a Canadian from CIDA for seven years, until 1996. Canada was the first country to adopt the Women at Risk program and has hosted international workshops on the program.

Seeking to retain legitimacy then, Valcourt reversed his original position on 'Nada', granting her asylum for humanitarian reasons. This decision opened the door to Canadian officials within IRB interested in gender equality. By 1992, an internal IRB working group released a draft discussion paper on gender-related persecution to various regional members and staff of the IRB. The paper—written in consultation with various interested parties, such as the UNHCR, the Canadian Council for Refugees (CAR), and the Inter-Church Council for Refugees—reinterpreted the Convention grounds from a gender perspective (Kuttner 1997); it was released in March 1993 as *Guidelines on Women Refugee Claimants Fearing Gender-Related Persecution.* This move enabled the Canadian government to maintain consistency between their 'global' face on gender equality and domestic commitments to gender equality under the Charter of Rights and Freedoms. It further added to the state's prestige and legitimacy on the issue in later years:

> During the preparatory process [of the Platform for Action adopted at the Beijing World Conference on Women]. . . . Canada was the only country which had adopted Gender based Guidelines for Refugee Claimants. . . . Prior to and during the final Preparatory Committee for Beijing, Canada had actively supported/pushed including references to women refugees and gender persecution

> in the [Platform for Action]. Buttressed by our strong domestic stance on the issue, Canadian negotiators were prepared to push the issue to the end. (e-mail exchange with DFAIT official, 1998)

Despite commitments to gender equality at home and abroad, the next section argues that the Guidelines and AWR program alone do little more than 'add women and stir' to the existing asylum system. Collectively, these efforts fail to recognize the root causes of displacement, the role of gender in the process of displacement, and the relationship between Canadian foreign policies and gendered displacements 'over there'. Thus even as feminist advocates and bureaucrats renegotiate gender within the context of Canadian foreign policy, the gendered political and economic structures which produce and restrict refugees, remain.

The Gendered Political Economy of Displacement: Challenging Canadian Commitments to Refugee Women

The Guidelines apply only to inland claims representing one-third of all asylum applications to Canada (Giles 1996: 44). Of the total of inland claimants, on average, 30 per cent are women (CIC 1998). The low number of female inland claims may be due to the fact that refugee women are less prone to flight across expansive territories because of gender roles and relations. Thus, 'successful claims by women to refugee status are affected less by issues of definition than by the fact that few women who might qualify for refugee status within an expanded interpretation of the definition of refugee or even in within its traditional definition are in a position to make such claims' (Connors 1997: 117). This observation demands an investigation of the gendered nature of refugee displacement and process for women.

A number of scholars and practitioners have begun to draw links between refugee displacement, the world capitalist economy, and development assistance (Giles et al. 1996; UNHCR 1995). For example, it is asserted that international financial institutions (IFIs) and structural adjustment policies (SAPs) have contributed to the conditions for conflict in Africa. Timothy Shaw concludes that, 'unless SAPs are modified and moderated before the end of this century, Africa's economic marginalization and peacekeeping proliferation is likely to continue well into the next century' (1997: 37). The UN Secretary General has himself called for a more peace friendly structural adjustment program, asking IFIs to relax the conditions they impose. Further, we are reminded of the gender implications of SAPs. Structural adjustment program have in fact burdened those perhaps least able to shoulder the weight of the transition: the poor, the majority of whom are women, must fill in the gaps left behind by receding social welfare programs and labour standards (Elson 1989; Bakker 1994b; Moghadam 1999; Enloe 1989). Traditional gender roles mean that women are most likely to fill in where the state recedes in social programs. How global, national, and local gendered structures work together to perpetuate women's vulnerability to persecution is evident in local gender relations, state complicity in failing to protect women, and the unwillingness of receiving states to extend protection where the state in the country of origin fails to do so.

The World Bank has gone some distance to recognize the importance of supporting 'women's work', and increasingly projects are targeted at women to ease the period of transition during structural adjustment. It is rather ironic that IFIs rely on women to carry out traditional gender roles to make SAPs work on the one hand, while on the other, embracing new income-generating projects specifically targeted at women to redress vulnerabilities produced by economic instability and thus making the burden of women's 'double day' even heavier. Thus as Giles, Moussa, and Van Esterik point out, efforts to integrate women into development fail to address underlying gender inequalities, and what is more, may be at the root of displacement:

> At the basis of the creation of most refugee movements world-wide is uneven development: most refugee movements are a product of colonialism, environmental degradation, the international capitalist market economy and structural adjustment policies of institutions such as the World Bank and the International Monetary Fund. However, the effect of these policies on the phenomenon of uneven development, as well as on economic relations themselves, are regarded as paramount, solitary and genderless. While gender relations along with those of ethnicity and race are integral to the organization of productive and reproductive activities, Smith and Ng point out that the separation of gender from the economy itself is a product of capitalist development. Further, Ng argues that the state in modern society is a central site of struggle among groups identified by their race/ethnicity, class, gender. We posit that this is undoubtedly the case for refugees. (1996: 16)

On this point, it is essential to deconstruct the ideas and assumptions guiding Canadian efforts to protect refugee women, and also what is not addressed in the Guidelines or AWR. For instance, such initiatives do not draw out the relationship between Canadian involvement in IFI's as a donor state, interests in keeping refugees 'over there' as a participant in multilateral forums, interests in keeping refugees out of Canada through increasingly restrictive measures, and global refugee-producing structures. The root causes of refugee displacement, and lack of access to asylum systems such as Canada's, are discursively erased. In addition, the Guidelines fail to recognize feminist critiques of Western liberal political and economic thought which produce hierarchies of inclusion and exclusion, beyond that of the public/private sphere case. As Valji (2001: 27) has argued, the 1951 Refugee Convention is also premised on a duality of the political and economic: 'The delineation is patently false when one observes, in the context of its relevance for women, the manner in which the political is filtered through economic persecution—such as the disproportionate effects structural adjustment policies have on women'. And as Valji continues, through this separation, a hierarchy of persecutory practices is created. Without bringing this broader feminist analysis into consideration, we are perhaps distracted from recognizing and addressing contradictions which exist, seemingly simultaneously, between Canadian commitments to gender equality on the one hand, and its role in producing or sustaining gender unequal relations on the other.

There are other ways the public/private challenge in the Guidelines does not go far enough, with the result of producing new binaries. For example, it has been argued elsewhere (Foster 2000, Macklin 1995; Razack 1995) that the 'subject' of the Guidelines is overwhelmingly Third World women, who are characterized by the fact that for them, 'oppression is a way of life' (Hossie 1993). As such, refugee women are constructed as homogeneously 'vulnerable and dependent' and in need of First World protection (Foster 2000: 45). A recent study (Razack 1995) has additionally found that where female applicants present themselves as 'particularly vulnerable and helpless' in IRB hearings, they have a much higher rate of acceptance. The case of Nada is representative of this attitude, in which where advocates focus on elements of an overtly patriarchal Muslim society to make their case—a stereotype that dismayed Nada herself (Macklin 1995).

As a result of this attitude, a separation between 'self' (Canada as refugee receiving and rights respecting) and 'other' (the Third World as refugee-producing and rights abusing) is manifest. Macklin has argued that this separation diverts attention away from contradictions between gender inequalities in Canada and international promises or prestige with respect to gender equality. Refugee women, 'arrive in Canada, having escaped gender violence in their own countries of origin to find that domestic violence is a common occurrence here, that women are confronted with racism and gender discrimination and sometimes harassment in education, at wage work, and in their access to a range of social and legal services' (Giles, Moussa, and Van Esterik 1996: 17).

How, then, do we draw the line between discrimination in Canada—for example, where women have often been beaten and murdered by husbands and unprotected by the state—and persecution 'over there'? Macklin's concern is that

> the line may be drawn by reference to whatever 'we' (the non-refugee producing country) do. What we do is discrimination. The more the claimant's state look different from ours, the more what 'they' do begins to look to 'us' like persecution. In other words, the fear is that cultural difference may become the yardstick from which discrimination to persecution will be measured. (1995: 265)

Yet it is with this very yardstick that gender related cases have been measured, and as such 'one is persecuted if the state cannot, or will not protect you, but only if Canada can or will protect you in similar circumstances' (1995: 266).

In these instances, the Guidelines may feed national, conservative discourse and practices that restrict asylum to only 'deserving' refugees. It further contributes to Canadian notions of leadership and moral or even cultural superiority. In emphasizing 'helpless victims' (read oppressed Third World Women) as legitimate applicants under the Guidelines and in the AWR program, it is implied that any applicant falling outside of this description is not a legitimate refugee. Both the Guidelines and the AWR reproduce refugee 'women' as a homogenous group and highlight 'cultural' practices leading to persecution, diverting one's attention away from critical questions regarding domestic and international policy responses to forced displacement that restrict asylum. It therefore enables the Canadian state to appear to uphold lofty principles of gender equality and humanitarianism on the one hand, while justifying the restriction of asylum and foreign policies contributing to the displacement of persons on the other. Further, this position masks the discrepancies between Canadian commitments to protect refugee women, and the government's inability to protect Canadian women in light of prevailing inequalities based on gender, race, sexual orientation, and ability as the case of Gillian Hadley reminds us. This construction of refugee women poses a further obstacle to refugee women exercising their rights, where the Canadian state can assume to have adopted a gender-positive approach while at the same time effectively silencing the issue of North-South relations that perpetuate gender inequalities.

Conclusions

In many ways, advocates for refugee women working both within and outside of the Canadian state have achieved remarkable things in the past decade. They have persuaded the Canadian government to adopt a position on gender-related persecution, making it possible for some women to escape domestic violence, rape, and oppressive social norms of their country of origin. This is a precedent that provides leadership to other countries as they begin to also recognize gender-related persecution. Gender advocates can thus use this development as a moral leverage with which to hold the Canadian state accountable to upholding refugee women's rights. At the same time, this optimism must be tempered.

A critical feminist critique (see Stienstra 1994; Whitworth 1994) can help 'make sense' of the contradictions highlighted throughout this chapter. Investigating the reasons why Citizenship and Immigration Canada adopted the Guidelines means examining the intersections of gendered external and domestic political actors and the structures shaping Canadian foreign policy making, and recognizing that such pressures are likewise imbued with contradictions regarding liberal principles to human rights, political sovereignty, and economic freedom. By investigating the ideas and assumption within the Guidelines, we make sense of how this move was in fact 'productive': it diverts attention away from, indeed legitimizes, Canadian interests in restricting asylum both within Canada and in overseas offices to only 'deserving refugees'. While the symbolic challenge is upheld as a symbol of Canadian commitment, the number of women getting in under the Guidelines is excruciatingly small: access to asylum is not enhanced, and discriminatory barriers remain well outside of Canada's borders and perceived responsibility. Finally, the Guidelines and other actions to support refugee women in Canada bolster the humanitarian image of that country on the one hand, while masking the contradiction between commitments to refugee women and its ability to uphold principles on gender equality on the other. Images of refugee women as homogenous and in need of rescue lend to this duality of 'good' and 'bad' states, upholding Canada as a rights respecting state.

The application of gender analysis in this chapter reveals a number of other important insights on displacement. It illustrates the gendered assumptions inherent in global and national political-economic forces leading to forced displacement, and how these same forces rely on traditional gender roles of women and men to 'make the centre hold' in times of displacement. Gender analysis likewise reveals the different experiences of men and women in the asylum process and ultimately, how values attached to gender determine who gets in. These findings affirm that until a transformation of Canadian interests along gender equality lines occurs, efforts to change the system will not fundamentally shift the numbers of refugee women getting into the country. In a word, while efforts to integrate refugee women 'open the door a crack' (Macklin 1995), critical gender analysis of Canadian foreign policy is required to swing the door more justly open, and to put Canadian principles on gender equality and humanitarianism into action.

Notes

1. I recognize the importance of the Guidelines to the individuals who have since gained access to Canada under them. This is not to diminish the relevance of their experiences, but rather to argue that more systemic change is required to promote access to the Canadian asylum process beyond an ad hoc, individual basis. I recognize too that the efforts of internal and external advocates for refugee women are limited by structural barriers and constraints, and from that point of view their accomplishments are indeed noteworthy. This chapter, then, is to prompt more reflection on asylum as a whole, and how such accomplishments are related to wider Canadian interests, globally and domestically.
2. Relief budgets nearly trebled between 1980 and 1990, from $353 million to just under $1 billion for the European Community (Macrae 1999: 4–5).
3. These developments should be viewed in relation to the boom in humanitarian interventions, peacekeeping and peace building since the Cold War. Between 1989 and 1997, the number of people deployed in such operations was more than double that of the previous forty years (Hicks-Stiehm 1999: 42).
4. In February of 1995, Canada introduced a $975 'head tax' for adult refugees seeking permanent residence, a particularly onerous amount for someone who has fled her or his country, often with few or no possessions. This tax was repealed in 1999 after a public outcry by refugee-rights activists.
5. 'Pro-men' groups often argue that refugee men and children together also constitute 80 per cent of any refugee population. This argument overlooks the fact that all over the world women are overwhelming responsible for the care of children and are therefore restricted in their economic, political, and social choices.
6. The introduction of the Guidelines or the Women at Risk Program have done little to change the proportion of women (or men) applying for or receiving asylum in Canada (Macklin 1995). Female claims under the Guidelines outnumber men by more that 7:1 (1,320 to 178), while the acceptance and rejection rates were roughly equal for the 1,500 gender-based claims between 1994 and 1998 (Jones 1999).
7. It was during the late eighties and early nineties that the Conservative government significantly cut funding to women's organizations.
8. Of course, women are also persecuted in the same ways as men, and in this case the Convention should be adequate. What feminist legal critics generally fail to point out is that men may also be persecuted in gender-related ways and for gender-specific reasons.
9. For example, advocates had good working relations with members of the Immigration and Refugee Board of Canada (IRB), including its chairperson, Judge Nurjehan Mawani.

Judge Mawani was active in promoting the adoption of Guidelines on Gender Related Persecution in Canada and promoted these Guidelines in international forums (see 1993a, b, and c). Alliances were also forged with staff working in the Canadian International Development Agency on the WID approach. CIDA would later fund the position of Senior Coordinator for Refugee Women in UNHCR.

10. The Senior Coordinator was responsible for developing a Policy on Refugee Women and acting as a catalyst to its implementation.
11. As a related aside, UNHCR and other humanitarian organizations working with refugees have likewise recognized the necessity of providing resources to women to help cope with the lack of state services directed at refugee populations in host countries.

Part IV

Women's Organizing

Chapter 12

'It's Time for Change': A Feminist Discussion of Resistance and Transformation in Periods of Liberal World Order

Teresa Healy

At the beginning of the twenty-first century, Canadian equality-seeking women's organizations have identified an old problem in need of renewed attention: 'The historical practice of discrimination against women results in ongoing inequality' (Canadian World March of Women 2000b: 15). This straightforward statement of a deeply rooted problem in Canadian society was issued by the Canadian Women's March Committee early in the year 2000. It was accompanied by an equally clear set of demands directed at the Canadian government. In short, a significant coalition of women's groups in Canada marked the new millennium by organizing to compel the federal government to 'respect and promote women's basic human rights'. In order to do so, they argued, the government must 'radically change its ways of governing, . . . actively promote the public interest and adopt specific measures that will move us forward in the progressive realization of women's rights' (CWMW 2000b: 11).

In this chapter, I will explore what this problem and ensuing debate among feminists have to do with the study and practice of Canadian foreign policy. I will argue that the Canadian coalition formed to support the World March of Women 2000 Against Poverty and Violence Against Women articulated aspects of post-colonial feminist politics that challenge, not just domestic policy, but Canadian foreign policy as well. In conjunction with the Québécoise organizers of the World March and their counterparts around the world, the Canadian Women's March Committee identified the state as a common site of struggle for feminist movements.

There are three aspects to this post-colonial feminist critique of the state. First of all, the political organizations of First Nations women and immigrant women especially, together with women of colour, working class women, disabled women, lesbians, and poor women, identify discontentment with their place in the Canadian 'nation'. Their critique challenges the definition of who exactly defines and acts in the 'national interest' and undermines the narrow definition of the 'national interest' in traditional approaches to Canadian foreign policy. This offers an opportunity to compare realism with post-colonial feminism. Secondly, given that the march identified women's knowledge of internationalization as a strength of feminist movements in Canada, the march took seriously the relationship between collective organizing and any possible transformation in the form of state. Women's experiences of colonialism in and elsewhere are seen as having the potential to become political expressions with transformative implications. In the second section of this chapter we can compare post-colonialism with neo-Gramscian international political economy. Thirdly, this feminist explanation of poverty and violence against women criticizes the Canadian government's support for a deregulated financial markets, structural adjustment, privatization, export-oriented development, free trade, and liberal investment agreements for women in the South, as well as the North. In this way, the march challenged the Canadian government's role in constructing a liberal, re-colonizing world order. Yet the march also perceived in international institutions the possibility of transforming the international system. This third section of the chapter discusses foreign policy directions for challenging the liberal (recolonizing) world order and allows us to examine feminist post-colonialism and idealism.

The Canadian Women's March 2000 was significant because it was organized by a diverse coalition of women's equality-seeking groups and was able to mobilize women across the country. Students of Canadian foreign policy may find the theoretical examination of the march interesting, insofar as it engages us in a feminist discussion of realist, critical, and idealist perspectives, together with post-colonial theory. But the most important reason to conduct this discussion and continue the reflection promoted by the Women's March 2000 is to strengthen women's movements. From my perspective, a dialogue between feminist post-colonial and neo-Gramscian approaches is the most fruitful for developing a global perspective on ending poverty and violence against women.

The National versus Women's Interests

The World March 2000 Against Poverty and Violence Against Women was organized by the Fédération des Femmes du Québec. It emerged out of the very successful 1995 Women's March Against Poverty, in which thousands of women marched for ten days in Quebec and won nine key demands in the area of economic justice (Canadian World March of Women 2000a). In 1996, women from across Canada organized the Women's March for Bread and Roses. In October 1998, in response to the Quebec women's invitation issued at the 1995 Beijing UN Conference on Women, 140 women from sixty-five countries met in Montreal to adopt a common platform of demands. Each national committee then organized national meetings and events. During 2000, women in 157 countries joined the World March to demand an end to poverty and to violence against women. Many national organizations sent representatives to meet at the United Nations on 17 October 2000, the International Day for the Eradication of Poverty (World March of Women in the Year 2000 2000: 2).

On 8 March 2000, the Canadian Women's March Committee (CWMC) launched a campaign to mobilize Canadian women's groups around the World March of Women 2000 Against Poverty and Violence Against Women. In Canada, women's groups at every level organized events to celebrate the march in each province and territory that included a march of 30,000 in Montreal, and 50,000 women on Parliament Hill in October.

In this chapter, I will focus on the written analysis that grew out of a consultative process led by the Canadian Women's March Committee in the year preceding the March on the Hill. I will review the set of demands directed at the federal government that was prepared by the twenty-four national women's equality-seeking organizations in the March Committee. 'It's Time for Change! Demands to the Federal Government to End Poverty and Violence Against Women' (CWMW 2000b) was drafted, circulated for extensive consultation with women across Canada, redrafted, and then used as the basis for education and political action during the campaign.

As a measure of its commitment to the struggle for representation in the Canadian state and justice in Canadian society, the CWMC demanded that any legitimate government in Canada account for itself before this broadly based coalition of women's equality-seeking groups. The Canadian Women's March condemned the Canadian government's colonial relations with the First Nations peoples. It saw in the government's support for neo-liberalism a strategy having the effect of re-colonizing the majority of the world's population. In an effort to respect the autonomy of the Quebec women's movement, as well as its definition of nation, the CWMC did not speak for women in Quebec.

Despite ideological pronouncements that neo-liberalism is in the general interest, the politics of globalization has constructed a boundary between the few who have been on the inside of the neo-liberal project and those who see themselves on the outside. The purpose of the research behind 'It's Time for Change' was to meet the needs of women who know themselves to be excluded. This suggests that the 'common sense' view of what is in the national interest is a contested one. The thousands of women who marched on Parliament Hill in October 2000, together with those across the country who marched, sang, yelled, drummed, painted, acted, designed web pages, quilted, wrote, spoke at meetings, prayed, took photos, organized, struck, bargained, raised banners, made art, cooked, wheeled their wheelchairs, and mobilized in innumerable other ways throughout the year were adamant in their message that globalization does not meet the general interests of the women of Canada.

At the heart of the march's demands was that women's interest in becoming free of violence and poverty be given priority in national and foreign policy. The demands were rooted in an explicit criticism of the growing inequality in Canadian society and the politics of exclusion upon which the liberal form of state now rests in Canada and in other countries as well:

> Creating more free markets, cutting taxes, reducing the size of government, privatising public institutions, deregulating work, removing rules that protect the environment, privatising health care, opening our schools to big corporations—none of these policies imposed around the world by the new global order benefit women. On the contrary, they force women into non-standard and precarious jobs, push our wages down, erode our health and safety, increase the number of poor, and condemn us all to much more unpaid work in the home.
>
> These policies threaten our very autonomy and safety, by, in effect, making us

> subject to the arbitrary power that men have enjoyed over women in the 'private' sphere for centuries. Less public intervention means less support to resist exploitative employers, harassing colleagues, violent partners, abusive doctors, teachers or clergy. Aboriginal women, Black women, women of colour and women with disabilities are disproportionately affected by these policies, since direct and systemic discrimination exacerbates the existing patterns of inequality with which all women are confronted. (CWMW 2000b: 19)

If, in effect, the Canadian government cannot represent the diversity of women's interests, then how can it be seen to be acting in the interests of the nation?

The feminist struggle to demystify the 'national' interest resonates well beyond the borders of Canada. In Vandana Shiva's eloquent analysis of the popular struggle in India against the construction of hydro-electric dams that are expected to displace thousands of people, we are offered a way to think of national level struggles in global terms. Shiva suggests that the 'national' interest is not tied to these mega-projects financed by the World Bank. The interests tied up in the success of these highly globalized dams are, in fact, those of a national elite whose interests converge with the 'narrow, local and parochial' interests of the most powerful countries of the G7. 'The real though subjugated national interest' emerges in the collective efforts of communities engaged in resistance to the dams. In this article, Shiva turns dominant discourse on its head: 'The global does not represent the universal human interest. It represents a particular local and parochial interest which has been globalized through the scope of its reach' (Shiva 1993b: 150).

The orthodox, or realist, position in international relations is that struggles over representation within national boundaries are not the concern of international relations. Liberal democracies, in fact, have a great deal of legitimacy to act in the international realm, since their positions are arrived at with the level of citizen participation deemed appropriate by the polity itself. Nevertheless, from a realist perspective, the national interest is articulated in the inter-state system by the representatives of any state that has been recognized by the international community, regardless of the quality of national level democratic participation. The national interest is the only interest that counts in a world order that is essentially insecure and prone to conflict and is built from the anarchic associations of rational, autonomous, and self-interested states.

Post-colonial feminists do not accept the realist view of the state or world order. Together with most feminist approaches to international relations, feminist post-colonial approaches ask *exactly whose* interests are served and whose are ignored as governments further the 'national' interest in the range of issues considered in inter-state institutional relations (Whitworth 1995: 85). This question helps uncover the artificial separation realists make between power relations at the national level and those in the international arena. Feminist post-colonial analyses consider the boundary between national and international politics to be steeped in a discourse of exclusion and inclusion (Pettman 1996: 4).

From a feminist and post-colonial perspective, not only do realists mislead by portraying the state as an autonomous, unitary, and purposive individual that acts in the international arena, but the realist state mirrors the image of the sovereign male political subject developed in European political theory, with all of its masculinist implications (Steans 1998: 43–59). Furthermore, post-colonial theorists share with critical theory the idea that the state is not a concrete entity that 'acts'. Rather, it is a place where struggles take place, where unequal social relations of power are given meaning and legitimacy and then institutionalized. Post-colonial feminists join with other critical feminists to consider the extent to which the masculinized and militarized state (Steans 1998: 87) defends state sovereignty, as well as the rule of the father, a highly globalized and racialized class hierarchy, and the acquired rights of corporations.

The specifically post-colonial questions emerge, however, when feminists dispute the complex histories of imperialism and colonialism which have shaped and continue to shape the nation, state, and world order (McClintock, Mufti, and Shohat 1997). So too do they lead towards investigations of conflicts over meanings ascribed to nation, state, and world order both within and between cultures, depending on national historical position within imperial configurations and their relations with other colonized nations (Narayan 1997: 151–4). The Canadian Women's March, by problematizing the 'national' interest in the ways it does, raises post-colonial questions which can make a significant contribution to an analysis of Canadian foreign policy.

Resistance and Transformation: State and Society

Although the dominant 'local' and 'parochial' interests have been globalized, women in Canada do not experience the results of globalization uniformly. Throughout the discussion paper 'It's Time for Change', the authors offer a feminist analysis of the multiple ways in which neo-liberal policy has devastated different communities of women in Canada. This is a rich analysis of the impact of poverty and violence on aboriginal women, young women, women with disabilities, lesbians, poor women, Inuit women, black women, and women in minority racial, ethno-cultural, or linguistic groups. In their discourse, we see evidence of the struggle that feminists undertook in the 1980s and 1990s to respond to the critique of women who had been left out of the mainstream of the Canadian women's movement. In an early document welcoming women to the World March 2000, CWMC argues it has good reason to believe that 'our movement will strengthen as we deal with the systemic racism and white supremacy, the sexism and patriarchy, the heterosexism and homophobia, the ableism, the educational and economic classism, and the ageism that exist here in Canada and hence, within our movement' (CWMW 2000c: 2).

As a result of this political renewal, CWMC's analysis of Canadian women undercuts the 'ethnocentric universalism' which Chandra Talpade Mohanty powerfully criticizes in much western feminist scholarship directed towards women in the Third World (Mohanty 1997: 258). Mohanty argues that western feminism tends to present western women as 'secular, liberated and having control over their own (1997: 273) as opposed to Third World women, who are seen 'as an already constituted, coherent group with identical interests and desires, regardless of class, ethnic or racial location, or contradictions' (1997: 258). Mohanty's argument is that 'a homogeneous notion of the oppression of women as a group is assumed' (1997: 258) in the case of Third World women, with the result that the Western feminist analysis ignores the complexity of material life, political choices, and discursive representations of Third World Women (1997: 269).

Emerging, as it does, after a long period of internal conflict, discussion, and debate over issues of race, class, sexuality, and nationalism within the Canadian women's movement, the CWMC may be seen as an expression of post-colonial political organization and analysis. The voices expressed in the demands of the CWMC are diverse. 'It's Time for Change' does not assume that Canadian women have been liberated whereas Third World women, in general, have not been. Rather, the writers acknowledge the basis for solidarity that exists precisely because equality-seeking women's groups in Canada and in other countries find themselves struggling with globalization promoted by their states within and across national borders. We are invited to consider the possibilities of a radical democratic political agenda informed by the varied experiences of women who have experienced the legacy of colonialism in Canada and in other countries as well. Thus we can affirm feminist approaches to foreign policy analysis that simultaneously reveal the partiality of dominant interests, and contrast those with the breadth of women's knowledge of international relations.

What is important about the politics of this criticism is that the Canadian Women's March Committee reclaims public space by bringing women to the forefront of women's concerns without renouncing its demands for a different form of activist state. This puts the Canadian women's movement in direct conflict with the dominant discourse on globalization that advocates a minimalist state, active primarily in the sphere of market expansion. In the Canadian Women's March Committee's 'Feminist Dozen', every one of the thirteen immediate demands to the federal government challenges the primacy of the market over Canadian society. For example, the CWMC demands the reinstatement of funding for a variety of equity-seeking groups so as to further their ability to represent themselves in the areas of legislative and policy reform. This demand stems from a critique of the market as well as a struggle for representation and justice that flows from an analysis of women's experiences of poverty and violence.

These demands arise out of a long struggle of many women's groups for democracy and draw on the historical memory of having fought for and won social guarantees in previous struggles with and in the state. Women in Canada are not likely to stop mobilizing if their demands are not met in the Liberal government's next Speech from the Throne. Moreover, women in Canada are likely to re-group even if a portion of the budget is re-allocated to meet some of their demands. The reason is that the demands presented to the government are unlikely to be satisfied in a liberal form of state. The CWMC is not just pushing the government to adopt alternative policies; it is actually mobilizing for a new form of state.

The significance of this point is that states are social structures that are changed over time through the conscious activity of humans acting collectively to create the world around them. Although the modern state can be said to have emerged in

Europe after 1648, it bears scarce resemblance to the modern state at the beginning of the twenty-first century. This is because states are products of social structure. It is not just that societies change over time and so states change with them. Rather, from a neo-Gramscian perspective, certain forms of state emerge depending on the character of the particular social bloc on which they are based (Cox 1987: 105). We can think of a social bloc as a particular alliance of social forces, or collective interests. If the bloc is built successfully, its members will be able to present their 'particular' interests as being in the general or 'national' interest, not least by striving to shape the characteristics of the state itself. This is not so easy to do. If groups outside of the privileged alliance make it clear that their interests are not represented through the state, then they will engage in a struggle to adapt the state to their needs (Cox 1996a: 124–43).

As an indication of the 'recolonizing' temper of the times, the minimalist liberal state has become the ideal form of state promoted by the most powerful social bloc in the United States and its allies, including Canada. In the past twenty years, national governments have turned towards privatization and downsizing through their domestic policy and international agreements if they can be convinced or, if coercion becomes necessary, by means of debt-servicing agreements and military aid. This minimalist form of state depends upon the extension of market relations into social services that had previously *taken out* of market relations (i.e. de-commodified), through the struggles of feminists and the working class. The increased economic marginalization of women and families who depended on public social services is one direct outcome. At times, through labour struggles or community organizing, workers and communities successfully mobilize to resist and return services to the public sphere. The increased expression of authoritarianism on the part of the state in ensuring these economic activities remain commodified is another possible outcome. Of course, the process is uneven and does not happen in exactly the same way in every country.

The negotiation of free trade agreements, however, is expected to consolidate the liberal form of state despite national level opposition (Gill 1996: 216; Clarke and Barlow 1997). Across the Americas, for example, governments and corporations are intensifying their efforts to conclude the proposed Free Trade Agreement of the Americas (FTAA) by the target year 2005. First proposed in a meeting in Miami at the Summit of the Americas in 1994 by the thirty-four government leaders, and followed up in subsequent meetings of heads of government and trade ministers, the proposed FTAA is intended to institutionalize a rules-based, open, and transparent regime in international trade in goods and services throughout the Americas. The FTAA has significant implications for the organization of finance and investment as well. This proposed agreement, if accepted, will not only alter the way in which goods, services, and capital are moved across borders, but will also have serious consequences for the movement and freedom of labour in the Americas. The specific effects on women will need to be considered.

As argued above, the main demands of the Women's March can be fulfilled only through the construction of a form of state other than the one that is being established by dominant forces in the current period, but no such change will occur without significantly restructured power relations at the level of civil society. From a neo-Gramscian perspective, any alternative to globalization presupposes an alternative to the neo-liberal form of state, which, in turn, depends upon political struggles at the national level. Furthermore, and contrary to the assumptions of western (feminist) neo-colonial discources, post-colonial feminism looks for expressions of resistance and social transformation on the part of post-colonial subjects (Marchand 1995: 57) both inside and outside of liberal democratic contexts. This perspective encourages opposition movements in one country to ally themselves with their counter-parts in other countries.

Along with Marxist and Gramscian approaches, many post-colonialist feminists are historicist in their use of concepts. Yet, because of its debt to postmodernism, feminist post-colonialism rejects universal explanations of historical dynamics. Rather, multiple overlapping histories of colonization and imperialism are told by, and with respect for, the perspectives of the people who were colonized (Tuhiwai Smith 1999: 27, 33). This is one of the ways post-colonialism confronts the dualism that sees the tradition-bound, irrational, underdeveloped Orient as the counterpart to the superior, modern, rational 'West' (Said 1979: 9–10, cited in Marchand and Parpart, 1995: 4).This is different from a 'dependency' attitude that underemphasizes the resistance of colonized peoples to the domination of northern economic, military, and political interests. Although post-colonialism has different meanings in different intellectual communities, here I follow Ania Loomba, who suggests that 'it is . . . helpful to think of postcolonialism not just as coming literally after colonialism and signifying its demise, but more flexibly as the contestation of colonial domination and the legacies of colonialism.' (Loomba: 1998, 12) While post-colonial feminist analyses might consider the material conditions of women's work in the market and non-market economy, they also recover the significance of ideas in structuring power relations and look to the many ways in which communities have sought to fight back against racism and imperialism constructed in external as well as internal ideological structures.

Post-colonial theorists argue that peoples of post-colonial states continue to resist the effects of empire; one of which is expressed in the idea that subordinated peoples cannot speak, act for, or represent themselves. They ask whether western intellectuals are willing to challenge the extent to which dominated peoples of the world are not seen as legitimate political subjects. Edward Said, in one of his most compelling statements, asserts that the relevant issue concerns 'the political willingness to take seriously the alternatives to imperialism, among them the existence of other cultures and societies' (Said: 1994, xiii).

The problem is not just one of individual volition. Stephen Slemon points out that it is difficult to raise these critical questions within institutions that 'have no abiding interest in the specifics of either colonist history or post-colonial agency' (Slemon 1995: 50). L.H.M. Ling argues that even critical international relations scholars 'reproduc[e] the ideological hegemony of the West even as [they try] to transcend it' (Ling 1996: 2), insofar as they assume a lack of agency on the part of non-western post-colonial states in the face of a totalizing capitalist world hegemony.

One way for feminists to reject this particular legacy of colonialism is to incorporate a concern with the dynamics of agency in our analyses as well as our political organizations. This is something that the Women's March enables us to understand. Beginning from the assumption that markets and forms of state are social creations, it actually matters *whether and how* we organize ourselves to contest them. Every time feminist organizations call attention to the anti-social interests cutting away at our public institutions, a deeper understanding of the constructed nature of social organization becomes possible. The notion that private markets and a limited state are 'natural' gives way to an analysis of how markets and states are historically constructed. As a result, alternative forms of social organization may be contemplated (Cox 1996a: 191–208). We can never assume that resistance will emerge spontaneously out of the contradictions of globalization. Women's opposition will not necessarily manifest itself. It may be violently repressed, or it may take unexpected forms. When it does appear, it is not an automatic effect of the imperatives of world order.

'Recolonization'

The Canadian Women's March Committee recognizes the power of international institutions such as the IMF, the World Bank, and the WTO to add to the difficulties faced by poor women through the erosion of public services. It offers a very sophisticated analysis that looks for the gendered impact of international finance and debt, structural adjustment, free trade, militarism, and war. The CWMC pays specific attention to the needs of immigrant and refugee women in Canada and, throughout the document, analyzes the international dimension of women's work, the global rights of lesbians, the need for public health care in all countries, the issues involved in the trafficking in women, and need for women to defend our full citizenship in this moment of market-led globalization.

The CWMC analysis shows how feminist critiques revealing the partiality of interests at the national level of Canadian politics may provide the basis for a powerful critique of these same, narrow, global interests as they are expressed through the Canadian state in international organizations such as the IMF, the World Bank, the ILO, and the UN system in general. This task is even more important given the apparent disparity between the Canadian government's promotion of human rights in international institutions and its lack of initiative in 'implementing, maintaining and living up to national and international standards that effectively guarantee the human rights of all women' (CWMW 2000b: 21). The reader is reminded that 'the Canadian government has argued for respect for women's human rights on the international scene' (CWMW: 2000b, 17). Furthermore, 'the federal and provincial governments have publicly and officially proclaimed their commitment to women's equality and declared their intention to eliminate violence against women.' The CWMC also points out: 'The recognition of women's rights in different international human rights instruments has resulted in an obligation on the part of the federal government to respect and promote women's equality and human rights' (CWMW 2000b: 12).

Noting Canada's record on the ratification of significant human rights covenants and anti-discrimination conventions, CWMC argues:

> All these international agreements hold the promise of a more equal society where women's basic security and dignity will be respected. They direct governments to take all necessary measures to ensure the promotion of women's human rights. However, current government policies sadly betray these international objectives and Canadian promises.' (CWMW: 2000b, 17–18)

Unfortunately, the Canadian government also is a member of the Group of 8, the International Monetary Fund, the World Trade Organization, and the Organization of American States, as well as being a party to the North American Free Trade Agreement. It is not hesitant to implement the directives emanating from these particular institutions, precisely because representatives of the Canadian government develop the very neo-liberal policies that become benchmarks for national state policies the world over (Panitch 1996: 86). Not only do our governments send representatives to formulate policy at the international level, but these institutions are a product of diplomatic and international agreements. They ought to be seen as creations of states (Cox 1996: 495). They bring into view the dual character of world order: the inter-state system and the world economy (Cox 1987: 107). They were created and have been continually reformed by representatives of the most powerful countries, including Canada, that also happen to be liberal democracies.

But this still does not explain how there could be such an apparent discrepancy between international human rights discourse and women's experiences of marginalization in Canada and other places as well. For such an explanation, we need to consider the character of this 'recolonizing' moment in history. In the current period, the US-led world order described by the phrase *pax americana* is highly globalized. Globalization is often defined in material terms as the liberalization of international trade, the deregulation of international finance, and the internationalization of production. It may also be defined in ideological terms as the dominant discourse, which limits the range of legitimate political activities by strengthening the general sense that there is no alternative to neo-liberal restructuring. Finally, globalization may be defined in institutional terms as the consolidation of neo-liberal restructuring through agreements like the North American Free Trade Agreement (NAFTA) or the proposed Free Trade Agreement of the Americas (FTAA). Over the past decade, globalization has conditioned the activities of those states that have been restructured along neo-liberal lines in the wake of struggles between social forces at the domestic level and at the level of world order.

As governments negotiate regional trade agreements or sign on to the World Trade Organization, the outcomes are not only economic, however devastating they may be. The liberal state is being presented as the protector of liberal political freedoms at the national level as well as at the level of world order. International declarations in support of the human rights of the individual are the political counterparts to the supposed fairness and predictability of international economics under an open, transparent, rules-based trading system. The international economic system is left fairly unencumbered by international human rights declarations because of the liberal requirement to maintain the separation of politics and economics, on the one hand, and its defence of the individual (male) subject, on the other. If the rights of the individual are protected in international human rights institutions, the representatives of the liberal state are legitimized in their efforts to negotiate international trade and investment treaties having serious negative impacts on the social structure of national societies. Government declarations of support for human rights at the level of world order can, moreover, have the effect of legitimizing inequalities in the national social order (Neufeld 1995: 17).

To the extent that feminist movements have pressured their governments to bring social and community rights to the international negotiations, they may have been able to undermine the power of dominant social forces. If feminist organizations can show how the promises of the 'social clauses' or UN declarations cannot be fulfilled by the minimalist liberal state in this era of globalization, then international institutions become contested terrain and the link between domestic and foreign policy is made apparent. In this respect, the contestation exhibited by the CWMC has the potential to examine potential 'cracks in the consent' (Marino: 1998, 22) which might help to uncover further contradictions in the relationship between the liberal state and the global market. If, however, women's movements turn uncritically to international institutions in addressing their demands, the transformative quality of their politics may be traded for liberal ideals.

The CWMC has, in concert with other national committees involved in the World March of Women, developed a set of 'World Demands' on Poverty and Violence Against Women (World March of Women in the Year 2000: 2000). The website of the World March of Women in the Year 2000 offers an advocacy guide with background analysis, a description of the six demands to eliminate poverty and the eleven demands to eliminate violence against women, as well as action sheets linked to each demand. It was meant to be a resource in the development of national campaigns and in preparation for the October meeting at the United Nations. The guide is a feminist teaching tool that could be incorporated into international-relations classes or used in economic and political literacy workshops.

In its feminist internationalism, the World March has taken on, not just the UN, but member states by calling on them to adopt, ratify, and implement international conventions and covenants relating to the rights of women and children. It also urges states to adopt other relevant human rights instruments that bear on the elimination of violence against women. On poverty and the 'sharing of wealth', the World March first demands that members of the UN 'adopt a legal framework and strategies aimed at eliminating poverty.' Once again, the demands begin with the state. The World Demands also include a tax on speculative currency transactions. The monies collected could then be used to create a social development fund. The World March document also includes demands for a return to the goal of 0.7 per cent of GNP from wealthy countries to be used in aid to poorer countries. It calls for the cancellation of Third World debt and outlines requirements that both international aid as well as national budgets be spent on social development. The World March demands a new international institution with power and authority to establish a fair, participatory world economic system founded on principles of solidarity, and an end to embargoes and blockades.

By making these demands, the World March increases the possibility that more women will come to know the limitations of the current United Nations system. The problem, however, is that the focus on the institutional reform of the UN system diminishes the post-colonial critique of globalization as 'recolonization'. Nowhere in these demands are the unfettered right of transnational corporations to extend the process of commodification and profit making challenged. The consensus which emerged through international consultation with feminist organizations seems to have taken shape on the familiar terrain of liberal (western) feminism. For example, a global re-distribution of income (through increased aid budgets), a tax on currency speculation, and measures aimed at poverty reduction are not the same thing as a redistribution of wealth, or efforts to prevent new supranational agreements from making economic policy making even less democratic than it already is.

One of the problems of working at the level of international institutions is that they tend to elicit an 'idealist' response from those who participate. Idealism, or liberal institutionalism, is based on the assumption that greater clarity in communication is the key to resolving conflicts. Education is thought to increase the capacity for modernization and rationality. International institutions are supposed to make a rules-based global order more transparent and facilitate co-operation between various state and non-state actors in the global system. Free trade agreements, for example, offer a rules-based, transparent mechanism for economic co-operation. In general, liberalism is optimistic about the role international institutions play in overcoming international conflict.

Post-colonial theorists, however, point out that the history of national capitalist development did not depend simply upon the extension of markets. Imperialism was central to its history and by no means led to co-operative international relations. Neither would feminist post-colonial theorists tend to see the current world order as characterized by progressive, globalized webs of interdependence. Rather, they are likely to be concerned with the structural legacy of colonialism, as well as current 'recolonization' (Alexander and Talpade Mohanty 1997: xxii) and the gendered and racialized dimensions structuring world order.

The post-colonial sensibility generated out of women's experiences in the national context may indeed force us to reflect further on the kind of international institutions we expect our states to create, but because the democratization of globalization is unlikely to occur by means of United Nations reform without a prior transformation of the minimalist liberal form of state and the globalized economic order, the foreign policy of the women's march would be strengthened if it were to develop in a different direction. The World March of Women organizes around changes at the level of the state, and this is a profound challenge to the globalization project. In terms of its own foreign policy or feminist internationalism, however, member coalitions of the march might consider building the capacity for communication and solidarity with counterparts who also have experiences of building new social alliances, thereby leading to possible new forms of state, rather than moving immediately to demands for UN reform.

Women's movements do not act merely within the globalized container that dominant social forces have created, but we do contend with the national contexts in which we find ourselves experiencing free markets and states built on the basis of a social bloc not of our choosing. As Cox argues with respect to counter-hegemonic forces more generally, a feminist post-colonial politics would likely be strengthened through the simultaneous and self-conscious organization of women struggling collectively against foreign and domestic policies that reproduce unequal social relations in our various countries (Cox 1996: 207).

Conclusion

The Canadian coalition which formed in support of the World March of Women in the Year 2000 is able to draw important links between the Canadian government's foreign and domestic policies because it is grounded in women's experiences. The CWMC is critical of structural adjustment at home, as it is critical of the Canadian government's promotion of economic globalization beyond the Canadian borders. The Canadian women's organizations making up the World March coalition do not accept the optimistic universalism of liberal discourse. Rather, they inquire into the specific interests served by a domestic restructuring program that has contributed to a rapid polarization of income and wealth, and a foreign economic policy that has the effect of exaggerating the same dynamic in countries of the post-colonial South where many women have to contend with even more precarious conditions, and still fight back. Despite these strengths, the World March initiative could be challenged to continue to explore the differences between liberal and post-colonial discourses on globalization and international institutions. Otherwise the foreign policy of the movement will often be at odds with the profound critique of national level restructuring.

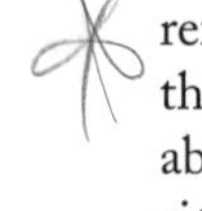

Because of the struggles within the women's movement (and movements) to reflect the diversity of women's voices, women's organizations are more likely than they were to engage the state as a place where hierarchies based on race, ethnicity, ability, age, and sexuality are constructed. By its very collective character, this opposition challenges the liberal definition of society as a simple aggregate of autonomous (male) individuals. It challenges the privileged position of the powerful forces supporting the foundation of the minimalist liberal state. Though their collective self-organization, women's organizations suggest future possibilities for the organization of society more generally. It is the post-colonial sensibility of the analysis presented by the Canadian Women's March Committee, together with the critique of the market, as well as the politics of engagement with the state, and its commitment to a diverse political practice that suggests creative avenues for feminist interrogation of foreign policy in an era of globalization. It is something to be welcomed, since it is indeed 'time for change'.

Chapter 13

Organizing for Beijing: Canadian NGOs and the Fourth World Conference on Women

Elizabeth Riddell-Dixon

Introduction

In September 1995—the year of the United Nations' fiftieth anniversary—delegates from 189 countries met in Beijing to attend the largest conference ever convened by the UN: the Fourth World Conference on Women. *The Beijing Declaration and Platform for Action*, which were unanimously adopted on the closing day of the conference, not only consolidated and reaffirmed gains for women realized at other recent world conferences, but also made significant advances on diverse issues ranging from the reaffirmation that rape is a war crime, to the delineation of state responsibilities to eliminate violence against women, to the affirmation of sexual and reproductive rights for women. Canadian non-government organizations (NGOs) as well as Canadian government officials were active both at the conference and at the preparatory meetings.

This chapter examines the government sponsored mechanisms that were established to facilitate NGO preparations in Canada for the Beijing Conference on Women.[1] It assesses the extent to which the government sponsored mechanisms in this case facilitated meaningful participation by NGOs, that is, participation that was taken seriously by the government and offered real opportunities for influencing policy. It further considers whose interests were served in the process. It concludes that the process did assist NGOs in developing their positions and that it facilitated a two-way flow of information between government officials and NGO representatives. The mechanisms did not, however, result in the NGOs having significant influence on Canada's positions.

Government efforts to facilitate participation by NGOs in the Beijing process must be seen in the context of broader efforts to democratize the making of Canadian foreign policy. In 1993 the Chrétien government came to power with a promise to democratize that process (Liberal Party of Canada 1993). To keep its campaign promise, the Liberal government undertook a series of activities to increase public involvement in foreign policy making, which included consultations across the country to hear the views of Canadians on policy issues and sponsoring mechanisms to help NGOs prepare for UN conferences and summits. Students of Canadian foreign policy have been skeptical of government efforts to democratize policy making. Kim Nossal describes 'stakeholder politics'—the strategy of providing the stakeholders (the attentive public) with opportunities to participate—as 'an excellent tool of political management':

> It ensures that those primarily affected by a policy area will have an opportunity to have their say, to comment on proposed policy changes, to register their objections or to offer their ideas. It thus not only protects state officials against future claims by stakeholders; it also binds the stakeholders more tightly to the policies eventually adopted (Nossal 1995: 38).

Students of Canadian foreign policy have been highly critical of the motivation for inviting NGOs participation in public hearings and consultations, which are frequently seen as opportunities to co-opt NGOs, or at least to dilute their opposition (Whitworth 1995; Neufeld 1999; Pratt 1983–4). Of particular concern are the government's dealings with the 'counter-consensus'—a term coined by Cranford Pratt to refer to the growing numbers of 'internationally minded public interest groups which are in serious opposition to many components of the present consensus that underlies Canadian foreign policy' (Pratt 1983–4: 100). The NGOs that make up the counter-consensus include groups concerned with labour, development, human rights, peace, women, indigenous peoples, and the environment (Pratt 1983–4: 117–29; and Neufeld 1999: 116 n19), all of which were involved with the Beijing Conference on Women. Cranford Pratt has described government strategies for dealing with NGOs as 'exercises in public relations, in the erosion of dissent, and in the cooption of dissenters' rather than as opportunities for meaningful dialogue in which NGOs can exert some influence (Pratt 1983–4: 120). Mark Neufeld argues that the very idea of democratizing the foreign policy making process was appropriated by the government from the NGOs in the counter-consensus, in order to co-opt the groups (Neufeld 1999: 104–7). Drawing on the work of Robert Cox, Neufeld argues that, in order to retain its hegemony, the ruling elite must at times co-opt its real critics (i.e., the leaders of key societal groups that oppose the overall direction and substance of its policies) by appropriating some of their 'dangerous' ideas:

> In the Canadian case, the leaders to be co-opted were those active in the social movements which formed the core of the counterconsensus. And the 'dangerous idea' to be assimilated and domesticated was the cojoining of 'democracy and foreign policy'. (Neufeld 1999: 104–5)

Neufeld is, however, quick to point out that the NGOs' demands for democratization have been accommodated only in form—not in substance. For instance, the government was able to retain its hegemony throughout the hearings of the Special Joint Committee Reviewing Canadian Foreign Policy by controlling the conditions under which they took place. The government determined the time and locations of the hearings, the groups invited to participate, the agenda, and the themes for discussion (Neufeld 1999: 106). Sandra Whitworth agrees that the hearings exemplify techniques in political management and attempts to manufacture consent (Whitworth 1995: 93). She concludes, however, that the government was not very effective in managing the views of women's groups which were largely ignored in the final report (94).

The counter-consensus challenges dominant class assumptions. It offers valuable critiques of public policies, and its participation in policy making ensures that matters frequently ignored in government circles are at least brought to the table. In providing opportunities for the attentive public to express its opinions, the government sponsored consultations and other mechanisms to facilitate the participation of civil society in the foreign policy making process contribute to greater—although by no means complete—democratization. Foreign policy is rarely an issue in elections; thus it is even more important that civil society has ways of making their views known to those formulating policy.

This analysis of government sponsored mechanisms to help NGOs prepare for the Beijing Conference on Women must, therefore, be seen in the context of broader debates about the democratization of Canadian foreign policy. They must also be considered in the context of pre-existing tensions between women's groups and the federal government.

Relations between feminist groups and the federal government have deteriorated since the late 1980s, when the Conservative government significantly cut funding for the Women's Program and withdrew financial support for the Court Challenges Program, which had provided feminist groups with crucial support in challenging Canadian laws that were deemed to discriminate against women (Burt 1994: 220). At the same time, the Conservatives began funding the anti-feminist group REAL Women (Burt 1994: 220).

From 1985 to 1988, the National Action Committee on the Status of Women (NAC) and other members of the counter-consensus actively opposed a central priority of the Mulroney government: negotiating a free trade agreement with the United States. During this period, the NAC's strategy shifted from its earlier emphasis on maintaining co-operative relations with government officials to a much more confrontational approach (Bashevkin 1989: 364). Tension continued to mount in the 1990s as the Conservatives persevered with policies inimical to woman's needs (e.g., cutting social services, especially support for child care), pursuing a North American Free Trade Agreement in spite of strong opposition from women's groups and other members of the counter consensus, and promoting the Charlottetown Accord, whose provisions were seen as weakening sexual equality in Canada and further undermining social programs (Burt 1994: 221). Feminist concerns fared no better after the Liberals came to power in 1993. Precious few references to women appeared in the government's 1995 policy document *Canada the World: Government Statement.*[2] In the very year of the Fourth World Conference on Women, the government's statement contains no substantial discussion whatsoever of women's rights or women's issues. Furthermore, the 1995 federal budget dramatically cut social programs of vital importance to women, slashed funding for women's groups, and disbanded the Advisory Council on the Status of Women. Thus by the time preparations for the Beijing Conference on Women were underway, relations between the government and women's groups were already strained. Government policies since the late 1980s had been undermining the gains that feminist groups had previously worked hard to achieve. The groups had responded with increased hostility, which did little to endear them or their causes to government decision makers. An awareness of these pre-existing tensions is necessary for an understanding of this case.

Feminist scholars have demonstrated the invisibility of women in the making of foreign policy:

> The study and practice of international relations in general, and foreign policy in particular, remain the most unrepresentative of women of feminist analyses; resistance to any change in this respect is dependent upon the assumed, and regularly asserted, gender neutrality of these areas. (Whitworth 1995: 84)[3]

Assumptions of gender-neutrality pervade analyses of Canadian foreign policy. In foreign policy, current practices, which are primarily defined by men and within a masculine framework, provide the norm for explaining foreign policy. That which is feminine and the areas where women predominate are considered to be outside the areas of 'real' foreign policy and thus have little effect on the analysis or practice of foreign policy (Stienstra 1994–5: 105).

This chapter examines a case that was unique: although the broader policy making process remained dominated by men, women were the key actors in the immediate decision making. It is, however, essential to recognize that there are tiers of power in government. At the top level, the Canadian government is dominated by men. This is the level at which power resides and at which women's issues do not constitute a top priority. At the lower level, the public servants formulating positions on women's issues are generally women and most are personally, as well as professionally, committed to ensuring women's equality with men and to enhancing the well-being of women. Yet, they are relatively few in number and they tend to be relegated to positions that carry less weight than those occupied by others pressing for competing objectives. For example, the position of Secretary of State for the Status of Women does not carry nearly the power or authority enjoyed by the Minister of Finance. Thus, Paul Martin, former Minister of Finance, was able to implement his 1995 budget, many of whose provisions directly contradicted the positions that Canada was advocating vis-à-vis the *Beijing Declaration and Platform for Action* (see also Chapter 14 in this volume). When push came to shove, the views of the Minister of Finance prevailed over those of Secretary of State for the Status of Women. The case supports the feminists' argument that the involvement of relatively small numbers of predominately elite women (i.e., white, well-educated women) has little effect on the overall structures of power (Stienstra 1994–5: 115).

Government-sponsored Mechanisms to Facilitate NGO Participation in the Beijing Process

On 4 June 1992, officials at Status of Women Canada convened a meeting in Ottawa for Canadian women's groups, at which the former informed the latter about the upcoming 1995 Beijing Conference of Women and urged them to begin preparing for it. Concrete plans for an NGO facilitating committee were developed by an NGO steering committee that coalesced at a conference organized in March 1993 by the Manitoba UN End of the Decade Committee. This was the only NGO in Canada to have held a conference every year, since the 1985 Third World Conference on Women to assess the progress being made in Canada in implementing the 1985 *Forward-looking Strategies for the Advancement of Women to the Year 2000.* The steering committee formed at the Manitoba conference drafted a proposal in consultation with the Women's Program[4] and SWC, for establishing government sponsored mechanisms to help NGOs prepare for the Beijing Conference on Women. The proposal received government approval, and two mechanisms were established: the Canadian Beijing Facilitating Committee (CBFC), and the Canadian Preparatory Committee (CPC). The former was to facilitate the participation of Canadian women's NGOs in the Beijing process. The specific mandate of the former as follows:

> The CBFC will use its seats on the Canadian Preparatory Committee (CPC) to lobby on behalf of women's groups in terms of process, access, and representation. In this capacity, it will bring Canadian women's voices to the CPC and will strive to influence the government's preparations.
>
> Through the Secretariat in Ottawa, the CBFC will serve as a clearinghouse for information in preparation for Beijing. The CBFC newsletter will play a crucial role in this networking. As well, the CBFC will be compiling a list of Canadians who will be going to New York and Beijing. (Canadian Beijing Facilitating Committee 1994: 23)

Thus, the CBFC had a mandate to distribute information relating to the Beijing Conference and to facilitate the participation of Canadian NGOs as well as lobbying on their behalf. In keeping with the strong preference of Canadian women's groups, the CBFC had its headquarters within the women's movement. For logistical and financial reasons, it was based in Ottawa. The Canadian Research Institute for the Advancement of Women, a national organization that encourages and promotes research by and for women in Canada, was the only Ottawa-based group to offer space, and some staff time; hence it became the headquarters for the CBFC. The CBFC elected two co-chairs, an anglophone, and a francophone.

The Canadian Preparatory Committee was established to facilitate consultations between members of the federal Interdepartmental Committee on the World Conference on Women and NGOs in the preparation of Canada's positions on documents pertaining to the UN Conference on Women. On 15 December 1993, the CPC held its first meeting to discuss the roles and responsibilities of the committee, the *Platform for Action*, Canada's preparations for the upcoming meetings of the UN Commission on the Status of Women, and the preparation of *Canada's National Report to the Fourth World Conference on Women*. In 1994 the CPC met after each of the major international negotiations pertaining to the Beijing Conference (e.g., the meetings of the UN Commission on the Status of Women and the Vienna regional meeting). By 1995 the CPC was also meeting before each of the international negotiating sessions.

To determine if these government mechanisms helped to democratize the process, it is important to consider several questions:

- Which NGOs participated in the government sponsored mechanisms?
- Did government facilitate meaningful participation?
- Whose interests were served by the government-sponsored mechanisms?

These questions are discussed below.

Which NGOs Participated in the Government-Sponsored Mechanisms?

The selection of the CBFC's membership was remarkably democratic. Letters were sent to 2,000 women's groups across the country soliciting nominations. From these nominations, national women's groups elected six representatives of national groups, provincial and regional groups elected six representatives from their ranks, and groups representing specific constituencies (such as indigenous women, visible minorities, lesbians, and immigrant women) elected eight representatives. The process was more democratic than that used for selecting members of the NGO coordinating committees established for the 1995 Copenhagen Summit on Social Development and the 1993 Vienna Conference on Human Rights, where lead groups in the field began the process and gravitated into the leadership positions.

The members of the CPC were government officials and representatives of NGOs. On the government side, its members were drawn from the four main departments on the interdepartmental committee: Status of Women Canada (SWC), the Department of Foreign Affairs and International Trade (DFAIT), the Canadian International Development Agency (CIDA), and Human Resources Development (i.e., the Women's Program).[5] On the NGO side, the committee's membership consisted of six representatives of the CBFC and eight representatives from labour, development, and human-rights groups. Since the government did not provide travel funds, groups had to pay to send their own representatives. Hence most of the groups represented on the CPC were based in Ottawa.

The NGOs involved in the Beijing process represented a large and diverse sector of the attentive public. Some were anglophone, others francophone. Their numbers included women's groups, indigenous groups, peace groups, human rights groups, development groups, environmental groups, and groups devoted to promoting the rights of lesbians, children, the disabled, women of colour, and seniors. In ideological terms, the vast majority of the participants were feminist in their orientation. Several prominent right-wing groups, including REAL Women, contacted government officials on numerous occasions and were on the CBFC distribution list. It is not surprising, however, that they did not exercise leadership roles in the government sponsored mechanisms, since the CBFC membership was elected and the right-wing groups made up a very small minority of those participating. Overall, the NGOs involved in the Beijing process represented large and diverse sectors of the counter-consensus. Thus, government efforts to facilitate this degree of participation clearly moved the process towards democratization.[6] The NGOs had valuable insights to contribute; hence their voices needed to be heard and taken seriously. Thus we turn our attention to the question: did the Canadian foreign policy making process allow them meaningful participation? As Sandra Whitworth states, 'democracy is not just a process, it is also an outcome' (Whitworth 1995: 94).

Did the Government Facilitate Meaningful Participation?

Sandra Whitworth's study of the Special Joint Committee Reviewing Canadian Foreign Policy illustrates how participation cannot be equated with influence. For diverse women's groups participated in the consultations, but their opinions were not recognized to any appreciable extent in the Committee's work: 'While women's organizations were invited to submit briefs and appear before the Special Joint Committee, their views were largely ignored in the final report' (1995: 84). These findings further confirm the pervasive view in the literature on Canadian foreign policy making: the dominant Canadian political culture may set broad guidelines within which government officials have to operate, but the latter, nonetheless, enjoy a large degree of autonomy from civil society in the formulation and implementation of Canada's foreign policies (Nossal 1995, especially 95–137; 1983–4; Pratt 1983–4; 1989, especially 51–2).

The question thus arises: did the government sponsored mechanisms facilitate NGO participation that affected policy outcomes? The answer in this case is a clear no: the members of the CBFC exerted very little influence over the direction and substance of Canada's positions. Neither the government officials nor the NGO representatives on the CPC thought NGOs had significantly influenced Canada's positions. There are several reasons for that.

On the NGO side, two factors undermined the effectiveness of their submissions to government: the timing and the format of the composite texts they submitted to government. The problem of timing was to a considerable extent due to external causes, although it was clearly exacerbated by fact that most members of the CBFC lacked UN experience. The UN system militated against early preparations. For example, the first substantial draft of the text that became the *Platform for Action* was issued only a little over a month before the final preparatory negotiations, which left NGOs as well as government representatives with little time to respond. Furthermore, the initial version was available only in English, federal civil servants had been working on the issues in the *Platform for Action* for years, and they were operating within guidelines set by established government policy. Their specific positions and strategies were in every case worked out interdepartmentally before the NGOs even presented their composite texts. The CBFC, for its part, failed to establish priorities early in the process or to develop a conceptual framework for assessing the evolving international texts. In every case, by the time NGOs had produced a composite text, the conference agenda and the government's objectives were already established.

A second set of problems was related to the format of the NGO submissions to government. These problems were due in large measure to inadequate time, although they were compounded by the fact that many of the CBFC leaders lacked UN experience. In contrast, the leaders of the NGO facilitating committees for the Copenhagen Summit on Social Development and the Vienna Conference on Human Rights had extensive international experience. UN negotiations are a world unto themselves. To conduct effective line-by-line analysis, one needs to know UN language, rules, procedures, and structures, to which government delegates and all participants must adhere. The first text that the CBFC submitted to the government was described by an experienced NGO representative as a 'higgeldy piggelty compilation'. Yet, as time went on, the CBFC developed more effective methods of drafting composite NGO texts, and their documents became more and more readable. Before the final international preparatory negotiations, for example, the CBFC used lead groups to co-ordinate its response to each of the twelve critical areas of concern in the *Platform for Action*. Upon receiving their sections of the document, the lead groups each solicited the views of thousands of women across Canada by fax and e-mail and drafted their responses. From these reports, the CBFC then compiled a 126–page composite text, which was submitted to the government within one month of the former having received the UN text. The CBFC, therefore, accomplished a great deal in short order. Nonetheless, the NGO text proposed numerous and extensive changes, which were not organized in the numerical order of the paragraphs in the *Platform for Action*. As a result, government officials would have needed to undertake the monumental task of comparing the NGO text and the *Platform for Action* if they wanted to fully understand the NGO positions. Shortly before the Beijing Conference, the CBFC produced another composite text that was much more coherent than its predecessors and that outlined four to six priorities for each issue area in the *Platform for Action*. Thus, with time, the CBFC texts became more effective, but the committee never achieved the desired goal of producing a concise, well-organized line-by-line analysis of the *Platform for Action*.

Yet, even if the NGOs had had perfect timing and had presented their positions in a completely friendly format, there is still the question of whether government officials would have been receptive. As mentioned earlier, the literature on Canadian foreign policy demonstrates that the Canadian government is fairly autonomous from civil society in general and from the counter-consensus in particular, in formulating foreign policy. Furthermore, it would be hard to argue that the government, as a whole, was particularly receptive to women's issues or to the well-being of women. At the same time that it was preparing for the Fourth World Conference on Women, the Canadian government was slashing funding for social programs of vital importance to women and ensuring the demise of the Advisory Council on the Status of Women. In sum, the government sponsored mechanisms in our case fulfilled one—but only one—of the criteria for assessing democratization: facilitating the participation of a large and diverse range of groups and allowing the voice of the counter-consensus to be heard. Yet if the interests of democratization were being only partially addressed, then whose interests were being served?

Whose Interests Were Served by the Government-Sponsored Mechanisms?

In response to this question, one would have to say that both NGOs and the government benefited from the arrangements. Government support of NGO participation was considerable. Within Canada, it included

- funding the CBFC to facilitate and co-ordinate the participation of NGOs,
- providing funds to assist NGOs in preparing their positions,
- establishing the CPC to facilitate consultations between the Interdepartmental Committee on the World Conference on Women and the NGO community, and
- disseminating information pertaining to the Fourth World Conference on Women, including comprehensive briefing packages for those attending the conference.

Thus, Canadian NGOs were assisted in several important ways. First, the mechanisms ensured that important information was distributed continually to the attentive public. The CBFC produced an informative newsletter, *Onward to Beijing*, which along with other relevant government and UN documents and briefing kits, was circulated to all who asked to be on its distribution list. The distribution list, however, was disappointingly small, comprising just over 2,000 group representatives and individuals. Since 2,000 women's groups—not private individuals—were contacted initially when the CBFC was being established, one would have expected the final list to have been appreciably longer. In light of the interest generated by conference and the high quality of the information distributed, the small circulation was regrettable. The database did, nonetheless, reflect considerable regional, linguistic, racial, and ideological diversity.

Secondly, the mechanisms promoted networking among a large number of diverse groups. They helped to strengthen the links among women's groups that shared common goals and between women's groups and other members of the counter-consensus. In particular, the CPC brought together women's groups with other members of the broader counter-consensus, including labour, development groups, and human rights groups.

Thirdly, the mechanisms facilitated the formulation of joint positions and lobbying strategies. The CBFC oversaw the development of NGO composite texts, which in turn, assisted them in presenting their positions to government officials at home and at the international negotiations and facilitated the assumption by the CBFC of leadership roles in the international NGO caucuses. Without government funding, it would not have been possible for such geographically dispersed and diverse groups to have worked together to develop composite texts.

Fourthly, the CPC provided a channel for presenting views directly to government officials before each of the preparatory meetings and the Beijing Conference. It guaranteed access, albeit somewhat limited, to those formulating Canada's positions.

Government support of NGO participation was not, however, purely altruistic. It did much to enable the Canadian government to retain control of the process. This government dominance was obvious in the CPC—the principal channel for NGOs to convey their concerns and their critiques of the *Platform for Action* to government officials. Government officials decided on the composition of the CPC, called and chaired its meetings, and set its agendas. The NGO representatives on the CPC expressed frustration at the way the meetings were structured, which left little time for substantial discussions between them and the government officials about Canada's positions.

Having the ability to decide who would get what information and when also gave considerable power to the government officials. This is not to say that they generally withheld information. Quite to the contrary, they shared a great deal of information about the conference with the NGOs. Such sharing was highly beneficial to the NGOs, but it also served the government's objectives. Public interest in, and support for, the conference bolstered the importance and legitimacy of the work being done in the government to prepare for it. Government officials were prompt in passing the draft conference document on to the NGOs. It was, after all, in the government's best interest to have the NGOs produce composite texts, which would serve as evidence of public support for moving the agenda ahead. Government officials did not, however, hesitate to withhold information, particularly the substance of its negotiating positions at the 1995 New York Preparatory Meetings, when this tactic seemed to serve its interests. Government officials may have had good reasons for making these decisions,[7] but the fact remains that control over the distribution of vital information is an important trump card.

The political management referred to by Kim Nossal was also exemplified by the ways in which the government sponsored mechanisms institutionalized participation, and thereby determined which voices were heard most clearly in the policy making process. Voices of dissent were not silenced, but they were frequently relegated to the sidelines. Throughout the Beijing process, relations between the NAC and the Canadian government were strained. Overall, the government had not given high priority to women's issues, and the NAC was very critical of the government's deficiencies in this regard. The already strained relationship was further eroded by the 1995 federal budget. Although the NAC and those within government who were drafting Canada's positions for the Beijing Conference shared many of the same concerns and broad objectives, relations between them were undermined by the pervasive tension and contentious nature of the relationship that existed between the NAC and the Canadian government, as a whole.

The way the CBFC was established was seen by many in the women's movement as a ploy to reduce the NAC's influence in the Beijing process. If government officials had worked out the details for the facilitating committee with the Group of 23—the umbrella group representing the vast majority of feminist groups in Canada and in which NAC was a prominent member—the NAC would have played a lead role—if not the lead role. The decision to work with the NGO steering committee that emerged in 1993 from the conference of the Manitoba UN End of Decade Committee meant that the NAC did not assume the lead of the CBFC.

In addition to serving as useful tools of political management, the government's provisions for facilitating the participation of NGOs helped the public servants to cope with their heavy workload. Having a CBFC to reply to inquiries and distribute information reduced the amount of time government officials had to spend dealing directly with NGOs. Government officials in all the key departments received numerous queries from the public, but many of these could be directed to the CBFC. Thus, governmental support for the NGOs clearly had some definite advantages for the government.

Assessing the extent to which co-option took place is more difficult. The vast majority of the groups involved agreed with the general direction of Canada's positions, so there was less need for co-option at the macro level than would have been case if the NGOs had been advocating a radically different direction to the one proposed by government. Yet the NGOs did not hesitate to level criticisms in areas where they thought the Canadian government should be more proactive. For example, Canadian Voice of Women for Peace wanted the Canadian government to be a vigorous advocate for the inclusion of strong disarmament provision in the *Platform for Action*. The NAC demanded that the Canadian government pledge additional resources for women's advancement and exert pressure to have the *Platform for Action* discuss the root causes of the structural inequalities inherent in capitalism. Participating in the CBFC and the CPC did not stop NGOs from criticizing Canada's stands. Madeleine Gilchrist, who had been centrally involved as a member of the CBFC and as a non-governmental observer on Canada's delegations to the preparatory meetings, resigned from Canada's delegation to the Fourth World Conference on Women explicitly because she had found government officials to be insufficiently forthcoming with information and too unreceptive to the idea of incorporating NGOs' recommendations into their official positions. She was clearly quite capable of criticizing a process in which she had been an active player. In general, however, those leading the CBFC tended to be less critical, particularly in public, of government officials than were some of those less close to the centre. This trend may, however, have been more indicative of the constructive relationship that already existed between the Canadian Research Institute for the Advancement of Women and the government than of the latter's control of the process.

One can conclude that the government sponsored mechanisms did much to facilitate the participation of NGOs, both in terms of the broad and diverse range of the groups involved and the amount of preparatory work they were able to achieve and the various levels on which they were able to participate. The mechanisms did not, however, enable them to influence the substance of Canada's official positions. The mechanisms did assist government officials in several ways. They helped cultivate interest and support for the conference, which was a high priority for those formulating Canada's positions. They institutionalized participation, thereby influencing which voices got central access. They did not stop the criticisms of the most vocal critics, but they did prevent them from playing the lead roles. The mechanisms could not control the NGOs, but they did assist the government in retaining control of the process.

These findings concur with those of other students of Canadian foreign policy who argue that government sponsored mechanisms to facilitate participation by

NGOs do little to influence policy but that they are significant in serving the interests of the governing elite. In her study of the Special Joint Committee Reviewing Canadian Foreign Policy, Sandra Whitworth (1995) concluded that women's groups were able to present their views but these views were not acknowledged or represented to any appreciable extent in the outcome of the process. In a similar vein, the CBFC and the CPC did much to help Canadian women's groups to develop their positions and to present them to government officials, but they did not result in significant influence over policy.

POSTSCRIPT

It is important to remember that the Beijing Conference on Women was part of a continuing process and that success of the government sponsored mechanisms should not be assessed solely in terms of the conference itself. In fact, the long-term benefits are perhaps the most important considerations. The most significant long-term gain has been the further growth and development of networks among women's groups in Canada. In preparing for, and participating in, the Beijing Conference on Women, groups gained greater knowledge of the workings and the demands of UN negotiations and significant experience in working together to analyze an international text and in lobbying co-operatively to influence policy. After the 1985 Nairobi Conference on Women, there was only one group in Canada—the Manitoba UN End of the Decade Committee—that was meeting regularly to assess Canada's progress in implementing the Nairobi *Forward-looking Strategies*. Such was not the case after Beijing. There is now a well-informed constituency to monitor the government's progress. These groups have invested too much time and energy and too many of their scarce resources to let the issues drop, and they expect action (see Chapter 12 in this volume)

Canadian NGOs continue to monitor the Canadian government's performance, as well as those of the provincial and territorial governments, and to lobby for greater compliance with the provisions of the *Platform for Action*. Many groups across the country that were involved with the Beijing process continue to hold regular meetings to assess progress made since Beijing and to plan lobbying strategies. In 2000 many were involved in activities relating to the 'Beijing +5' conference, which the UN convened in June 2000 to assess the achievements realized during the five years since the Fourth World Conference on Women. Canadian NGOs, for example, were active participants in a series of Internet working groups entitled 'Beijing +5 Global Forum', which were organized by the United Nations' Women Watch web site. The workshops examined areas where progress has been made in order to identify factors promoting success. They also identified obstacles to progress and developed strategies for overcoming these barriers. In short, the networks among Canadian women's groups and between them and other NGOs that were forged and strengthened during the Beijing process continue to flourish. The government sponsored mechanisms in the Beijing case did much to facilitate the development of valuable expertise and of more effective lobbying networks, which continue to help women's groups in their struggle to hold the government responsible to the commitments it made at the Fourth World Conference on Women.

NOTES

1. This case study is explored in greater depth in Elizabeth Riddell-Dixon (2001); *Canada and the Beijing Conference on Women' Governmental Politics and NGO Participation* (Vancouver: University of British Columbia Press). The author wishes to thank the Social Sciences and Humanities Research Council of Canada for its support of this research.

   Although beyond the scope of this paper, it is important to note that the Canadian government also provided considerable support for NGOs at the international negotiations. This support included having nongovernmental observers on Canada's official delegations, funding some NGO representatives to attend the negotiations and providing in-depth daily briefings for the NGOs.
2. The references to women included a mention of the Fourth World Conference on Women (26), a sentence saying that Canada is 'associated internationally with the promotion of the rights of women and children' (34), and two references to the need to ensure women's full and equal participation in economic development (40 and 42).
3. See also *Feminism and International Relations: Towards a Political Economy of Interstate and Non-governmental Organizations* (London: Macmillan, 1994). In recent years, several other students of Canadian foreign policy have sought to break the silence. The macro-level problem was clearly outlined by Deborah Stienstra (1994–5) in 'Can the Silence be Broken: Gender and Canadian Foreign Policy', *International Journal* 50, no. 1: 103–27. Others have chosen to focus on particular areas of foreign policy. For example, Kimberly Manning and Barbara Arneil examine 'one essential aspect of peace building that has hereto been neglected—gender.' See 'Engendering Peacebuilding', *Canadian Foreign Policy* 5, no. 1 (1997): 51–7, and 'Gender and Peacebuilding: Report on a Roundtable', *Canadian Foreign Policy* 5, no. 1 (1997):. 69–72. In 'Gender, Race and the Politics of Peacekeeping,' Sandra Whitworth highlights the consequences of ignoring gendered and racial distinctions. See Edward Moxon-Browne, ed, *A Future for Peacekeeping?* (Basingstoke: Macmillan, 1998), 176–91.
4. The Women's Program is 'the primary government source of financial and advisory assistance to women's groups and other voluntary organizations working to improve the status of women' (Canada, Secretary of State 1985: 5).
5. The Women's Program was first part of the Department of Secretary of State, then part of Human Resources Development, and subsequently moved to Status of Women Canada on 1 April 1995.
6. This finding coincides with Sandra Whitworth's conclusion regarding the hearings of the Special Joint Committee Reviewing Canadian Foreign Policy: 'The direct involvement of Canadian citizens in the consultation process is at least a partial step toward greater democratization' (1995: 94).
7. There were legitimate concerns that Canada's positions might get into the hands of conservative states and right wing groups, which would use this information to undermine Canada's negotiating positions.

Chapter 14

Gendered Dissonance: Feminists, FAFIA, and Canadian Foreign Policy

DEBORAH STIENSTRA

> Canada can and must take advantage of the tremendous opportunity offered by a world without borders in which there is a free flow of knowledge and cultures, a global society where information reigns supreme, generates innovation and stimulates creation, and an international economy where the number one challenge is to design and develop regulating instruments on a world scale.
>
> *–Lloyd Axworthy, former Minister of Foreign Affairs (1997)*

> We should refine and strengthen our understanding of the ways in which the current unrestrained capitalist agendas impact on women in the north and south in different, similar or related adverse ways. We are determined that women's economic contributions and needs be recognized, realizing that this will mean a restructuring and re-evaluation of work and family life. We support a quality of life whereby every person has access to meaningful work, quality education and an adequate standard of living. The economic potential of all Canadian women must be valued, recognized and supported. *–Making Connections (CRIAW 1998)*

In 1997, representatives of about 40 Canadian women's groups came together to assess whether and where they could go together after the 1995 Fourth World Conference on Women in Beijing. They agreed that, especially in response to the changes in the world as a result of globalization, it was critical to act together to ensure that women's equality is enhanced, not eroded. In many ways, the commitments made by the women's groups in 1997 echoed earlier activist fervour against the free trade agreements with the United States and later with Mexico. But the work that followed from that 1997 meeting was also substantially different, embodying a new commitment to work together as a strategic alliance and to use the international arena as a means to pursue greater equality within Canada.

This chapter will illuminate feminist tools of analysis that reframe and challenge Canadian foreign policy by examining the goals and work of the Canadian Feminist Alliance for International Action (FAFIA). By exploring four different areas of critique—identity, international human rights standards and regulation, the economy, and gender—I will illustrate the disparity between Canadian foreign policy and what Canadian foreign policy might look like if it were established by women's groups. I will also highlight the significance of recognizing differing interpretations of what Canadian foreign policy is, who participates in defining it, and where we find it.

Fractured Discourses

Over the past twenty years, the discourses of most Canadian women's groups on foreign policy has been fractured and erratic. Few women's groups have made a sustained response to the federal government's foreign policy, and those that have have commented when specific issues, particularly military issues and international trade, have drawn their attention. Women's groups have also commented on foreign policy as it has responded to women's concerns, as in the world conferences on women and the international instruments related to women's equality. The responses of groups have been individual, each group responding as it was able. There have been few, if any, attempts to develop a cohesive response to Canadian foreign policy.

The oldest, and most persistent, group involved in commenting on Canadian foreign policy is the Canadian Voice of Women for Peace (VOW). Since its creation in 1960, it has provided a continuing criticism of Canadian foreign policy, especially in connection with militarism and, increasingly in the 1990s, the environment. In 1998 it presented its position on Canada's nuclear policy to the Parliamentary Standing Committee on Foreign Affairs and International Trade and in 1999 its views on a culture of peace to the peace-building consultation.

The National Action Committee on the Status of Women (NAC), Canada's largest umbrella women's group, which represents over 700 women's groups, has turned its considerable attention to foreign policy in certain cases. The most well-known is its very public opposition to the Free Trade Agreement (FTA) with the United States and later, to the North-American Free Trade Agreement (NAFTA) (Gabriel and Macdonald 1994; 1996). In the summer of 1990, other women's groups, including Voice of Women, the Canadian Federation of University Women, and the Women's International League for Peace and Freedom, also presented their views on investment policy at public consultations on the Free Trade Agreement of the Americas (FTAA) and World Trade Organization (WTO). But even when there has been an issue of common interest, such as trade, there has been no co-ordination between the various groups on their positions.

Women's groups have also commented on Canadian foreign policies at the four world conferences on women held between 1975 and 1995, becoming, with each conference, more sophisticated in their engagement with policy development and analysis (Roberts 1996; Chapter 13, this volume).

Women's groups have especially drawn attention to the Canadian government's implementation (or lack thereof) of international commitments, including the United Nations *Convention on the Elimination of All Forms of Discrimination against Women* (CEDAW) and the *Beijing Platform for Action*. In 1990 NAC prepared an alternative report on Canada's implementation of CEDAW. It argued that 'Canadian women are just beginning to feel the adverse effects of the government's deficit reduction strategies and an export-led economic adjustment plan which privileges the market and proposes that social programs are irresponsible spending' (National

Action Committee 1990: 1). Stienstra and Roberts (1995), drawing on the experiences of about thirty women's groups, analyzed the Canadian implementation of the *Forward-looking Strategies*, adopted at the third world conference on women in Nairobi in 1985. They argued that the federal government in implementing the FTA violated the Nairobi Strategies. Other groups have since written alternatives to the official government response, addressing its implementation of international commitments. Waldorf and Bazilli (2000) detail those developed in response to CEDAW.

Women's groups also addressed the development of, and their involvement in, foreign policy in the 1995 Foreign Policy Review. Whitworth argues that while three times as many women's groups submitted briefs or made presentations to the Special Joint Committee in 1995 as in the 1986 foreign policy review, 'the issues raised by women's groups appear in the Committee's Report in only a few instances, and where they do they are supported with little detail and few recommendations' (1995: 84).

Many areas of Canadian foreign policy, including agricultural trade policies, development assistance, environmental policies, and cultural exchanges, have received little or no attention from women's groups. In the few areas of foreign policy that have been addressed, the scattered responses to specific foreign policy areas, and the lack of attention to many areas of foreign policy can be seen a lack of consistency on the part of women's groups. In addition, when a number of groups were interested in the same issue, such as trade, there were no attempts to develop a coherent position or speak with one voice. [1]

Several explanations can be given for this lack of consistency and coherence among women's groups. The most obvious is that women's groups are interested only in a limited range of foreign policy issues and different groups are interested in different issues. There is some truth to this argument. But Sandra Whitworth's analysis suggests that even when women want to contribute to the overall development and direction of foreign policy, as in the Foreign Policy Review process, their voices remain unheard and their concerns ignored. This, she suggests, is because of different views of foreign policy:

> Women's organizations make explicit the gendered nature of particular foreign policies, while the Special Joint Committee opts for gender neutrality; women's groups see a clear relationship between trade agreements, the promotion of manufactured exports and the working conditions of women who are locked in factories and risk death, while the Report acknowledges no such connections; women's groups explain the relationship between gender equity in UN staffing and civil societies while the Report simply names gender equity as something to be considered; and so on. (Whitworth 1995: 94)

As we will see in the following sections, despite the rise of a more coherent discourse on foreign policy among women's groups, they remain in significant dissonance with the Canadian government as to what foreign policy is and where we find it.

ESTABLISHING FAFIA

The 1997 meeting of women's groups in Canada and the subsequent formation of FAFIA is one attempt to create not only a stronger group of women who could speak knowledgeably on Canadian foreign policy, but to draw together the disparate threads of women's activism around foreign policy. This work created what we can call a feminist discourse on foreign policy, relying on specific analytic tools like an integrated feminist analysis and a transformative agenda, and on feminist practices including transparency and accountability. Using these tools, FAFIA began to develop its feminist discourse on foreign policy in several reports.

The establishment of FAFIA drew on the expertise of those who had been most involved with addressing women's concerns in foreign policy. Initially, the Canadian Research Institute for the Advancement of Women (CRIAW) had housed the non-governmental co-ordinating body for the Beijing women's conference (Chapter 13, this volume) and continued its leadership in the post-Beijing work. The co-ordinating group, including CRIAW, eventually became FAFIA.

Using the remaining funds from the office of the North American focal point (an off-shoot of the UN-based Coordinating Group of NGOs for facilitating the presence of NGOs from North America), CRIAW established a virtual clearing house of post-Beijing activities. In 1997, it organized a meeting called 'From Beijing to the Millennium', which was attended by forty-five women from across the country. The participants were chosen from groups that had been involved in specific activities connected with the Beijing conference or were lead groups for one of the areas in the *Beijing Platform for Action.*[2] The objectives of the meeting were

- to assess what had and had not been done to date in terms of follow up,
- to strategize on what are the most effective and efficient means of establishing follow up mechanisms including the monitoring of the implementation of the *Platform for Action* in Canada,
- to provide training on how to work more effectively with UN documents, agreements and conventions and to involve a greater number of young women in the post-Beijing process. (CRIAW 1997: 2–3)

The 1997 meeting was a historic breakthrough, especially in terms of clarity among the participants on the resistance to the existing economic and political agenda required for women's equality in Canada. To ensure that this agreement could be used for political action by the participants, a 'Ginger Group' (a small working committee) was established to draft a set of principles that would act as a basis for unity. The Common Values statement (quoted in part above) was drafted in 1998, together with a proposal for funding further collective action on the work of Beijing. The proposal, entitled 'Making Connections: Canadian Women Act on Beijing' (CRIAW 1998), included the creation of a national steering committee, a national consultation, and co-ordination of Canadian non-governmental participation at the 1999 meeting of the United Nations Commission on the Status of Women.[3]

In 1999, a national consultation was held, and at it the Canadian Feminist Alliance for International Action (FAFIA) was born.[4] The steering committee, unlike the Canadian Beijing Facilitating Committee, was not intended to be composed of representatives of different groups in the Canadian women's movement. Rather, the members 'came to the Committee as individuals and not as representatives of organizations, thus the position was not understood to be an organizational position' (*Canadian Women* 1999: 6). This practice has caused considerable controversy in the women's community because it challenged both the notion of representation of organizations in national coalitions, and the *de facto* practice in some past coalitions of identity politics.[5]

The mandate of the Steering Committee illustrated the beginnings of a feminist discourse around foreign policy. Its mandate was to

- work at the international level in a way that is more political, strategic and coordinated.
- work to improve conditions for women in Canada in a way that also supports women internationally.
- keep as a priority the impact of economic policies, both domestic and international, on women.
- work with an integrated feminist analysis and transformative agenda. (Canadian Women 1999: 8)

At the basis of FAFIA's work is a commitment to an integrated feminist analysis (IFA). This type of analysis 'recognizes and takes into account the multiple and intersecting impacts of policies and practices on different groups of women because of their race, class, ability/disability, sexual orientation, religion, culture, refugee or immigration status, or other status. It links the domestic and the international' (*Canadian Women* 1999: 8). It is at the core of the feminist discourse FAFIA pursues. The integrated feminist analysis argues that in order to address women's equality our analysis must be complicated by the diverse experiences of being a woman in Canada as well as contrasting women's experiences in Canada with those of women across the world.

The use of an integrated feminist analysis in feminist organizing parallels the rise of attention to women's diversities in academic analyses. Chandra Mohanty was one of the first to show how our analytic tools have too often made women homogenous and have created women from the Third World as 'other'. Too often, western feminist scholars have undertaken analysis 'which seeks to uncover a universality in women's subordinate position in society' (Mohanty 1991: 69). Our tools, she and other post-colonial authors argue, need to reflect the range of identities, based in their historical, geographic, and other locations. 'Strategic coalitions which construct oppositional political identities for themselves are based on generalizations and provisional unities, but the analysis of these group identities cannot be based on universalistic, ahistorical categories' (Mohanty 1991: 69).

The move to an integrated feminist analysis shifts the discourse among Canadian women's groups in at least two significant ways. First it is explicitly feminist; that is, it recognizes that it is not enough to be for women, but that the work needs to be equality-seeking for women. This definition of feminist is built at the barest minimum on the explanations of what it takes to reach women's equality in the *Beijing Platform for Action*. Secondly, the IFA shifts the discourse among women's groups from an exclusive women-centred focus to one which addresses the intersections between gender and race, ability, class, sexual orientation, and many other statuses. This is a clear rejection of the women-only model often pursued in the women's movement in Canada. The IFA rejects the perception that women necessarily have any thing in common. Rather it argues that all women's lives are complicated by their race, class, sexual orientation, refugee status, or disability and it embraces the complexity that results. It states explicitly that there may be times when the needs of different groups of women are at odds as a result of using this complex tool and seeks to address this through a second tool, the transformative agenda.

As always, feminist work is fundamentally committed to seeking change, and FAFIA chose to be explicit about the type of change they were seeking by using the tool of a transformative agenda. 'As opposed to change which focuses on working within existing structures, frameworks, etc., transformative change is directed towards altering these structures and frameworks as well as presenting alternatives. Inherent in this action is the understanding that existing institutions, structures, policy frameworks are patriarchal, racist, homophobic . . .' (*Canadian Women* 1999: 8). Thus, FAFIA spoke within the feminist tradition of Canada not only to engage with Canadian foreign policy, but to change it.

A final, although less explicit, plank of the FAFIA agenda was to promote transparency and accountability both from government and within its own membership. FAFIA called on governments to ensure greater consultation with women's equality-seeking non-governmental organizations, specifically on the implementation of Canada's commitments on international instruments and well as more generally on international gender equality work. Consultation was seen, not as the corrective for years of lack of accountability, but rather as a way of getting the government to identify its own priorities early enough in the process for NGOs to decide how to engage with them. FAFIA called for greater transparency about the ways in which NGOs were appointed as members of Canada's delegations to international meetings and greater accountability of NGO delegates to the equality-seeking women's community in Canada. Finally, FAFIA called on governments to be honest about their own successes and failures when reporting to international bodies. Too often Canadian reports paint a picture of all that has been done. Rarely does Canada admit where the gaps are or where there have been failures.

FAFIA also took the goals of transparency and accountability into its own structures so that it could as much, as possible, lead by example. Those who participate in FAFIA activities, whether in the steering committee, at national consultations, or on delegations to international meetings, agree to be accountable to the women's equality-seeking groups and to ensure that information about the work they are doing is shared as broadly as possible within those communities. A key part of the initial proposal was 'to build an engaged community of women who understand the interconnectedness of global and national issues and can act effectively at local, regional, provincial and national levels' (CRIAW 1998: 13). This meant that in addition to newsletters, a website and other information-sharing resources, there would be training sessions on the United Nations structures, human rights instruments, and the role of NGOs at each national consultation, with the hope that the sessions would become part of a stand-alone workshop available to women's groups for the sharing of that knowledge.

FAFIA and Canadian Foreign Policy

FAFIA used these tools of feminist discourse on Canadian foreign policy to address specific issues in Canadian foreign policy, especially related to immigration and refugee policies, foreign domestic workers, human rights, military policy, trade policies, macro-economic policies, and globalization. Two major reports were prepared for FAFIA and were widely distributed among its members and to the relevant policy makers. The first, *The Other Side of the Story* (FAFIA 1999), provides an alternative analysis of the picture for women in Canada based on the answers Canada submitted to the United Nations questionnaire on the implementation of the *Beijing Platform for Action*. The second, *Alternative Report on Canada* (FAFIA 2000), provided substantial commentary in three key areas (human rights, economic equality, and violence against women) on what Canada's position should be at the Beijing +5 Special Session in June 2000. The recommendations were formulated at a consultation with the FAFIA members in February 2000. The *Alternative Report* was also included in the *NGO Alternative Global Report* prepared by the Committee of Non-Governmental Organizations in Consultative Relationship with the United Nations.

While the FAFIA documents never specifically use the phrase 'Canadian foreign policy', they consistently take the position that there is currently a great divide between policies relating to domestic and international concerns that needs to be addressed. Indeed, it may be that the reason they do not refer specifically to foreign policy is the fear that their work may be separated from the domestic concerns. The tools of feminist discourse used by FAFIA also provide insights that help to identify some of the key concerns of a gendered analysis of Canadian foreign policy in several specific areas: identity, human rights instruments, the economy, and gender.

Identity

FAFIA brings forward several critiques of identity tensions around foreign policy within the Canadian government—the identity of Canada internally on women's equality as well as the tensions between parts of the Canadian government when addressing gender externally. First, it chastises the government for its unwillingness to be serious in addressing women's equality within Canada by ensuring high-level representation (such as a minister with access to Cabinet) to women's equality. 'Canada is self-congratulatory about equality issues. Women's equality is a minor file to be relegated to a junior minister with no real influence over finance and trade, where many of the decisions most affecting women's lives are made' (FAFIA 1999: 43). This marginalization of the women's portfolio within the federal government has had the effect of limiting the capacity of the government to integrate gender analysis effectively in its own decision-making structures. One of the best tools in government for ensuring gender analysis across departments, including DFAIT, is gender-based analysis. Yet as its own report to the United Nations suggests, the adoption of gender-based analysis has proceeded very slowly (Status of Women 1999: 26).

Canada's identity tensions around gender are further exacerbated by its separation of the foreign policy work on economic and on civil or political matters. This is most evident in the dual mandate of the Department of Foreign Affairs and International Trade (DFAIT). The two sides—foreign affairs with responsibility for human security and human rights, and international trade—have separate mandates and do not seem to work together. Officials in the department have admitted that the two sides of DFAIT are two solitudes. A further separation of political and social from economic can be seen when we recognize the role of the Department of Finance in the work of international financial institutions. This separation of identities has had serious repercussions for the cohesion of Canada's foreign policy, especially in its attention to both human rights commitments and international trade agreements.

The Government of Canada thus has several separate identities, each with its own levels of power within the development of foreign policy. These various identities have significant implications for foreign policy, especially that related to women. Delegations to international meetings related to women are appointed by the Minister for Foreign Affairs, whose officials have senior authority over the position taken by Canadian delegations at international meetings. Yet this means that those officials with substantive experience in gender analysis, such as those in Status of Women Canada, the main agency promoting gender-based analysis, are sidelined and their Minister remains subordinate to the Minister for Foreign Affairs when Canada pursues gender issues internationally. Though government officials might argue that there is interdepartmental co-ordination and adequate preparation and that this is normal process, the evidence indicates otherwise.

Canada has taken leadership in many international forums on gender issues, and yet it fails to recognize the consequences for the equality of women of its even stronger positions on international trade or the economy. Indeed, Canada fails to take gender into account when negotiating trade agreements or working with international financial institutions (Chapter 4, this volume). FAFIA illustrates this by considering the Canadian commitment to promoting women's health and its additional commitments to international trade agreements and the privatization of health research:

> Canada's ability to enact and enforce environmental and health protection laws are restricted by two forces: international trade agreements and the increasing 'cost-recovery' system of turning health research and quality control over to private business with financial interests in the outcomes. . . . This is a good example of the

> interdependence of women's equality issues. Women's economic inequality leads to inequality in decision-making apparatus which leads to inequality in health, as well as destructive trade, industry and environmental policies. (FAFIA 1999: 41)

The lack of attention to gender analysis in the development of Canada's trade and economic policies became more pointed when FAFIA invited government officials from both the trade side of DFAIT and the Department of Finance to attend their national consultations. None attended. The DFAIT officials who were sent were those from the 'social' side, where the International Women's Equality desk is based. These identity tensions undermine foreign policy even further when we consider some of the directions of foreign policy, including in the area of human rights standards.

International Human Rights Standards

Canada has been a leader in international human rights, especially of women's human rights (Chapter 9, this volume). It has signed many significant human rights treaties, but it has also set as a priority the establishment of international rules and agreements in the neo-liberal global economy. The former Minister of Foreign Affairs, Lloyd Axworthy, is quoted at the beginning of this chapter as saying that Canada is part of 'an international economy where the number one challenge is to design and develop regulating instruments on a world scale' (1997). Yet in many cases, these economic agreements have been adopted at the expense of international human rights treaties. By using an integrated feminist analysis to examine this area we will highlight some of the ways in which Canadian foreign policy is gendered.

The FAFIA *Alternative Report* suggests that 'because of the importance of their subject matter, . . . international human rights treaties have a natural primacy over other international laws and agreements. Governments cannot contract out of human rights obligations by signing on to multilateral or bilateral trade agreements or other agreements, or by taking measures to comply with the requirements of international financial institutions or trade regulating bodies' (FAFIA 2000: 63). The current situation in Canada is not as rosy as this recommendation. FAFIA suggests that the government is 'contracting out' of its international human rights agreements since 'most of the so-called initiatives listed in Canada's response (to the United Nations questionnaire on Beijing +5) are actually . . . undermined by trade, economic, environmental and other policies' (1999: 44).

The failure to implement its international human rights obligations has been increasingly brought up as an issue at the United Nations. For example, the National Association of Women and the Law (NAWL) presented the United Nations treaty bodies with a thorough analysis of Canada's implementation of its obligations under the *International Covenant on Civil and Political Rights* in 1999 and on its implementation of the *International Covenant on Economic, Social and Cultural Rights* in 1998. And Josephine Grey and the group Low Income Families Together (LIFT) presented their report on the situation in Ontario as regards adherence to both of these Covenants in 1998 and 1999 (Waldorf and Bazilli 2000: 48,

52). After the submission of the 1998 report, the United Nations Committee called on Canada, given its strong economic status, to correct some of the critical gaps including the adoption of

> the necessary measures to ensure the realization of women's economic, social and cultural rights, including the right to equal pay for work of equal value; direct a greater proportion of budgets to measures to address women's poverty and the poverty of their children, affordable day care, and legal aid for family matters; implement measures that will establish adequate support for shelters for battered women, care-giving services and women's NGOs. (Committee on Economic, Social and Cultural Rights 1998)

Similar criticisms were made by the Human Rights Committee when it called on Canada to 'assess the impact of recent changes in social programs on women and redress any discriminatory effects of these changes' (1999).

These criticisms are echoed in the FAFIA reports, but the analysis used links the lack of implementation of these human rights instruments to neo-liberal economic policies adopted by the government in its attempts to facilitate Canada's integration into the global economy and illustrates the effects for women in Canada and around the world. They describe the disparity between their vision and the neo-liberal economic approach taken by the government as a

> disturbing values conflict with current governments. Women seek a balanced economy, one that sets human rights obligations at its centre and seeks to design budgets, fiscal and trade policy in such a way as to ensure both economic stability and prosperity and a fair distribution of economic opportunities and benefits. (FAFIA 2000: 71–2)

The consequences of Canadian policy as illustrated with the integrated feminist analysis are twofold. First, the neo-liberal policies in Canada exacerbate the poverty of women as a group 'and of particular groups of women who are more oppressed economically and socially because they are Aboriginal, women of colour, immigrant women, migrant women, lesbians, disabled women, elderly women or single mothers' (FAFIA 2000: 72). But these policies also have significant effects for women around the world, and FAFIA argues the government needs to recognize how the policies are making their situations worse.

> Trade and other policies which alter traditional local ways of earning a living and perpetuate the economic exploitation of women's labour and natural resources in developing countries either force women to migrate or make them want to migrate to developing countries to improve their conditions and the conditions of their families. (FAFIA 2000: 72)

To reduce these disparities, FAFIA argues for the primacy and implementation of international human rights standards, including those specifically on women's equality, before we enter into new international economic agreements. The current situation illustrates how far the discourses of the women's movements are from those of the Canadian government.

The Economy

The gap between understandings of Canadian foreign policy among Canadian feminists and the federal government seems widest when we consider their understandings of the economy and how Canadian foreign policy views the economy and more particularly globalization. Sjolander (this volume) has identified some of the elements of the federal government's statements about globalization. In this section I will examine FAFIA's critique and the constraints that create this gap.

The coalition of women's groups which are represented in FAFIA want a different kind of economy than that pursued currently by the Canadian government. They are seeking policies which 'support and foster equality, social justice, improvements in the lives of citizens, and a healthy economy. The concept of the citizen as a fully and richly participating member of a political and cultural community has been lost' (FAFIA 2000: 71). In its place, FAFIA argues, the government is pursuing a neo-liberal agenda 'which elevates the value of market freedom and devalues a balanced, people-centred approach' (FAFIA 2000: 71).

Specifically, the FAFIA critiques propose that spending priorities be shifted towards resources for women's equality programs and services; ensuring that all trade agreements respect international covenants that promote women's equality; adopting regulations for the international market; cancelling the debt of the fifty-three poorest countries; and promoting local production for local consumption.

Why is the gap here so great? In large part the gap is a result of profoundly different understandings of the economy and tools for economic analysis. The federal government is using neo-liberal economic analysis, with its emphasis on the market, its valuation of laissez-faire politics, and its promotion of policies which enhance a more globalized economy. This, however, is not the lens used by the women's groups. Feminist analysis wants to put the people back in politics, especially women and those most disadvantaged by economic policies.

The impact of neo-liberal economics is not only the exclusion of many voices, but a systematic undervaluing of some of the key areas where women are present. Steans (1999) argues that what feminist analysis brings to the study of global political economy is the rethinking of the private sphere and how it is included in our analysis. Sassen (2000) illustrates how women's survival strategies in the shadows of the global economy, including the remittances of foreign domestic workers and illegal trafficking in women have provided considerable economic support to that same economy. These and many other feminist authors have documented the real contributions of women to the economy, including in areas not considered part of the economy like unpaid work, child-rearing, volunteer work, and agricultural production—what Marilyn Waring (1997) has referred to as 'shit work'.

In Canadian foreign policy, these areas have been rendered either invisible or illegitimate. They are not considered part of economic policies, and women's groups are thought naive to suggest the changes they propose. But the neo-liberalism adopted by the Canadian government also actively works to 'frame' women's equality in its own image. Globalization is seen to be a positive force for women that provides increased opportunities for them in the labour force. Anne Sisson Runyan quotes from a draft platform adopted by the Economic Commission for Europe in 1994 which says, 'Feminization of the labour force contributed to economic growth and brought many women a measure of economic and social independence. Globalization, privatization, technological change and the development of new activities in dynamic sectors, such as service industries, provided opportunities for fostering this contribution' (1999: 213). This framing was also abundantly evident at the Beijing +5 meetings in June 2000 as the countries of the North resisted the inclusion in the final Outcomes document of a recommendation for changes to globalization to ensure women's equality. Instead the agreement was to call for actions to 'enhance the capacity of women and empower them to be able to meet the negative social and economic impacts of globalization' (United Nations 2000: 51, par. 101c).

A reliance on neo-liberal economics and its tools of analysis by the Canadian government makes it nearly impossible to address many of the concerns of feminist activists around the economy. The gap between the two positions is a result of fundamentally different understandings of the economy, each of which seeks to benefit different groups in the economy. But, finally, the disagreement between FAFIA and Canadian foreign policy is also evident in how each understands and addresses gender.

Gender

Over the past decade there has been considerable movement in the federal government to introduce gender as an organizing principle for policy analysis. In 1995, just before the Beijing conference on women, it adopted its federal plan for gender equality with eight major objectives. The first objective was to introduce gender-based analysis throughout all federal departments and agencies. That was followed by a commitment to improving women's economic autonomy (objective 2) and promoting and supporting global gender equality (objective 7) (Status of Women Canada 1995). Unfortunately, the implementation of these commitments, especially in Canadian foreign policy, is lagging far behind. This lack of implementation illustrates the undervaluing of gender in Canadian foreign policy.

The federal plan for gender equality has as its basis the commitment to implementing gender based analysis (GBA). Put simply, GBA is

> a process that assesses the differential impact of proposed and/or existing policies, programs and legislation on women and men. It makes it possible for policy to be undertaken with an appreciation of gender differences, of the nature of relationships between women and men and of their different social realities, life expectations and economic circumstances. It is a tool for understanding social processes and for responding with informed and equitable options. (Status of Women Canada 1996: 4)

Each federal department is responsible for implementing GBA, and Status of Women Canada acts as a resource to departments in this work.

As a tool and with appropriate implementation, GBA could have significant impact, assisting in the inclusion of gender in policy development. But GBA has been criticized both by the women's movements in Canada and in the academic community for excluding women's organizations from the assessments, not using explicitly feminist analyses, and failing to recognize the diversity of women's experiences (W. Williams 1999). Women's movements have expressed concern that the drive for gender-based analysis with its push to bring gender into the mainstream in policy may simply change the language without changing the content. Williams quotes one feminist, 'After main streaming gender, will the new stream look like the old stream?' (1999). FAFIA suggests that governments should consider relying on the expertise of women's groups in implementing GBA, since the government admits they are finding that implementation has been slowed by decision makers who lack the skills. 'Women's organizations have the skill, experience and expertise to do gender analysis of policy, and in fact have been doing it for decades. However, they are viewed by Government as suspect, biased, unrealistic and unskilled' (FAFIA 1999: 36).

Of the federal government departments primarily responsible for Canadian foreign policy, only the Canadian International Development Agency (CIDA) has substantively addressed GBA. CIDA has been using this type of analysis for the past ten years and has made the inclusion of women and development an agency-wide priority. DFAIT has made no public statement of how it plans to implement GBA. Yet the Canadian government has continued to promote GBA as an important tool for all countries of the world. In the federal plan for gender equality it argues, 'Canada has continually promoted the integration and mainstreaming of gender analysis in the work of all international fora including . . . the United Nations, the OECD, the Commonwealth, La Francophonie, and the OAS' (Status of Women 1995: 67). Furthermore, in a description of Canadian priorities for the Habitat II conference in 1996, the government said, 'A key Canadian objective is the integration of a gender perspective throughout the Habitat Agenda. . . . An important step in ensuring that this takes place is through the development of tools and methodologies for applying gender-based analysis which will lead to more informed and improved policies in this area' (DFAIT 1999g). Again, an interdepartmental committee in preparation for the International Conference on Population and Development +5 recommended that Canada's priorities include:

> continuing to support the development of analytic tools, methodologies and mechanisms to conduct gender-based analysis in order to ensure the development and implementation by governments and UN bodies (including the Commission on Population and Development) of policies and programs that effectively address the needs and concerns of women. (DFAIT 1998b)

While GBA appears to be a cornerstone for Canadian federal policy outside of Canada, the government seems reluctant to make that same commitment to linking gender analysis and its own international activities.

In the federal plan for gender equality, the second objective is to improve women's economic autonomy and well-being. The commitments made by government departments, including Finance, fail to make any link between their promotion of a neo-liberal global economy and facilitating Canada's participation in it and this objective. In fact, in a commitment specifically made by Finance, it is clear that there is little understanding of gender-based analysis. 'Fiscal policy is established for the Canadian economy as a whole with the ultimate goal of maximizing the economy's growth potential. A strong economy works to the advantage of men and women. It is the government's aim to ensure that fiscal and economic initiatives do not further disadvantage low-income Canadians' (Status of Women 1995: 22–3). There is no recognition here of the diverse situations that women or men may find themselves in, nor of the fact that a disproportionate number of the poor are women.

The only place that links are made between the global situation and the situation in Canada is in the discussion under objective 7. There the government commits to 'focus attention on women's issues' (Status of Women Canada 1995: 67) in various multilateral fora. Unfortunately, the reality of this has been a substantive separation between gender equality and other areas of work. The government has been very good at promoting gender equality in women's areas of international work, as well as in those that could be seen as 'social', including social development and health. It has ignored gender or marginalized its importance to economic and trade considerations.

Thus we see a contradiction in the federal government in relation to gender. The government affirms regularly its commitment to the use of gender-based analysis, the incorporation of gender analysis in international organizations, and the pursuit of global gender equality. But it fails to bring these commitments into what some may call the 'hard' issues of foreign policy, especially the economy and trade. Thus it works against itself, committing in one arena to promote gender equality, while in another pursuing economic policies that will fundamentally undermine gender equality.

Women's groups, including FAFIA, address women's situations, not gender, in their analysis. That is the purpose of integrated feminist analysis. They recognize the need for gender analysis, but want to make sure that the voices of women are not lost in the pursuit of gender. But they also go further. The IFA is a tool for ensuring not only that women's voices are included, but that the complexity of women's situations are addressed. That means addressing the situations of Aboriginal women, women with disabilities, women of colour, black women, poor women, and the women who fit into more than one of these categories. At present the tools that exist cannot fully analyze all these diversities. As Williams suggests,

> much public policy is developed using statistics. These statistics are not collected to reflect the diversity of women. For example, there are almost no statistics on lesbians. How will diversity be addressed in this process? . . . Some women thought race and gender must be dealt with at the same time and that this separation of gender was a feature of a dominant white culture.' (1999)

Finally, the use of integrated feminist analysis is a recognition that women's situations in Canada are affected by and affect the lives of women around the world. Thus FAFIA calls for the government to recognize and support the transnational activism of women's groups in Canada. For example, 'Women's Program initiatives are not awarded for initiatives taking place outside Canada, for capital expenditures or for travel and other expenses incurred outside of Canada' (FAFIA 1999: 33). There is currently no funding for Canadian women's groups to promote gender equality in developing countries. CIDA's program criteria generally exclude domestic women's groups, and DFAIT has no funding program for international gender equality (Stienstra 1999: 79). Joan Grant-Cummings, formerly a member of the FAFIA steering committee and president of the National Action Committee on the Status of Women, suggests that it was through the leadership of women from the South exploring the impact of economic restructuring on their lives that women in Canada became aware of and active on these issues (Stienstra 1999: 76).

Despite the Canadian government's increased commitment to the inclusion of gender-based analysis in its policy making, there remains a substantial rift between the understanding of gender in Canada and gender-identified foreign policy, and what are perceived by many as the most important areas of foreign economic policy and trade policy. Women's groups have called for policies that respond to the multiple voices of women from their many locations within and outside Canada.

Conclusions

In the context of the 1995 Foreign Policy Review, Sandra Whitworth argued that women's organizations made explicit the gendered nature of particular foreign policies. FAFIA, in its own analysis of Canadian foreign policy, argued that it had a disturbing values conflict with Canadian foreign policy. We have seen in each of the four areas of FAFIA critique an overwhelming dissonance between what government pursues and what women's groups identify as priorities. This is clear evidence of the gendered nature of Canadian foreign policy, an approach which systematically excludes or diminishes the contributions of feminist analysis, speaks with multiple and conflicting voices on Canadian foreign policy, and makes commitments to gender equality while pursuing practices which increase the poverty or human rights abuses of many women.

This analysis also highlights the contested definitions of Canadian foreign policy and who is involved in it. FAFIA does not refer to the work it has done as part of Canadian foreign policy. This is a serious omission for our understanding of Canadian foreign policy. It reminds us that there are significant differences in our understandings of where we find Canadian foreign policy. Most government officials and many foreign policy analysts consider the Department of Foreign Affairs and International Trade as *the* site for the creation of foreign policy. FAFIA's analysis illustrates that foreign policy is created and debated in lesser government offices, including Status of Women Canada, and by non-governmental organizations. This analysis also illustrates there are hidden locations for the creation and maintenance of foreign policy, in this case notably the Department of Finance, which sets and implements the macro-economic frameworks for government policies in addition to its own work with international financial organizations. The omission of any reference to Canadian foreign policy by FAFIA illustrates a distrust of the standard ways of describing Canadian foreign policy and an attempt to outline an alternative.

What are the implications of these gendered discourses and practices for women's organizing in Canada and for Canadian foreign policy? At this time the Canadian government is incapable of bridging the great divide between its views and those of women's groups because of its faith in and reliance on neo-liberal economics. This approach continues to exclude women's situations and rejects the possibility of incorporating women's experiences. Its own multi-faced identity in relation to gender policies illustrates the marginalization of the status-of-women machinery in government. Thus there is little hope that the gender-based analysis initiative will sustain any fruit. At best, it will keep the crumbs of gender on the table. At worst, it will co-opt the language of feminism without any of the transformational agenda that is required to put it into practice.

For women's groups, this is a pivotal time. While the commitments made by governments are clearly not going to be implemented fully, groups may ask what the purpose of work in this area is. One message of this analysis is that unless women's groups hold governments accountable to the commitments they have already made, the commitments will be ignored. The move to work as an alliance across the women's movement is a significant venture. It provides a sustained voice for the women's movement and more consistency in policy positions. Yet the future of this initiative is uncertain, largely because the government fails to recognize (or is unwilling to support) the on-going work of the Canadian women's movement to ensure links between the global and the local. One vision of the future would be to have a self-sustaining feminist centre to study both foreign policy and discourses and practices. This would create an alternative place for women-focused work to be done, for an integrated feminist analysis to be used on government policy, for the creation and maintenance of expertise within the Canadian women's movement on Canadian foreign policy. Alternative sources of funding, support, and links will be needed to ensure that a integrated feminist analysis of Canadian foreign policy is sustained.

Appendix on Methodology

My research for this chapter is influenced in large part by the role I played on the national steering committee of FAFIA between its inception and August 2000, when I resigned. This article was written well after my resignation. Data were gathered in part through participant observation. But I have used only documents available to members of the Alliance and have not used any internal correspondence or documents to develop this argument. I have shown drafts of this chapter to the national steering committee of FAFIA and tried to respond to the concerns that they have raised. This, however, remains my analysis of these discourses and practices.

That being said, the role of participant observer in research is not an easy one and often causes as many problems for the researcher as for those with whom she participates and whom she observes. This is especially true for a feminist academic who works as an activist and writes about or analyses her experiences. It raises important questions about feminist research methods and practices.

From the vantage point of the people she works with, the participant-observer relationship can have some benefits, but can also cause difficulties with identity, trust, and power. The benefits of the relationship are the contributions the researcher makes to the collective work, using her knowledge, privilege, and resources. These can all bring much needed support to often under-resourced activist work. But it can also create identity problems for those involved. For example, is the researcher part of us when she writes about us? If so, should we have something to say about what she writes? If not, can she write what she does without talking to the other members? It can cause disagreements about knowledge and power as well. Whose knowledge is it to write about, and who controls who can or cannot write about the collective experiences? Finally, it raises significant issues around the more general, and often difficult, relationships between activists and academics, a relationship often misused by academics who fail to remain accountable to the communities they work with. Does a feminist academic bring her research or other academic work as 'collateral' to the table in the same way professional feminist organizers do in collective work? And can she take back to her paid work some of the 'benefits' of the collective work, as do other feminist professionals by writing about it? Or is her work, that is, that of analyzing, writing, and publishing, of such a different stripe that she cannot? Have academics in the past so misused their relationships that no academic should be trusted to be part of collective feminist work unless they agree to separate their activist and academic selves?

The question of participant observation is equally difficult when discussed from the vantage point of the academic community. It was not too long ago that research was limited to what we know call 'scientific' or positivist research. This approach valued the separation of the researcher from the subject under investigation, promoted 'neutral' third-party analysis of situations, and often made those researched into objects, unable to participate in the research. In many areas of the social sciences, this method has been challenged by post-positivist approaches, with feminist research methods at the forefront of this challenge. Yet in disciplines like political science, especially foreign policy analysis, post-positivism is still a marginal phenomenon. It remains risky for an academic to use methods like participant observation (or at least admitting to it in print), that challenge the neutrality of the researcher, enhance the capacity of those researched to participate in the research process, and engage the researcher in the process of creating the situations under study. The resulting work may be undervalued or rejected as not legitimate research, the author may be called on to 'teach' his or her colleagues about the value of these methodologies and may be excluded from discussions of research in the area. Academics often face a 'chilly climate' for using these methods.

Yet part of what this chapter, and this collection as a whole, is seeking to do is to create new ways of studying Canadian foreign policy. And from time to time, we need to rethink not only what we say about our subject, but how we do our research.

Notes

1. Some may argue that this sort of strategic co-ordination takes place in the National Action Committee as it negotiates its public stands, trying to address the needs and interests of its many member groups.
2. As Riddell-Dixon (Chapter 13, this volume) notes, the CBFC identified lead groups in each of the twelve priority areas. After Beijing, each group contributed to a collection of essays, *Taking Action for Equality, Development and Peace* (1996), that explored ways in which this document could be used in the everyday work of women's groups.
3. The Commission on the Status of Women was co-ordinating the United Nations five-year review of the Beijing conference commonly called Beijing +5; it was seen by Canadian NGOs as a critical location where decisions on women's equality would be made.
4. The National Consultation agreed to a permanent steering group but was unable to choose a name. The name FAFIA was adopted at a steering group meeting.
5. While this is a very interesting point when one is considering the development of women's organizing in Canada, it is not directly related to this discussion of women's organizing around foreign policy.

Bibliography

Abendroth, W. 1972. *A Short History of the European Working Class*. London: New Left Books.

Adamson, N., et al. 1988. *Feminist Organizing for Change*. Toronto: Oxford.

Adjin-Tettey, E. 1997. 'Defining a Particular Social Group Based on Gender'. *Refuge* 16, no. 4: 22–5.

Alexander, M., and C. Mohanty, eds. 1997. *Feminist Genealogies, Colonial Legacies, Democratic Futures*. New York: Routledge.

Allison, L., ed. 1993a. *The Changing Politics of Sport*. Manchester: Manchester University Press.

———. 1993b. 'The Changing Context of Sporting Life'. In Allison (1993a).

Anderson, B. 1991. *Imagined Communities*. Rev. edn. London: Verso.

Ashcroft, B., G. Griffiths, and H. Tiffin, eds. 1995. *The Post-colonial Studies Reader*. New York: Routledge.

Ashworth, L.M., and L. A. Swatuk. 1998. 'Masculinity and the Fear of Emasculation in International Relations Theory'. In Zalewski and Parpart.

Axworthy, L. 1997a. 'Canada and Human Security: The Need for Leadership'. *International Journal* 53, no. 2 (Spring): 183–96.

———. 1997b. 'Between Globalization and Multipolarity: The Case for a Global, Human Canadian Foreign Policy'. <http://www.dfait_maeci.gc.ca/english/foreignp/humane.htm>.

———. 1998. Notes for an address by the Minister of Foreign Affairs to the Canadian Institute of International Affairs Foreign Policy Conference, Ottawa, 16 Oct.

———. 1999a. 'Human Security and Canada's Security Council Agenda'. Notes for an Address by the Minister of Foreign Affairs to the Société des Relations Internationales de Québec, Quebec City, 25 Feb.

———. 1999b. 'Kosovo and the Human Security Agenda'. Notes for an Address by the Honourable Lloyd Axworthy, Minister of Foreign Affairs, to the Woodrow Wilson School of Public and International Relations, Princeton University, 7 Apr.

———. 1999c. 'Message from the Honourable Lloyd Axworthy, Minister of Foreign Affairs to the Hague Appeal for Peace', 13 May.

———. 2000. 'Notes for an Address by the Honourable Lloyd Axworthy Minister of Foreign Affairs to the University of Calgary Law School on Canada and Human Security'. 17 Feb. <http://webapps.dfait-maeci.gc.ca/minpub/Publication.asp?FileSpec=/Min_Pub_Docs/103033.htm>.

———, and S. Taylor. 1998. 'A Ban for All Seasons'. *International Journal* 53, no. 2 (Spring): 189–203.

Axworthy, L., and K. Vollebaek. 1998. 'Now for a New Diplomacy to Fashion a Humane World'. *Herald International Tribune*, 21 Oct.

Baines, E. 2000. 'The Elusiveness of Gender-Related Change in International Organizations: Refugee Women, UNHCR and the Political Economy of Gender'. Ph.D. Dissertation, Dalhousie University, Halifax.

Bakkan, A., and D. Stasiulis. 1997. 'Negotiating Citizenship: The Case of Foreign Domestic Workers in Canada'. *Feminist Review* 57 (Autumn): 112–39.

Bakker, I. 1994a. *Rethinking Restructuring: Gender and Change in Canada.* Toronto: University of Toronto Press.

———. 1994b. *The Strategic Silence: Gender and Economic Policy*. London: Zed Books.

———. 1997. 'Integrating Paid and Unpaid Work into Economic Growth and Human Development Strategies'. Paper presented to the Workshop on Integrating Paid and Unpaid Work into National Policies, Seoul, 28–30 May.

Barry, K. 1979. *Female Sexual Slavery*. New York: Avon.

Bashevkin, S. 1989. 'Free Trade and Canadian Feminism: The Case of the National Action Committee on the Status of Women'. *Canadian Public Policy* 15, no. 4: 363–75.

Beier, M., and A.D. Crosby. 1998. 'Harnessing Change for Continuity: The Play of Political and Economic Forces behind the Ottawa Process'. In Cameron, Lawson, and Tomlin.

Beneria, L., and S. Feldman, eds. 1992. *Unequal Burden, Economic Crisis, Persistent Poverty and Women's Work*. Oxford: Westview Press.

Beneria, L., and A. Lind. 1995. 'Engendering International Trade: Concepts, Policy, and Action'. Gender, Science and Development Programme Working Paper Series, 5 July. United Nations Development Fund for Women.

Benoît, L. 1999. 'Letter from the Rt.-Hon. Léon Benoît, MP'. <http://www.interchange.ubc.ca/adamj/atrisk.htm>.

Bercuson, D. 1996. *Significant Incident: Canada's Army, the Airborne, and the Murder in Somalia*. Toronto: McClelland and Stewart.

Bery, R. 1995. 'Media Ethics: No Magic Solutions'. In Slocum, Wichhart, Rocheleau, and Thomas-Slayter.

Bickerton, J.P, and A. Gagnon, eds. 1994. *Canadian Politics*. 2nd edn. Toronto: Broadview.

Biersteker, T., and C. Weber, eds. 1996. *State Sovereignty as Social Construct*. Cambridge: Cambridge University Press.

Black, D.R., and H.A. Smith. 1993. 'Notable Exceptions? New and Arrested Directions in Canadian Foreign Policy Literature'. *Canadian Journal of Political Science* 26, no. 4 (December): 745–75.

Black, D.R. and C. Turenne Sjolander. 1996. 'Multilateralism Re-constituted and the Discourse of Canadian Foreign Policy'. *Studies in Political Economy* 49 (Spring): 7–37.

Blacklock, C. 2000 'Women and Trade in Canada: An Overview of Key Issues'. Discussion paper prepared for Status of Women Canada, Ottawa (August).

Boal, A. 1979. *Theatre of the Oppressed*. London: Pluto.

———. 1992. *Games for Actors and Non-Actors*. London: Routledge.

Booth, K.1991. 'Security and Emancipation'. *Review of International Studies* 17, no. 4: 313–32.

———. 1998. *Statecraft and Security: The Cold War and Beyond*. Cambridge: Cambridge University Press.

———. Forthcoming. *Security, Community and Emancipation: Critical Security Studies and Global Politics*. Boulder: Lynne Riemer.

Boyd, M. 1993. 'Gender Concealed, Gender Revealed: The Demography of Canada's Refugee Flows'. Paper presented at the conference 'Gender Issues and Refugees: Development Implications'. Toronto, 9–11 May.

Bradley, B. 1999. 'Stop the Backlash against Refugees: They're Welcome Here'. *Socialist Worker*, no. 316, 15 Sept.<http://webhome.idirect.com/~sworker/316–12–refugees.html>.

Brod, H., and M. Kaufman, eds. 1994. *Theorizing Masculinities*. London: Sage.

Brodribb, S., ed. 1999. *Reclaiming the Future: Women's Strategies for the 21st Century*. Charlottetown: Gynergy.

Brown, S. 1988. 'Feminism, International Theory, and International Relations of Gender Inequality'. *Millennium: Journal of International Studies* 17, no. 3: 461–77 (special issue: Women and International Relations).

Burstyn, V. 1999. *The Rites of Men: Manhood, Politics, and the Culture of Sport*. Toronto: University of Toronto Press.

Burt, S. 1994. 'The Women's Movement: Working to Transform Public Life'. In Bickerton and Gagnon.

Cagatay, N., D. Elson, and C. Grown, eds. 1995. 'Gender, Adjustment and Macroeconomics'. Special Issue of *World Development* 23, no. 11 (November).

Cahn, S.K. 1994. *Coming on Strong: Gender and Sexuality in Twentieth-Century Women's Sports*. New York: Free Press.

Caldwell, G., S. Galster, J. Kanics, and N. Steinzor. 1999. 'Capitalizing on Transition Economies: The Role of the Russian Mafia in Trafficking Women for Forced Prostitution'. In Williams (1999a).

Cameron, M.A., R.J. Lawson, and B.W. Tomlin, eds. 1998. *To Walk without Fear*. Toronto: Oxford University Press.

Cameron, M.A., and M.A. Molot, eds. 1995. *Canada Among Nations 1995: Democracy and Foreign Policy*. Ottawa: Carleton University Press.

Cameron, M.A., and B.W. Tomlin. 2000. *The Making of NAFTA: How the Deal Was Done*. Ithaca: Cornell University Press.

Canada. Commission of Inquiry into the Deployment of Canadian Forces to Somalia. 1995. *Document Book No. 8, Racism*. Ottawa: Canadian Government Publishing.

———. 1997a. *Information Legacy: A Compendium of Source Material from the Commission of Inquiry into the Deployment of Canadian Forces to Somalia*. Ottawa: Canadian Government Publishing.

———. 1997b. *Dishonoured Legacy: The Lessons of the Somalia Affair*. Final report of the Commission. Ottawa: Minister of Public Works and Government Services Canada.

Canada. Department of Citizenship and Immigration (CIC). n.d. *Statistics*. <http:/www.cic.gc.ca/english/refugee/index.html>.

———. 2000. 'Landing Fee Eliminated for Refugees'. News release, 28 Feb. <http://www.cic.gc.ca/english/press/00/0006–pre.html>.

———. 1998. *Facts and Figures at a Glance*. <http://www.cic.gc.ca/english/index.html>.

Canada. Department of Foreign Affairs and International Trade (DFAIT). 1995a. *Canada in the World*. Ottawa: Publishing, Public Works and Government Services Canada.

———. 1995b. 'The Promotion of Prosperity and Employment'. In Department of Foreign Affairs and International Trade (1995a). <http://www.dfait-maeci.gc.ca/english/foreignp/cnd-world/chap3.htm>.

———. 1997a. *Agenda 2000: A Sustainable Development Strategy for the Department of Foreign Affairs and International Trade*. Ottawa: DFAIT.

———. 1997b. *An Agenda for Mine Action* (Ottawa), 2–4 Dec.

———. 1998a. *Canada World View* Ottawa, 20 Oct.

———. 1998b. 'Proposed Canadian Objectives and Priorities: ICPD +5 and Beyond'. <http://www.dfait_maeci.gc.ca/human_rights/paper_e.asp#Gender>.

———. 1998c. *Marchi Launches Internet Site Dedicated to Canadian Businesswomen*. Press release No. 150, 8 June. <http://www.dfait-maeci.gc.ca/english/news/press_releases/98_press/98_150e.htm>.

———. 1999a. 'Axworthy Announces Progress on Human Security Agenda' News Release 117, 20 May. <http://198.103.104.118/minpub/Publication.asp?FileSpec=/

Min_Pub_Docs/100335.htm>.

———. 1999b. *Implementing the Outcomes of the World Summit on Social Development*. Ottawa: DFAIT. <http://www.dfait-maeci.gc.ca/human_rights/909_e.pdf>.

———. 1999c. *Human Security: Safety for People in a Changing World*. Ottawa: DFAIT.

———. 1999d. *Marchi Welcomes New Data on Businesswomen Exporters*. Press Release No. 49, 8 March 8<http:///www.dfait-maeci.gc.ca/english/news/press_releases/99_press/99_049–e.htm>.

———. 1999e. 'Special Edition on Human Security'. *Canada World View*, Fall. Also available at <http://www.dfait-maeci.gc.ca>.

———. 1999f. 'Statement: Notes for Address by the Honourable Lloyd Axworthy Minister of Foreign Affairs to the Opening of the NGO Peacebuilding Consultations', 2 Mar. <http://198.103.118/minpub/Publˇ?/FileSpec=/Min_Pub_Docs/100235.htm>.

———. 1999g. 'Canadian Priorities and Objectives for the Habitat Agenda'. <http://www.dfait-maeci.gc.ca/english/foreign/social/habitat.htm>.

2000a. *Freedom From Fear: Canada's Foreign Policy for Human Security*. <http://www.dfait.maeci.gc.ca/foreignp/humansecurity/HumanSecurity Booklet-3.asp>.

———. 2000b. 'Foreign Policy: Social Issues: Humanitarian Affairs: Migration Issues'. <//www.dfait-maeci.gc.ca/menu-e.asp>.

Canada. Office of the Auditor General. 1997. <http://www.oagbvg.cg.ca/domino/cesd>.

Canada. Office of the Auditor General, and the Commissioner of the Environment and Sustainable Development. 2000. 'The Auditor General of Canada Announces the Appointment of the New Commissioner of the Environment and Sustainable Development'. News Release. 21 Aug. Ottawa. <http://www.oag_bvg.gc.ca/domino/media.nsf/html/00comm_e.html>.

Canada. Secretary of State. 1985. *The Women's Program and the Role of Women's Voluntary Organization in Promoting Change*. Ottawa: Secretary of State.

———. Special Joint Committee on Canada's Defence Policy. 1994. 'Security in a Changing World'. Report of the Committee. Ottawa: Public Works and Government Services Canada.

———. Special Joint Committee Reviewing Canadian Foreign Policy. 1994. *Canada's Foreign Policy: Principles and Priorities for the Future*. Report of the Committee. Ottawa: Public Works and Government Services Canada.

———. Standing Committee on Foreign Affairs and International Trade. 2000. *Testimony*, P. Martin. Ottawa: House of Commons, 18 May.

———. Standing Committee on National Defence and Veterans Affairs. 1993. 'The Dilemmas of a Committed Peacekeeper: Canada and the Renewal of Peacekeeping'. Ottawa: Public Works and Government Services Canada.

———. Working Group on Transnational Crime. 1999. *Solicitations for Research Proposals*. Ottawa: Canadian Government Publishing.

Canadian Beijing Facilitating Committee. 1996. *Take Action for Equality, Development and Peace: A Canadian Follow-up Guide to Beijing '95*. Ottawa: The Committee.

———. 1994. *Onward to Beijing: For Equality, Development and Peace*. Newsletter 1, no. 2 (Dec.).

Canadian Council for Refugees. 2000. *Report on Systemic Racism and Discrimination in Canadian Refugee and Immigration Policies*. <http://www.web.net/~ccr/antiracrep.htm>.

Canadian Human Rights Act Review Panel. 2000. *Promoting Equality: A New Vision*. Ottawa: Minister of Justice.

Canadian International Development Agency (CIDA). 1997. 'Combatting Desertification: Meeting the Challenge: Canada's Commitment to the United Nations Convention to Combat Desertification'. <http://www.acdi-cida.gc.ca/cida_ind.nsf>.

———. 1999. <http://www.acdi_cida.gc.ca/agency_e.htm>.

Canadian Labour Congress (CLC). 1997. *Women's Work: A Report*. Ottawa: CLC.

Canadian Research Institute for the Advancement of Women (CRIAW). 1997. 'From Beijing to the Millennium: Report of a meeting held on May 30/31, 1 June, organized by the Canadian Research Institute for the Advancement of Women'. Ottawa: CRIAW.

———. 1998. *Making Connections: Canadian Women Act on Beijing*. Project Presented to the Women's Program, Status of Women Canada. Ottawa: CRIAW.

Canadian Women's Studies, Les Cahiers de la Femme (CWS/CF). 1999. Special issue, 'Immigrant and Refugee Women'. 19, 3.

Canadian World March of Women. 2000a. 'History of the Canadian Women's March Committee'. <http://www.canada.marchofwomen.org/en/history/international.html>.

———. 2000b. 'It's Time for Change: Demands to the Federal Government of Canada'. < http://www.canada.marchofwomen.org/en/demands/intro.html>.

———. 2000c. 'Welcome: Marching United for Our Future'.<http://www.canada.marchofwomen.org/en/welcome>.

Carney, P. 2000. *Trade Secrets: A Memoir*. Toronto: Key Porter.

Carpenter, B. 2000. *Re-Thinking Prostitution: Feminism, Sex and the Self*. New York: Peter Lang.

Carty, L., ed. 1993. *And Still We Rise: Feminist Political Mobilizing in Contemporary Canada*. Toronto: Women's Press.

Castel, J. 1992. 'Rape, Sexual Assault and the Meaning of Persecution'. *International Journal of Refugee Law* 4, no. 1: 39–56.

CBC News. 1999a. 'An International Concern, Chinese Boat People: Human Cargo'. <http://cbc.ca/insidecbc/newsinrevi...099/Boat%20People/Internatonal.html>.

———. 1999b. 'Change Immigrant Law: Reform.' <http://(wysiwg://53/htt://cbc.ca/cgi-bin...cgi?/news/1999/09/02/reform990902>, 2 Sept.

———. 1999c 'Chinese Boat People: Human Cargo: The System'. <http://cbc.ca/insidecbc/newsinrevi...099/Boat%20People/System.html>.

———. 1999d. 'Ottawa Offers Illegal Migrants Deal', 8 Nov. < http://cbc.ca/cgi-bin/templates/view.cgi?category=Canada&story=news/1999/11/27/immcaplan9>.

Cheney, P. 1994. 'Canada ... Canada'. *The Toronto Star*, 10 July, F1.

Chimni, B.S. 1993. 'The Meaning of Words and the Role of UNHCR in Voluntary Repatriation'. *International Journal of Refugee Law* 5, no. 3: 442–60.

Chopra, J. 1998. 'Introducing Peace-Maintenance'. *Global Governance* 4, no. 1: 1.

CIDA. *See* Canadian International Development Agency.

Cipriani, L. 1993. 'Gender and Persecution: Protecting Women under International Refugee Law'. *Georgetown Immigration Law Journal* 7: 511–48.

Citizens for Public Justice. 1999. *Statement on Boat People*. <http://www.web.net/~ccr/cpjboats.htm>.

Citizens' Inquiry into Peace and Security. 1992. *Transformation Moment: A Canadian Vision of Common Security*. (Report of the inquiry.) Waterloo, Ont., Mar.

Clark, J. 1997. 'The First International Country'. *International Journal* 52, no. 4 (Autumn): 539–45.

Clarke, T., and M. Barlow. 1997. *MAI: Multilateral Agreement on Investment and the Threat to Canadian Sovereignty*. Toronto: Stoddart.

Clement. W., ed. 1996. *Building on the New Canadian Political Economy*. Montreal: McGill-Queen's University Press.

Cohen, M.G. 1987. *Free Trade and the Future of Women's Work: Manufacturing and Service Industries*. Toronto: Garamond.

Cohen, R., and F. Deng. 1998. *The Forsaken People: Case Studies of the Internally Displaced*. Washington, DC: Brookings Institution Press.

Connell, R.W. 1995. *Masculinities*. Berkeley: University of California Press

Connors, J. 1997. 'Legal Aspects of Women as a Particular Social Group'. *International Journal of Refugee Law*, Special Issue, 9 (Autumn): 114–28.

Convention on the Elimination of All Forms of Racial Discrimination. 1966. UNGA Res. 2106 (XX).

Convention on the Elimination of All Forms of Racial Discrimination against Women. 1981.GA Res. 34/180, UN GAOR, 34th Session (Supp. No. 46).

Cooper, A.F. 1997. *Canadian Foreign Policy: Old Habits and New Directions*. Scarborough: Prentice Hall Allyn and Bacon.

Corner, L. 1996. *Women, Men and Economics: The Gender-Differentiated Impact of Macroeconomics*. New York: UNIFEM.

Coulon, J. 1998. *Soldiers of Diplomacy: The United Nations, Peacekeeping, and the New World Order*. Toronto: University of Toronto Press.

Cox, R.W. 1986. 'Social Forces, States and World Orders: Beyond International Relations Theory'. In Keohane.

———. 1987. *Production, Power and World Order: Social Forces in the Making of History*. New York: Columbia University Press.

———. 1996a. 'The Global Political Economy and Social Choice'. In Cox and Sinclair (1996).

———. 1996b. 'Multilateralism and World Order'. In Cox and Sinclair (1996).

———. 1999. 'Civil Society at the Turn of the Millennium'. *Review of International Studies* 25, no. 1: 3–28.

———, and L. Axworthy. 2000. 'Correspondence: The Crisis in Kosovo'. *Studies on Political Economy* 63 (Autumn): 133–52.

———, and T.J. Sinclair, eds. 1996. *Approaches to World Order*. Cambridge, U.K.: Cambridge University Press.

———, and C.T. Sjolander. 1998. 'Damage Control: The Politics of National Defence'. In Pal.

Craske, N. 1998. 'Remasculinization and the Neoliberal State'. In Randall and Waylen.

CRIAW. *See* Canadian Research Institute for the Advancement of Women.

Crosby, A. D. 1998a. *Dilemmas in Defence Decision-Making: Constructing Canada's Role in NORAD, 1958–96*. Houndsmills, U.K.: Macmillan.

———. 1998b. 'Defining Security Environments for Global Governance: Canada and the U.S. "Global Protection System."' *Global Governance* 4: 331–53.

Dale, A., and J.B. Robinson, eds. 1996. *Achieving Sustainable Development*. Vancouver: UBC Press.

Dale, S. 1993. 'Guns 'n' Poses: The Myths of Canadian Peacekeeping'. *This Magazine* 26 (Mar.–Apr.), pp. 11–16.

———. 1999. *Lost in the Suburbs: A Political Travelogue*. Toronto: Stoddart.

Daley, K. 1998. Assistant to N. Mawani, Chairperson of the IRB. Personal interview with E. Baines. 21 May, Ottawa.

Das, L.S. 1997. *Awakening the Buddha Within*. New York: Broadway.

Day, S., and G. Brodsky. 1998. *Women and the Equality Deficit: The Impact of Restructuring Canada's Social Programs*. Ottawa: Status of Women Canada.

de Goede, Marieke. 2000. 'Mastering "Lady Credit": Discourses of Financial Crisis in Historical Perspective'. *International Feminist Journal of Politics* 2, no.1 (Spring): 58–81.

de Larringa, M., and C.T. Sjolander. 1998. '(Re)presenting Landmines from Protector to

Enemy'. In Cameron, Lawson, and Tomlin.

Desbarats, P. 1997. *Somalia Cover-Up: A Commissioner's Journal.* Toronto: McClelland and Stewart.

De Stoop, C. 1994. *They Are So Sweet, Sir: The Cruel World of Trafficking in Filipinas and Other Women.* Trans. F. Hubert-Baterna and L. Hubert-Baterna. Manila: Limitless Asia.

DFAIT. *See* Canada. Department of Foreign Affairs and International Trade.

Dion, S. 1997. 'Canada is Going to Make it After All!' Notes for an address by the Honourable S. Dion, President of the Privy Council and Minister of Intergovernmental Affairs at the biennial conference of the Association for Canadian Studies in the United States, Minneapolis, Minnesota, 21 Nov.

Dobell, P.C. 1972. *Canada's Search for New Roles: Foreign Policy in the Trudeau Era.* London: Royal Institute of International Affairs.

Dobrowolsky, M.A. 2000. *The Politics of Pragmatism: Women, Representation and Constitutionalism in Canada.* Toronto: Oxford University Press.

Doezema, J. 1998. 'Forced to Choose: Beyond the Voluntary v. Forced Prostitution Dichotomy'. In Kempadoo and Doezema.

———. 1999. 'Loose Women or Lost Women: The Re-emergence of the Myth of White Slavery in Contemporary Discourses of Trafficking in Women'. Paper delivered to the International Studies Association annual meeting, Washington, DC.

Dornan, C. 1995. 'Scenes from a Scandal'. *The Globe and Mail.* 21 Jan.

Doty, R.L. 1996. 'Sovereignty and the Nation: Constructing the Boundaries of National Identity'. In Biersteker and Weber.

———. 1997. *Imperial Encounters: The Politics of Representation in North-South Relations.* Minneapolis: University of Minnesota Press.

Draimin, T., and B. Tomlinson. 1998. 'Is There a Future for Canadian Aid in the Twenty-First Century?' In Hampson and Molot.

Dunne, T. 1997. 'Colonial Encounters in International Relations: Reading Wight, Writing Australia'. *Australian Journal of International Affairs* 51, no. 3: 309–23.

Durano, M.F.B. 1999. 'Gender Issues in International Trade'. Women's Strategic Planning Seminar on Gender and Trade. Organized by the Centre of Concern and DAWN Caribbean, Grenada, West Indies, 8–11 Dec.

Dyck, N. 1991. *What Is the Indian Problem: Tutelage and Resistance in Canadian Indian Administration.* St. John's: Institute of Social and Economic Research.

The Economist. 1996. 'Tomorrow's Second Sex'. 28 Sept.

Eggleton, A. 1997. Notes for an Address by the Honourable Art Eggleton, Minister for International Trade, on the Occasion of the International Conference of the World Association of Women Entrepreneurs. Toronto, 3 May.

Elson, D. 1989. 'The Impact of Structural Adjustment on Women: Concepts and Issues'. In Ominode.

———. 1992. 'From Survival Strategies to Transformation Strategies: Women's Needs and Structural Adjustment'. In Beneria and Feldman.

———, and R. Pearson. 1981. 'Nimble Fingers Make Cheap Workers: An Analysis of Women's Employment in Third World Export Manufacturing'. *Feminist Review*, no. 7: 87–107.

Enloe, C. 1989. *Bananas, Beaches and Bases: Making Feminist Sense Out of International Relations.* London: Pandora.

———. 1993. *The Morning After: Sexual Politics at the End of the Cold War.* Berkeley: University of California Press.

———. 1996. 'Margins, Silences and Bottom Rungs: How to Overcome the Underestimation of Power in the Study of International Relations'. In Smith, Booth, and Zalewski.

———. 2000. *Maneuvers: The International Politics of Militarizing Women's Lives.* Berkeley: University of California Press

Environment Canada. 1997. *Sustainable Development Strategy: Summary Document.* Ottawa: Public Works and Government Services Canada.

Evans, P., and G. Wekerle, eds. 1997. *Women and the Canadian Welfare State.* Toronto: University of Toronto Press.

FAFIA (Canadian Feminist Alliance for International Action). 1999. *The Other Side of the Story: A Feminist Critique of Canada's National Response to the UN Questionnaire on the Implementation of the Beijing Platform for Action.* Ottawa: FAFIA.

———. 2000. *Alternative Report on Canada: Prepared for the Special Session of the United Nations General Assembly June 2000 to review progress in implementing the Beijing Platform for Action.* Ottawa: FAFIA.

Federal/Provincial/Territorial Ministers of Energy and Environment. 2000. 'Background to the National Implementation Strategy on Climate Change: International Context'. <http://www.nccp.ca/nccp/pdt/media/book_3_en.pdf>.

Feldman, A. 2000. 'Rational Ambivalence: The UNHCR Responses to Internal Displacement Emergencies'. Paper presented at the International Studies Association, Los Angeles, 14–18 Mar.

Foster, P. 2000. 'The Gender Guidelines: From Margins to the Centre?' *CWS/CF* 19, no. 3: 45–50.

Francis, D. 1997. *National Dreams: Myth, Memory and Canadian History.* Vancouver: Arsenal Pulp Press.

Gabriel, C., and L. Macdonald. 1994. 'NAFTA, Women and Organising in Canada and Mexico: Forging a Feminist Internationality'. *Millennium: Journal of International Studies* 23, no. 3 (Winter): 535–62.

———. 1996. 'NAFTA and Economic Restructuring: Some Gender and Race Implications'. In Bakker (1994a).

Galtung, J. 1971. 'A Structural Theory of Imperialism'. *International Journal of Peace Research* 8: 81–118.

George, J., and D. Campbell. 1990. 'Patterns of Dissent and the Celebration of Difference: Critical Social Theory and International Relations'. *International Studies Quarterly* 34: 269–93.

Gibb, H. 1997. *Gender Front and Centre: An APEC Primer.* Ottawa: North-South Institute.

Giles, Wenona. 1996. 'Aid Recipients or Citizens? Canada's Role in Managing the Gender Relations of Forced Migration'. In Giles, Moussa, and Van Esterik (1996).

———, W., H. Moussa, and P. Van Esterik, eds. 1996. *Development and Diaspora: Gender and the Refugee Experience.* Dundas, Ont.: Artemis Enterprises.

Gill, S. 1996. 'Globalization, Democratization and the Politics of Indifference'. In Mittelman.

———, and J. H. Mittelman, eds. 1997. *Innovation and Transformation in International Studies.* Cambridge: Cambridge University Press.

Ginifer, J., ed. 1997. *Beyond the Emergency: Development within UN Peace Missions.* London: Frank Cass.

Gluck, S., and D. Patai. 1991. *Women's Words: The Feminist Practice of Oral History.* New York: Routledge.

Gordon, L., ed. 1990. *Women, the State and Welfare.* New York: Routledge.

Grandea, N. 1997. 'Engendering the Asia-Pacific Economic Cooperation (APEC Forum). Document #WLN-CAN97–003, produced for Session 2 of the Women Leaders Network meeting, Ottawa-Hull, 13–16 Sept.

Greatbatch, J. 1989. 'The Gender Difference: Feminist Critiques of Refugee Discourse'.

International Journal of Refugee Law 1, no. 4: 518–27.

Grinspun, R., and R. Kreklewich. 1994. 'Consolidating Neoliberal Reforms: "Free Trade" as a Conditioning Framework'. *Studies in Political Economy* 43 (Spring): 269–93.

Gutierrez, E. 1995. 'Women—Latin America: Integration . . . for Men?' *Inter Press Service*, 12 Sept.

Gwinnett, B. 1998. 'Policing Prostitution: Gender, the State and Community Politics'. In Randall and Waylen.

Haglund, D. 1999. 'Grand Strategy—or Merely a Geopolitical Free-for-all'. In Hampson, Hart, and Rudner.

Hallock Johnson, S. 1999. 'An Ecofeminist Critique of the International Economic Structure'. In Meyer and Prügl.

Hammerstad, A. 2000. 'Whose Security? UNHCR, Refugee Protection and State Security after the Cold War'. Paper presented at the International Studies Association annual meeting, Los Angeles, 14–18 Mar.

Hampson, F., M. Hart, and M. Rudner, eds. 1999. *Canada Among Nations, 1999: A Big League Player?* Toronto: Oxford University Press.

———, and M.A. Molot, eds. 1998. *Canada Among Nations 1998: Leadership and Dialogue.* Toronto: Oxford University Press.

———, and D. Oliver. 1998. 'Pulpit Diplomacy: A Critical Assessment of the Axworthy Doctrine'. *International Journal* 53, no. 3 (Summer): 379–406.

Harrison, D., and L. Laliberté. 1994. *No Life Like It: Military Wives in Canada.* Toronto: James Lorimer.

Hay, Robin Jeffrey. 1999. 'Present at the Creation? Human Security and Canadian Foreign Policy in the Twenty-First Century'. In Hampson, Hart, and Rudner, eds.

Heinbecker, P. 1999. 'Human Security'. *Peace Magazine.* Summer, pp. 13–14.

Heininger, J.E. 1994. *Peacekeeping in Transition: The United Nations in Cambodia.* New York: Twentieth Century Fund Press.

Hemispheric Social Alliance. 2001. *Alternatives for the Americas.* Discussion draft # 3, revised for the 2nd People's Summit of the Americas (April).<http://www.asc-hsa.org/pdf/altering2.pdf>.

Hicks-Stiehm, J. 1999. 'United Nations Peacekeeping: Men's and Women's Work'. In Meyer and Prügl.

Hobe, S. 1998. 'Global Challenges to Statehood: The Increasingly Important Role of Nongovernmental Organizations'. *Global Law School Journal* 5, no. 1. <http://www.law.indiana.edu/glsj/vol15/no1/hobe.html>.

Hobsbawm, E.J. 1968. *Industry and Empire.* Penguin.

Homer-Dixon, T. 1994. 'Environmental Scarcities and Violent Conflict: Evidence from Cases'. *International Security* 19, no. 2: 5–40.

hooks, b. 1994. *Teaching to Transgress: Education as the Practice of Freedom.* New York: Routledge.

Hooper, C. 1998. 'Masculinist Practices and Gender Politics: The Operation of Multiple Masculinities in International Relations'. In Zalewski and Parpart.

Hossie, L. 1993. 'For Women, Oppression Is a Way of Life.' *Globe and Mail*, 5 Feb.

Human Rights Watch. 1996. *No Guarantees: Sex Discrimination in Mexico's Maquiladora Sector'* 8, no. 6 (August).

Hyndman, J. 1996. 'International Responses to Human Displacement: Neo-liberalism and Post–Cold War Geopolitics'. *Refuge* 15, no. 3: 5–9.

———. 1997. 'Managing and Containing Displacement after the Cold War: UNHCR and Somali Refugees in Kenya'. *Refuge* 16, no. 5: 6–10.

Ignatieff, M. 2000. *Virtual War: Kosovo and Beyond*. Viking.

Indiana Journal of Global Legal Studies. 1996. 'Special Issue on Feminism and Globalization: The Impact of the Global Economy on Women and Feminist Theory'. 4, 1 (Fall).

Indra, D. 1987. 'Gender: A Key Dimension of the Refugee Experience'. *Refuge* 6:6.

———. 1989. 'Ethnic Human Rights and Feminist Theory: Gender Implications for Refugee Studies and Practice'. *Journal of Refugee Studies* 2, no. 2: 221–41.

International Committee of the Red Cross (ICRC). 1996. *Anti-personnel Landmines: Friend or Foe?* Geneva: ICRC.

International Convenant on Civil and Political Rights. 1966. UN GA Res. 2200A (XXI), 21 UN GAOR (Supp. No. 16) 52, UN Doc. A/6316.

International Convenant on Economic, Social and Cultural Rights. 1966. GA Res. 2200A (XXI) UN Doc. A/6316. Came into force 3 Jan. 1976.

International Organization for Migration. 1995. 'Trafficking and Prostitution: The Growing Exploitation of Migrant Women from Central and Eastern Europe'. <http://www.iom.int/iom/Publications/entry.htm>.

Jakobsen, J. 1998. *Working Alliances and the Politics of Difference*. Bloomington: Indiana University Press.

Jimenez, M., and S. Bell. 2000. '650 Charges in Canadian Sex Slave Trade'. *National Post*. 14 Apr.

Jockel, J.T. 1994. *Canada and International Peacekeeping*. Washington: Center for Strategic and International Studies.

Joekes, S. 1995. 'A Gender Perspective on Development and International Trade'. *ICDA Journal* 3, no. 2: 81–93.

———, and Ann Weston. 1994. *Women and the New Trade Agenda*. New York: UNIFEM.

Jones, A. 1999. 'Pity the Innocent Men.' *The Globe and Mail*, 20 Feb.

Kaplan, T. 1997. *Crazy for Democracy: Women in Grassroots Movements*. New York: Routledge.

Keeble, E., and H. Smith. 1999. *(Re)Defining Traditions: Gender and Canadian Foreign Policy*. Halifax: Fernwood.

Keller-Herzog, A. 1996. 'Globalisation and Gender: Development Perspectives and Interventions'. Prepared for Women in Development and Gender Equity Division, Policy Branch, Canadian International Development Agency, Dec.

Kelly, N. 1993a. 'Assessing Gender-Based Persecution Claims'. Paper delivered to conference 'Gender Issues and Refugees: Development Implication', 9–11 May, Toronto.

———. 1993b. 'Gender-Related Persecution: Assessing the Asylum Claims of Women'. *Cornell International Law Journal* 26: 565.

Kelson, G. 1999. 'Recognizing Gender-Based Persecution in Canada: Are Canada's Guidelines Being Used Consistently?' *CWS/CF* 19, no. 3: 149–53.

Kempadoo, K., and J. Doezema, eds. 1998. *Global Sex Workers: Rights, Resistance and Redefinition*. New York: Routledge.

Keohane, R.O., ed. 1986. *Neorealism and Its Critics*. New York: Columbia University Press.

Kerr, J. 1994. *Expert Group Meeting on Women and Global Economic Restructuring. Final Report*. Ottawa: North-South Institute.

Kettel, B. 1996. 'Putting Women and the Environment First: Poverty Alleviation and Sustainable Development'. In Dale and Robinson.

Kien, S.P. 1995. 'The Lessons of the UNTAC Experience and the Ongoing Responsibilities of the International Community for Peacebuilding and Development in Cambodia'. *Pacifica Review* 7, no. 2: 129–33.

Kofman, E., and G. Youngs, eds. 1996. *Globalization: Theory and Practice*. London: Pinter.

Krause, J. 1994. 'The International Dimension of Gender Inequality and Feminist Politics:

A New Direction for International Political Economy?' Paper to be presented at the conference 'Global Politics: Setting Agendas for the Year 2000', Nottingham Trent University, 25–27 July.

Kuttner, S. 1997. 'Gender-related Persecution as a Basis for Refugee Status: The Emergence of an International Norm'. *Refuge* 16, no. 4 (Oct.): 17–21.

Lakey, B. 1995. *Grassroots and Nonprofit Leadership: A Guide for Organizations in Changing Times*. Gabriola Island, BC: New Society Publishers.

Lambert, H. 1997. 'New Directions in Refugee Protection: Yugoslavia as a Precedent for Response to Future Crises'. Paper presented at the International Studies Association, Toronto, 18–22 Mar.

Liberal Party of Canada. 1993. *Creating Opportunity: The Liberal Plan for Canada*. Ottawa: The Party.

Liebich, F., and J. Ramirez. 1996. 'A History of Institutional Change: The IRB Working Group on Refugee Women'. In Giles, Moussa, and Esterik.

Lim, L. 1998. *The Sex Sector: The Economic and Social Bases of Prostitution in Southeast Asia*. Geneva: International Labour Office.

Ling, L.H.M. 1996. 'Hegemony and the Internationalizing State: A Post-colonial Analysis of China's Integration into Asian Corporatism'. *Review of International Political Economy* 3, no. 1: 1–26.

Lipshutz, R. 1992. 'Reconstructing World Politics: The Emergence of Global Civil Society'. *Millennium* 21, no. 3: 389–420.

Loomba, A. 1998. *Colonialism/Postcolonialism*. London: Routledge.

Luke, C. 1996. 'Feminist Pedagogy Theory: Reflections on Power and Authority'. *Educational Theory* 46, no. 3 (Summer): 283–302.

Lynch, C. 1999. 'The Promise and Problems of Internationalism'. *Global Governance* 5: 88–101.

McClintock, A., A. Mufti, and E. Shohat, eds. 1997. *Dangerous Liaisons: Gender, Nation and Postcolonial Perspectives*. Minneapolis: University of Minnesota Press.

McCoy, A.W., 1995. '"Same Banana": Hazing and Honor at the Philippine Military Academy'. *Journal of Asian Studies* 54, no. 3 (Aug.): 689–726.

———. 1997. 'Ram Boys: Changing Images of the Masculine in the Philippine Military'. Paper Presented at the International Studies Association Annual Meetings, Toronto, 18–22 Mar.

Macdonald, L. 1995. 'Unequal Partnerships: The Politics of Canada's Relations with the Third World'. *Studies in Political Economy* 47 (Summer).

———. 1999. 'Trade with a Female Face: Women and the New International Trade Agenda'. In Taylor and Thomas.

———. 2000. 'Democracy, Human Rights and the Transformation of Civil Society in the New North America'. In Thomas.

McDonald, L., B. Moore, and N. Timoshkina. 2000. 'Migrant Sex Workers from Eastern Europe and the Former Soviet Union: The Canadian Case'.<http://www.swc-cfc.gc.ca/publish/research/001115–0662653351>.

MacDonald, M. 1996. 'Promises, Promises: Canadian Campaign Rhetoric, *Agenda 21*, and the Status of Women'. In Dale and Robinson.

MacKenzie, Major General (retired) L. 1996. *Testimony to the Commission of Inquiry into the Deployment of Canadian Forces to Somalia*. 1 Feb. Ottawa: Canadian Government Publishing.

———. 2000. 'Airborne Never Received a Sliver of the Credit It Earned'. *The Ottawa Citizen*, 15 July, A6.

Macklin, A. 1995. 'Refugee Women and the Imperative of Categories'. *Human Rights Quarterly* 17, no. 2: 213–77.

———.1996. 'Opening the Door to Refugee Women: A First Crack'. In Giles, Moussa, and

Van Esterik.

———. A. 1997. 'Gender Based Persecution in Armed Conflict: Focus on Refugee and Internally Displaced Women'. Paper presented to the UN Expert Group Meeting on Gender-based Persecution, 9–12 Nov, Toronto.

MacLaren, R. 1995. Statement 95/2. 'Canada's Trade Policy for the 21st Century: The Walls of Jericho Fall Down'. Notes for an Address by the Honourable Roy MacLaren, Minister for International Trade, to the Centre for International Studies and the Centre for International Business, University of Toronto, Toronto, 18 Jan.

McLellan, A. 2000. 'Notes for a Speech by the Honourable Anne McLellan Minister of Justice and Attorney General of Canada to 10th Congress on Prevention of Crime and the Treatment of Offenders on Women in the Criminal Justice System', 14 Apr. Vienna. <http://www.canada.justice.ca/en/news/sp/2000>.

McMichael, P. 2000. *Development and Social Change*, 2nd edn. Thousand Oaks, Calif.: Pine Forge Press.

Macpherson, K. 1994. *When in Doubt, DO BOTH: The Times of My Life*. Toronto: University of Toronto Press.

MacRae, J. 1999. 'Aiding Peace ... and War: UNHCR, Returnee Reintegration, and the Relief Development Debate', *New Issues in Refugee Research*. Working Paper No. 14. Geneva: UNHCR.

Malone, D. 1999. 'The Global Issues Biz: What Gives?' In Hampson, Hart, and Rudner.

Manalo, R.G. 1997. 'The Experience and Challenge of Engendering APEC'. Document #WLN-CAN97–021 for Session 2, Strategies to Integrate Gender Perspectives into APEC. 13–16 Sept. Ottawa and Hull: Women Leaders Network.

Manley, J. 2000. Notes for an Address by the Honourable John Manley, Minister of Foreign Affairs, to the Third Annual Diplomatic Forum 'Canada's Foreign Policy Agenda and Priorities', Winnipeg, 20 Oct. <http://198.103.104.118/minpub/Publication.asp?/FileSpec=/Min_Pub_Docs/103808.htm>.

Manson, General P. D. 1988. 'Peacekeeping in a Changing World'. Address to the Empire Club of Canada, 17 Nov., Toronto. *Canadian Speeches*, 2, 8 (Dec.): 35–41.

Marchand, M. 1995. 'Latin American Women Speak on Development: Are We Listening Yet?' In Marchand and Parpart.

———. 1998. 'Different Communities/Different Realities/Different Encounters: A Reply to J. Ann Tickner'. *International Studies Quarterly* 42, no. 1: 199–204.

———. 2000. 'Gendered Representations of the "Global": Reading/Writing Globalization'. In Stubbs and Underhill.

———, and J.L. Parpart, eds. 1995. *Feminism, Postmodernism, Development*. London: Routledge.

Marchi, S. 1997. 'Notes for an Address by the Honourable Sergio Marchi, Minister for International Trade, to the Luncheon for William Daley, U.S. Secretary of Commerce, Offered by the Canadian Businesswomen's International Trade Mission'. 13 Nov. Washington, DC. <http://198.103.104.118/minpub/Publication.asp?FileSpec=/Min_Pub_Docs/101766.htm>.

———. 1998. 'Notes for an Address by the Honourable Sergio Marchi, Minister for International Trade, to the Centre for Trade Policy and Law', 13 Feb. Ottawa. <http://www.dfait-maeci.gc.ca/english/news/statements/98_state/98_008e.htm>.

———. 1999a. 'Notes for an Address by the Honourable Sergio Marchi, Minister for International Trade, to the Business Networking Luncheon co-hosted by the Ireland-Canada Business Association and the Canadian Embassy', Dublin, 14 June.<http://198.103.104.118/minpub/Publication.asp?FileSpec=/Min_Pub_Docs/101433.htm>.

———. 1999b. 'Notes for an Address by the Honourable Sergio Marchi, Minister for

International Trade to the Canada-U.S.A. Businesswomen's Trade Summit, Toronto, 18 May<http://198.103.104.118/minpub/Publication.asp?FileSpec=/Min_Pub_Docs/100232.htm>.

———. 1999c. 'Canada and the World Trade Organization: Opening Opportunities around the World'. A Statement by the Honourable Sergio Marchi Minister for International Trade to the House of Commons Standing Committee on Foreign Affairs and International Trade, 9 May, Ottawa. <http://198.103.104.118/minpub/Publication.asp?FileSpec=/Min_Pub_Docs/100222.htm>.

Marino, D. 1998. *Wild Garden: Art, Education and the Culture of Resistance.* Toronto: Between the Lines.

Marsden, L. 1992. *Timing and Presence: Getting Women's Issues on the Trade Agenda.* Working Paper Series: Gender, Science and Development Programme 3, July, Toronto: International Federation of Institutes for Advanced Study.

Martin, P., and M. Fortmann. 1995. 'Canadian Public Opinion and Peacekeeping in a Turbulent World'. *International Journal* 50, no. 2 (Spring): 370–400.

Mathias, P. 1999. 'Refugee Program Biased Towards Women'. *The National Post*, 20 Feb.

———. 1993b. 'The Factual and Legal Legitimacy of Addressing Gender Issues'. *Refuge* 13, no. 4: 7–10.

———. 1993c. 'The Convention Definition and Gender-Related Persecution: The IRB Perspective'.Conference paper presented to 'Gender Issues and Refugees: Development Implications', 10 May. North York : York University, Centre for Refugee Studies and Centre for Feminist Research.

Mawani, N. 1995. 'Violations of the Rights of Refugee Women in the Refugee Context'. *National Journal of Constitutional Law* 5: 5.

Mertus, J. 1998. 'The State and the Post-Cold War Refugee Regime'. *International Journal of Refugee Law* 10, no. 3: 321–48.

Meyer, M., and E. Prügl, eds. 1999. *Gender Politics in Global Governance.* Lanham, Md.: Rowman and Littlefield.

Mies, M. 1986. *The Lace Makers of Narsapur: Indian Housewives Produce for the World Market.* London: Zed Books.

———. 1993. 'The Myth of Catching-Up Development'. In Mies and Shiva (1993).

———, and V. Shiva. 1993. *Ecofeminism.* London: Zed Books.

Miles, A. 1996. *Integrative Feminisms.* New York: Routledge.

Miller, B. 2000. 'Chinese Migrants Deported'. *Prince George Citizen*, 11 May.

Miller, L. 1990. *Global Order: Values and Power in International Politics.* Boulder: Westview Press.

Mills, K. 1997. 'United Nations Intervention in Refugee Crises in the Post-Cold War World'. Paper presented at the International Studies Association, Toronto, 18–22 March.

Mitchell, B., ed. 1995. *Resource and Environmental Management in Canada: Addressing Conflict and Uncertainty.* 2nd edn. Toronto: Oxford University Press.

Mittelman J., ed. 1996. 'Globalization: Critical Reflections'. *International Political Economy Yearbook* 9. Boulder: Lynne Reimer.

Moghadam, V. 1999. 'Gender and the Global Economy' in M. Marx Ferre, J. Lorber, and B. Hess., eds. *Revisioning Gender.* London: Sage.

Mohanty, C.T. 1991. 'Under Western Eyes: Feminist Scholarship and Colonial Discourses'. In Mohanty, Russo and Torres.

———. 1997. 'Under Western Eyes: Feminist Scholarship and Colonial Discourses'. In McClintock, Muftis, and Shohat.

———, A. Russo, and L. Torres., eds. 1991. *Third World Women and the Politics of Feminism.* Bloomington: Indiana University Press.

Molot, M.A. 1990. 'Where Do We, Should We, or Can We Sit? A Review of Canadian Foreign Policy Literature'. *International Journal of Canadian Studies* 1–2.

Moran, B. 1988. *Stoney Creek Woman: The Story of Mary John*. Vancouver: Arsenal Pulp Press.

Morgan, D.H.J. 1994. 'Theater of War: Combat, the Military, and Masculinities'. In Brod and Kaufman.

Morrison, D. 1998. *Aid and Ebb Tide: A History of CIDA and Canadian Development Assistance.* Waterloo: Wilfrid Laurier University Press in association with the North-South Institute.

Mosher, J. 2000. 'Managing the Disentitlement of Women: Glorified Markets, the Idealized Family, and the Underserving Other'. In Neysmith.

Mottram, M., and D. Lague. 1999. 'Why doors are shutting on the world's homeless'. Saturday, 27 Nov. <http://www.theage.com.au/news/19991127/A1341-1999Nov26.html>.

Moxon-Browne, E., ed. 1998. *A Future for Peacekeeping?* Basingstoke: Macmillan.

Murphy, A.B. 1996. 'The Sovereign State System as Political-Territorial Ideal'. In Biersteker and Weber.

Murphy, C. 1996. 'Seeing Women, Recognizing Gender, Recasting International Relations'. *International Organization* 50, no. 3 (Summer): 513–38.

———. 1998. 'Six Masculine Roles in International Relations and Their Interconnection: A Personal Investigation'. In Zalewski and Parpart.

Musa, E.T. 1993. 'Actions of the International NGO Working Group on Refugee Women 1991–93'. Paper prepared for the Refugee Desk, Anglican Church of Canada.

NAC. *See* National Action Committee on the Status of Women.

Nagel, S., and A. Robb, eds. 2001. *Handbook of Global Social Policy.* New York: Marcel Dekker.

Narayan, U. 1997. *Dislocating Cultures: Identities, Traditions, and Third World Feminism.* New York: Routledge.

Nash, J. 1994. 'The Challenge of Trade Liberalization to Cultural Survival on the Southern Frontier of Mexico'. *Indiana Journal of Global Legal Studies*, 1, no. 2: 367–95.

National Action Committee on the Status of Women (NAC).1990. *Parallel Report to the Second Report of Canada to the U.N. Committee on the Elimination of All Forms of Discrimination Against Women.* Ottawa: NAC.

———. 2000a. 'Women, Globalization and Trade'. Unpublished paper. Toronto, March.

———. 2000b. *Women 's Cry for Help Falls on Deaf Ears—Our Failing justice System Allows Yet Another Man to Murder Another Woman.* Press release. 23 June. <http://www.nac-cca.ca/about/news2000_e.htm>.

National Association of Women and the Law (NAWL). 1998. 'Canadian Women and the Social Deficit'. <http://www.nawl.ca/geneva.htm>.

———. 1999a. 'The Civil and Political Rights of Canadian Women'. <http://www.nawl.ca/civalpolit99.htm>.

———.1999b. *Gender Analysis of Immigration and Refugee Protection Legislation and Policy.* March. Ottawa: NAWL.

National Council of Welfare. 1998. *Poverty Profile 1996.* Ottawa: The Council.

National Film Board. 1992. *The Voice of Women: The First Thirty Years.* Montreal.

NAWL. *See* National Association of Women and the Law.

Neack, L., J. Hey, and P. Haney. 1995. *Foreign Policy Analysis: Continuity and Change in its Second Generation.* Englewood Cliffs, NJ: Prentice-Hall.

Nesmith, C., and P. Wright. 1995. 'Gender, Resources, and Environmental Management'. In Mitchell.

———. 1999. 'Working Globally for Gender Equality'. *Canadian Development Report 1999*. Ottawa: North-South Institute.

Neufeld, M. 1995a. 'Hegemony and Foreign Policy Analysis: The Case of Canada as a Middle Power'. *Studies in Political Economy*, 48 (Autumn): 7–29.

———. 1995b. *The Restructuring of International Relations Theory*. Cambridge, UK: Cambridge University Press.

———. 1999. 'Democratization in/of Canadian Foreign Policy: Critical Reflections'. *Studies in Political Economy* 58 (Spring): 97–119.

———. Forthcoming. 'Pitfalls of Emancipation and Discourses of Security: Reflections on Canada's "Security with a Human Face"'. In Booth.

Neufeld, M., and S. Whitworth. 1996. 'Image(in)ing Canadian Foreign Policy'. In Clement.

Newland, K., and D.W Meyers. 1999. 'Peacekeeping and Refugee Relief'. In Whitman.

Neysmith, S. 2000. *Restructuring Caring Labour*. Toronto: Oxford University Press.

Niva, S. 1998. 'Tough and Tender: New World Order Masculinity and the Gulf War'. In Zalewski and Parpart.

Nossal, K.R. 1983–4. 'Analyzing Domestic Sources of Canadian Foreign Policy'. *International Journal*, 39 (Winter): 1–22.

———. 1995. 'The Democratization of Canadian Foreign Policy: The Elusive Ideal'. In Maxwell and Appel Molot.

———. 1997. *The Politics of Canadian Foreign Policy*. 3rd edn. Scarborough: Prentice Hall.

———. 1998–9. 'Pinchpenny Diplomacy: The Decline of Good International Citizenship in Canadian Foreign Policy'. *International Journal* 54, no. 1 (Winter): 88–105.

———. 2000. 'Home-Grown IR: The Canadianization of International Relations'. *Journal of Canadian Studies* 35, no.1 (Spring): 95–116.

Ó Tuathail, G. 1996. *Critical Geopolitics: The Politics of Writing Global Space*. Minneapolis: University of Minnesota Press.

Off, C. 2000. *The Lion, The Fox and the Eagle: A Story of Generals and Justice in Yugoslavia and Rwanda*. Toronto: Random House Canada.

Oliver, D. 1998. 'The Canadian Military After Somalia'. In Hampson and Molot.

Ominode, B., ed. 1989. *The IMF, The World Bank and the African Debt*. Zed Books.

Ontario. Attorney General. 2002. 'Refugee and Immigration Law'. http://www.attorney-general.jus.gov.on.ca/html/OLAR/ch12.html.

Organisation for Economic Co-operation and Development (OECD). 1997. OECD Conference on Women Entrepreneurs in Small and Medium Enterprises. <http://www.oecd.org/dsti/sti/industry/smes/act/smeconf.htm>.

———. 2000. *Women Entrepreneurs in SMEs: Realising the Benefits of Globalisation and the Knowledge-based Economy*. <http://www.oecd.org/dsti/sti/industry/smes/news/women2000.htm>.

Orser, B., E. Fischer, S. Hooper, R. Reuber, and A. Riding. 1999a. *Beyond Borders: Canadian Businesswomen in International Trade*. Complete Research Report. <http://www.infoexport.gc.ca/businesswomen/book/menu-e.asp>.

———. 1999b. 'Executive Summary'. In Orser, Fischer, Hooper, Reuber, and Riding (1999a).

———. 1999c. 'Report'. In Orser, Fischer, Hooper, Reuber, and Riding (1999a).

———. 1999d. 'Research Findings: Where are Canadian Women doing Business?'. In Orser, Fischer, Hooper, Reuber and Riding (1999a).

———. 1999e. 'The Development of Export Markets: Findings from In-Depth Interviews with Women Business Owners'. In Orser, Fischer, Hooper, Reuber, and Riding (1999a).

The Ottawa Citizen. 1995. 'Soldier Confirms Airborne Held Massacre Party'. 9 Nov.

———. 1996. 'U.S. Soldier Discharged for Refusing to Serve UN'. 25 Jan.

Oziewicz, E. 1993. 'No Plan to Accept Victims of Sex Bias'. *Globe and Mail*, 16 Jan. 16.

Pal, L., ed. 1998. *How Ottawa Spends 1998–99: Balancing Act: The Post-Deficit Mandate*. Toronto: Oxford University Press.

Panitch, L. 1996. 'Rethinking the Role of the State'. In Mittelman.

Parpart, J. 1998. 'Conclusion: New Thoughts and New Directions for the 'Man' Question in International Relations'. In Zalewski, Marysia and Parpart.

Pasic, A. and T.G. Weiss. 1997. 'Yugoslavia's Wars and the Humanitarian Impulse'. *Ethics and International Affairs* 11: 105–50.

Paul, D.E. 1999. 'Sovereignty, Survival and the Westphalian Blind Alley'. *Review of International Studies* 25, no. 2 (Apr.): 217–32.

Pedrero, M., T. Rendon, and A. Barron. 1995. 'Desigualdad en el Acceso a Oportunidades de Empleo y Segregacion Ocupacional por Genero: Situacion Actual en Mexico y Propuestas'. In UNIFEM.

Pellerin, H. 1996. 'Global Restructuring and International Migration: Consequences for the Globalization of Politics'. In Kofman and Youngs.

Persaud, R.B. 1997. 'Franz Fanon, Race and World Order'. In Gill and Mittelman.

Peterson, V.S., ed. 1992a. *Gendered States: Feminist (Re)Visions of International Relations Theory*. Boulder: Lynne Rienner.

———. 1992b. 'Security and Sovereign States: What Is at Stake in Taking Feminism Seriously?'. In Peterson (1992a).

———. 1992c. 'Introduction'. In Peterson (1992a).

———, and A.S. Runyan. 1993. *Global Gender Issues: Dilemmas in World Politics*. Boulder: Westview Press.

———, and J. True. 1998. 'New "Times" and New Conversations'. In Zalewski, Marysia and Parpart.

Pettigrew, P.S. 2000a. 'Notes for an Address by the Honourable Pierre Pettigrew, Minister for International Trade, to the Canadian Bar Association'. 19 May. Ottawa. <http://198.103.104.118/minpub/Publication.asp?/FileSpec=/Min_Pub_Docs/103416.htm>.

———. 2000b. 'Notes for an Address by The Honourable Pierre S. Pettigrew, Minister for International Trade, on Seattle: A Collision Between Two Worlds to the Global Forum 2000'. 15 May. Washington, DC. <http://198.103.104.118/minpub/Publication.asp?/FileSpec=/Min_Pub_Docs/103338.htm>.

Pettman, J. J. 1996. *Worlding Women: A Feminist International Politics*. New York: Routledge.

Pettman, R. 1998. 'Sex, Power, and the Grail of Positive Collaboration'. In Zalewski and Parpart.

Philips, A., ed. 1998. *Feminism and Politics*. New York: Oxford.

Philippine Women Centre of BC. 2000. 'Canada: The New Frontier for Filipino Mail-Order Brides'. (November). <http://www.swc-cfc.gc.ca/publish/research/001115-0662653343>.

Polanyi, K. 1957. *The Great Transformation: The Political and Economic Origins of Our Time*. Boston: Beacon Press.

Prah, P. 1997. 'Charges that Mexico Fails to Enforce Sex Discrimination Laws Focus of Hearing'. Daily Labor Report, 224, 20 Nov.

Pratt, C. 1983–4. 'Dominant Class Theory and Canadian Foreign Policy: The Case of the Counter-Consensus'. *International Journal* 39 (Winter): 235–58.

———. 1989. *Internationalism Under Strain: The North-South Policies of Canada, the Netherlands, Norway and Sweden*. Toronto: University of Toronto.

———. 1990. *Middle Power Internationalism: The North-South Dimension*. Montreal: McGill-Queen's University Press.

———, ed. 1994a. *Canadian International Development Assistance Policies: An Appraisal.* Montreal: McGill-Queen's Press.

———. 1994b. 'Humane Internationalism and Canadian Development Assistance Policies'. In Pratt (1994a).

———. 1996. 'Competing Perspectives on Canadian Development Assistance Policies'. *International Journal* 51, no. 2: 235–58.

———.1998. 'DFAIT's Takeover Bid of CIDA: The Institutional Future of the Canadian International Development Agency'. *Canadian Foreign Policy* 5, no. 2 (Winter): 1–13.

Prince George Citizen. 2000a. 'Emotional Departure for Migrants'. 11 May.

———. 2000b. 'Last of 7 Migrant Escapees Captured'. 6 June.

———. 2000c. 'Mailbox: Your Letters'. 23 June.

——— . 2000d. 'Migrants: Our Health Risk'. 6 July.

Project Ploughshares. 1996. *Report to Donors*. Waterloo, Ont. Feb.

Projet de Société. 1995. *Canada and Agenda 21*. Winnipeg: IISD. <http://iisd.ca/worldsd/canada/projet/c24.htm>.

Pronger, B. 1990. *The Arena of Masculinity: Sports, Homosexuality, and the Meaning of Sex.* Toronto: Summerhill Press.

Prouse, R. 2000. 'The Dark Side That Emerged in Somalia Is Inside All Canadians'. *The Ottawa Citizen,* 15 July.

Prügl, E., and M.K. Meyer. 1999. 'Gender Politics in Global Governance'. In Meyer and Prügl (1999).

Pugliese, D. 1995. 'Somalia: What Went So Wrong?' *The Ottawa Citizen*, 1 Oct.

———. 1996. 'Airborne Again'. *The Ottawa Citizen*, 15 Apr.

Pulkingham, J., and G. Ternowetsky, eds. 1996. *Remaking Canadian Social Policy: Social Security in the Late 1990s.* Halifax: Fernwood.

Rai, S., and G. Lievesley., eds. 1996. *Women and the State: International Perspectives.* London: Taylor and Francis.

Ramazanoglu, C. 1989. *Feminism and the Contradictions of Oppression.* London: Routledge.

Randall, V. 1998. 'Gender and Power: Women Engage the State'. In Randall and Waylen.

———, and G. Waylen, eds. 1998. *Gender, Politics and the State*. London: Routledge.

Raustiala, K. 1997. 'States, NGOs, and International Environmental Institutions'. *International Studies Quarterly* 41, no. 4: 719–40.

Rayman, R. 1999. *Beyond Borders: Canadian Businesswomen in International Trade.* Summary Report. <http://www.infoexport.gc.ca/businesswomen/beyond_borders/report-e.pdf>.

Razack, S. 1995. 'Domestic Violence as Gender Persecution: Policing the Borders of Nation, Race, and Gender'. *Canadian Journal of Women and the Law* 8: 45–88.

———. 1996. 'The Perils of Story Telling for Refugee Women'. In Giles, Moussa, and Esterik.

Reardon, B. 1985. *Sexism and the War System*. New York: Teachers College Press.

Reif, L. 1998. 'Environmental Policy: The Rio Summit Five Years Later'. In Hampson and Molot.

Ribbens, J., and R. Edwards, eds. 1998. *Feminist Dilemmas in Qualitative Research: Public Knowledge and Private Lives.* London: Sage.

Richard, A. 2000. 'International Trafficking in Women to the United States: A Contemporary Manifestation of Slavery and Organized Crime'. *DCI Exceptional Intelligence Analyst Program* (April).

Richmond, A.H. 1994. *Global Apartheid: Refugees, Racism, and the New World Order.* Toronto: Oxford University Press.

Riley, M., and R. Mejia. 1996. 'Gender in the Global Trading System: Analysis and Strategies from a Gender Focus'. Paper submitted to the 1996 WTO Ministerial Conference. Washington, DC: Center of Concern.

Rioux J.F., and R. Hay. 1998–9. 'Canadian Foreign Policy: From Internationalism to Isolationism?' *International Journal* 54, no. 1 (Winter): 57–75.

Roberts, B. 1996. 'Taking Them at Their Word: Canadian Government's Accountability for Women's Equality'. *Canadian Woman Studies/Les Cahiers de la femme* 16, no. 3 (Summer): 25–8.

Robinson, P. 1999. 'Ready to Kill But Not to Die: NATO's Strategy in Kosovo'. *International Journal* 54, no. 4 (Autumn): 671–82.

Rosenberg, J. 1994. *The Empire of Civil Society*. London: Verso.

Ross, D. A. 1996–7. 'Canada and the World at Risk'. *International Journal* 52, no. 1 (Winter): 1–24.

Rubinstein, R. A. 1993. 'Cultural Aspects of Peacekeeping: Notes on the Substance of Symbols'. *Millennium* 22, no. 3: 547–62.

Ruggie, G. 1993.'Territoriality and Beyond: Problematizing Modernity in International Relations'. *International Organization* 47, no. 1: 137–74.

Russ, J. 1998. *What Are We Fighting For?* New York: St. Martins Press.

Runyan, A.S. 1996. 'The Places of Women in Trading Places: Gendered Global/Regional Regimes and Inter-nationalized Feminist Resistance'. In Kofman and Youngs.

———.1999. 'Women in the Neo-Liberal 'Frame'. In Meyer and Prügl.

Sachs, W., ed. 1993. *Global Ecology: A New Arena of Political Conflict*. London: Zed Books.

———. 1999. *Planet Dialectics: Explorations in Environment and Development*. Halifax: Fernwood.

Said, E. 1994. *Culture and Imperialism*. New York: Vintage.

Sassen, S. 2000. 'Women's Burden: Counter-geographies of Globalization and the Feminization of Survival'. *Journal of International Affairs* 53, no. 2 (Summer): 503–24.

Sen, G. 1991. 'Macroeconomic Policies and the Informal Sector: A Gender Sensitive Approach'. Working paper no. 13, written for the UN INSTRAW Conference on Macroeconomic Policies towards Women in the Informal Sector, April.

Sens, A.G. 1997, *Somalia and the Changing Nature of Peacekeeping: The Implications for Canada*. A Study Prepared for the Commission of Inquiry into the Deployment of Canadian Forces to Somalia. Ottawa: Minister of Public Works and Government Services.

Servaes, J., T.L. Jacobson, and S.A. White, eds. 1996. *Participatory Communication for Social Change*. London: Sage.

Shannon, S. 1999. 'Prostitution and the Mafia: The Involvement of Organized Crime in the Global Sex Trade'. In P. Williams (1999a).

Shaw, T. 1997. 'Beyond Post-Conflict Peacebuilding: What Links to Sustainable Development and Human Security?' In Ginifer.

Shiva, V. 1988. *Staying Alive: Women, Ecology and Survival in India*. London: Zed Books.

———. 1993a. 'Homeless in the Global Village'. In Mies and Shiva (1993).

———. 1993b. 'The Global Is Not Planetary'. In Sachs (1993).

Shrewsbury, C.M. 1997. 'What Is Feminist Pedagogy?' *Women's Studies Quarterly* 25, no. 1: 166–73.

Shue, H. 1999. 'Global Environmental and International Inequality'. *International Affairs* 75, no. 3: 531–45.

Sjolander, C.T. 1998. 'Critical World Politics: Defining Territory in a "Placeless" Discipline'. *Journal of Interdisciplinary Education* 2 (Fall): 135–46.

Slemon, S. 1995. 'The Scramble for Post-Colonialism'. In Ashcroft, Griffiths, and Tiffin.

Slocum R., L.Wichhart, D. Rocheleau, and B. Thomas-Slayter, eds. 1995. *Power, Process and Participation: Tools for Change.* London: ITP.

Smith, L.T. 1999. *Decolonizing Methodologies: Research and Indigenous Peoples.* London: Zed Books.

Smith, M. J. 1998. 'Humanitarian Intervention: An Overview of the Ethical Issues'. *Ethics and International Affairs* 12: 63–79.

Smith, S., K. Booth, and M. Zalewski, eds. 1996. *International Theory: Positivism and Beyond.* Cambridge: Cambridge University Press.

Sokolsky, J.J. 1995. 'Great Ideals and Uneasy Compromises: The United States Approach to Peacekeeping'. *International Journal* 50, no. 2 (Spring): 266–93.

Somalia Inquiry. *See* Canada. Commission of Inquiry into the Deployment of Canadian Forces to Somalia.

Sparr, P. 1994a. 'Feminist Critiques of Structural Adjustment Programs'. In Sparr (1994b).

———, ed. 1994b. *Mortgaging Women's Lives: Feminist Critiques of Structural Adjustment.* London: Zed Books.

Spencer-Nimmons, N. 1994a. 'The Emergence of Refugee Women as a Social Issue: 1978–1988'. Ph.D. dissertation, Department of Sociology. Toronto: York University.

———. 1994b. 'Canada's Response to the Issue of Refugee Women: The Women at Risk Program'. *Refuge* 14, no. 7.

Stairs, D. 1998a. 'The Media and the Military in Canada'. *International Journal* 53, no. 3 (Summer): 544–81.

———. 1998b. 'Of Medium Powers and Middling Roles'. In Booth (1998).

———. 1999. 'Canada and the Security Problem: Implications as the Millennium Turns,' *International Journal* 54, no. 3 (Summer): 386–403.

Standing, G. 1989. 'Global Feminization Through Flexible Labour'. *World Development* 17, no. 7: 1077–95.

Stanford, J. 1999. *Paper Boom: Why Real Prosperity Demands a New Approach to Canada's Economy.* Toronto: James Lorimer.

Statistics Canada. 2000. *Women in Canada.* Ottawa: Canadian Government Publishing.

Status of Women Canada. 1995. *Setting the Stage for the Next Century: The Federal Plan for Gender Equality.* Ottawa: SWC.

———. 1996. *Gender-Based Analysis: A Guide for Policy-making.* Updated version (1998). Ottawa: Status of Women Canada. Online.

———. 1999. *Canada's National Response to the UN Questionnaire on Implementation of the Beijing Platform for Action.* Ottawa. <http://www.swc_cfc.gc.ca/beijing5/quest-e>.

Steans, J. 1998. *Gender and International Relations: An Introduction.* New Brunswick, NJ: Rutgers University Press.

———. 1999. 'The Private is Global: Feminist Politics and Global Political Economy'. *New Political Economy* 4, no.1: 113–28.

Stienstra, D. 1994–5. 'Can the Silence Be Broken? Gender and Canadian Foreign Policy'. *International Journal* 50 (Winter): 103–27.

———. 1999a. 'Of Roots, Leaves and Trees: Gender, Social Movements and Global Governance'. In Meyer and Prügl.

———. 1999b. 'Working Globally for Gender Equality'. *Canadian Development Report 1999.* Ottawa: North-South Institute.

———. 2000. 'Cutting to Gender: Teaching Gender in International Relations'. *International Studies Perspectives* 1: 233–44.

———. 2001. 'Recasting Foreign Policy Analysis Using a Gender Analysis: Where to Begin?' In Nagel and Robb.

Stienstra, D., and B. Roberts. 1995. *Strategies for the Year 2000: A Woman's Handbook*. Halifax: Fernwood.

Strange, S. 1996. *The Retreat of the State: The Diffusion of Power in the World Economy*. Cambridge, UK: Cambridge University Press.

Stuart, S., and R. Bery. 1996. 'Powerful Grass-roots Women Communicators'. In J. Servaes, T. Jacobson, and S.A. White.

Stubbs, R., and G.R.D. Underhill, eds. 2000. *Political Economy and the Changing Global Order.* Toronto: Oxford University Press.

Sustainable Development Research Institute. 1994. Conference paper presented to 'Women and Sustainable Development: Canadian Perspectives', Vancouver 27–31 May.

Sylvester, C. 1996. 'The Contributions of Feminist Theory to International Relations'. In Smith, Booth, and Zalewski (1996).

Taylor, A., and C. Thomas, eds. 1999. *Trade and the New Social Agenda*. London: Routledge.

Tesfay Musa, Elsa 1993. 'Actions of the International NGO Working Group on Refugee Women 1991–93'. Paper prepared for the Refugee Desk, Anglican Church of Canada.

Tester F.J., and P. Kulchyski. 1994. *Tammarniit (Mistakes): Inuit Relocation in the Eastern Arctic, 1939–63*. Vancouver: UBC Press.

Thakur, R. 1999. 'The United Nations and Human Security'. *Canadian Foreign Policy* 7, no. 1 (Fall): 51–60.

Thomas, K. 2000. *International Political Economy Yearbook*. Special issue on regionalism. Boulder, Colo.: Lynne Rienner Press.

Thompson, E.P. 1968. *The Making of the English Working Class*. Harmondsworth: Penguin.

Tickner, J.A. 1992. *Gender in International Relations: Feminist Perspectives on Achieving Global Security*. New York: Columbia University Press.

———. 1997. 'You Just Don't Understand: Troubled Engagements Between Feminist and IR Theorists'. *International Studies Quarterly*, 41, 4: 611–32.

———. 1998. 'Continuing the Conversation'. *International Studies Quarterly* 42, no.1: 205–10.

Tilman, R., ed. 1993. *A Veblen Treasury*. Armonk, NY: M.E. Sharpe

Tokman, V. 1989. 'Policies for a Heterogeneous Informal Sector in Latin America'. *World Development* 17, no. 7: 67–76.

Townson, M. 2000. *A Report Card on Women and Poverty*. Ottawa: Canadian Centre for Policy Alternatives.

Trade Commissioner Service. 1997. *Businesswomen in Trade—News and Press Releases: Trade Research Coalition*. Ottawa: Department of Foreign Affairs and International Trade.<http://www.infoexport.gc.ca/businesswomen/news-trc-e.asp>.

Tremblay, M., and C. Andrew, eds. 1998. *Women and Political Representation in Canada*. Ottawa: University of Ottawa.

Tucker, M. 1980. *Canadian Foreign Policy: Contemporary Issues and Themes*. Toronto: McGraw-Hill.

Tuhiwai Smith, L. 1999. *Decolonizing Methodologies: Research and Indigenous Peoples*. New York: Zed Books.

UNDP. 1994. *Human Development Report 1994*. UNDP.

UNHCR. *See* United Nations High Commissioner for Refugees.

UNIFEM. 1995. *The Human Cost of Women's Poverty: Perspectives from Latin America and the Caribbean*. Mexico City: UNIFEM.

United Nations. 2000. *Report of the Ad Hoc Committee of the Whole of the Twenty-third Special Session of the General Assembly* A/S-23/10/Rev.1. New York: UN.

United Nations Committee on Economic, Social and Cultural Rights. 1998. 'Concluding Observations of the Committee: Canada' E/C.12/1/Add. 31. New York: UN.

United Nations High Commissioner for Refugees (UNHCR).1995. *The State of the World's Refugees: In Search of Solutions*. New York: Oxford University Press.

———. 1997. *The State of the World's Refugees: A Humanitarian Agenda*. Oxford: Oxford University Press.

———. Statistics. 1998.<http://www.unhcr.ch/statist/98oview/tab3_1.htm>.

———. 2000. 2000 Global Appeal. <http://www.unhcr.ch/fdrs/ga2000/pdf/factfigs.pdf>.

———. Executive Committee. 1990. *Conclusion on Refugee Women and International Protection*, No. 64.

United Nations Human Rights Committee. 1999. 'Concluding Observations of the Human Rights Committee: Canada' CCPR/C/79/Add.105.

UNRISD. 1997. *Working Towards a More Gender Equitable Macro-economic Agenda*. Report of the UNRISD/CPD Workshop. Geneva: UNRISD.

USAID, Office of Women in Development. Gender Reach Project 1999. 'Women as Chattel: The Emerging Global Market in Trafficking'. *Gender Matters Quarterly*, Feb.

Valji, N. 2001. 'Women and the Refugee Convention: Fifty Years of Seeking Visibility'. *Refuge: Canada's Periodical on Refugees* 19, no. 5: 25–35.

Vancouver Status of Women. 1997. *Women Oppose Corporate Globalization*. Vancouver, BC.

Veblen, T. 1993. 'Why Is Economics Not an Evolutionary Science?' In Tilman.

Waldorf, L., and S. Bazilli. 2000. 'Country Papers: Canada'. In *The First CEDAW Impact Study*. Toronto: Centre for Feminist Research and International Women's Rights Project, York University.

Walker, R.B.J. 1990. 'Security, Sovereignty and the Challenge of World Politics', *Alternatives* 15: 3–27.

Waring, M. 1997. *Three Masquerades: Essays on Equality, Work and Hu(man) Rights*. Toronto: University of Toronto Press.

Waylen, G. 1998. 'Gender, Feminism and the State: An Overview'. In Randall and Waylen.

Weber, C. 1998. 'Something's Missing: Male Hysteria and the U.S. Invasion of Panama'. In Zalewski and Parpart.

WEDO (Women's Environment and Development Organization). 1999. <http://www.wedo.org>.

Wendt, A. 1992. 'Anarchy Is What States Make of It', *International Organization* 46, no. 2: 33–67.

Wenek, Major R.W.J. 1984. *The Assessment of Psychological Fitness: Some Options for the Canadian Forces*. Technical Note 1/84, Ottawa: Directorate of Personnel Selection, Research on Second Careers, July in Commission of Inquiry into the Deployment of Canadian Forces to Somalia (1995). Ottawa: Canadian Government Publishing.

White, M. 2002. 'Making Trade Work for Women: Opportunities and Obstacles'. Washington, DC: Women's EDGE. <http://www.womensedge.org/trade/trade-primer.htm>.

White, S. 1994. *Participatory Communications: Working for Change and Development*. London: Sage

Whitman, J., ed. 1999. *Peacekeeping and the UN Agencies*. London: Frank Cass.

Whitworth, S. 1994. *Feminism and International Relations*. Houndsmills: Macmillan Press.

———. 1995. 'Women, and Gender, in the Foreign Policy Review Process'. In Cameron and Molot.

———. 1997. 'The Ugly Unasked Questions about Somalia'. *The Globe and Mail*, 14 Feb.

———. 1998. 'Gender, Race and the Politics of Peacekeeping'. In Moxon-Browne.

———. 2000. 'Theory and Exclusion: Gender, Masculinity, and International Political Economy'. In Stubbs and Underhill.

———. Forthcoming. *Warrior Princes and the Politics of Peacekeeping: A Feminist Analysis.* Boulder: Lynne Riemer.

Wilkinson, Ray. 2000. 'Cover Story', *The Americas: Debate over Asylum in the U.S. and Canada.* 2, 119. <http://www.unhcr.ch/>.

Williams, P., ed. 1999a. *Illegal Immigration and Commercial Sex: The New Sex Trade.* London: Frank Cass.

———. 1999b. 'Trafficking in Women and Children: A Market Perspective'. In Williams (1999a).

Williams, W. 1999. 'Will the Canadian Government's Commitment to Use a Gender-Based Analysis Result in Public Policies Reflecting the Diversity of Women's Lives?' Conference paper presented to 'Made to Measure: Designing Research, Policy and Action Approaches to Eliminate Gender Inequity', Halifax, 3–6 Oct. Halifax: Maritime Centre of Excellence for Women's Health.

Winslow, D. 1997. *The Canadian Airborne Regiment in Somalia: A Socio-Cultural Inquiry.* A Study Prepared for the Commission of Inquiry into the Deployment of Canadian Forces to Somalia. Ottawa: Government Services Canada.

Wolf, D., ed. 1996. *Feminist Dilemmas in Fieldwork.* Boulder: Westview.

Women Leaders Network (WLN). 1997. 'Statement and Recommendations of the Women Leaders Network at its Second Meeting—The Economic Impact of Women in the APEC Region'. Ottawa and Hull, 13–16 Sept.

Women Working Worldwide. n.d. 'World Trade is a Women's Issue: Promoting the Rights of Women Workers in a Changing World Economy'. Unpublished briefing paper. Manchester.

Women's Strategic Planning Seminar on Gender and Trade. 1999. Organized by The Center of Concern and DAWN Caribbean, Grenada, West Indies, 18–19 Dec.

Wood, A. 1991. 'North-South Trade and Female Labour in Manufacturing: An Asymmetry'. *Journal of Development Studies* 27, no. 2: 168–89.

World March of Women in the Year 2000. 2000. 'Advocacy Guide to Women's World Demands'. <http://www.ffq.qc.ca/marche2000/en/cahier/index.html>.

Woroniuk, B. 1999. 'Women's Empowerment in the Context of Human Security: A Discussion Paper'. Background document for 'Women's Empowerment in the Context of Human Security', a joint workshop held by the United Nations Inter-Agency Committee on Women and Gender Equality and the OECD/DAC Working Party on Gender Equality, 7–8 Dec., Bangkok.

Worthington, P., and K. Brown. 1997. *Scapegoat: How the Army Betrayed Kyle Brown.* Toronto: McClelland Bantam.

Yeatman, A. 1994. *Postmodern Revisionings of the Political.* New York: Routledge.

Young, G. 1993. 'Gender Inequality and Industrial Development: The Household Connection'. *Journal of Comparative Family Studies* 24, no. 1 (Spring): 1–2.

Zajdow, G. 1995. *Women and Work: Current Issues and Debates.* Geelong, Australia: Deakin University Press.

Zalefwski, M., and J. Parpart, eds. 1998. *The 'Man' Question in International Relations.* Boulder: Westview Press.

Index

* Hard to address feminism because there is no accepted, concrete definition. So many different theories injecting/inferring their own beliefs into feminism